B

TH

STUDIES IN GOVERNMENT
AND PUBLIC POLICY

BY ORDER
OF THE
PRESIDENT

The Use and Abuse of
Executive Direct Action

Phillip J. Cooper

University Press of Kansas

© 2002 by the University Press of Kansas

Published by the University Press of Kansas (Lawrence, Kansas 66049), which was
organized by the Kansas Board of Regents and is operated and funded by Emporia
State University, Fort Hays State University, Kansas State University, Pittsburg State
University, the University of Kansas, and Wichita State University

Library of Congress Cataloging-in-Publication Data
Cooper, Phillip J.
    By order of the president : the use and abuse of executive direct
  action / Phillip J. Cooper.
        p. cm. — (Studies in government and public policy)
    Includes bibliographical references and index.
    ISBN 0-7006-1179-7 (cloth : alk. paper) — ISBN 0-7006-1180-0 (pbk. : alk.
  paper)
      1. Executive orders—United States—History.   2. Executive
  power—United States—History.   I. Title.   II. Series.
    KF5053 .C578 2002
    342.73'06—dc21   2001008168

British Library Cataloguing in Publication Data is available.

Printed in the United States of America

10 9 8 7 6 5 4 3 2 1

The paper used in this publication meets the minimum requirements of
the American National Standard for Permanence of Paper for Printed
Library Materials Z39.48-1984.

Once again it is necessary and appropriate to dedicate a volume to public servants who have been lost in the service of their country and their communities. Those who died in the terrorist attack on the United States on September 11, 2001 left behind loving families, devoted friends, and a grateful nation. Many more did not die but have endured more than anyone should have to bear in the aftermath of the attack. Still others have gone back to work across the nation with heavy hearts and a renewed commitment to labor in the public interest for all of us. Thank you one and all.

CONTENTS

Preface   ix

Acknowledgments   xiii

ONE
The Tools of Presidential Direct Administration   1

TWO
Executive Orders: Directing the Executive Branch   15

THREE
Strategies, Tactics, and Political Realities of
Executive Orders   39

FOUR
Presidential Memoranda:
Executive Orders by Another Name and Yet Unique   81

FIVE
Presidential Proclamations: Rule by Decree   117

SIX
National Security Directives:
Secret Orders, Foreign and Domestic   143

SEVEN
Presidential Signing Statements:
A Different Kind of Line Item Veto   199

EIGHT
Presidential Direct Action and Washington Rules:
The Dangers of Power Tools   231

Notes   245

Bibliography   279

Opinions Cited   287

Index   291

PREFACE

Democracy is in the details. In other words, there is indeed an interdependence between ends and means. Although that is a veritable truism, there seems to be a need to remind Americans, including professionals, of the importance of that relationship every now and again. Many presidents have found themselves embroiled in legal, political, and policy difficulties as much for the means they chose as for the ends they sought to achieve. That has been true from the days of George Washington to the most recent occupants of the White House.

Many of the most important White House controversies have involved presidential direct action, the use of executive orders and proclamations to carry out policy. These are situations in which the president simply issues statements, many having the force of law, with no requirement for any particular processes such as those required to enact legislation or even to adopt administrative rules. As new presidents come to the White House, their administrations learn from their predecessors' actions just how these tools of presidential power can be used. Indeed, in recent decades, each administration seems to find new devices and new ways of using them to achieve policy goals, including goals they know they are unlikely to accomplish if they call upon Congress for help.

Today, these presidential power tools include not only executive orders and proclamations but also presidential memoranda, national security directives, and presidential signing statements. It is not just that these little-known devices exist and are not really understood by most participants in the public policy process, let alone citizens, that is important. Neither is it alone the fact that some of these devices need not be disclosed to Congress, much less published for the general public, that matters most. Nor is it the fact that these tools are often used together in combinations that can be confusing, to be charitable, and just plain deceptive, in a number of instances, that should be cause for attention. There is virtually no significant policy area in which presidents operate that has not been shaped to one degree or another by the use or abuse of these tools. It is for all these reasons and more that attention really must be paid to presidential direct action and the tools used for that purpose. Yet for all that, even professionals are only belatedly beginning to notice even the most obvious of these devices.

James Madison was right in pointing out that ignorance in a democracy is but a "prologue to a farce." If so, then it is past time to provide essential knowledge about these instruments—all of them. They are different, and each has its unique characteristics. The task is not simply to understand what they are, but also how they can be used, what purposes presidents have sought to serve by using them, and what advantages they offer as mechanisms to accomplish those purposes. There is one other major concern that must be addressed. It is the difficulties that can arise from their use. These downsides range from the trivial to the extraordinarily serious, from inside-the-Beltway spats to deadly international clashes, and from the near-term to the long-run future of the nation.

In seeking to address all of these issues, this book is about power, how it is used and abused, even where the ends for which it is employed are laudable in themselves. Because it attempts to provide a broad and integrative understanding of these tools of presidential direct action, it can really only begin a much larger and longer conversation about the subject. At the same time, it seeks to add to several academic literatures, to provide some degree of civic education, and to inform policymakers at all levels, professional public managers and elected officials. The use of these tools has affected all levels of government, from international to local policies. They have long been a major factor since the beginning of the nation in policies affecting Native Americans. They have also had pervasive impacts on most areas of the business community. It may be too much to hope, but it would be the author's fondest wish that this book might even in some small way encourage conversations not only within these different groups but among them as well.

There are a number of policymakers and informed citizens who have some knowledge of at least executive orders, if not all the tools considered in this book. But it is surprising to find how many people, including highly educated citizens and experienced professionals, know little if anything about them. For these readers, chapter 1 provides critically important foundation information that may seem familiar to many academic readers.

Within the academic community, I hope that this book can offer a contribution to the literatures on the presidency, public law, public policy, and public administration. In the most general sense, it is about what have come to be known as policy tools, but the tools come into their true usefulness and dangerousness as we understand how they have been—and are being—applied.

As this book went into production, Kenneth R. Mayer's new work on executive orders, *With the Stroke of a Pen* (Princeton: Princeton University

Press, 2001), was just emerging. I was told by another scholar of the presidency who saw it before I did that the two books were very different. When
I read his new work, I found that the two are different indeed. Our approaches
are very different and we consider very different material. In particular, this
work focuses on a wide range of tools of presidential direct action and their
interrelationships. As will become clear as readers move through this book,
there are many reasons why executive orders and other tools of presidential
action need to be understood together. There are many other differences as
well, but for now suffice it to say that I hope both will together make useful
additions in an area long in need of attention.

In the roughly two decades over which I have studied these mechanisms,
each administration has found many uses for them. Democratically controlled
Congresses have complained bitterly about the use and abuse of power by
Republican presidents, only to be replaced by a Republican-dominated Congress equally frustrated by a Democratic president. In this game of power,
any number can play, and both parties have been more than ready to use the
tools of presidential direct action. This book, then, is also about relationships
and the damage that has been done to critical Washington workways by con-
servatives and liberals alike, in both political parties, who have been too ready,
whether they would admit it or not, to let the ends justify the means.

ACKNOWLEDGMENTS

There is no way to write a little book like this about such a big topic with material that spans the entire history of the nation without feeling humbled, and I do. I am grateful to the many people who have done so much to help me with the research and writing of this book. Among the most important of these are Louis Fisher, Morton Rosenberg, Ron Moe, and Harold Relyea of the Congressional Research Service (CRS). These dedicated public servants have for many years made it their business to try to keep the importance of the instruments, institutions, and processes of American governance and public management in the view of those who fashion policy as well as those who seek to understand it. What they, and their CRS colleagues, do is of far greater value to the maintenance of democracy than most Americans will ever know. Their assistance has been invaluable to my own understanding and to this book.

In the years over which this book has evolved, many colleagues have discussed the subject and shared helpful insights. They include William Richardson, University of South Dakota; Thomas Lauth, University of Georgia; John Rohr, Virginia Polytechnic Institute and State University; Neil Kerwin, American University; and Charles Wise, Indiana University. A number of colleagues at the University of Vermont have been helpful in offering suggestions or in reading portions of the manuscript. They include Howard Ball, Frank Bryan, John Burke, and Gregory Gause.

Many students have suffered through hearing more about presidential power tools than they ever wanted to know, and I appreciate what they offered in return on the subject. Two students, Betty Castle and Jennifer Heston, not only helped with research in the early years of the project but have done their own scholarship in the area. Their assistance is gratefully acknowledged.

The staff of the Reference and Government Documents divisions of the Bailey/Howe Library at the University of Vermont has been of great assistance in the preparation of this manuscript. In particular Scott Schaeffer, Martha Day, Trina Magi, and Bill Gill have worked diligently to help me find arcane documents from long ago and equally hard-to-locate documents of more recent vintage. Their efforts and helpful spirit are gratefully acknowledged.

Mike Briggs and his colleagues at the University Press of Kansas are known to many for their sensitivity to the scholarly enterprise, sincere inter-

est in the ideas considered by their authors, and infinite patience. I have bene-
fited more than once from these qualities, and I am grateful for all of them.
Fred Woodward's efforts as director, along with Mike's work as editor in
chief, have managed to keep a major press that cares in an increasingly glo-
balized and impersonal field. For that we should all be grateful.

Some material included in chapter 4 appeared in "Presidential Memoranda
and Executive Orders: Of Patchwork Quilts, Trump Cards, and Shell Games,"
Presidential Studies Quarterly 31 (2001): 126–141, published by Sage.

Finally, thank you to Claudia, who dislikes public acknowledgments, but
whose love, help, and support in this and all other things are too important
not to mention. Beyond that, she is a fine scholar and editor who contributed
much to this book.

Of course, none of the fine people acknowledged bear any responsibility
for any errors in the book.

ONE

THE TOOLS OF PRESIDENTIAL DIRECT ADMINISTRATION

Suppose a call came in from a recently elected president's transition staff. The president had asked the transition team to prepare to instruct her and her inner circle about just what kinds of tools were available to make things happen. This president was an outside-the-Beltway person, as were a number of her close aides.

This new team is fully aware of the importance of putting forth a legislative agenda in the now famous (even trite) first hundred days of the administration. Indeed, much of the brief time between November and January has been consumed with thoughts about what ought to go into that agenda. Even more time has been spent trying to staff the key cabinet and subcabinet jobs. Then, of course, there is the budget, but most new administrations inherit a proposed budget developed by their predecessor, and it may take as much as a year to develop a financial plan that is fully the new president's plan. Finally, coming fresh from the campaign (and with a number of campaign staff members now in the White House), the new team certainly understands that the president can take a limited number of important issues to the people around the Washington establishment in an effort to force action.

To be sure, these tasks present difficulties. In an era of divided government, sending an agenda to the legislature is but the beginning of a protracted process (possibly a battle) that may yield relatively little at the end of the day. Even presidents who have had a legislature controlled by their own party have found it difficult to get what they sought. Although the White House has more leverage over the budget preparation process, it is still dependent on a complex appropriations process that ultimately requires congressional support and involves large numbers of stakeholders with their own power centers on the Hill.[1]

Certainly, there have been administrations that have elected to employ a model that is often described as the "administrative presidency" in an effort to achieve their goals.[2] This approach suggests the use of reorganization, personnel management techniques, or counterstaffing to move agencies in the desired direction, whether they want to go there or not, with or without congressional involvement.[3] Of course, most presidents who start by declaring their commitment to pick good people and then give them the room to do the job, often under the banner of cabinet government, end up changing their minds when they become convinced, rightly or wrongly, that their people have been co-opted by the agencies they were supposed to change or when they become frustrated by the reality that things are just taking too long and producing too few results.[4] They often then move away from their avowed commitment to cabinet government and toward a more direct approach.

What many of the new arrivals may not fully appreciate is that in addition to these more or less well-known challenges, they will also inherit a large body of executive orders and other pronouncements that remain in effect unless and until they are amended, superseded, or rescinded. If they are like most administrations in recent years, at least reaching back to the late 1970s, once they learn about the number, range, importance, and uses of these instruments, they will want to use them. Even those who have experience with executive orders begin to see that these tools and other instruments have been evolving and can be used in new and creative, if sometime problematic, ways.

All of these factors, and a desire to make an impact quickly, can lead an administration to employ tools of presidential direct action. These include executive orders, presidential proclamations, presidential memoranda, signing statements, and national security directives. What should the outside adviser tell the White House about the nature, uses, benefits, and dangers of these instruments? Though it is certainly the case that presidents since George Washington have employed a wide range of devices in an effort to move the government quickly and decisively, the constellation of tools and the ways in which they have been employed have evolved over the years.

WHAT'S NEW, WHAT'S NOT, AND WHAT COUNTS?

Curiously, the literature on the presidency largely ignores the tools of presidential direct action, as if the way that the president uses this power matters little.[5] The emphasis is almost completely focused on what the new administration wants to achieve and how it can organize, staff, and position itself with potential political allies to accomplish that agenda. However, even a relatively quick look at history suggests that many presidents have run into difficulties as much for how they did what they did as because of the policies themselves. And a proper sensitivity for this fact requires an understanding of the tools that presidents have at their disposal to carry out the work. It seems to be a truism that must be relearned every so often that ends and means are inextricably interrelated. Even if their significance is not obvious or immediate, the impacts are quite real and meaningful.

Another problem that one finds in much of the literature on why presidents succeed or fail has to do with perspective. In Washington, and in the literature about it, there is a sense that one must be a White House person or a Capitol Hill advocate. And, as anyone who has spent much time in Washington knows, it can often be a very long distance between both ends of the avenue. These biases are understandable and sometimes even necessary. There has for many years been a tendency of the Congress not to defend its institutional character and authority against White House challenges to its processes and powers.[6] At the same time, presidents have become increasingly frustrated by the difficulties they find in dealing with the numerous ways in which members of Congress, their committees, or their institutional rules delay or even bury important policies. President Bill Clinton expressed this frustration as he announced a new policy on privacy protections: "I am taking this action today because Congress has failed to act and because a few years ago Congress explicitly gave me the authority to step in if they were unable to deal with this issue. I believe Congress should act. Members of Congress gave themselves 3 years to pass meaningful privacy protections, and then gave us the authority to act if they didn't. Two months ago their deadline expired. After 3 full years there wasn't a bill passed in either Chamber."[7] Even on the Hill itself, there are frustrations about partisanship or the influence of campaign finance pressures that seem to prevent the most dedicated member from focusing on the nation's most pressing problems. Any number of members of Congress have decided in recent years not to seek reelection in part because of these dynamics.

For longtime Washington insiders, much of this is old news. Congresses and presidents have been battling for years, and partisan wrangling is not a recent invention. Neither is the presence of strongly held ideology on one end of the spectrum or the other. That having been said, the climate does seem to be changing, and the change is sorely felt. Call it the erosion of Washington rules. These rules are not codified anywhere. Political scientists address them, if at all, most often as informal relationships among institutions. To professionals, these are the understood norms that for many years made it possible for staff people and elected officials to work together even though they had strong institutional, partisan, or even ideological differences. These understandings have long been the warp and woof on which policy is woven and programs function. These rules make it possible for those who lose badly to continue to work with the victors and for institutions to wage pitched battles and yet retain the ability to cooperate with one another.

FOCUSING ON THE CRITICAL CORE

The task, then, is to examine the use and abuse of presidential instruments of direct action so as to better understand their nature, strengths, and dangers. The object is not only to see these devices in terms of their legality or for the wisdom of the ends they are used to attain but also to understand how their use affects the critical institutions, processes, and actors involved in the policy process. These include what were once called Washington rules.

The purpose here is analytic, but there are several relatively obvious normative implications that flow from it. The thesis that emerges is that there is substantial justification for the rise and use of most of the tools of presidential direct action, but that they have been used in increasingly problematic ways that present constitutional, institutional, procedural, and policy difficulties. These negative effects operate in both the formal and informal spheres and have contributed to the erosion of the Washington rules that make effective working relationships possible.

THE ESSENTIAL PREMISES OF PRESIDENTIAL DIRECT ACTION

With all that in mind, consider the challenge of advising the new administration. Clearly, each of the instruments is complex and requires individual attention. However, even before that, it is essential to establish some foundations against which to assess each of the presidential tools. They include at least four critical dimensions: the prerogative debate, the constitutional dialogue, interorganizational and intergovernmental complexity, and the presence of international and emergency pressures. For many scholars, this may be but a reminder of important premises. For the uninitiated, these four aspects are necessary foundations for further understanding and use of the tools.

The Problematic Prerogative Argument

It is well understood that different presidents have held quite different understandings of their own role and authority.[8] And it is certainly the case that to speak of the political power of the presidency is not the same as speaking of the president's legal authority.[9] Even so, the fact is that executive orders and proclamations, among other devices, are formal instruments of government action. As such, their validity rests on the constitutional or statutory authority advanced to support them.[10] In the background of many debates over just how much power the president has to issue such orders is the argument over the executive prerogative concept. This becomes particularly important when the traditional power sharing among institutions breaks down or when there is a legal challenge by someone outside government.

The prerogative theory is the idea that the chief executive is not limited to delegations of authority from the Constitution or statutes.[11] The argument is not merely about what the president may be able to do politically but claims that there is formal authority for broad action and apparent legal warrant for it. The prerogative idea derives from the British royal prerogative under which the monarch issued a variety of orders and proclamations, citing the authority of the Crown as the basis for the action.

However, the prerogative is both misunderstood and misapplied by presidents and their supporters as a formal constitutional claim to authority for the issuance of executive orders and other directives in the United States. Because presidential decrees have their distant origins in the prerogative idea and because presidents still assume such power, it is important to consider it briefly. Although a full-blown argument about the prerogative is beyond the present purpose, it is important to understand at least four critical points. First, the assumptions about the prerogative powers of the British monarch are often incorrectly stated. Second, after independence, the newly formed states reacted against assertions of prerogative powers by creating weak executives. Third, at the time the Constitution was drafted and the campaign for its ratification was waged, great pains were taken to deny that the new presidency would have the broad powers that had been understood to lie at the heart of the prerogative power of the king. Finally, there are necessary cautions to be observed regarding discussions of John Locke's treatment of the prerogative in the American context.

Even in British law, the Crown did not at the time of the American colonization, much less in the days of independence, have the absolute authority to produce decrees having the force of law on any subject he or she chose.[12] For example, in 1611, the *Proclamations Case* held that "the King cannot change any part of the common law, nor create any offence by his proclamation, which was not an offence before, without Parliament."[13] Indeed, American colonists were more than ready to argue precisely that fact in opposition to the British Orders in Council and other directives imposed on the colonies.[14]

After independence was declared, the new states continued to react against abuses by the Crown and the royal governors. One of the forms that this took was the creation of weak chief executives in state governments who were made quite dependent on the legislature.[15] Two states specifically denied their chief executives the prerogative in their new state constitutions.[16] "In the Virginia constitution of 1776 it was stipulated, as if out of abundant caution, that 'the executive powers of government' were to be exercised 'according to the laws' of the commonwealth, and that no power or prerogative was ever to be claimed 'by virtue of any law, statute, or custom of England.'"[17] It is a matter of some interest that while state constitutions have changed over the years, many still seek to maintain constraints on governors.[18]

It is certainly true that by the convention of 1787 there was a frustration with weak executives and the abuses of state legislatures. Indeed, in *Federalist* no. 48 James Madison had reminded his readers that those who crafted the state constitutions "seem never for a moment to have turned their eyes from the danger, to liberty, from an overgrown and all-grasping prerogative" of the king to such an extent that they forgot the dangers that might emanate from strong legislatures and excessively weak executives.[19] And there clearly was by that point a desire to ensure a more energetic and efficacious executive. Even so, the framers frequently reiterated their desire that the presidency would not be based on the British monarchical model and that a number of the powers generally regarded as central to the royal prerogative would be denied to the president or at least divided between the executive and the legislature.

James Wilson began the debate on the Virginia design for the presidency on June 1, 1787. At the outset, he dismissed the fears that had been expressed regarding the proposal for a single executive by rejecting "the Prerogative of the British Monarch as a proper guide in defining the Executive Powers."[20] Indeed, the debates make clear the fact that the framers did not want the presidency to be modeled on the British monarchy and that they knew that charges that the president would merely represent the replacement of one king with another of the homegrown variety could jeopardize the new Constitution.

Certainly the push for a strong and effective executive knew no more committed advocate than Alexander Hamilton, who, after all, argued that "A feeble executive implies a feeble execution of government. A feeble execution is but another phrase for a bad execution; and a government ill executed, whatever it may be in theory, must be, in practice, a bad government."[21] But Hamilton, like Wilson and Madison, knew that the advocates of the new Constitution would have to address the fears of an excessively powerful chief executive. And those charges were indeed leveled during the ratification debate.[22] It was for that reason that Hamilton wrote *Federalist* no. 69, in which he explained in detail the differences between the powers of the president and the royal prerogative.[23]

In their design for the presidency, the framers went beyond a general rejection of the prerogative power to carve up the powers that were at the heart of the British prerogative. The power of the monarch to create offices and to appoint officials to fill them was split, with Congress retaining the authority to create important offices and an additional check added, requiring the advice and consent process, or what we simply refer to today as Senate confirmation. The president was denied an absolute veto over legislation, with Congress retaining the authority to override. The military power was also split, with the power to declare war and to raise and support the military going to the Congress and the authority of the commander in chief left to the president. Authority over foreign affairs was made subject to confirmation by an extraordinary majority in the Senate. Revenue measures were required to be initiated in the most numerous branch of the Congress. These were fields in which the Crown had exercised prerogative authority, to the anger of the colonists and, one might add, to the consternation of many British citizens as well.[24] Where an element of prerogative had been given to the president, as in the case of the pardon power, it was specifically enumerated and, even in this area, there was a qualification with respect to impeachments.[25]

John Locke, in his *Second Treatise on Civil Government,* supported the idea of the prerogative, however. And given the influence of Locke in the founding period, there is a tendency to consider that this provides strong support for the prerogative in the American context. Locke wrote:

> The good of the society requires that several things should be left to the discretion of him that has the executive power. . . .
> This power to act according to discretion for the public good, without the prescription of the law and sometimes even against it, is that which is called "prerogative"; for since in some governments the lawmaking power is not always in being, and is usually too numerous and so too slow for the dispatch requisite to execution, and because also it is impossible to foresee, and so by laws to provide for, all accidents and necessities that may concern the public, or to make such laws as will do no harm if they are executed with an inflexible rigor on all occasions and upon all persons that may come in their way, therefore there is a latitude left to the executive power to do many things of choice which the laws do not prescribe.[26]

Yet it was understood at the time of the framing that Locke was writing in the context of British experience and not working with a positive Constitution in the American tradition. Therefore, great care needs to be exercised in seeking to apply Locke directly and broadly in the latter setting. Madison made this point quite specifically with respect to the prerogative:

Writers such as Locke, and Montesquieu, who have discussed more the principles of liberty and the structure of government, lie under the same disadvantage of having written before these subjects were illuminated by the events and discussions which distinguish a very recent period. Both of them, too, are evidently warped by a regard to the particular government of England, to which one of them owed allegiance; and the other professed an admiration bordering on idolatry. . . . The chapter on prerogative shows how much the reason of the philosopher was clouded by the Royalism of the Englishman.[27]

Presidents and commentators would later debate the narrower aspect of Locke's prerogative argument with respect to true emergencies, but the framers were at pains both during the debate on the presidency and in the ratification debate to distance themselves from the concept and certainly from the broad use of it laid out in Locke's expansive language.

That having been said, many presidents have felt the need to reach out with executive orders or proclamations, creating some of the most important debates over executive action and some of the most important policy moves in our history.[28] From George Washington's Neutrality Proclamation through Abraham Lincoln's many direct actions during the Civil War (including the Emancipation Proclamation) to more than seventeen hundred executive orders issued by Woodrow Wilson before, during, and after World War I, to the executive orders that were used to engineer the Tea Pot Dome debacle, to the raft of orders issued by Franklin Delano Roosevelt to implement the National Industrial Recovery Act, to his use of Executive Order 9066 as the basis for the exclusion and later incarceration of Asian Americans during World War II, to Harry Truman's order desegregating the military, to Truman's and later Dwight Eisenhower's orders launching the ill-fated loyalty-security program, to Eisenhower's national security directive launching the overthrow of the Arbenz regime in Guatemala, to John F. Kennedy's order attacking housing discrimination, to Lyndon Johnson's order mandating affirmative action in government contracting, to Richard Nixon's imposition by orders and proclamations of a wage and price freeze, to Jimmy Carter's oil import fee order, to Ronald Reagan's regulatory review and security classification orders, to George Bush's national security directives supporting the Iran-Contra imbroglio, to Clinton's order attempting to block striker replacements, to George W. Bush's order calling for military arrests, detention, and trial of noncitizens in the wake of the September 11 attack, these tools of presidential direct action have been at the heart of the good, the bad, and the ugly of the presidency. Broad assumptions about the existence or scope of a prerogative power in the presidency will not resolve such difficulties, either politically or constitutionally.

The Importance of the Constitutional Dialogue

Despite the difficulties involved in getting into court to challenge the use of presidential direct action instruments, there have been many cases that have addressed the limits of executive action or that have come about because of executive directives. The important point here is to understand that what is involved, as Louis Fisher argues, is not simply a set of presidential actions and legal reactions but an ongoing "constitutional dialogue."[29] It is a continuing conversation not only about particular policies but also about the presidency, its powers, and its relationships to other key participants in the governing process.

Though it is certainly the case, as James David Barber has argued,[30] that there is great opportunity for each occupant of the White House to place his or her distinctive stamp on the office, the presidency is an institution. And as Michael Sandel has reminded us, "Political institutions are not simply instruments that implement ideas independently conceived; they are themselves embodiments of ideas."[31] Institutions are not merely mechanisms to accomplish particular purposes; they are repositories and maintainers of values. And the temporary occupant of the presidency can by his or her actions affect the institution for good or ill. "Beyond the character and times of individual presidents, and the vagaries and coherence of their appeal and advisory systems, there is the ongoing office. Each incumbent fleshes out the presidency in a different way."[32] The constitutional dialogue that takes place over time, involving the president and the other branches, not only affects the resolution of particular policy disputes but also the nature and powers of the presidency itself.

When the president relies for his or her authority to issue an order or proclamation on the Article 2 executive powers of the Constitution, major constitutional debates can occur, and their results can have long-lasting effects. President Truman's seizure of the steel mills during a labor dispute provides an important case in point. In that incident, the debate was well under way even before Truman issued his Executive Order 10349 on April 8, 1952.[33] The president had fought a losing battle with Congress over labor legislation with the passage of the Taft-Hartley Act. Looking back on previous experiences with seizures, Congress had considered granting the president seizure authority under certain conditions in labor disputes but had rejected the proposal. Even so, the president was convinced that the commitments of the nation to European reconstruction and to the troops on the battlefields of Korea, along with a number of historical examples of seizures, would provide him with the support needed to sustain his claim to constitutional authority. For several members of the Supreme Court, the fact that Congress had spoken and had rejected the president's call for support was critically important. The Court's majority spoke through Justice Hugo Black, overturning Truman's seizure of the steel mills, but Justice Robert Jackson's concurring opinion was to have an important impact for the future.[34] Jackson analyzed the president's action not principally by an examination of Article 2 powers but in a wider framework that asked whether the circumstance was one in which the president was in agreement with Congress, acting in the absence of any legislative statement on the type of action taken by the chief executive, or whether the president was acting in a way that had been rejected by Congress.

A young clerk who had worked for Jackson, William Rehnquist, learned much from the justice and would later turn Jackson's approach into the controlling standard in a case arising from the executive agreements and executive orders, issued first by President Carter and then by President Reagan, concerning the resolution of the Iran Hostage crisis. Applying, and even expanding upon Jackson's framework, Associate Justice Rehnquist found that the failure of Congress to reject the actions of the two presidents, coupled with what were considered to be similar examples of international settlement agreements, constituted acquiescence in the president's actions.[35]

Of course, the interbranch dialogue that Fisher has described is often even more active and continuous when statutory authority is involved. And since presidents have most often claimed either direct statutory authority or mixed statutory and constitutional foundations for their actions, such a rich, complex, and ongoing dialogue involving the three branches is common, at least in those instances in which the president's actions are controversial inside or outside of government.

The Many Players in the Contemporary Game: Interorganizational and Intergovernmental Complexity

In order to understand the full significance of the use of these presidential policy tools, it is necessary to remember at all times that the conversation includes many participants in addition to the Congress and the Supreme Court. It includes all the stakeholders in the policy communities that are affected directly and sometimes even indirectly by presidential directives. Just as such groups offer legislators draft legislation in an effort to get their causes onto the public agenda and to move them toward acceptable policy resolutions, so there are interest groups that press the White House for direct action.

Even beyond the variety of Washington voices in the dialogue, however, it is important to consider the discussion outside the Beltway. Indeed, it is essential to consider the intergovernmental dimensions of presidential direct action. In some instances, state and local governments, and the contractors who work with them in the delivery of public services, are positively affected by presidential direct action. Thus, when President Carter sought to ensure that agencies provided more notice through a wider variety of means and increased opportunity to participate in agency rulemaking, it became more feasible for state and local voices to be heard in the policy process.[36] On the other hand, those voices beyond the Beltway have been growing stronger and more critical as the demands have increased on states and localities to accept greater responsibility for implementation of national policies while resources to support those obligations have declined.[37] State and local officials have reacted with increasing anger in those instances in which they have concluded that executive orders or other presidential instruments have increased what they perceive to be the federal government's intrusion into their affairs.[38]

Intergovernmental issues were often recognized as important in the areas of health, education, and welfare, which the federal government has traditionally addressed through grants, with a host of regulations attached. Presidents have recognized that participants in these programs could often be reached by executive orders associated with grantees or contractors.[39] However, what is not as widely understood is the growing importance, since the late 1970s, of an intergovernmental model of regulation.[40] Under this approach, states have been permitted to develop their own standards for regulated activities (provided they are at least as rigorous as the federal standards and are approved by the national agency involved) and to enforce the standards as well. If they are unable or unwilling to set their own standards, they may nevertheless be approved to implement the federal standards themselves. Only if they will not do either will the federal government step in and operate the programs directly. Thus, state and local governments are more intimately involved than ever before in federal programs, including those governed or at least shaped by presidential direct action. For this reason, among others, they are important participants in the constitutional dialogue.

International and Emergency Pressures

There is one additional set of baseline concerns in any discussion of the use of the tools of presidential direct action. These relate to the traditional deference granted to presidents in international matters and in emergency situations. Though the framers of the Constitution clearly intended that the president should not possess the powers of the king with respect to treaties and the ability to commit the nation to war, it has also been the case that presidents have traditionally been granted considerable freedom of action in the foreign policy arena, even in situations in which Congress or the courts might have asserted their own powers. Certainly the latitude afforded President George W. Bush after the September 11 attacks on the World Trade Center and the Pentagon is a clear example. Legislators of both parties have often felt the need to rally around the president when troops have been sent into the field, even in the absence of a declaration of war. Indeed, it has been common over the course of American history for Congress to pass a war powers resolution after the outbreak of hostilities to ratify presidential orders and proclamations, sweeping though they often were.

The Supreme Court has usually avoided head-on confrontations with the chief executive in crisis conditions, as in the case of the initial challenges to the World War II–era Japanese exclusion orders issued by General John DeWitt pursuant to Executive Order 9066.[41] The Court has frequently repeated the famous (or infamous, depending on one's point of view) dictum that the president is the sole organ of foreign policy and great deference is owed to his actions in that arena.[42] Indeed, when the Court reviewed Abraham Lincoln's actions at the outbreak of the Civil War, it found that not only was he authorized to take such actions but that he also was in fact constitutionally obligated to do so.[43] And in the contemporary world, the other participants in the constitutional dialogue have been willing, within limits, to recognize natural disasters and even economic emergencies as deserving of some of the same kinds of deference that have been accorded the president in military and foreign policy settings.

That having been said, it is also true that after the high point of a crisis passes, the president had better be prepared for two kinds of important reactions. First, the Congress and the courts may rather quickly shed their deferential approaches. Second, the fallout from emergencies is often intense and may very well have long-lasting consequences for the institutional presidency.

With respect to the first problem, although the Supreme Court has rarely taken the chief executive on in the intense moments of crisis, it has been willing after the immediate emergency passes to rule against the president.[44] The mere fact that a president claims there is an economic emergency does not mean that the judiciary or the Congress will consent, as President Carter learned when he tried to impose fuel import charges on grounds of the economic impact of the energy crisis[45] or as occurred in the attempt by the Reagan administration to block rulemaking on a claim that it was required first to meet soaring inflation and then to respond to the recession.

However, advocates of a strong presidency may answer that such late responses really count for little, since by the time they issue forth, the president could not care less, the crisis having been successfully met. On the other hand, this is the kind of situation in which the actions of one president may lead to responses that are troublesome for future administrations. Thus, there is little question that the perceived abuses of emergency powers claims and military or other foreign policy necessities during the Johnson and Nixon years led to a string of legislative responses in the 1970s. The National Emergencies Act, the War Powers Resolution, and the Congressional Budget and Impoundment Control Act are among the more obvious, though by no means the only, examples.

A FEW WORDS ABOUT NUMBERS

There was a good deal of discussion in the news media during the Clinton years, much of it poorly informed, about executive orders. The media tend to use that term to describe a wide range of presidential tools that apply to very different people in significantly varied ways. At the core of much of the commentary has been the assertion that presidents are using executive orders more than ever before. The immediate tendency is to count the numbers of orders. Unfortunately, that is an unhelpful exercise. In fact, the numbers of orders issued by recent administrations show no significant increases, and in a number of cases, actually indicate decreases over earlier periods, particularly when compared to presidents from Wilson through Truman. That said, a mere counting tells us little. The issue goes more to content than to quantity. Further, recent administrations, particularly those of George Bush, Bill Clinton, and George W. Bush, have tended to increase significantly the use of presidential memoranda and to use them interchangeably with executive orders or even side by side with executive orders on the same topic. This has become so common that presidents like Clinton have made public statements about the issuance of a new executive order that turned out to be a memorandum. The same kinds of problems exist with respect to national security directives, only in that case we have only partial information about some administrations, since significant portions of material from some administrations remain classified. The fact that the Federation of American Scientists and some presidential libraries have provided numbers and approximate titles tells us relatively little. Presidential signing statements have been common for most modern administrations, but there is no question that their substance and import have changed since the Reagan years. For all these reasons, running the numbers really tells us very little and we will not focus on it.

It should also be noted, however, that it was possible to locate and use literally thousands of executive orders, proclamations, memoranda, national security directives, and signing statements for this analysis. Each chapter speaks to the problems of accessing each of the types of materials in question, though some are obviously much easier to locate than others. There is also a brief source note at the end of the book that provides additional guidance. While the emphasis is on the postwar presidencies, the study drew on materials dating all the way back to George Washington, where that provided useful insights. One of the surprises in the research was that it was possible to obtain a large body of national security directives dating back to the Truman years and including even some declassified portions of directives from the Clinton years. Even so, there is a variety of difficulties in obtaining some of the materials analyzed here, and those problems will be discussed as each of the tools is considered.

CONCLUSION

The chapters that follow will examine each of the power tools available to the president. Each will ask a number of questions. What is it? How is it used? Why are such devices used? What are their potential strengths? What difficulties might they engender? How has their use changed over time? After this individual tool-by-tool consideration, the concluding chapter considers some more general lessons to be learned from these analyses. These lessons are important for presidents, their administrations, legislators, scholars, and citizens.

TWO
EXECUTIVE ORDERS:
DIRECTING THE EXECUTIVE BRANCH

President Clinton's first official act after taking the oath of office was not to prepare the State of the Union address, to send the names of nominees for cabinet appointments to the Senate for confirmation, or to transmit his legislative package to congressional leaders. His first official act was to sign an executive order, specifically Executive Order 12832.[1] It was not an action mandated by the Constitution or by statute. This order was not adopted to deal with a national emergency that required action to protect the country against attack or to move federal resources to deal immediately with a natural disaster. Indeed, it was no small bit of irony that the order concerned a set of ethical commitments to which all new appointees would have to subscribe, the violations of which could result in removal from office.

When George W. Bush replaced Clinton, he moved quickly to issue his own political executive orders in his first week in office. With great fanfare, Bush launched his so-called faith-based service initiative, for example, aimed at increasing federal government partnerships with faith-based organizations in human services programs, with two executive orders.[2]

The idea that the president could move to govern in no small part by decree is a concept of which most Americans are blissfully unaware. If they were alert to the practice, many would most likely be aghast that the president could, in effect, write law without benefit of the normal constitutional processes or even the requirements for administrative rulemaking mandated by statute.[3] Some might indignantly claim that this is a constitutional travesty on a magnitude that would cause the founders to roll over in their graves. Others might insist that this is an unprecedented action of presidential ego. Nevertheless, a number of the framers were very much involved in the development of the executive order, and although one might or might not find some of President Clinton's actions to be based on a highly developed sense of himself, there was certainly nothing new in making quick use of the executive order as a device to enact policy and to communicate political messages. Indeed, he was following the lead of his Republican and his Democratic predecessors.

Rule by presidential decree has been the subject of serious controversy since the administration of George Washington, however, and the debates continue. Even though it is a little known fact, the truth is that some kind of presidential direct action has been at the root of some of the most intense debates in American history. It should be noted that executive orders issued by governors and mayors have also been at the heart of major controversies. Examples include orders issued by Florida governor Jeb Bush and California governor Pete Wilson seeking to end affirmative action programs and a number of controversial orders issued by New York City mayors, like Ed Koch and Rudolph Giuliani.[4]

There are many reasons why executive orders have been used throughout American history by presidents of all parties and ideologies. In some instances, indeed, presidents are mandated by law or by circumstance to issue such orders. Few knowledgeable observers, even those who are quite critical of some of the uses and abuses of presidential decrees, are prepared to suggest that executive orders should be banned outright. For a new administration, then, the challenge is to understand what executive orders are, how they are used, why they are employed, what potential strengths they offer, and what difficulties they may engender.

WHAT ARE EXECUTIVE ORDERS?

Among the available tools of presidential direct action, the one about which members of a new administration are most likely to be aware is the executive order. There is a tendency, particularly by the news media, to use the term broadly and generically to include the whole family of presidential power tools. Executive orders are directives issued by the president to officers of the executive branch, requiring them to take an action, stop a certain type of activity, alter policy, change management practices, or accept a delegation of authority under which they will henceforth be responsible for the implementation of law. The most commonly cited definition comes from a 1957 study on executive orders done for the House Committee on Government Operations: "In the narrower sense Executive Orders are written documents denominated as such. . . . Executive orders are generally directed to, and govern actions by, Government officials and agencies. They usually affect private individuals only indirectly. Proclamations in most instances affect primarily the activities of private individuals."[5] This traditional interpretation has held that executive orders are used internally while proclamations are directives issued to those outside the government. For reasons that will be made clear, however, the situation in practice is somewhat more complex and not nearly so neatly defined.[6]

The form of executive orders has varied dramatically over time. "The earliest Executive Orders sometimes took the form of hastily scribbled Presidential endorsements on legal briefs or upon the margins of maps. Presidents wrote, 'Approved,' 'Let it be done,' or other short comments and these jottings sufficed to stamp a proposal with the authority of the Presidential imprimatur."[7] Many were not even signed by the president but by the secretary of state or some other cabinet officer.[8] In fact, there was no serious effort to establish any uniformity of style until President Ulysses S. Grant imposed one by executive order in 1873.[9] However, even after that the Supreme Court expressed a reluctance to entertain claims brought against an executive order on grounds that it was not of proper form.[10]

President Herbert Hoover issued an order of his own in 1929, establishing a process for the development of executive orders, and several succeeding presidents have added their own changes to that process.[11] It often comes as a surprise to people called upon to work with orders today that the current governing guidelines for the issuance of executive orders are themselves from an executive order issued by President Kennedy. Executive Order 11030 was first promulgated in 1962, though it has been amended by a number of later orders issued during the Johnson, Carter, and Reagan administrations.[12] These orders require that proposed executive orders, originating outside the White House, be submitted to the director of the Office of Management and Budget (OMB). If approved by the OMB, the proposed order goes to the attorney general for consideration of its legality and to the Office of the Federal Register for a review as to form. If these steps are cleared, the proposed order or proclamation goes to the president for signature.

For many administrations, this simple process of promulgating authoritative policies is far more attractive than the arduous effort needed to move a bill through the Congress. It is also far simpler than what administrative agencies must accomplish to promulgate a regulation. There is no requirement for notice and public participation. Indeed, the Supreme Court has held that the president is not covered by the Administrative Procedure Act (APA)[13] that applies to other executive agencies.[14] It was largely because of this simplicity, and in an effort to avoid the other more standard vehicles for developing policies—and the political disputes that sometimes accompany them—that former vice president Al Gore's National Performance Review (NPR) recommended that President Clinton should proceed as much as possible by presidential directive rather than by statute or by administrative rulemaking.[15]

The only general statutory requirement is for publication of executive orders and proclamations in the *Federal Register*. The Federal Register Act, which mandates publication of most official pronouncements by executive agencies as well as executive orders and proclamations, was adopted in 1935.[16] The legislation came about largely as a result of difficulties engendered by executive orders.

The National Industrial Recovery Act was passed in June 1933 as part of the attack on the Great Depression by the newly installed administration of Franklin Delano Roosevelt (FDR). The act, among other things, authorized the affected industries to develop codes of fair competition, which acquired the force of law when signed by the president. By the end of 1933, no less than two hundred fifty executive orders had been issued promulgating or amending National Recovery Administration (NRA) codes of competition. On November 27 a record twenty-three such executive orders were issued in one day. Indeed, there were so many NRA orders that the administration ultimately issued E.O. 6497 in December 1933, exempting NRA orders from the ordinary procedures, minimal though they were, for issuing executive orders.[17] And since there was no orderly process for making or disseminating NRA orders, it came as no surprise that both the government and the businesses that were supposed to live by the codes became confused.

An executive order was issued in August 1933 setting forth the requirements of the code governing the petroleum industry, including one provision that applied criminal penalties to violations of the quotas established by the code. Two oil companies sued in October, seeking injunctions to block enforcement of that part of the order. However, although another executive order had been issued in September that had eliminated the part of the code they were challenging, neither government lawyers nor the companies realized that fact.[18] The case wound its way through the system and all the way to the U.S. Supreme Court. While the case was moving through the courts, in September 1934, the provision in question was reinstated by another executive order. In seeking to untangle the confusion in the case before it, the Court observed:

> That assumption was that this section still contained the paragraph (eliminated by the Executive Order of September 13, 1933) by which production in excess of assigned quotas was made an unfair practice and a violation of the Code. Whatever the cause of the failure to give appropriate public notice of the change in the section, with the result that the persons affected, the prosecuting authorities, and the courts, were alike ignorant of the alter-

ation, the fact is that the attack in this respect was upon a provision which did not exist.[19]

Unfortunately, because the Federal Register Act evolved in this way, it ultimately proved a limited tool for addressing concerns raised by presidential decrees. The language of the act spoke only to executive orders and proclamations:

> **44 U.S.C. SEC. 1505. DOCUMENTS TO BE PUBLISHED IN FEDERAL REGISTER**
>
> (a) Proclamations and Executive Orders; Documents Having General Applicability and Legal Effect; Documents Required to Be Published by Congress. There shall be published in the Federal Register—
>
> (1) Presidential proclamations and Executive orders, except those not having general applicability and legal effect or effective only against Federal agencies or persons in their capacity as officers, agents, or employees thereof;
>
> (2) documents or classes of documents that the President may determine from time to time have general applicability and legal effect; and
>
> (3) documents or classes of documents that may be required so to be published by Act of Congress.

Partly in an effort to escape even these minor requirements, modern administrations have learned to accomplish their tasks without necessarily labeling a particular decree as an executive order (or a proclamation). Even some directives that were executive orders were not required to be published because they were security classified. Their existence was revealed by publication of an executive order number, usually with a letter suffix but nothing more. Even that much disclosure has been avoided by many presidents in the postwar years by turning what might have been executive orders into national security directives (see chapter 6). Other matters related to international affairs were also exempted from the publication requirements by the Register Act itself: "This chapter does not apply to treaties, conventions, protocols, and other international agreements, or proclamations thereof by the President."[20] Thus, large numbers of decrees that were for all intents and purposes executive orders could be promulgated without ensuring that their existence or their terms would be made publicly known through publication in the *Federal Register*.

But publication is only the beginning of the discussion about ensuring the availability of presidential directives to the Congress and the public. As is true of statutes and regulations, the mere chronological publication of presidential decrees is of little help, since the sheer volume of information is overwhelming. The real need is to provide a codification of the materials that brings together all related orders and updates them so that it is possible to have in one place all the current orders applicable in any given situation. Such a codification was done twice, most recently in 1989 to cover only proclamations and orders from April 1945 through January 1989, but it has not been produced since then.[21] It is true that the Code of Federal Regulations, Part 3, contains presidential actions and that libraries that obtain it often have back issues, but that is still only a chronological listing for a particular period of time and not a codification. In fact, the Federal Register Act specifically exempts executive orders from the kind of codification that is required for other authoritative administrative actions.[22]

An understanding of the full body of presidential pronouncements has been even more difficult because the numbering process that is used to label and organize orders did not begin until 1907. At that time the Department of State began numbering orders that were then sent to the department as the official depository for such decrees. The orders were backnumbered to take into account those historical orders on hand; thus, Executive Order 1 was designated to be an order issued by President Lincoln in 1862 that established military courts in Louisiana.[23] A compilation of those orders was not published until 1944, the result of a Works Projects Administration (WPA) project of the New Deal.[24] Of course, there were many orders issued before the State Department began its number and filing system. It has been estimated that there were anywhere between fifteen thousand and fifty thousand orders that were never accounted for.[25] Another WPA project attempted to collect summaries of as many of the unnumbered orders as possible. That study provides useful information but certainly is not complete.[26]

There has been an attempt by the National Archives to clarify the current status of executive orders through what are termed Executive Order Disposition Tables,[27] but this effort is not really a codification of executive orders and proclamations, let alone a full integration of the several different types of instruments of presidential direct action. The tables provide only chronological listings of orders issued by presidents since Eisenhower and indications as to whether they have been altered or rescinded. The disposition tables were necessary because executive orders remain in force until they are replaced, amended, or rescinded by the president that issued them or a successor. One of the important tasks for any new administration then is to attempt to understand the orders that it has inherited from its predecessors and to determine what should be done with them.

However, for the preceding reasons, it is often quite difficult to find all the relevant authoritative pronouncements applicable to a particular agency and program. That is true not only for people who must interact with the executive branch but also for Congress and even for the White House itself. Indeed, one of the first tasks for an incoming administration is to get a clear picture of what orders are in place in what fields and how they relate to statutes and to other policy statements issued by executive branch agencies.

HOW ARE EXECUTIVE ORDERS USED?

Among the reasons executive orders are so difficult to master is that they are used in a variety of ways and for a plethora of reasons. Consider first how they are employed. Let us be candid about this challenge. Plowing through the how and why of executive orders can seem a rather tedious task, but it is only by knowing what the tool is and how it can be used that an administration can employ it effectively and avoid some of the dangerous consequences that can flow from using it badly or in the wrong situations. As many power brokers have learned, it is precisely because most people will not make the effort to delve into the details that there is often so much room to maneuver.[28]

Vehicles for Issuing Binding Pronouncements to Units of the Executive Branch

In the most general sense, the primary use of executive orders is to make legally binding pronouncements. There are many ways for a chief executive to communicate his or her wishes to subordinates, but executive orders are intended to be authoritative and lasting. In order to make use of the tool in this way, it is essential to understand the nature of the authority carried by orders.

The legal force of an executive order derives from the statutory or constitutional authority cited by the president in issuing the decree.[29] Indeed, many orders are issued pursuant to statute. In cases where the Congress has not specifically called for executive orders, presidents have usually claimed at least implied statutory authority for their actions, even when they were certain that they also had independent constitutional authority under Article 2's executive powers of the Constitution for their orders. If valid, presidential orders have also been recognized as acceptable authority for the issuance by executive agencies of substantive rules (rules having the force of law).[30]

Many of the disputes over executive orders arise with respect to whether the authority the president claims can fairly be implied from the statute in question. This point about real as compared with claimed authority has become more of an issue over the years as various administrations have identified a number of statutes that seem to offer a great deal of latitude to a president seeking to issue an executive order. Classic examples would include the Trading with the Enemy Act, which has been used for everything from actual wartime situations to President Nixon's imposition of wage-price controls and President Carter's failed attempt to impose a fuel surcharge.[31] Another open-textured provision is a statute that grants the president broad discretion to subdelegate authority and to assign tasks and responsibilities to executive branch officials.[32]

Whether the claim is that statutory authority for an order is expressly stated or implied, it can stand only if the statute itself is valid. That requires both that the statute be within the constitutional authority of the Congress and that it not be in violation of the Constitution. The Supreme Court has on rare occasions added yet a third requirement: that the statute must not violate the so-called nondelegation doctrine. In the *Yakus v. United States* case, concerning E.O. 9250 issued by FDR under the Emergency Price Control Act of 1942, the Court laid out the general requirements for an appropriate delegation of authority: "The Act is thus an exercise by Congress of its legislative power. In it Congress has stated the legislative objective, has prescribed the method of achieving that objective—maximum price fixing—, and has laid down standards to guide the administrative determination of both the occasions for the exercise of the price-fixing power, and the particular prices to be established."[33] However, in the *Panama Refining* case, the Court concluded that, in the National Industrial Recovery Act (NIRA), the Congress "declares no policy as to the transportation of the excess production. So far as this section is concerned, it gives to the President an unlimited authority to determine the policy and to lay down the prohibition, or not to lay it down, as he may see fit. And disobedience to his order is made a crime punishable by fine and imprisonment."[34]

In the famous "sick chicken case," also brought to test the NIRA, the Court concluded, "Congress cannot delegate legislative power to the President to exercise an unfettered discretion to make whatever laws he thinks may be needed or advisable for the rehabilitation and expansion of trade or industry."[35] In other words, Congress is not to provide standardless delegations of authority to the president or other officers of the executive branch. However, given the fact that the Supreme Court has been unwilling to impose the nondelegation doctrine as a barrier since the New Deal, it remains to be seen whether it could be successfully invoked today to challenge a statute or a presidential order issued under it.[36]

More recently, the tendency has been for presidential actions to be viewed from the perspective offered by Justice Jackson in his concurring opinion in the steel seizure case, when he framed the assessment of presidential actions in relational terms. Justice Rehnquist summarized the approach:

> Justice Jackson's concurring opinion elaborated in a general way the consequences of different types of interaction between the two democratic branches in assessing Presidential authority to act in any given case. When the President acts pursuant to an express or implied authorization from Congress, he exercises not only his powers but also those delegated by Congress. In such a case the executive action "would be supported by the strongest of presumptions and the widest latitude of judicial interpretation, and the burden of persuasion would rest heavily upon any who might attack it." *Id.,* at 637. When the President acts in the absence of congressional authorization he may enter "a zone of twilight in which he and Congress may have concurrent authority, or in which its distribution is uncertain." *Ibid.* In such a case the analysis becomes more complicated, and the validity of the President's action, at least so far as separation-of-powers principles are concerned, hinges on a consideration of all the circumstances which might shed light on the views of the Legislative Branch toward such action, including "congressional inertia, indifference or quiescence." *Ibid.* Finally, when the President acts in contravention of the will of Congress, "his power is at its lowest ebb," and the Court can sustain his actions "only by disabling the Congress from acting upon the subject." *Id.,* at 637–638.[37]

In the case of executive orders, federal courts have found that congressional-executive agreement could be expressed in a number of ways. In addition to adopting a statute that specifically authorized future presidential decrees, the Congress could ratify presidential action after the fact.[38] The classic example of this approach has come during times of war, when Congress has adopted a war powers bill, approving actions taken to that point in an emergency and authorizing further and often broad presidential actions.[39] (Legislators have also overturned executive orders that had previously been issued when they disagreed with the president's actions.) But there have been other occasions on which courts have been willing to accept less direct evidence of legislative support. For example, there have been a number of cases in which the Supreme Court has taken the fact of continued funding for particular programs as evidence of congressional ratification, particularly if the president's actions were specifically mentioned during the appropriations process.[40]

There is another way that orders have been sustained. In an opinion by Rehnquist, the Supreme Court upheld orders issued by Presidents Carter and Reagan in settling the Iran Hostage crisis.[41] The settlement was accomplished by executive agreement (not by treaty) and through executive orders implementing that agreement. Among other provisions, the orders effectively blocked efforts by American businesses to proceed through U.S. federal courts to satisfy their claims against Iranian assets in the United States that had been frozen during the hostage crisis. The agreement established a claim procedure that was to be handled internationally to resolve all claims. In this instance the Court found that although some of the presidents' actions were supported by statutes, others were not. Even so, the justices considered the orders to be examples of executive action in that so-called "twilight area" mentioned by Justice Jackson, in which there was neither congressional support nor legislative opposition. Rehnquist concluded that the presidents' actions could be sustained in significant measure because Congress had acquiesced. Even though there was no disagreement within the Court on this point, it was a matter of considerable concern to the businesses involved that a president could take dramatic action that had the effect of blocking litigation in the federal courts and have that action upheld largely because Congress did nothing.

Of course, the Court has also recognized that the president has independent constitutional authority under Article 2 that can be used to justify an order in appropriate circumstances, whether Congress disagrees with or supports the chief executive.[42] At the same time, presidents are not relieved of their constitutional obligation to respect properly enacted statutes, and courts can intervene to issue findings on the validity of presidential actions.[43]

Indeed, there have been a variety of cases in which courts have found that presidents violated constitutional or statutory provisions. Many officials have certainly heard of the constitutional battle lost by President Truman when he ordered the seizure of steel mills, but most are not aware that such rulings against presidential orders can be traced to the early years of the Republic[44] and are as contemporary as the ruling of the U.S. Circuit Court for the District of Columbia rejecting President Clinton's striker replacement order in *Chamber of Commerce v. Reich*.[45]

Despite the long history of battles over presidential direct action, new questions continue to arise about basic issues as to the legal status of orders.

For example, it was only in 1999 that the Supreme Court for the first time considered whether executive orders are severable, as is true of statutes, such that one portion of an order could be struck down while leaving other portions intact. The Court concluded at that time that they were indeed severable. Even so, the Court's 1999 ruling struck down an 1850 executive order issued by President John Tyler, revoking rights granted to an Indian tribe in an 1837 treaty on grounds that that particular order was not severable because it was one unified policy statement.[46] The lesson here is that the vulnerabilities of executive orders are many, varied, and real. Though it can be difficult for critics to get an order into court, there are any number of presidents who have lost significant cases.

Making Policy in Fields Generally Conceded to the President

Exactly how and how much particular chief executives use executive orders may be a matter of recurring conflict, but many of the uses of the tool are widely accepted. This expectation that the president will act by decree sometimes stems from the fact that certain important functions must be carried out, despite the lack of legislation, or out of inertia related to a continuing practice by previous administrations of both parties.

Probably the most prominent example is in the area of security classifications. Presidents since the days of Franklin Roosevelt have made the issuance of executive orders on security classification an important order of business. Although policies were generated dealing with security issues as early as 1869,[47] Congress did not adopt legislation authorizing security classifications for more than a century after that. While World War I–era legislation made it a crime to disclose classified information, it did not set out a classification system or speak directly to the president's power to do so.[48]

Franklin Roosevelt issued the first executive order laying out the classification system and process in 1940 as World War II was unfolding in Europe, with U.S. involvement a virtual certainty.[49] President Truman followed with his own orders on the subject.[50] Interestingly, Congress missed another clear opportunity to address the security classification issue when it adopted the landmark National Security Act of 1947. Dwight Eisenhower inherited a large and expanding body of classified material as the cold war nuclear regime and the work of the national security policy agencies established in the postwar period grew. The Eisenhower and later the Kennedy administrations adopted executive orders on the subject.[51]

By the time Richard Nixon came to the White House, issues of national security, in both its foreign and domestic aspects, had become an extremely controversial subject and were about to become more so. Even though Senator Joseph McCarthy had long since departed the scene, the cold war–era attacks on anyone or anything considered subversive continued well past the 1950s. Critics of the civil rights and antiwar movements of the 1960s and 1970s painted those groups as subversive. Given Nixon's tendency to see enemies and adversaries all around, it was not surprising that the intensity of security concerns escalated, often with worrisome consequences, as in the case of the domestic surveillance program.[52] When the misdeeds of the administration became public as the Watergate-related publicity spread the stories across the newspapers and television screen, Congress reacted with a strengthened Freedom of Information Act and a New Right to Privacy Act, but, interestingly enough, not with a statute directly on the subject of classification.

It was therefore no surprise that by the time President Carter came to office in 1977 there was pressure to address problems of overclassification and the need for declassification of existing classified materials. Not only did the Carter people seek to adopt a new classification policy, replacing President Nixon's Executive Order 11652,[53] but they went at it in a new and participative fashion, resulting in Executive Order 12065.[54] The Carter order adopted a "when in doubt, don't classify (or declassify)" presumption. On the other hand, it was also no great surprise when, in April 1982, President Reagan issued Executive Order 12356, which replaced the Carter order and reversed the approach.[55] What engendered considerable conflict at that time was the fact that the Reagan administration's development of its security classification order was done in a manner that was far less open and participative than the Carter effort, including allegations that the administration deliberately froze Congress out of the process.

Even so, it was not until 1994 that Congress acted, specifically authorizing, and indeed requiring, presidential issuance of an executive order on classification. It came as an amendment to the National Security Act of 1947 and provided that "not later than 180 days after the date of enactment of this title, the President shall, by Executive order or regulation, establish procedures to govern access to classified information which shall be binding upon all departments, agencies, and offices of the executive branch of Government."[56] President Clinton then issued Executive Order 12958, revoking the Reagan order and again making a significant change, moving in the direction of reduced classification and increased attention to the need for appropriate declassification.[57]

Security classification is probably the best-known example of a field largely ceded to governance by executive order, but it is certainly not the only one. Other examples include ongoing governance of civil servants, foreign service and consular activities, operation and discipline in the military, controls on government contracting, and, until recently, the management and control of public lands. Although there are statutes in all these areas, there has been a tradition over many administrations of the use of executive orders as primary or at least as important policy and management tools.

Initiating or Directing Regulation

At the other end of the spectrum from the typically accepted uses of executive orders are those cases in which the administration uses them as mechanisms of regulation, not only of agencies but also of businesses or citizens through the technical device of orders to government officials. The traditional understanding has been that the device generally used to address the behavior of those outside the executive branch is the presidential proclamation. However, executive orders have been used from the earliest days to initiate regulation or to implement regulatory programs enacted by Congress. George Washington issued an order for implementation of U.S. sanctions against trade with French interests. Unfortunately, for one of the captains enforcing the policy, Washington's order was found by the Supreme Court to have exceeded the congressional mandate and a Captain George Little was ordered to pay some eight thousand dollars as a fine for trespass to the owner of a vessel he seized.[58] President Lincoln issued a range of orders dealing with control over Civil War–era trade practices. Battles raged over the effects on railroad company rights of way affected by presidential orders concerning reservation lands in the late nineteenth century.[59] And in the 1920s, executive orders were used to control and restrict airspace and to assign some radio frequencies.[60]

Regulatory orders have ranged from specific orders aimed at particular businesses or people to more general directives that nevertheless call for broad regulatory efforts. Though President Truman's famous steel seizure order was directed to the secretary of commerce, the intended targets of the order were clear and specific: the recalcitrant steel firms. More recently, the Supreme Court has recognized such obviously regulatory orders as directives to the secretary of state setting forth rules governing passports.[61]

One of the most dramatic uses of executive orders for regulatory purposes occurred during the Nixon administration. In 1971, President Nixon issued Executive Order 11615 imposing a wage-price freeze.[62] While it did establish an administrative agency with responsibility for implementation of the order, plainly it spoke directly to the public:

> Section 1. (a) Prices, rents, wages, and salaries shall be stabilized for a period of 90 days from the date hereof at levels not greater than the highest of those pertaining to a substantial volume of actual transactions by each individual, business, form or other entity of any kind during the 30-day period ending August 14, 1971, for like or similar commodities or services. If no transactions occurred in that period, the ceiling will be the highest price, rent, salary or wage in the nearest preceding 30-day prior in which transactions did occur. No person shall charge, assess, or receive, directly or indirectly in any transaction prices or rents in any form higher than those permitted hereunder, and no person shall, directly or indirectly, pay or agree to pay in any transaction wages or salaries in any form, or to use any means to obtain payment of wages and salaries in any form, higher than those permitted hereunder, whether by retroactive increase or otherwise.
>
> Each person engaged in the business of selling or providing commodities or services shall maintain available for public inspection a record of the highest prices or rents charged for such or similar commodities or services during the 30-day period ending August 14, 1971.

Formally known as the economic stabilization program, the freeze was extended by executive order until May 1, 1972. Despite its dramatic reach and importance, the program was authorized by statute, and that broad delegation of power was upheld against challenges.[63]

A Device to Delegate Authority to Other Agencies or Officers

Many of the executive orders issued by presidents have been delegations of authority originally conferred on the president by statute to various agencies or officers of the executive branch. Although these are rarely controversial matters in the contemporary era, they were matters of contention in earlier times. For one thing, it is more common now for Congress to assign statutory obligations directly to specific agencies, sometimes precisely for the purpose of preventing White House frustration of legislative intentions. In an earlier period, particularly up to and through World War II, Congress often assigned responsibilities to the president as head of the executive branch. Although it was understood that no president could personally attend to all of these duties, there was concern about the legality of subdelegations to subordinate officials and, more generally, about the possible loss of account-ability that could result if authority drifted out of the very visible office of the president and down into the bureaucracy. These concerns were exacerbated by the Brownlow Commission's warnings about the loss of integration and effective organizational control of the executive branch by the president.[64] The problem seemed to grow more worrisome during the war years when a host of agencies was created to govern wide-ranging domestic activities as well as military and war production functions. In the early postwar years, there was a wave of legislation that presented the president with many new obligations, including creation of what is now known as the national security agencies. By the late 1940s, it was becoming clear that the president had responsibilities under some eleven hundred different statutes.[65]

It was against this background that the White House sought legislation that would provide a broad-based authority for the president to subdelegate to subordinate officials virtually all legal obligations assigned to the Oval Office. The legislation, 3 U.S.C. §301, provides that

the President of the United States is authorized to designate and empower the head of any department or agency in the executive branch, or any official thereof who is required to be appointed by and with the advice and consent of the Senate, to perform without approval, ratification, or other action by the President (1) any function which is vested in the President by law, or (2) any function which such officer is required or authorized by law to perform only with or subject to the approval, ratification, or other action of the President: Provided, That nothing contained herein shall relieve the President of his responsibility in office for the acts of any such head or other official designated by him to perform such functions. Such designation and authorization shall be in writing, shall be published in the Federal Register, shall be subject to such terms, conditions, and limitations as the President may deem advisable, and shall be revocable at any time by the President in whole or in part.

Congress retained the requirement that the subdelegation could go only to officers who were confirmed by the legislature and ensured that the president retained ultimate responsibility for the manner in which the assigned tasks were carried out.

This statute does not confer on the president any substantive authority but merely the power to delegate authority provided in other legislation. That is significant because it is common today for presidents to cite this provision of law along with the powers conferred on them by the "Constitution and laws of the United States" as the authority to support an order. To those unfamiliar with this legislation, it may appear that the president has an independent source of statutory authority to support his actions, but that is not the case.

A Tool to Reorganize Agencies, Eliminate Existing Organizations, or Create New Ones

With the centuries-long debates over the intent of the framers with respect to the separation of powers, there is little if any dispute that they deliberately targeted three sets of authority that had previously been central to the prerogative powers of the British Crown to be limited, broken apart, and controlled by checks and balances. The memory of the use of military and international powers to plunge the country into wars and other political adventures abroad, the full control by the Crown of the ability to raise and spend money to support them, and the monarch's power to create offices and fill them with persons whose support the king sought to obtain or retain was clear. Thus, though the president was given the appointment power, Congress was left with the power to create various kinds of offices, with the appropriations authority needed to fund them, and the check of Senate advice and consent for many, though certainly not all, significant executive branch positions.

Even so, many presidents have taken it upon themselves to create new agencies, eliminate existing organizations, and reorganize others by executive order with or without congressional approval. Louis Fisher points out that there was so much of this activity during the New Deal that Senator Richard Russell sponsored legislation to prevent the use of executive orders to create new agencies without legislative support and requiring that funds could not be used to support such an agency for more than one year in order to give Congress authority to consider the action and to give or withhold its consent.[66] According to Fisher, "Although Russell was a Democrat, like Roosevelt, he said that the President was not vested: 'with one scintilla of authority to create by an Executive Order an action agency of Government without the approval of the Congress of the United States.' Reviewing the language of one of Roosevelt's executive orders, Russell concluded that 'it has not a leg to stand on or even a finger with which to catch hold of anything.'"[67]

Eventually, the process for handling reorganization plans was worked out and used for decades thereafter. However, as Fisher has pointed out, that process fell into disuse because it required reorganization plans to be supported with a joint resolution of approval. The Reagan administration avoided the process, and the Clinton administration tended to use executive orders and other devices to meet its needs.

Even so, postwar administrations continued to use executive orders for these organization-building activities with and without congressional involvement. Thus, for example, President Kennedy created the Peace Corps by Executive Order 10924 in 1961.[68] Nixon made significant use of the reorganization authority and other legislative vehicles as bases for his executive orders establishing the Cabinet Committee on Environmental Quality and ultimately the Council on Environmental Quality a year later, following passage of the National Environmental Policy Act. Among Nixon's uses of executive orders in conjunction with reorganization plans was his reorganization of the Executive Office of the President. At its core was the establishment of the Office of Management and Budget, which has had its authority expanded through executive orders by every president since then.

More recently, the debate over the president's use of directives to create and reorganize surfaced during the Reagan and Bush administrations as those two presidents sought to alter existing units and create new ones to do battle with regulatory agencies. The Paperwork Reduction Act (PRA) was an initiative of the Carter administration aimed at limiting sweeping agency requests for information that was expensive to collect and often unnecessary or ineffectively used. It created the Office of Information and Regulatory Affairs (OIRA) within the Office of Management and Budget. Its primary task initially was to screen agency requests for information for compliance with the PRA. However, when the Reagan administration came to Washington, one of its first actions was to issue Executive Order 12291, which effectively transformed the OIRA into the lead agency for deregulation by delegating sweeping authority to the OMB to interdict agency rulemaking efforts and to maintain ongoing control over their operations.[69] That authority was augmented in early 1985 by E.O. 12498, issued after Reagan's reelection victory.[70] Executive Order 12291 also created the Vice President's Task Force on Regulatory Relief, a body that was placed over the OIRA to address these regulatory control issues.

These efforts continued into the Bush years, but a new dimension was added when the Vice President's Task Force on Regulatory Relief was replaced by the Council on Competitiveness, which came to be known as the Quayle Commission. It is interesting to note that not only was there no statutory authority for this organization but that the president did not even take the trouble to issue a formal executive order creating it. Rather, its existence was announced in a White House press release in April 1989, and direction was finally given to agencies concerning the council in a memorandum from the office of the cabinet secretary more than a year later in June 1990.[71] The administration continued the operation of both the council and the OIRA well after Congress refused to reauthorize the Paperwork Reduction Act. Indeed, the OIRA continued to operate well into the first Clinton administration until an agreement was reached with Congress and the amended PRA legislation passed.

The Clinton administration continued the tradition of presidentially mandated creation and reorganization of various bodies. Clinton's second executive order, E.O. 12835,[72] was a creation of the National Economic Council, an important step in his effort to respond to his campaign focus of "It's the economy, stupid."[73]

George W. Bush made creation of a cabinet-level Office of Homeland Security a leading element in his response to the September 11 terrorist attack. Although Congress was moving at breakneck speed to give the president virtually whatever he asked for at the time, Bush chose to use Executive Order 13228 to create the office. Moreover, he did not rely on any of the congressional resolutions or other statutes available to create the office but relied, as he said, on "the authority vested in me as President by the Constitution and the laws of the United States of America."

Management of Federal Personnel

One of the more common uses of executive orders is in the management of civil service, foreign service, and military personnel. Such orders not only provide broad policy for federal personnel management but also concern specific personnel actions. This has been true even though the Pendleton Act and the more recent Civil Service Reform Act provided a statutory framework for civil service administration and created implementing agencies.

One of Clinton's first orders was his commitment in E.O. 12839 to cut one hundred thousand positions from the federal service. Far less visible but much more frequent have been orders by presidents issued to alter pay grades,[74] address regulation of the behavior of civil servants,[75] outline disciplinary actions for conduct on and off the job,[76] and establish days off, as in the closing of federal offices.[77] Orders have also often been used over the years to exempt named individuals from mandatory retirement, to create individual exceptions to existing policies governing pay grades and classifications, and to provide for temporary reassignment of personnel in times of war or national emergency. Executive orders have frequntly been used as a form of private bill to make exceptions from normal operations, particularly with respect to civil service requirements and restrictions. Orders are also used to announce temporary or even sometimes permanent appointments.

Presidents are by no means the only chief executives who use executive orders for these purposes. Governors and some mayors have taken similar actions. Thus, former New York governor Mario Cuomo moved to stop sexual harassment in the state civil service using an executive order.[78] Chicago mayor Richard Daley imposed ethics requirements on city employees involved in contracting.[79] Public service management orders have sometimes proved to be extremely controversial. For example, when California governor Pete Wilson moved to block affirmative action hiring, his efforts met with protests and legal challenges.[80] Florida governor Jeb Bush faced similar reactions when he barred affirmative action in state employment in Executive Order 99-281.[81] The matter went further still when Illinois governor James Thompson used an executive order to create a partisan patronage-control operation (through the medium of a hiring and promotion freeze) and set up a unit within his own office to authorize exemptions to the freeze. These actions were later struck down by the U.S. Supreme Court.[82]

To Control the Military, Provide for Its Discipline, and Manage Its Resources

Among the standard executive orders issued by each administration is a variety of actions concerning military personnel, including adjustments of rates of pay and allowances for the uniformed services[83] and amendments to the Manual for Courts-Martial.[84] Particularly during periods of heightened national security activity, orders are regularly used to transfer responsibility, people, or resources from one part of the government to the military or the reverse. Many orders have been used to manage public lands, but it is often not recognized that frequently the lands are parts of military reservations or sites. In fact many of the orders issued by presidents in times of war or national emergency are very focused actions of this sort. Even in peacetime there are manifold organizational issues too detailed for statutes but that require action beyond the Department of Defense. President Clinton's order of succession of officers to act as secretary of the army is a typical example.[85]

An Instrument of Foreign Policy

Among the factors that makes control of the military, its organization, people, and operations particularly complex is that it functions around the world, often with peacetime routine, emergency alert, and possibly even combat under way at the same time in different places. The same can be said of the development and management of foreign policy and the organizations central to it.

Beyond the obvious realities of its operations, the well-established cultures of organizations from the Department of State through the Central Intelligence Agency (CIA) present special challenges for the chief executive. The flexibility and relative simplicity of the executive order make it a useful tool that can target the special problems of particular postings abroad. This category also includes management of intelligence agencies. While control of the operations of these organizations is also handled through national security directives, the executive order provides a more or less public way to provide information on the structure, operation, and governance of intelligence agencies. This was a particular theme during the Carter administration in the post-Vietnam period.[86] Yet even the Carter approach did not always mean the imposition of new restrictions on the agencies. Thus, he issued E.O. 12139, setting forth the authority of a range of officials to approve foreign intelligence electronic surveillance.[87]

Foreign policy is often made using a combination of statutes, treaties, executive agreements, executive orders, national security directives, and sometimes proclamations. George Washington's Neutrality Proclamation, the subject of so much controversy in the nation's early years, is an example (see p. 123). The Iran Hostage settlement and the Haitian refugee orders discussed later provide more recent examples. At other times, presidents have relied heavily on claimed constitutional authority to make foreign policy, even in some instances where there was ambiguous legislation on the subject, or none at all, for that matter. In *Haig v. Agee*[88] the Supreme Court was asked to assess the Carter administration's authority to revoke the passport of Philip Agee for disclosing information about U.S. intelligence operations and agents abroad, apparently resulting in attacks on U.S. personnel. The Passport Act of 1926 did not specifically indicate any authority in the White House or any agency to revoke a passport. In upholding the government's action, the Supreme Court pointed to an "unbroken string" of executive orders issued by the president, beginning in 1903, that delegated authority to the secretary of state to issue passports under such conditions as the secretary would set. The other half of that inquiry examined the general assumption that the president had the constitutional authority to issue such orders to the secretary. Chief Justice Warren Burger's opinion for the Court ultimately concluded that the president's and the secretary's actions were legislatively authorized by acquiescence, but in truth he plainly based the opinion on the long line of executive orders and on deference to the president's foreign policy powers.[89] As it has so often, the Court, citing dictum from the *Curtiss-Wright* case, suggested that judges should not even be evaluating the president's actions in the field of foreign policy: "In this vast external realm, with its important, complicated, delicate and manifold problems, the President alone has the power to speak or listen as a representative of the nation. . . . As Marshall said in his great argument of March 7, 1800, in the House of Representatives, 'The President is the sole organ of the nation in its external relations, and its sole representative with foreign nations.' "[90] This deferential language was gratuitous and unrelated to the core of the *Curtiss-Wright* ruling, as has often been noted, since that case involved a situation in which there was clear congressional authorization for the president's actions.

Justice Rehnquist, writing in the Iran Hostage challenge, *Dames & Moore v. Regan,* cited the *Curtiss-Wright* dictum but added that the president must of course act within the Constitution and that this so-called "plenary and exclusive" executive power was not intended to grant the president a kind of kingly prerogative.[91] In a later phase of the implementation of the Iran Hostage agreement, the Sperry Corporation challenged the constitutionality of the application by the Treasury Department, under an executive order delegation from the president, of a tax equaling 2 percent on amounts recovered by American companies from Iran in the settlement process. In this case, the company sued because it claimed that the levy was an unconstitutional tax. The Court upheld the fee requirement, terming it a user fee that could be levied even though the company had negotiated a private settlement without moving through the claims process operated by the government.[92]

As globalization increases, there can be implications for state and local governments from this kind of application of executive orders. These connections stem from the efforts by state and local officials to advance economic development in their jurisdictions by building international connections and from the increasing tendency of these governments to become active market participants. These factors combined recently to produce a Supreme Court ruling on the subject concerning contracting policy in Massachusetts.

The Commonwealth of Massachusetts adopted a policy under which it would not contract with firms that did business with Myanmar (formerly known as Burma). Later the Congress adopted legislation calling upon President Clinton to determine when and whether it was necessary to impose sanctions against the repressive Myanmar regime. He did so, issuing Executive Order 13047 in 1997, imposing a ban on investments there. In support of his order, he cited not only P.L. 104-208 adopted in 1996 and aimed at Burma but also the more general foreign affairs authority under the International Economic Powers Act, the National Emergencies Act, and the general sub-delegation statute 3 U.S.C. §301.[93]

A trade group, several of whose members were covered under the Massachusetts policy, filed suit, asserting state interference with national foreign affairs authority, preemption by the congressional and presidential actions, and state violation of the interstate commerce clause of Article 1. The federal government supported the challenge, as did the European Union and a number of individual countries. The Supreme Court ruled against the state.[94] In the process, Justice Souter observed:

> The President has been given this authority not merely to make a political statement but to achieve a political result, and the fullness of his authority shows the importance in the congressional mind of reaching that result. It is simply implausible that Congress would have gone to such lengths to empower the President if it had been willing to compromise his effectiveness by deference to every provision of state statute or local ordinance that might, if enforced, blunt the consequences of discretionary Presidential action.[95]

To Set Aside, Manage, or Allocate Resources or to Dispose of Physical Assets or Real Property

Although contemporary critics have challenged decisions by the Clinton administration setting aside property, it is a practice with a long history. Of course, it is also a history that has produced many controversies. Even so, the Supreme Court has often upheld such actions, even in the absence of statutes supporting the action. The best known of such cases is *United States v. Midwest Oil Co.*[96] In response to challenges to the president's authority to take action on lands in the absence of statutory support, the Court examined the records of presidential land decrees and concluded there was an overwhelming and consistent record of support for the president's actions. The Court's findings on the point are worthy of quotation at some length.

> Scores and hundreds of these orders have been made; and treating them as they must be . . . , as the act of the President, an examination of official publications will show that (excluding those made by virtue of special congressional action), . . . he has during the past 80 years, without express statutory authority—but under the claim of power so to do—made

a multitude of Executive Orders which operated to withdraw public land that would otherwise have been open to private acquisition. They affected every kind of land mineral and nonmineral. The size of the tracts varied from a few square rods to many square miles and the amount withdrawn has aggregated millions of acres. The number of such instances cannot, of course, be accurately given, but the extent of the practice can best be appreciated by a consideration of what is believed to be a correct enumeration of such Executive Orders mentioned in public documents. They show that prior to the year 1910 there had been issued 99 Executive Orders establishing or enlarging Indian Reservations; 109 Executive Orders establishing or enlarging Military Reservations and setting apart land for water, timber, fuel, hay, signal stations, target ranges and rights of way for use in connection with Military Reservations; 44 Executive Orders establishing Bird Reserves.

In the sense that these lands may have been intended for public use, they were reserved for a public purpose. But they were not reserved in pursuance of law or by virtue of any general or special statutory authority. For, it is to be specially noted that there was no act of Congress providing for Bird Reserves or for these Indian Reservations. There was no law for the establishment of these Military Reservations or defining their size or location. There was no statute empowering the President to withdraw any of these lands from settlement or to reserve them for any of the purposes indicated.

Congress did not repudiate the power claimed or the withdrawal orders made. On the contrary it uniformly and repeatedly acquiesced in the practice and, as shown by these records, there had been, prior to 1910, at least 252 Executive Orders making reservation for useful, though non-statutory purposes.[97]

The Court's language seems rather flippant, given the importance and scope of the presidents' actions, but any examination of the WPA lists of orders quickly confirms the fact that presidential powers in this area were broadly accepted over many decades. The politics of the contemporary West, sometimes referred to as the sagebrush rebellion, though dramatic, has essentially injected new controversy into what had been a common and generally accepted practice.

CONCLUSION

It is clear, then, that the significant use of executive orders is by no means a recent development. They have been used in many ways over time. To speak of their uses and scope, however, does not really explain why presidents have elected to issue executive orders. Neither does it explain their advantages and disadvantages. These are the topics considered next.

THREE
STRATEGIES, TACTICS, AND POLITICAL
REALITIES OF EXECUTIVE ORDERS

Presidents have a wide range of choices as to how to make and implement policy. Just what prompts presidents to select one tool over another in a given situation or why administrations have elected to use a number of tools together is a complex inquiry. There are a variety of answers to that question. Some of them have to do with the particular strengths and weaknesses of each of these devices.

WHY ARE EXECUTIVE ORDERS EMPLOYED?

Consider first some of the available explanations as to why presidents choose to use executive orders. Some of the reasons are intimately connected to the politics of the presidency and its relationships to other institutions, but others seem almost to have been dictated by circumstances.

To Respond to Emergencies

It is common to think of executive orders as devices that are used to deal with emergencies, as in Lincoln's use of this tool during the Civil War. Indeed, emergencies have often triggered the use of presidential decrees. President Wilson issued many of them to deal with World War I challenges, from control over military assets to war mobilization.[1] But not all emergencies have involved military conflicts. Indeed, some emergencies may be declared in part at least to assist an administration in accomplishing its own goals when Congress might not otherwise be supportive.

Most Americans would be surprised to know that the nation operated under a continuous state of emergency from 1933 until 1976, and the majority of those years certainly were not periods of declared war. The emergency terminated at that time simply because that was the date set by the National Emergencies Act of 1974 to terminate all pending emergency declarations.[2] Thereafter, all emergencies declared by the president would automatically terminate after two years. In the work leading to that legislation, the Senate Special Committee on the Termination of the National Emergency found that some 470 special emergency powers had accumulated as a result of claimed emergencies from the Truman administration to the Nixon years and that "this vast range of powers, taken together, confer enough authority to rule the country without reference to normal constitutional procedures."[3]

Franklin Roosevelt took office on March 4, 1933, with the nation spiraling downward. With some 12 to 14 million unemployed and gross farm income less than half what it had been in 1929, the social as well as the economic impacts of the Great Depression were already devastating.[4] His Inaugural Address is still well known for its soft, humane, supportive side, as FDR reassured the people that "the only thing we have to fear is fear itself"; but what is generally forgotten is that he also served notice that he intended to attack the depression as if it were a military invader. And if the Congress would not do what was necessary to repel the invader, then he would do it himself:

> It is to be hoped that the normal balance of executive and legislative authority may be wholly adequate to meet the unprecedented task before us. But it may be that an unprecedented demand and need for undelayed action may call for temporary departure from that normal balance of public procedure.
>
> I am prepared under my constitutional duty to recommend the measures that a stricken nation in the midst of a stricken world may require. These measures, or such other measures as the Congress may build out of its experience and wisdom, I shall seek, within my constitutional authority, to bring to speedy adoption.
>
> But in the event that the Congress shall fail to take one of these two courses, and in the event that the national emergency is still critical, I shall not evade the clear course of duty that will then confront me. I shall ask the Congress for the one remaining instrument to meet the crisis—broad Executive power to wage a war against the emergency, as great as the power that would be given to me if we were in fact invaded by a foreign foe.[5]

First Lady Eleanor Roosevelt knew that this was not mere rhetorical flourish. She told FDR's biographer Frank Friedel that she knew that the president saw Wilson's use of presidential decrees to take the nation through World War I as a model of how to mobilize to meet not merely the military side of national emergencies but the economic dimensions as well.[6] The new president had been a part of the Wilson administration that had issued some 1,791 orders.[7]

The day after his speech, Roosevelt called an emergency session of Congress. Meeting on March 9, it adopted the equivalent of a war powers resolution, which concluded, "The actions, regulations, rules, licenses, orders and proclamations heretofore or hereafter taken, promulgated, made, or issued by the President of the United States or the Secretary of the Treasury since March the 4th, 1933 . . . are hereby approved and confirmed."[8] Meanwhile, he had already declared a bank holiday and on March 10 issued regulations for bank operations upon their reopening.[9] Shortly thereafter, he continued the national emergency in banking, even though the banking holiday had ended. He also used executive orders to prohibit trading or hoarding of gold (requiring that it be turned over to the Federal Reserve Banks),[10] prohibited the export of gold, and set up rules for international financial transactions.[11] Congress at each point came behind the president to ratify his actions, including those associated with the gold restrictions and currency valuations, moves the Supreme Court upheld.[12] As Arthur Schlesinger has pointed out, the Congress seemed as though it could not wait to adopt the administration's banking bill, moving the legislation through both houses and onto the president's desk in less than eight hours.[13] This was but the beginning. In the following fifteen months, the president issued some 674 executive orders.[14] And from 1933 to 1945, during the Great Depression and World War II, Roosevelt issued altogether some 3,723 such orders.[15]

Harry Truman issued an additional 137 orders between Roosevelt's death and the end of 1945. Truman was happy to see the end of the fighting, but within a very short time he found himself looking back fondly on the era of common commitment and sacrifice that characterized the war years.[16] There was a strong desire by virtually everyone to be freed from wartime constraints, even though there was much to do to demobilize and reorient the economy. Government canceled some $15 billion in defense contracts in one month, so that more than 60,000 employees were laid off by just two firms, and this at a time when millions of returning veterans needed civilian employment.[17] Demobilization legislation and executive orders were needed to address some of the problems. For example, housing had to be found for the nearly 12 million returning veterans and their families when there was already a housing shortage.[18] There was considerable fear that the economy would dive back toward depression-era levels. However, at the same time there was concern about postwar inflation pressures in the form of demands by industry for major price increases and by unions to receive the wage hikes they had forgone during the war. The result of these tensions was a wave of strikes from fall 1945 through much of 1946. At some point during that period there were 800,000 steel workers, 200,000 meat packers, 175,000 General Motors auto workers, 60,000 lumber workers, 27,000 oil workers, 15,000 elevator operators, 3,500 electrical workers, and even coffin makers on strike.

President Truman used executive orders not only to address the effects of the strikes but also as a tool to pressure management and labor to settle.

While Truman's seizure of the steel mills is remembered and frequently discussed, it is often forgotten that he issued orders seizing towing operations in New York Harbor[19] as well as coal mines[20] and railroads.[21] In the case of the railroads, the tactic had the effect of causing a delay in the strike date. The threat to the union was obvious in that the seizure would break the strike. The concern for management was that the government, while in control of a business, would give employees a raise or otherwise change working conditions so that, when negotiations resumed, the conditions on the ground would have changed significantly. When the negotiations broke down, Truman took the even more draconian step of addressing Congress, attacking both labor and management and requesting authority to draft striking workers into the military. The parties got the message and reached a settlement while Truman was in the midst of his speech to the Congress.[22]

Later, John L. Lewis, head of the United Mine Workers, took his union out on strike, notwithstanding the seizure order as well as the Krug-Lewis operating agreement, which provided favorable terms for the coal miners. Lewis paid heavily for his hubris, or, more accurately, made his union pay for it. The White House saw this as a golden opportunity to make an important point, and they took it.[23] Lewis served notice of his intention to abrogate the agreement unless it was renegotiated to his liking, doing so even though the government had obtained a temporary restraining order against his threatened strike. The administration pressed both civil and criminal contempt actions against Lewis and the union, resulting in fines of $10,000 against Lewis and $3.5 million against the union. The Supreme Court upheld the contempt findings but reduced the fine against the union to $700,000, with the additional $2.8 million to be ordered if the union failed to take prompt action to end the strike and purge itself of contempt.[24]

To Transition to or from Governance in Times of War or Other National Emergency

The fact that these battles over the impact of labor disputes took place after the war presents another important aspect of emergency orders. The Supreme Court has recognized on a number of occasions that just because the conditions giving rise to an emergency may have ended does not mean that any orders issued to deal with it necessarily end as well. Indeed, the Court has recognized that the consequences of emergencies may require continued use of emergency powers for some time after the emergency itself has been terminated, such as when a war ends. Thus, the Court affirmed the validity of the presidential actions associated with the Food Relief Program headed by Herbert Hoover as part of war relief following World War I.[25] Truman received considerable support from the Court for his use of emergency orders to address demobilization and recovery from World War II, even though he received little support from Congress on his postwar programs, particularly after the 1946 congressional elections.[26] His orders included establishment of the Wage Stabilization Board,[27] liquidation of wartime agencies,[28] reestablishment of the Office of Economic Stabilization,[29] and many more. As the Court held in a 1947 case, "The cessation of hostilities does not necessarily end the war power. . . . The war power includes the power 'to remedy the evils which have arisen from its rise and progress' and continues during that emergency."[30] In a case challenging an executive order transferring powers from the Office of Price Administration to the attorney general, the Court concluded, "There can be no question but that the President as a step in the winding-up process had power to transfer any or all of the price administration functions to the Attorney General."[31]

Presidents have long understood the utility of the order as an instrument to get through difficult times. The kinds of actions that are needed during the transition are often the kinds of specific, often unique problems that Congress would be unlikely to address, particularly since the circumstances are temporary. Presidents are aware that those special circumstances and the need for prompt action often mean support for their use of executive orders.

In some instances, executive orders have even been considered as tools with which to anticipate possible emergencies. President Clinton was urged to take action in anticipation of the Year 2000 (Y2K) scare, given the uncertainty as to what might occur if government computers malfunctioned as a result of software design problems on January 1, 2000. In a Congressional Research Service Report for Congress, Harold Relyea warned, "The emergencies resulting from possible Y2K malfunctionings are likely to be of a character similar to those resulting from such natural disasters as a hurricane or an earthquake—e.g., loss of electric, gas, and water service, breakdowns in emergency police, fire, and health assistance, and limitations on food and medical supplies due to transportation disruptions."[32] Clinton did issue E.O. 13010 in 1996, creating the President's Commission on Critical Infrastructure Protection, which came to be used in connection with the Y2K problem though it was created to address other problems.[33] The following year, Clinton issued E.O. 13073, creating a President's Council on Year 2000 Conversion, to address both the possibilities of Y2K disaster and to take actions to prevent it. Citing nothing more specific than "the authority vested in me as President by the Constitution and the laws of the United States of America," Clinton ordered his new council and the agencies of the executive branch to achieve certain policy objectives:

It shall be the policy of the executive branch that agencies shall:
1. Assure that no critical Federal program experiences disruption because of the Y2K problem;
2. Assist and cooperate with State, local, and tribal governments to address the Y2K problem where those governments depend on Federal information or information technology or the Federal Government is dependent on those governments to perform critical missions;
3. Cooperate with the private sector operators of critical national and local systems, including the banking and financial system, the telecommunications system, the public health system, the transportation system, and the electric power generation system, in addressing the Y2K problem; and
4. Communicate with their foreign counterparts to raise awareness of and generate cooperative international arrangements to address the Y2K problem.[34]

To Strike Hard and Fast in Foreign Policy Matters

National emergencies have been declared since the National Emergencies Act went into effect. All of the emergencies declared between 1976 and 1999 involved foreign policy actions, ranging from Carter's response to the Iran hostage crisis to the Clinton administration's actions on Kosovo and Afghanistan (see Table 3.1). There are several reasons why executive orders are weapons of choice for a president who wants to hit hard in the foreign policy arena.

For one thing, the president who acts by order in foreign policy actions starts in most cases from a strong foundation of legal and political authority. Unfortunately, many administrations have jumped from this general authority to make broad and dangerous assertions of power, even in the face of contradictory congressional action. For reasons already indicated, the Supreme Court has historically deferred to such actions, at least in situations in which the president could assert a foreign policy emergency. Further, there have been a number of enactments, such as the International Emergency Economic Powers Act, that offer the president a wellspring of statutory authority to take emergency actions in the foreign policy arena. In an effort to prevent abuses of this wide-ranging authority, Congress provided in the National Emergencies Act for the possibility of a legislative veto that would terminate an emergency. However, the Supreme Court struck down the legislative veto in

1983.[35] Although the Congress responded by amending the Emergencies Act in 1985 to provide for a veto by joint resolution,[36] that meant little since a joint resolution must go to the president for signature.

There are other characteristics that make the tool attractive. It is a device that sends a powerful message. It can be done quickly and can mobilize a variety of agencies. Indeed, such executive orders can in many important respects control access to the marketplace and to the U.S. economic infrastructure that is central not only to American firms but also to the operation of multinational firms and the financial activities of many governments around the world. It also controls access to technology. The use of the executive order, relative to many diplomatic techniques, is a very public and therefore a powerful move.

To Address Private Disputes with a Public Impact

Like foreign affairs issues, labor disputes often present temporary but often serious concerns for the entire nation, and presidents are expected to take action to address such situations. Executive orders provide a useful and simple means to take action without necessarily putting the president squarely in the middle of the conflict. And perhaps more important, they can buy the president time during which to encourage settlement. The president can claim to have taken decisive action without really committing to any particular position.

Many presidents of both parties have used executive orders to create emergency boards to investigate labor management disputes under the Railway Labor Act. President Kennedy found himself in the middle of several such disputes as he came to the White House. Less than a month into his administration Kennedy issued E.O. 10919,[37] invoking the provisions of the Railway Labor Act in the pending dispute between Pan American Airlines and the Flight Engineers International. Only four days later, he issued another order, E.O. 10921,[38] including American Airlines, TWA, Eastern, National, and Flying Tigers, in this case simply asserting "the authority vested in me as President of the United States," with no reference to statute. He issued another order two days later, adding Western Airlines,[39] and another the day after that, expanding the investigations to include Northwest Airlines.[40] He issued similar orders with respect to a New York Harbor–based merchant marine dispute[41] (later expanded to deal with a nationwide strike addressed by E.O. 10949[42]) and to address a national railway workers clash involving some seventy-nine railroad companies.[43] All of this transpired in his first five

Table 3.1. Declared National Emergencies, 1976–1999

Declaration	Date	Title	Citation
E.O. 12170	11/14/79	Blocking Iranian government property	3 C.F.R. (Comp. 1979): 457–458
E.O. 12211	04/17/80	Further prohibitions on transactions with Iran	3 C.F.R. (Comp. 1980): 253–255
E.O. 12444	10/14/83	Continuation of export control regulations	3 C.F.R. (Comp. 1983): 214–215
E.O. 12470	03/30/84	Continuation of export control regulations	3 C.F.R. (Comp. 1984): 168–169
E.O. 12513	05/01/85	Prohibiting trade and certain other transactions involving Nicaragua	3 C.F.R. (Comp. 1985): 342
E.O. 12532	09/09/85	Prohibiting trade and certain other transactions involving South Africa	3 C.F.R. (Comp. 1985): 387–391
E.O. 12543	01/07/86	Prohibiting trade and certain other transactions involving Libya	3 C.F.R. (Comp. 1986): 181–182
E.O. 12635	04/08/88	Prohibiting certain transactions with respect to Panama	3 C.F.R. (Comp. 1988): 563–564
E.O. 12722	08/02/90	Blocking Iraqi government property and prohibiting transactions with Iraq	3 C.F.R. (Comp. 1990): 294–295
E.O. 12730	09/30/90	Continuation of export control regulations	3 C.F.R. (Comp. 1990): 305–306
E.O. 12735	11/16/90	Chemical and biological weapons proliferation	3 C.F.R. (Comp. 1990): 313–316
E.O. 12775	10/04/91	Prohibiting certain transactions with respect to Haiti	3 C.F.R. (Comp. 1991): 349–350
E.O. 12808	05/30/92	Blocking "Yugoslav Government" property and property of the governments of Serbia and Montenegro	3 C.F.R. (Comp. 1992): 305–306
E.O. 12865	09/26/93	Prohibiting certain transactions involving UNITA	3 C.F.R. (Comp. 1993): 636–638
E.O. 12868	09/30/93	Restricting the participation by U.S. persons in weapons proliferation activities	3 C.F.R. (Comp. 1993): 650–651
E.O. 12923	06/30/94	Continuation of export control regulations	3 C.F.R. (Comp. 1994): 916–917
E.O. 12924	08/19/94	Continuation of export control regulations	3 C.F.R. (Comp. 1994): 917–918

Table 3.1, *continued*

Declaration	Date	Title	Citation
E.O. 12930	09/29/94	Measures to restrict the participation by U.S. persons in weapons proliferation activities	3 C.F.R. (Comp. 1994): 924–925
E.O. 12934	10/25/94	Blocking property and additional measures with respect to the Bosnian Serb-controlled areas of the Republic of Bosnia and Herzegovina	3 C.F.R. (Comp. 1994): 930–932
E.O. 12938	11/14/94	Proliferation of weapons of mass destruction	3 C.F.R. (Comp. 1994): 950–954
E.O. 12947	01/23/95	Prohibiting transactions with terrorists who threaten to disrupt the Middle East peace process	3 C.F.R. (Comp. 1995): 319–320
E.O. 12957	03/15/95	Prohibiting certain transactions with respect to the development of Iranian petroleum resources	3 C.F.R. (Comp. 1995): 332–333
E.O. 12978	10/21/95	Blocking assets and prohibiting transactions with significant narcotics traffickers	3 C.F.R. (Comp. 1995): 415–417
Proc. 6867	03/01/96	Regulation of the anchorage and movement of vessels with respect to Cuba	3 C.F.R. (Comp. 1996): 8–9
E.O. 13047	05/22/97	Prohibiting new investment in Burma	3 C.F.R. (Comp. 1997): 202–204
E.O. 13067	11/03/97	Blocking Sudanese government property and prohibiting transactions with Sudan	3 C.F.R. (Comp. 1997): 230–231
E.O. 13088	06/09/98	Blocking property of the governments of the Federal Republic of Yugoslavia (Serbia and Montenegro), the Republic of Serbia, and the Republic of Montenegro and prohibiting new investment in the Republic of Serbia in response to the situation in Kosovo	3 C.F.R. (Comp. 1998): 191–193
E.O. 13129	07/04/99	Blocking property and prohibiting transactions with the Taliban	64 *Fed. Reg.* 36759–36761 07/07/99

Source: Harold C. Relyea, "National Emergency Powers," *CRS Report for Congress,* July 22, 1999, 13–15.

months in office. Between June 1961 and his assassination in November 1963, Kennedy issued another twenty-six orders in labor disputes.

To Generate Favorable Publicity

There is little question that presidents use executive orders in the face of strikes for public relations purposes as well as out of concern for the impact of the work stoppages themselves. Many presidents have employed executive orders to build or protect their image. President Clinton took several such actions as he came to office. His decision to make the first action of his presidency (even before leaving Capitol Hill after inauguration) the signing of an executive order on ethics,[44] his order calling for the elimination of one hundred thousand public service positions,[45] and his order mandating elimination of one-half of all executive branch internal regulations[46] are classic examples of the tactic. The signing of such orders is often done with great flourish as a media event, as when President Clinton and Vice President Gore crossed the White House lawn to stand between two forklifts laden with what were presumably federal documents to sign the order calling for elimination of half the government's internal regulations. Of course, what the president did not say was that he was not taking action to reduce the number of executive orders that imposed significant burdens on the ability of executive branch agencies to carry out their duties. Not only did Clinton retain the orders imposed by his predecessors, but he even added to the requirements agencies had to meet, forcing, among other things, more of the mountains of paper that the White House lawn ceremony decried.

Paying Debts, Rewarding Supporters, Answering Critics, and Sending Signals

Often presidents issue executive orders in what may appear to be a public relations event for reasons other than those announced when the order is issued. Presidential orders can be effective devices for paying political debts, demonstrating action for a constituency, responding to adversaries, or sending political signals—real or symbolic. Orders that are largely symbolic rewards for support often make strong statements of policy but provide no new resources. They typically call for awareness by federal authorities of some concern and frequently create interagency or advisory committees for consultation, but they rarely require much beyond consultation and reporting. They also commonly contain clauses serving notice that the order establishes no legally cognizable rights that would justify judicial review.

This is not to say that orders responding to constituents or supporters are all symbolic. President Clinton's order barring federal contracts with firms that engage in permanent replacement of striking employees is a clear example of a significant action taken on behalf of that most traditional of Democratic groups, organized labor. Clinton was under considerable pressure to do something for labor in early 1995. There was a strong sense that the administration had forgotten its friends. Its early focus on deficit reduction, program cutting, attacks on entitlement programs, and government jobs elimination (all matters on which Clinton issued executive orders) hardly seemed to organized labor and other traditional Democratic constituents as typical behavior from a president of their party.[47] On top of that, there was the all-out White House push for ratification of the North American Free Trade Agreement (NAFTA), along with executive orders to implement it. To make matters worse, the Federal Reserve, with the tacit support of the administration, had increased interest rates for the first time in five years in February 1995, raising fears of an economic slowdown. The Clinton White House knew that many of these developments would set the stage for the reelection contest in 1996.

The administration's efforts to move legislation opposing permanent replacement of striking workers had failed in 1994 when supporters twice failed to break a Senate filibuster.[48] That, together with NAFTA, marked two major defeats for labor in a year. Moreover, these events came at a time when organized labor was seeking to reassert itself with strikes against a number of firms. Just prior to the issuance of Clinton's order, the Bridgestone/ Firestone Corporation and a number of other employers had moved to employ striker replacements. (Ironically, this tactic was later cited as a possible reason for the manufacture of tires that were recalled because of a number of serious accidents.)

The battle over striker replacement had raged nationwide during 1994 and 1995. A year before President Clinton issued his executive order on the subject, the Minnesota Supreme Court had struck down state legislation banning striker replacements on grounds that it was a national problem to be addressed by Congress.[49] In June, the United Auto Workers struck against Caterpillar on the striker replacement issue.[50] In January 1995, replacement workers at Doe Run, the nation's largest lead company, voted out the striking union, after the National Labor Relations Board (NLRB) found that the replacements could vote and strikers could not.[51] Then the major league baseball strike and the threat by owners to employ striker replacements kept this issue before the public on a daily basis and in virtually every newscast.

It was against this background that Clinton issued Executive Order 12954, "Ensuring the Economical and Efficient Administration and Completion of Federal Government Contracts,"[52] commonly known as the striker replacement order. Citing his authority under the Constitution and laws of the United States and the Federal Property and Administrative Services Act (FPASA), the general statute on federal government contracting, Clinton ordered government agencies not to contract with firms using permanent striker replacements. The secretary of labor was required to examine cases of alleged striker replacement in firms with more than one hundred thousand dollars in federal contracts and was delegated discretion to terminate existing contracts for the convenience of the government and to debar such employers from eligibility to bid on other government contracts in the future. As the president asserted,

> Efficient economic performance and productivity are directly related to the existence of cooperative working relationships between employers and employees. When Federal contractors become involved in prolonged labor disputes with their employees, the Federal Government's economy, efficiency, and cost of operations are adversely affected. In order to operate as effectively as possible, by receiving timely goods and quality services, the Federal Government must assist the entities with which it has contractual relations to develop stable relationships with their employees.
> An important aspect of a stable collective bargaining relationship is the balance between allowing businesses to operate during a strike and preserving worker rights. This balance is disrupted when permanent replacement employees are hired. It has been found that strikes involving permanent replacement workers are longer in duration than other strikes. In addition, the use of permanent replacements can change a limited dispute into a broader, more contentious struggle, thereby exacerbating the problems that initially led to the strike. By permanently replacing its workers, an employer loses the accumulated knowledge, experience, skill, and expertise of its incumbent employees. These circumstances then adversely affect the businesses and entities, such as the Federal Government, which rely on that employer to provide high quality and reliable goods or services.[53]

The business community was ready to challenge the order. The nation's leading promanagement interest groups, including the Chamber of Commerce, the National Association of Manufacturers, the Labor Policy Association, and the American Trucking Association, joined in the suit by Bridgestone/ Firestone. The U.S. District Court for the District of Columbia rejected their request for a preliminary injunction, but they were more successful in the Court of Appeals, which found the order reviewable and concluded that it was in conflict with the National Labor Relations Act.[54]

The striker replacement order was only one of many similar efforts to speak to constituencies during the Clinton years. Of course, in this the administration was following in the steps of its predecessors, both Republican and Democratic. One of the best-known examples of such a presidential response was Franklin Roosevelt's reaction to demands by A. Philip Randolph and Walter White that the president issue an executive order to address discrimination in the military and in other aspects of war industries. When Roosevelt dragged his feet, Randolph threatened a massive march on Washington, to take place in July 1941. Roosevelt capitulated and issued an order in June, creating the Fair Employment Practices Committee. The planned march was called off.[55]

More recently, George W. Bush made careful use of executive orders, along with appointments in the administration, to respond to the right wing of the Republican party. Bush had worked hard to maintain a moderate image while maintaining the support of the far right. Soon after taking office, he used Executive Orders 13198 and 13199 to launch the so-called Faith-Based Initiative designed to increase contract delivery of various kinds of programs in cooperation with religiously affiliated organizations. He also issued five executive orders reversing Clinton prolabor policies and instituting measures responsive to concerns of the far right of his party.

However, administrations occasionally have issued orders not so much to assist supporters as to respond to threats or criticisms by adversaries, and doing so has sometimes brought unfortunate results. Perhaps one of the most significant examples was Truman's E.O. 9835, which established the loyalty/security program for federal employees.[56] Truman's trusted lieutenant Clark Clifford referred to the program as "a response to the temper of the times" and recalled that "it was a political problem. . . . Truman was going to run in '48, and that was it."[57] Truman's biographer, David McCullough, concluded that there were several reasons—all of them political and none having anything to do with his concern about Communists in government. First, he had just given the famous Truman Doctrine speech some nine days earlier and could not be seen to be less concerned with Communism at home than he was with its activities abroad. Second, the right-wing Republicans in Congress were about to act, and he could control the worst excesses of a possible policy from the Hill by moving decisively and rapidly before the legislature could do so. Finally, he felt a need to establish his anti-Communist credentials, particularly in light of his support for people like TVA administrator David Lilienthal, who had been a target of red hunters, and given his well-

known distaste for those congressional extremists.[58] Truman later acknowledged that his policy was undertaken "under the climate of opinion that then
existed" but later admitted that "it was terrible."[59]

Sometimes, the White House can go on the offensive with executive orders, seemingly launching outright attacks on its opponents. An example was
the Reagan administration's action in two executive orders (and subsequent
Office of Personnel Management [OPM] rules) modifying the eligibility of
various groups to participate in the federal employees' charitable-giving program, the Combined Federal Campaign. Opinions were divided among many
observers about which groups should have access to the program and what
controls should be exercised by the Office of Personnel Management and the
White House. To many critics, the Reagan administration was using its control over the program to attack groups on its list of adversaries by denying
them access to funds. The administration denied those assertions and its actions were ultimately upheld by the Supreme Court.[60]

Responding by Studying the Problem—The Investigatory Commission Gambit

Executive orders are the tool used by virtually all modern presidents to launch
investigations, usually through the creation of commissions. There are circumstances that seem to demand such action. Thus, Lyndon Johnson, who
initially opposed the idea of a national commission, became convinced he
had to take action in the wake of the Kennedy assassination. However, he
was also fully aware of just how complex and politically volatile his creation
of the Warren Commission might be. Johnson was convinced at first that the
locally initiated Texas blue-ribbon commission investigation and the FBI
criminal investigation would allow for a federal presence but avoid the problems that would be caused by sending in what he referred to as "a bunch of
carpetbaggers" in the form of a national commission.

A number of people in the Justice Department were lobbying for a
national commission or a high-level Justice Department review of the FBI
report on grounds that the rest of the nation would not be satisfied with
(or accord credibility to) an internal Texas investigation or a report from
J. Edgar Hoover's agency. Columnist Joseph Alsop listened to Johnson's
arguments against a national commission but warned in a telephone conversation with the president that from a public relations standpoint it would
be most important to have some review of the FBI report and that it should
be done by a small group of credible people.[61] It would not do to have the

attorney general conduct such a review of the assassination of his own brother. Alsop also warned that there was growing editorial sentiment at the *Washington Post* and elsewhere in the media that there had to be some national report.

Johnson relented and created the Warren Commission by Executive Order 11130 four days later on November 29, 1963.[62] Knowing how politically complex the situation was, the new president spent a great deal of time getting politically essential commission members and key congressional leaders on board. Johnson explained in a telephone conversation with the Republican whip Senator Thomas Kuchel (R-Calif.) that he was naming the commission and who would be appointed to it. He noted that he had obtained agreement from Senator James Eastland to call off Senate hearings on the assassination, and House leaders had concurred. Johnson badgered Earl Warren into accepting the chair of the commission, explaining that "wild people" were spouting conspiracy theories "charging Khrushchev killed Kennedy and Castro killed Kennedy and everybody" and that this could lead to miscalculations. "Khrushchev [might] move on us, he could kill 39 million in an hour, and we could kill a hundred million of his people in an hour."[63] When Richard Russell refused to serve with Earl Warren on the commission, Johnson explained that he was worried about what might happen if he did not establish such a commission and staff it with the right people. When Russell resisted, the president informed him, "You're God damned sure going to serve! We're going into a lot of problems. . . . You're going to lend your name because you're head of the CIA Committee in the Senate. This thing is breaking faster than you think. . . . The Secretary of State came over here this afternoon and he's deeply concerned. . . . You're gonna serve your country!"[64]

Quite apart from such extreme cases, it is well known that creating a presidential commission is a way of deflecting pressure, since the reports of commissions often come back well after the immediate pressure for action passes, only to be received with great ceremony and then deposited on the shelf with little future attention. However, executive orders used to launch such inquiries are not always issued with such cynical intentions and sometimes do produce significant results. For example, even the Supreme Court recognized that: "The Social Security Act received its impetus from the Report of the Committee on Economic Security, which was established by executive order of President Franklin D. Roosevelt to study the whole problem of financial insecurity due to unemployment, old age, disability, and health."[65]

That is not to suggest that many such commissions result in major policy change in the short term, but they can produce important responses in the longer term. And even if they do not produce specific policy, they often provide important information that can become the focus of ongoing consideration, both within government and in public opinion. Examples include President Johnson's creation by E.O. 11365 in July 1967 of the National Advisory Commission on Civil Disorders, later known as the Kerner Commission;[66] Carter's E.O. 13130, creating the President's Commission on the Accident at Three Mile Island in 1979;[67] and Reagan's E.O. 12546, issued February 3, 1986, creating a commission to study the space shuttle *Challenger* disaster.[68] Reagan resumed this approach with E.O. 12575 on December 1, 1986, when he created the President's Special Review Board, later known as the Tower Commission, to investigate Iran-Contra.[69]

After Clinton, George W. Bush made use of an executive order to create the President's Commission to Strengthen Social Security. This body was clearly designed to do more than to provide information on the debate over what to do about Social Security issues. It was clearly intended, given the makeup of the commission, to ensure that there would be recommendations for at least partial privatization of Social Security accounts. Indeed, the mission of the commission as set forth in Executive Order 13210 both provides political cover and yet indicates where the administration wants the group's report to go.

> Sec. 3. Mission. The mission of the Commission shall be to submit to the President bipartisan recommendations to modernize and restore fiscal soundness to the Social Security system according to the following principles:
>
> (a) Modernization must not change Social Security benefits for retirees or near-retirees;
>
> (b) The entire Social Security surplus must be dedicated to Social Security only;
>
> (c) Social Security payroll taxes must not be increased;
>
> (d) Government must not invest Social Security funds in the stock market;
>
> (e) Modernization must preserve Social Security's disability and survivors components; and
>
> (f) Modernization must include individually controlled, voluntary personal retirement accounts, which will augment the Social Security safety net.

To the public, however, it will be a bipartisan commission that will determine what its policy recommendations will be, not the president. This mode of action, therefore, takes some of the criticism from the president and provides a forum for discussion of controversial policy options that is at arm's length from the Oval Office.

The work of the Advisory Committee on Human Radiation Experiments, established by President Clinton's E.O. 12891 in 1994, began a process of investigation and disclosure, with various kinds of policy responses that continue to be discussed at the time of this writing.[70]

End Runs Around Congress

Not only have orders often been issued as responses to Congress or legislative friends or foes, but they have also been used in order to accomplish an end run around Capitol Hill. Certainly Clinton's striker replacement order was a classic example. Then there was Lyndon Johnson's famous Executive Order 11246, Equal Employment Opportunity (EEO), the basis for federal affirmative action contracting programs.[71]

By the time Johnson came to office, there was a well-established record of presidential executive orders on equal opportunity with respect to the military, other federal agencies, federal programs, and government contracts, from the first such order issued by FDR in 1941 through a number issued by Truman, Eisenhower, and Kennedy. But several circumstances changed between Kennedy's Executive Order 10925, creating the President's Committee on Equal Employment Opportunity (directing all executive agencies to examine their personnel practices with respect to equal opportunity and remedy the problems they found, and requiring equal opportunity employment practices by contractors) and Johnson's order on the same subject in September 1965.[72] Johnson had chaired Kennedy's EEO Committee, and he knew its limitations and that of the other civil rights policies in the federal government. Moreover, he had made passage of civil rights legislation a major theme of his administration, beginning with his commitment to enactment of the bill introduced in 1963 that ultimately became the Civil Rights Act of 1964. That legislation was bottled up by a Senate filibuster that was ultimately broken after the minority leader, Senator Everett Dirksen (R-Ill.), fashioned a compromise. To supporters of the bill, the language that was added merely sought to reassure business leaders and others that they would retain control of critical personnel management concerns as long as they did not discriminate on the basis of race. To those on the other side of the debate willing to sign on to the compromise, the new language, including §703(j), erected a barrier to affirmative action programs. The filibuster was broken, and the legislation was signed in July 1964.

However, the civil rights battles continued both in Washington and in the streets around the nation even as Johnson continued the fight for what became the Voting Rights Act of 1965. By spring 1965, Johnson was expanding his own awareness that merely outlawing segregation would be inadequate to ensure real civil rights and equal opportunity. Following the infamous Pettus Bridge attack by Alabama law enforcement officers on civil rights marchers in Selma, Johnson had not only sent in troops but also convened a special session of Congress. In his speech to the joint session, he made clear his intention to get the voting rights act through but to go beyond that in order to ensure that equal opportunity meant real opportunity. Daniel Patrick Moynihan's controversial study on the relationships between civil rights and poverty was one factor in the president's expanding view of what was needed. Johnson also assigned Vice President Hubert Humphrey the task of determining how to deal with the many equal opportunity programs operating in various parts of the government. In June, Johnson gave the Howard University speech (drafted in part by Moynihan), "To Fulfill These Rights," committing the administration to a more affirmative and active approach to civil rights.[73] In one of the most memorable passages, he said:

> You do not wipe away the scars of centuries by saying: Now you are free to go where you want, and do as you desire, and choose the leaders you please.
> You do not take a person who, for years, has been hobbled by chains and liberate him, bring him up to the starting line of a race and then say, "you are free to compete with all the others," and still justly believe that you have been completely fair.
> Thus it is not enough just to open the gates of opportunity. All our citizens must have the ability to walk through those gates.
> This is the next and the most profound stage of the battle for civil rights. We seek not just freedom but opportunity. We seek not just legal equity but human ability, not just equality as a right and a theory but equality as a fact and equality as a result.[74]

He announced the calling of a White House conference, "To Fulfill These Rights," to take action toward this end. The summer marked his signing of the Voting Rights Act, but it was also a period that made "Watts" a household word, after that part of Los Angeles erupted in violence.

Vice President Humphrey produced his memorandum for the president on the administration of civil rights functions in the executive branch in September,[75] and Johnson moved promptly, issuing Executive Order 11246.[76] The order replaced Kennedy's E.O. 10925. Taking the vice president's recommendation, Johnson eliminated the President's Committee on Equal Employment Opportunity, the broad purposes of which were covered by the Equal Employment Opportunity Commission created by the 1964 Civil Rights Act. The new order assigned civil rights responsibilities to all executive branch agencies. However, it assigned particular government-wide responsibilities to two agencies. It delegated responsibilities for federal government employment, including authority to issue regulations as well as for adjudication of discrimination complaints, to the Civil Service Commission. But the parts of the order that lit a political fuse were the sections in which Johnson delegated specific authority and responsibility to the secretary of labor to issue rules for and to enforce the civil rights policy on government contractors. Although §202 of the order that obligated contractors to "take affirmative action" with respect to equal opportunity was actually taken directly from the Kennedy order, it clearly had a new significance in 11246, given the context in which it was issued. Indeed, affirmative action opponents insisted that any effort to use that language specifically to seek to hire minorities was no longer permissible in light of the language of Title VII of the 1964 Civil Rights Act. Affirmative action opponents were sure that the order was more than a mere reassignment of EEO responsibilities and that the administration intended to implement the president's commitment to a broad understanding of equal opportunity, beyond the compromise that existed at the time of the enactment of the 1964 act and well beyond any measure that would have any chance of passage in Congress at that time.

While the battle over other civil rights issues raged, the secretary of labor set to work implementing the executive order. The explosion came when the Labor Department responded to complaints about discrimination in the construction unions, with particular attention to construction projects in Philadelphia. The department issued orders in 1969 (by then under the Nixon administration) implementing 11246 and requiring affirmative action programs that mandated minority hiring goals to be submitted by contractors bidding on federally financed construction projects. The comptroller general promptly issued an opinion, concluding that the orders violated the Civil Rights Act while the Justice Department issued an Attorney General's opinion in support of it.[77] Senator Sam Ervin convened hearings to challenge the action.[78] However, the U.S. Court of Appeals for the Third Circuit rejected broad challenges brought by contractors to what had by that time become known as the "Philadelphia Plan."[79]

Republican presidents have also used orders to accomplish by other means what they could not extract from Congress. Indeed, postwar Republican presidents, until 2001, have faced Democratically controlled legislatures. Ronald Reagan used executive orders to carry out end runs around Congress in a variety of ways. For example, he issued orders on "the family" (E.O. 12606),[80] "federalism" (E.O. 12612),[81] intergovernmental review of programs (E.O. 12372),[82] and governmental taking of private property (E.O. 12630).[83] These were subjects that had been part of Reagan's and the Republican party's domestic agenda but that he could not move through Congress. For the most part, the approach used to implement the policies was to compel agencies to take the administration's edicts on each of these subjects into consideration in agency rulemaking. Agencies were required to indicate in the preamble to their proposed policies whether a pending regulation fell into any of these categories and, if so, how they complied with the executive orders. The OMB was then free to evaluate the agency's analysis and compliance before the rulemaking process could move forward.

Quick, Convenient, and Relatively Easy Ways to Launch Significant Policy Initiatives

Executive orders are often used because they are quick, convenient, and relatively easy mechanisms for moving significant policy initiatives. Though it is certainly true that executive orders are employed for symbolic purposes, enough has been said by now to demonstrate that they are also used for serious policymaking or to lay the basis for important actions to be taken by executive branch agencies under the authority of the orders. Unfortunately, as is true of legislation, it is not always possible to know from the title of orders which are significant and which are not, particularly since presidents will often use an existing order as a base for action and then change it in ways that make it far more significant than its predecessors.

The relative ease of the use of an order does not merely arise from the fact that presidents may employ one to avoid the cumbersome and time-consuming legislative process. They may also use this device to avoid sometimes equally time-consuming administrative procedures, particularly the rulemaking processes required by the Administrative Procedure Act.[84] Because those procedural requirements do not apply to the president, it is tempting for executive branch agencies to seek assistance from the White House to enact by executive order that which might be difficult for the agency itself to move through the process. Moreover, there is the added plus from the agency's perspective that it can be considerably more difficult for potential adversaries to obtain standing to launch a legal challenge to the president's order than it is to move an agency rule to judicial review. There is nothing new about the practice of generating executive orders outside the White House. President Kennedy's executive order on that process specifically provides for orders generated elsewhere.

Nevertheless, it is common for the White House to find itself facing difficulties later for such third-party directives. Probably the worst example of this problem was the Teapot Dome scandal during the Harding administration. Investigations concluded that it resulted from Secretary of the Interior Albert B. Fall's acceptance of some four hundred thousand dollars in bribes from two oil companies to lease oil rights in the Naval Oil Reserves (originally created by executive order and upheld in *United States v. Midwest Oil Co.*).[85] In order for Fall to acquire the control needed to make the deal, he had to ensure that the authority over the oil was transferred to his office. He had Assistant Secretary Edward Finney develop a memorandum indicating what powers could be given to him. It explained how the president could delegate authority over leasing to him through an executive order. Fall then drafted a proposed executive order and cover letter, which he sent to the recently appointed secretary of the navy, with whom he had discussed the deal. Secretary Edward Denby went through the formality of having the draft reviewed by his people, most notably Assistant Secretary of the Navy Theodore Roosevelt Jr.[86] However, when Roosevelt and his colleagues recommended against transferring the control to Interior, Denby indicated that the president had already decided the matter and sent the materials forward. The president signed the order at the end of May. Fall, with the cooperation of Denby, then set about the business of issuing the leases to two companies, Monmouth Oil and Pan American. When the sweetheart deals were discovered, the government nullified the contracts on grounds of fraud and corruption and recovered the lands and rights involved in the deal.

To Control the Executive Branch or To Deal with Interagency Tensions—Control of Agency Policymaking

The Teapot Dome scandal clearly is the most extreme example. A much more common example in recent times of the temptation to use orders generated elsewhere is the increased complexity of other more standard policymaking processes. One of the reasons why rulemaking has come to be so cumbersome and time consuming is precisely because of the requirements that have been piled on top of the basic statutory process by executive orders.

Part of the reason for the rulemaking orders was ideological and policy-based; but in some administrations, and the Reagan, Bush, and Clinton years stand out in particular, the orders were part of a larger concern with control over the executive branch. In his Inaugural Address, Reagan declared, "Government is not the solution to our problem; government is the problem."[87] The administration launched a series of actions that included counterstaffing,[88] special training for new political appointees on dealing with the bureaucracy,[89] expanding the reach and scope of political appointments in what had generally been regarded as career civil service positions,[90] and more direct actions in the form of executive orders, such as control over agency rulemaking in his now famous executive order 12291.[91] While most administrations, dating at least as far back as FDR's, have appointed outside commissions to reinforce the message that presidents needed more control over the executive branch, the Reagan administration moved more dramatically than its predecessors to take control. The Office of Management and Budget was made the center of that effort, with E.O. 12291 and 12498 providing a great deal of authority for agency oversight. Indeed, the charges that the control based in these executive orders was intentionally and increasingly heavy-handed generated criticism from the Hill and the judiciary.[92]

These and other control-oriented orders included a clause that held that the agencies were constrained to follow the order "to the extent permitted by law," which enabled the White House to claim that the order itself was lawful. At the same time, if there were difficulties under the order, the agency was on notice that it was to obey the order but not in such a way as to violate the law. Indeed, when the Office of Management and Budget was called upon to respond to congressional critics, James C. Miller (director of the Office of Information and Regulatory Affairs of the OMB and later OMB director) testified:

> President Reagan's Executive order imposes on the agencies only "to the extent permitted by law" and only to the extent that its terms would not "conflict with deadlines imposed by statute or by judicial order." The limited application of [EO 12291] is a crucial point, one that insures [its] legality and the legality of actions pursuant to [it]. . . . If a statute or a court order establishes a date for a rulemaking action, the Executive Order 12291 cannot delay that action.[93]

Administrators, however, have often found themselves in a squeeze between congressional mandates and the actual behavior of the Executive Office of the

President, which may differ significantly from the language of the order. This tension was such a problem during the Reagan administration that some agencies found it necessary to protect themselves by creating logs to show that the agency met its obligations but that it had been prevented from carrying out statutory requirements by the OMB. When, for example, the Environmental Protection Agency (EPA) was challenged for failure to produce regulations on leaking underground storage tanks on time, the Court found:

> EPA submitted 169 regulations to OMB which were subject to statutory or judicial deadlines, and on 86 occasions OMB extended its review beyond the time periods outlined in EO 12291. OMB's propensity to extend review has become so great that EPA keeps a running record of the number of its rulemaking actions under extended review by OMB and the resulting delays. The average delay per regulation is 91 days; total delays were more than 311 weeks.[94]

Despite its rhetoric about freeing agencies and their people from the controls of the Reagan and Bush years, the Clinton administration kept virtually all of the Reagan/Bush orders in place and even added additional control mechanisms of its own. It is true that some of the administration's orders that were issued as part of the reinventing government initiative did provide more flexibility, most notably those associated with government contracting. However, over the course of its eight years, it seemed clear that the Clinton administration had its own interest in controlling the executive branch and was perfectly prepared to use executive orders to operationalize that concern.

The Transition Question: Use of the E.O. to Change Course from a Previous Administration

The discussion of the Reagan orders reveals another important reason that presidents use executive orders. They can be used effectively to transition from one administration to another. Even so, it seems that not since Franklin Roosevelt has a president been as conscious of the use of executive orders in the transition as the new Reagan administration was. If we recall that Reagan did not arrive in the midst of a dramatic national emergency as did Roosevelt, the attention to the use of orders to shape a new administration was even more dramatic. The Reagan team was the first to make a really systematic process of revoking orders from the previous administration; in this instance some thirty-nine orders were revoked by the end of 1981, most of them issued by the Carter administration.

In some instances, it was an effort to get rid of policies the new administration opposed. The Carter administration had been active in its use of executive orders and, given its dramatic differences with that administration, the Reagan people were ready with a series of orders to eliminate Carter's policies. Thus, Reagan's first executive order, E.O. 12287,[95] eliminated controls on crude oil and refined petroleum products by revoking the price and allocation regulations imposed in Carter's E.O. 11790 and 12038. His second order terminated the wage and price regulatory program then operating under Carter's Executive Order 12092.[96] On the same theme of eliminating economic controls, the new administration issued E.O. 12290[97] on February 17, 1981, revoking 12264 on export restrictions.

The new administration also moved to address issues of organization and operation. For the Reagan administration, one of the priority areas was the Foreign Service and intelligence operations. The issuance of orders 12292[98] and 12293,[99] following the Foreign Service Act of 1980, provided a context for some of that work. These orders amended nine existing executive orders and revoked another thirteen that had been issued between 1944 and 1980. Over the course of the following year, the administration issued orders on intelligence operations[100] and on the management of classified information.[101] These represented significant changes in direction from the Carter administration. Not surprisingly, there was sharp reaction from Congress to an administration that sought to reassert executive control in these fields.

Establishing changes in domestic operations was also important. Thus, the Reagan White House restructured Federal Regional Councils.[102] The new administration also promptly eliminated a variety of advisory committees from the Carter years,[103] and various organizational and operational changes followed in due course.

Then there was the replacement of Carter's orders on agency rulemaking in Reagan's E.O. 12291.[104] In addition to the earlier comments about this important directive, there is one other dimension worth noting. The Reagan administration drew on Carter's E.O. 12044[105] as a foundation for its own order and then built upon it in significant ways. Thus, for example, the Carter order had called for regulatory analysis in the form of a cost-benefit analysis. That is, administrators were to be alert to the potential impacts of their actions. The Reagan order took that idea several important steps further. It required a positive cost-benefit analysis and defined what was to be included in that calculus so as to make it much more difficult to produce the required positive result.

Section 2. General Requirements. In promulgating new regulations, reviewing existing regulations, and developing legislative proposals concerning regulations, all agencies, to the extent permitted by law, shall adhere to the following requirements:

(a) Administrative decisions shall be based on adequate information concerning the need for and consequences of proposed government action;

(b) Regulatory action shall not be undertaken unless the potential benefits to society for the regulation outweigh the potential costs to society;

(c) Regulatory objectives shall be chosen to maximize the net benefits to society;

(d) Among alternative approaches to any given regulatory objective, the alternative involving the least net cost to society shall be chosen; and

(e) Agencies shall set regulatory priorities with the aim of maximizing the aggregate net benefits to society, taking into account the condition of the particular industries affected by regulations, the condition of the national economy, and other regulatory actions contemplated for the future.

When the Clinton administration came to town, having campaigned against the burdens on policymaking imposed by Reagan and Bush, it took a full eight months to replace the Reagan orders. But even more interesting is the fact that Clinton's E.O. 12866 actually expanded the requirements placed on agencies instead of reducing them (see below). These orders provide one example of the decree inertia principle: the tendency of a line of executive orders of a particular type to continue from administration to administration and grow in size and complexity in the process. This principle is demonstrated in many fields. Another widely influential string of orders of this type is the set of security classification orders.

In sum, the Reagan White House certainly demonstrated that if an administration comes to Washington having carefully examined existing executive orders, statutory requirements, and its own policy priorities, it can, with relative ease and dispatch, employ executive orders to facilitate its transition to power. In so doing, the administration can rapidly dispose of many of its predecessor's policies, organization, and management practices if it wishes to do so.

CLINTON EXECUTIVE ORDER 12866, REGULATORY STANDARDS

Section 1. Statement of Regulatory Philosophy and Principles.

(a) *The Regulatory Philosophy.* Federal agencies should promulgate only such regulations as are required by law, are necessary to interpret the law, or are made necessary by compelling public need, such as material failures of private markets to protect or improve the health and safety of the public, the environment, or the well-being of the American people. In deciding whether and how to regulate, agencies should assess all costs and benefits of available regulatory alternatives, including the alternative of not regulating. Costs and benefits shall be understood to include both quantifiable measures (to the fullest extent that these can be usefully estimated) and qualitative measures of costs and benefits that are difficult to quantify, but nevertheless essential to consider. Further, in choosing among alternative regulatory approaches, agencies should select those approaches that maximize net benefits (including potential economic, environmental, public health and safety, and other advantages, distributive impacts, and equity), unless a statute requires another regulatory approach.

(b) *The Principles of Regulation.* To ensure that the agencies' regulatory programs are consistent with the philosophy set forth above, agencies should adhere to the following principles, to the extent permitted by law and where applicable.

(1) Each agency shall identify the problem that it intends to address (including, where applicable, the failures of private markets or public institutions that warrant new agency action) as well as assess the significance of that problem.

(2) Each agency shall examine whether existing regulations (or other law) have created, or contributed to, the problem that a new regulation is intended to correct and whether those regulations (or other law) should be modified to achieve the intended goal of regulation more effectively.

(3) Each agency shall identify and assess available alternatives to direct regulation, including providing economic incentives to encourage the desired behavior, such as user fees or marketable permits, or providing information upon which choices can be made by the public.

(4) In setting regulatory priorities, each agency shall consider, to the extent reasonable, the degree and nature of the risks posed by various substances or activities within its jurisdiction.

(5) When an agency determines that a regulation is the best available method of achieving the regulatory objective, it shall design its regulations in the most cost-effective manner to achieve the regulatory objectives. In doing so, each agency shall consider incentives for innovation, consistency, predictability, the costs of enforcement and compliance (to the government, regulated entities, and the public), flexibility, distributive impacts, and equity.

(6) Each agency shall assess both the costs and the benefits of the intended regulation and, recognizing that some costs and benefits are difficult to quantify, propose or adopt a regulation only upon a reasoned determination that the benefits of the intended regulation justify its costs.

(7) Each agency shall base its decisions on the best reasonably obtainable scientific, technical, economic, and other information concerning the need for, and consequences of, the intended regulation.

(8) Each agency shall identify and assess alternative forms of regulation and shall, to the extent feasible, specify performance objectives, rather than

specifying the behavior or manner of compliance that regulated entities must adopt.

(9) Wherever feasible, agencies shall seek views of appropriate State, local, and tribal officials before imposing regulatory requirements that might significantly or uniquely affect those governmental entities. Each agency shall assess the effects of Federal regulations on State, local, and tribal governments, including specifically the availability of resources to carry out those mandates, and seek to minimize those burdens that uniquely or significantly affect such governmental entities, consistent with achieving regulatory objectives. In addition, as appropriate, agencies shall seek to harmonize Federal regulatory actions with related State, local, and tribal regulatory and other governmental functions.

(10) Each agency shall avoid regulations that are inconsistent, incompatible, or duplicative with its other regulations or those of other Federal agencies.

(11) Each agency shall tailor its regulations to impose the least burden on society, including individuals, businesses of differing sizes, and other entities (including small communities and governmental entities), consistent with obtaining the regulatory objectives, taking into account, among other things, and to the extent practicable, the costs of cumulative regulations.

(12) Each agency shall draft its regulations to be simple and easy to understand, with the goal of minimizing the potential for uncertainty and litigation arising from such uncertainty.[106]

Use of Internal Practices and Contracting Power to Leverage Change Outside Government

Presidents do not use executive orders solely or even primarily to control the operation of executive branch agencies. In fact, presidents sometimes elect to employ executive orders that are nominally directed to government officials in order to leverage a much larger change in the society as a whole. The federal government (and states and localities at their levels) represents a large and important employer and a major participant in the economy, particularly when members of the armed services are included in the count. When government issues significant policy changes with respect to employment, it sets out markers that influence demands in the private sector as well. Similarly, when government establishes contracting requirements or even simply lays out purchasing preferences, it can significantly affect business practices across the nation. Chief executives are well aware of that leverage and have used it to achieve important policy impact without the need to fight pitched congressional battles or to depend on executive branch agencies to generate regulations.

The Clinton administration's striker replacement order was certainly designed to make use of that leverage, as was Johnson's affirmative action order. Jimmy Carter, too, sought to work that lever when he issued his Executive Order 12092 on November 1, 1978, Prohibition Against Inflationary Procurement Practices.[107]

Carter inherited an economic nightmare, given the dramatic impact on the economy from the Vietnam War demobilization and from a roughly 400 percent increase in fuel prices during the same period. And it was a period in which the presidency itself had been significantly weakened as a result of the Watergate debacle and the revelations both domestic and international that flowed from it.

Like Nixon, Carter faced demands to take dramatic action, but unlike his ill-fated predecessor, Carter did not have the congressional support to impose such dramatic measures as wage and price controls. While asserting that his order was intended "to provide for the procurement by Executive agencies and Military Departments of personal property and services at price and wage rates which are noninflationary," Carter also made clear that it was designed "to encourage noninflationary pay and price behavior by private industry and labor." The government did not deny that the intent of the order was broad and was expected to influence the wider economy but argued that the president's actions were authorized by the Council on Wage and Price Stability Act (COWPSA) and the Federal Property and Administrative Services Act of 1949.

The Wage and Price control statute did allow the council to generate "nonbinding pay and price standards and actions to publicize inflationary activities," but it did not provide any specific authority for sanctions. However, the Carter program provided for the effective debarment of contractors in that it prevented them from bidding on contracts over $5 million. Although the order itself did not impose that sanction, it authorized the council to issue guidelines for noninflationary wages and prices, monitor business compliance, and "take such other action as may be necessary and consistent with" the order. Using that power, the Office of Federal Procurement Policy, pursuant to the council's decision, announced that businesses not in compliance with the council's standards would be barred from bidding on the $5 million or larger contracts. The reviewing court later determined, "The $5 million threshold directly covers approximately 50 percent of all government procurement dollars, but will actually influence up to 65 to 70 percent because many of the companies that must certify compliance for contracts exceeding

$5 million also routinely bid on smaller government contracts."[108] While the court accepted that the president had the authority to assign tasks to the council, the legislation did not authorize the council or the president to impose sanctions such as debarment of contractors. The court also rejected the White House claim that the policy was justified by the FPASA, the general statute covering federal contracting. Indeed, the court concluded that the Congress had specifically rejected the idea of using this legislation to support economic controls on prices.[109]

The White House then turned to the previous civil rights order to support the Carter policy. The court rejected that argument, claiming that in the cases of the affirmative action orders Congress had at least acquiesced in the executive action and had provided evidence of support. It did so, said the court, by rejecting direct efforts to nullify the orders, by continuing appropriations to support the executive branch enforcement of the programs, and by more direct support in various pieces of legislation. Congress had discussed and rejected the idea of providing the kind of wage-price controls enacted during the Nixon administration.

The White House also employed the standard argument that, as a contractor, the government is free to choose with whom it will do business.[110] The decisions by potential contractors who may choose to comply with the conditions or not is a voluntary act and the conditions cannot therefore be considered mandatory controls. The court rejected that argument as the worship of form over substance:

> For the defendants to urge this position is simply to blink at reality. The fact remains that if a company seeking a government contract fails to comply with the guidelines, it faces a very genuine possibility of being declared ineligible to compete. It would be difficult to convince a business executive or anyone faced with a decision to comply or lose a substantial government contract that such a program is voluntary. The debarment threat serves as an effective lever and a none too subtle deterrent to any company which does business with the government. The government annually contracts for many billions of dollars in goods and services. These contracts represent a substantial share of the business of many companies. An element of compulsion is inherent and ever present. Further, the President's program is unlimited in duration and scope and carries with it the possibility of expanded coverage of both business firms and a larger segment of the national labor force. The Executive Order's purpose and intended effects remove it from the benign jaw-boning efforts authorized by COWPSA or from the efficiency and economy objectives of the Procurement Act. Finally, as to the defendants' argument that no one has a right to a government contract, the plain-

tiffs do not assert such a right. The issue is rather whether the President has the power to control incomes through the procurement process.[111]

Though recognizing that "inflation is a vexing and festering domestic problem" and that the president's efforts might indeed be "well-intentioned and commendable," the court concluded that E.O. 12092 exceeded the chief executive's power and violated the separation of powers.

Thus, executive orders can be and have been used as policy levers, but there are limits to the willingness of courts to tolerate such strategies. That is particularly true where Congress has either opposed the policy in question outright, where it has provided no tacit support, and where there is no evidence of acquiescence.

Nevertheless, there is little doubt that some of these leverage strategies have worked well. Certainly the Reagan administration's Drug-Free Workplace order not only supported an expanded use of drug testing in the public sector, but it also was plainly intended to send strong signals to private-sector employers. The order begins with the president's finding:

> Drug use is having serious adverse effects upon a significant proportion of the national work force and results in billions of dollars of lost productivity each year. . . .
> The Federal government, as the largest employer in the Nation, can and should show the way towards achieving drug-free workplaces through a program designed to offer drug users a helping hand and, at the same time, demonstrating to drug users and potential drug users that drugs will not be tolerated in the Federal workplace.[112]

And indeed, the order launched a national effort by employers both public and private to implement various types of employee-testing programs.

WHAT BENEFITS DO EXECUTIVE ORDERS OFFER AND WHAT PROBLEMS DO THEY POSE?

Clearly, then, there are many reasons why a president chooses to employ executive orders. What then are their benefits and what difficulties do they present? The benefits are relatively obvious, but perhaps for that very reason it is often difficult to ensure that adequate attention is paid to the potential downsides.

The Advantages of Executive Orders

The careful use of executive orders offers several advantages of timing and impact. Orders can be used effectively as part of the transition not merely to fulfill campaign promises but to stake out important policy positions in critical areas. The review of existing orders is one of the tasks that could easily be done during the campaign itself or, at a minimum, in the early days following an election. Certainly the Reagan team demonstrated how effectively this can be done.

Executive orders can also be used to hit quickly with policies aimed at important problems, providing a strong and immediate sense of momentum for a new administration. These messages are sent to reassure an administration's supporters that the issue positions for which they campaigned are going to be acted upon. In the case of symbolic orders, which are often used for this purpose, the reward can be given to allies without a serious commitment of political resources in Congress, legal resources in administrative rulemaking, or financial resources associated with building really substantive programs. They also serve to send a message to potential adversaries that the administration is truly in charge and moving. Those seeking to mobilize opposition in such conditions find themselves reactive and defensive.

This rapid use of executive orders can be particularly significant under conditions of emergency. Roosevelt's rapid action on the bank system and budget cutting at breakneck pace had an immediate and dramatic positive effect. When the banks and markets opened the week after his actions, it was clear that their high visibility improved investor confidence rapidly. Arthur Schlesinger points out that "a Treasury bond issue on March 13 was oversubscribed in a single day. On the 15th, the securities markets, closed during the bank holiday, reopened in a bullish mood. In the meantime, banks were reopening, and deposits were exceeding withdrawals."[113] Executive orders can also be effective stopgap measures that can be used during a transition into or out of emergency situations.

Executive orders are particularly useful to address specific problems or temporary situations when there is no time for legislation. It is not always necessary to declare an emergency in order to take such actions, but it is in an administration's best interest to rescind the orders as soon as the emergency or special situation passes. They are useful to institute investigations or studies aimed at future policymaking in a way that can calm politically troubled waters without committing the administration to any particular course of action. To point this out is not to support the cynical use of such commissions, but there have been any number of important commissions that led to significant policy development.

Orders are also useful to a president who feels the need to take significant policy risks for what he or she regards as an action that is simply the right thing to do, whether there is political support for it or not. Truman's desegregation of the military is an example. It may sound odd, but one of the earliest of what might be called civil rights orders in the numbered series came in 1908 when E.O. 984 was issued, opening civil service examinations to "deaf mutes"[114] some eighty-three years before society was ready to support an Americans with Disabilities Act.

Orders are effective devices for getting at executive branch departmental operations. Of course, they cannot be used in ways that violate the many statutory obligations of any particular agency or of public servants generally. It must also be said that the fact that they are effective for this purpose does not mean they are without the downsides discussed below.

Few people regard executive orders as important, which has made them a vehicle that can be used to take significant actions that are at least technically, but that are unlikely in most instances, to attract much attention, unless they are particularly sweeping in character. It is the presidential policymaking version of hiding in plain sight. Moreover, unless there is a formal legal challenge, there appears to be a tendency not to look too closely at the authority claimed by the president to support an order. There are often a variety of statutes that can be cited as authority for executive action in addition to the claim of a president to act under the authority granted by "the Constitution and laws" as the frequently used assertion of power. If an action is challenged, the tendency of the courts to look toward congressional acquiescence means that the odds are in the president's favor, unless there is significant legislative opposition on the record. That is particularly true when foreign policy–based orders are issued, even if their impact is domestic, as in the case of the Iran Hostage agreement orders. Even to make it to the point of a substantive legal evaluation of an order, the challengers often have a difficult time establishing standing to sue and a basis for judicial review of an order. That is even more true now that the Supreme Court has dramatically limited, or perhaps more accurately, all but eliminated legislative standing for members of Congress.[115]

Potential Dangers of Governance by Executive Order

Significant problems can accompany the use of executive orders. In general terms, they include creating or exacerbating interbranch and intergovernmental tensions, inviting external criticism of the White House, weakening cabinet department credibility and effectiveness, undermining the administrative law system, possibly exposing administrators and the government more broadly to liability, and being seen in certain instances as taking the easy way out.

The practice of using executive orders to make an end run around Congress has a mixed record of success, as the saga of the Clinton striker replacement order demonstrates. Indeed, Clinton, Reagan, Carter, Nixon, and Johnson, among recent presidents, encountered significant difficulties, both political and legal, by challenging the legislature using executive orders. It is true that if an administration's primary purpose is to put up a symbolic fight in defense of a constituent group, the White House may not consider it all bad to wage a battle, knowing full well that the administration will ultimately lose.

In some instances, the administration may effectively dare Congress to act, as when Truman issued his steel seizure order but sought congressional action even as he did so. This tactic did not help to save his order. In general, with the passage of time, so many statutes have accumulated that there is not quite as much room for a president to succeed with deliberate attempts to evade or confront Congress except in cases of foreign policy or under conditions of emergency. Not only is there a need for the president to avoid direct legislative pronouncements that run counter to an order, but he or she must also identify the claimed basis of authority to support an action. In matters of foreign or military affairs there is a good deal of freedom in this respect, but the same often cannot be said for domestic matters. Still, presidents have found other ways to challenge Congress by direct action and get away with it.

Presidents clearly have been more than willing to declare emergencies in order to justify their action, and the temptation to do so can be overwhelming. Although the courts have often been willing to accept such assertions in military or foreign policy contexts, they have had greater difficulty with assertions of economic emergency, at least in the absence of supporting statutes. Jimmy Carter learned that the hard way.

Quite apart from judicial challenges, there are other concerns about the use and abuse of orders based on claims of emergency conditions. For one thing, a willingness to claim emergencies when conditions truly do not warrant such a declaration undermines credibility. Efforts during Reagan's early years to suggest the need to abandon normal administrative rulemaking proceedings in order to deregulate administratively, on grounds of economic emergency, undermined the administration's reputation in several areas and served only to support critics who charged that what was really at stake was partisanship and ideology. These claimed emergency orders can be particularly troublesome when the White House asserts that the information about the emergency must be restricted on the grounds of national security.[116] Indeed, the combination of a willingness to employ special presidential edicts and to assert national security and executive privilege to block inquiries into White House action had a good deal to do with the passage of the National Emergencies Act, the War Powers Resolution, the Congressional Budget Impoundment and Control Act, the Right to Privacy Act, the 1974 Freedom of Information Act amendments, and a number of other pieces of legislation aimed at control over the use and abuse of the intelligence agencies.

Even when there is real cause for emergency orders, there are reasons for caution. For example, experience over time suggests that emergency actions frequently leave messes to be cleaned up after the fact that can be troublesome in instances where the emergency actions did not contemplate these future normalization issues. That was certainly the case in the New Deal period and in wartime. This holds true even after the real emergency ends. It is not always clear just when the effects of the emergency really end. When Congress enacts legislation that supports presidential actions at the time of an emergency, the legislation is often written quickly and in loose terms. Such legislation can remain in the statute books long after the emergency that gave rise to it has ended.[117] The fact that the legislation that granted some of the powers accorded FDR to deal with the depression has never been repealed is now used by some of the conspiracy theorists on the far right to justify their attacks on government.

Another danger of legislation and executive orders developed during emergencies is the tendency to craft broad provisions on grounds that the special actions will only or primarily affect the military, for example, or others at the center of a problem. Many of the war-related orders do address the military and governmental agencies, but numbers of them affect civilians directly. Thus, President Wilson issued E.O. 2604 on April 28, 1917, which imposed censorship on all telegraph and telephone lines, with authority given to the War Department.[118] Similarly, these orders suspended civil service hiring rules (E.O. 2600) and waived the eight-hour workday (2605).[119] It is interesting that in the first war year, land orders outstripped direct war orders 102 to 76 and that named civil service decisions and exceptions affecting named individuals amounted to almost as many orders (69) as the direct war orders. They may have been clearly war related, it is true, but they were far from limited military directives.

Quite apart from conflict that may be engendered with the Congress, executive orders can create intergovernmental tensions. One of the clearer

examples of this problem came with mixed messages from the Clinton administration. As early as fall 1993, Clinton underscored in Executive Order
12875 the administration's concern for "Enhancing the Intergovernmental
Partnership." The White House asserted: "Federal requirements . . . have
hindered State, local, and tribal governments from tailoring Federal programs
to meet the specific or unique needs of their communities. These governments
should have more flexibility to design solutions to the problems faced by
citizens in this country without excessive micromanagement and unnecessary regulation from the Federal Government." The order therefore required
federal agencies "to reduce the imposition of unfunded mandates upon State,
local, and tribal governments; to streamline the application process and increase the availability of waivers to State, local, and tribal governments; and
to establish regular and meaningful consultation and collaboration with State,
local, and tribal governments on Federal matters that significantly or uniquely
affect their communities." However, many state and local governments were
complaining that federal burdens at their levels were increasing, not decreas-
ing, and that there was a variety of important instances in which agencies
indicated little or no interest in state and local input. Clinton issued a new
federalism order, E.O. 13083, in May 1998[120] that replaced the 1993 directive and set off a storm of protest in the process, so much so that in August
the White House issued E.O. 13095, suspending the earlier directive.[121] Although E.O. 13083 told federal agencies that they were generally to defer to
states, to be sensitive to the imposition of federal mandates, and to involve
them in federal policymaking, there were a number of conditions under which
it was appropriate to assert federal authority over state objections:

> It is important to recognize the distinction between matters of national or
> multi-state scope (which may justify Federal action) and matters that are
> merely common to the States (which may not justify Federal action because
> individual States, acting individually or together, may effectively deal with
> them). Matters of national or multi-state scope that justify Federal action
> may arise in a variety of circumstances, including:
>   1. When the matter to be addressed by Federal action occurs interstate as
> opposed to being contained within one State's boundaries.
>   2. When the source of the matter to be addressed occurs in a State differ-
> ent from the State (or States) where a significant amount of the harm occurs.
>   3. When there is a need for uniform national standards.
>   4. When decentralization increases the costs of government thus impos-
> ing additional burdens on the taxpayer.
>   5. When States have not adequately protected individual rights and
> liberties.

6. When States would be reluctant to impose necessary regulations because of fears that regulated business activity will relocate to other States.

7. When placing regulatory authority at the State or local level would undermine regulatory goals because high costs or demands for specialized expertise will effectively place the regulatory matter beyond the resources of State authorities.

8. When the matter relates to Federally owned or managed property or natural resources, trust obligations, or international obligations.

9. When the matter to be regulated significantly or uniquely affects Indian tribal governments.

This was broadly understood by the states and some local officials as a significant shift in the administration's thinking, accompanied by a list of ways to undermine its claimed concern for federalism. They took their complaints to Congress, which promptly moved to deny funding to implement the order,[122] a tactic that Congress has used in response to a number of direct presidential actions over the years.[123] This time it lasted only three months. Both the orders were replaced a year later by E.O. 13132, which eliminated the offending language and reinforced the commitment to decentralization.[124] Another example is the handling of Clinton's E.O. 12898, Environmental Justice for Minority Populations[125] (see chapter 4).

Even more broadly, the decision to act by executive order rather than through a cabinet agency by rulemaking, for example, often makes the White House the lightning rod for criticism. It is one thing for critics to fight limited conflicts with agencies over particular actions, but quite another when the White House decides to interpose itself into the fray.

Related to that difficulty is the possibility that it may appear to those outside the executive branch that the president is doing an end run around his or her own cabinet officers. They may or may not have been involved in the development of an order, depending on the politics of the issue in question. Whether they are or not, if the order does draw fire, there is no question that they will be expected to go to the Hill in defense of the White House action and to support it within their own organizations. Then there is the tendency to call upon all agencies to participate in new activities and committees with no additional resources. Executive orders can easily become unfunded mandates for cabinet agencies. Further, the use of the presidentially appointed investigative commission strategy is understandable, but it may be better to connect the work of such commissions using executive branch agencies that will not go away when the commission ceases to exist and can continue with the policy development and implementation work that is so often lost when a commission or advisory group is terminated. Failure to involve the relevant agencies in appropriate ways sends a loud message about how the president sees his or her own people.

In addition to these internal and external responses to orders, there is also the fact that proceeding by orders undermines the administrative law processes that have been developed over the years to serve a variety of important purposes. For some people in the White House, this hardly sounds like a downside to the use of presidential decrees. Indeed, Vice President Gore's National Performance Review argued for the use of presidential directives because of a desire to avoid those processes. However, while it may seem that this is the appropriate strategy, it carries with it a number of difficulties. It is also worth noting that administrative law processes are so burdensome and time consuming these days in no small part because of the burdens placed on them by a series of executive orders from Carter through Clinton.

Administrative law processes were designed to ensure that the authority on which important actions are taken is clear. They were also intended to ensure that when the executive branch adopts rules having the force of law, the process for creating them is open, orderly, and participative. When government brings its power to bear on particular persons or organizations, administrative law is expected to ensure that the rudiments of due process are available. Finally, administrative law provides a means for judicial review, not only to provide a check on administrative arbitrariness and abuses but also to integrate important decisions that emerge from executive branch agencies into the larger body of law by reconciling them to appropriate constitutional and statutory provisions. And through all of that extends a concern to have a process that provides an appropriate level of deference to expert and professional civil servants charged with implementation of a host of legislation in technically difficult and politically contentious fields.

The nature of executive orders and the processes by which they are issued run in a very different direction. They are usually not open, provide little or no procedural regularity, and have limited participation. Indeed, they invite political appeals to do off the record and behind closed doors that which would be on the record and public in an agency proceeding. Executive orders often not only do not pay heed to these important concerns, but they also often create problems. For example, they can muddy the discussion of legislative history. Claims to authority can be an issue, not merely because of what the White House does today but as a result of past practice by other administrations. It was with no small bit of irony that the Supreme Court in 1989 reached back to an executive order promulgated by President Kennedy more than a decade before the Federal Advisory Committee Act (FACA) was passed to interpret the statute.[126] Among the many ironies in that case was the fact that the act was passed to deal with the complete failure of the executive order to protect the public interest. Moreover, the Court had to recognize that the interpretation it sought to place on the statute plainly violated a literal reading of the legislation in favor of the failed executive order's approach.[127] Recent presidents have moved in quite a different direction from a concern with the real validity of their actions to assert broad claims to constitutional authority or implied statutory authority. As we have seen, that can create more difficulties than it solves.

It is ironic but true that at various points of tension, some individuals in the White House and in Congress seem to forget that it is likely that the other party or officials with different ideological tendencies will be moving into and out of power in their institutions over time. The party in power in the White House will at some point be interested in maintaining accountability when the other party occupies the presidency, and the same is true in Congress. The basic relationships need to be maintained throughout if the tasks of government are to be accomplished.

It certainly cannot be said that there is anything open, orderly, or participative about orders. It is ironic that presidents often issue orders mandating various types of consultation but usually do not undertake such consultations before issuing the order. As the preceding comments about intergovernmental tensions noted, state and local officials provide perfect examples of this problem. However, even at the federal government level, there have been serious tensions over this problem. Thus, the decision by the Reagan administration to freeze key members of Congress out of discussions over significant changes in the order governing national security classification drew sharp criticism from the legislature. The tendency to use executive orders to provide special exemptions or benefits to individuals or groups exacerbates the tendency to believe that the White House is nothing more than a focal point for partisanship and arbitrariness.

The difficulties involved in getting judicial review tend to support those suspicions. There have been a number of difficulties in obtaining judicial review. Certainly the tightening of the standing doctrine has in several respects made an already difficult situation that much more complex. Although it is appropriate to craft reasonable rules of standing to protect against frivolous litigation or litigation that does not otherwise satisfy the case or controversy requirements of the Constitution, there seems little reason why such presidential actions should not be subject to review. A reading of the opinion for the D.C. Circuit in the striker replacement order case, *Chamber of Commerce v. Reich,*[128] reveals some of the existing difficulties. Another case, *Xin-Chan Zhang v. Slattery,*[129] provides a slightly different lesson. In that case, the U.S. Circuit Court of Appeals for the Second Circuit blocked efforts by the plaintiff to force the government to honor its own executive order. Thus, in addition to standing to sue, there is a question whether an aggrieved party should be able to compel an agency to honor a lawful executive order that has been issued to it. There is also a question of the degree to which a reviewing court would consider that review is precluded because the statutory authority claimed by the president appears to grant broad discretionary authority.[130] In the short term, these weaknesses may seem to make executive orders even more attractive to an administration, but that is short-term thinking.

Despite the apparent deference by the judiciary to the president's orders, this chapter has plainly demonstrated any number of instances in which the White House has lost in court. Executive orders, both legal and illegal, can expose officials to liability. It is an old argument, developed long before the battle over the so-called Nuremberg defense, that illegal orders do not insulate a public official from liability for his or her actions. The classic example harks back to *Little v. Barreme*[131] during the Washington administration. Even legal orders can expose the government to liability. Though the federal courts have often upheld dramatic actions taken by the president during difficult periods, they have not been hesitant to support claims against the government later. The many cases that were brought involving the U.S. Shipping Board Emergency Fleet Corporation after World War I provide examples of just how long such postorder legal cleanup can take and how much it can cost.[132] Later, in a 1951 case, the Supreme Court subjected government to claims by business for the damages done to their interests during the government's operation of the coal mines during World War II after FDR seized the mines in 1943.[133] Thus, the legal issues that may arise are concerned with both the validity of orders and with addressing the consequences of admittedly legitimate decrees.

There is also a set of difficulties that can be clustered under the heading of taking the easy way out. The first of these is that the ease and speed with which one administration can issue orders is equaled by the facility with which the next administration can undo those actions. Of the twenty-two orders issued by Jimmy Carter unrelated to the Iran Hostage crisis between the 1980 election and the arrival of Ronald Reagan, thirteen were revoked, superseded, or amended during the Reagan administration, and these were not even particularly significant. Even when the orders are not revoked, they are often dramatically modified. This is one of the factors giving rise to the decree-inertia principle under which orders in a direction in a policy space tend to expand in size and complexity over time, unless acted upon by an outside force.

It has been tempting for a long time now to seek to get control of agencies and hamstring them so that they cannot act, on the theory that they will then be unable to resist the policies promulgated by the president. Unfortunately, that also means that these agencies and the people who staff them cannot serve the political appointees of the administration either. There has been far more at issue than the question of whether any president really believes in cabinet government.

The use of executive orders as private bills, exempting individuals from various requirements of civil service and other restrictions, may seem like a harmless enough set of actions, but they can be troublesome. First, there is the danger of a significant mistake with important consequences, as in President Johnson's decision to exempt J. Edgar Hoover from mandatory retirement. There is also the clear risk of an appearance of arbitrariness and potential favoritism in this kind of practice.

The use of executive orders may be arbitrary and discriminatory and encourage that kind of behavior by others. Perhaps one of the best-known examples here is President Roosevelt's Executive Order 9066, which led to curfews, removal from homes and businesses, and ultimately incarceration in what were euphemistically called "relocation centers" but were in fact concentration camps. Roosevelt claimed no other authority for this order than his power as president of the United States and as commander in chief.[134] The order was later affirmed by Congress.[135] The result was that one hundred seventeen thousand Japanese Americans were placed in the camps.[136] It denied the people victimized by it even the barest rudiments of due process. Executive Order 9066 was not actually rescinded until 1976,[137] and it was another dozen years after that before Congress finally acknowledged wrongdoing and provided some limited recompense for the survivors of the camps.[138] Other exclusionary practices also were carried out through executive orders. Thus, E.O. 589 issued in 1907 prohibited Japanese and Korean laborers who had passports that permitted entry to Hawaii, Mexico, or Canada from entering the continental United States.[139]

The risk of orders prepared outside the White House can be very problematic, particularly if there is not a process in place by which to ensure that no troublesome orders slip through because they are not carefully and consistently scrutinized. That also implies that if executive orders are to be used well and effectively, then the White House must have a significant capacity to manage them. There is little evidence that such systematic and substantively adequate capacity exists. This can be a significant problem during situations of emergency. For example, at the end of the hostage crisis, Carter issued nine orders (E.O. 12277 through E.O. 12285) on one day, January 19, 1981, to implement the provisions of the settlement.

The building of this capacity should begin during transition and continue as the uses of these devices evolve during the administration. There is also some question whether the capacity is best maintained in the OMB. That agency has become so politicized that there is some question whether the function could be placed there without compounding political difficulties. From a practical standpoint there is also a question whether it would ever receive the attention it deserves in that office. It might be better placed in the office of the White House counsel.

Quite apart from the question of embarrassment, another kind of damage can come from using the order to respond to friend and foe alike: it can produce bad policy. Orders that are adopted to address political pressures of the moment can have long-term and far-reaching consequences, even if they survive immediate legal challenges, as in the case of Truman's loyalty-security program. The courts did not strike down the program per se, but it caused great damage to many individuals and fed the growing national hysteria of the second red scare. It also produced waves of litigation over the nature and operation of the program, such as *Joint Anti-Facist Refugee Committee v. McGrath*,[140] in which the Court struck down as arbitrary the process by which groups were placed on the dreaded Attorney General's List of Subversive Organizations.[141] Eisenhower issued his own loyalty-security order after Truman's orders and after Congress legislated on the subject. However, the Court found the administrative process established by his order to be in violation of the very statute he claimed to be implementing.[142]

To support steps born of political expediency, many administrations have looked for barn-door statutes, the broad terms of which can be used to justify a wide range of policy actions. From the Trading with the Enemy Act to the International Economic Emergency Act to the general delegation statute to the broad general management authority conferred by Title 5, this practice, along with the frequent use of executive orders to make significant policy decisions or to alter organizations or allocate responsibilities, can create a hodgepodge of potentially contradictory actions or confused organizations, with no one watching the big picture and no counterbalance from other interests along the way.

Then there is the question of the president as the role model for chief executive officers at other levels of government. There have been mixed experiences with the use of executive orders by governors and mayors around the nation. There is evidence that a number of governors, such as Jeb Bush in Florida and Pete Wilson in California, have been increasingly willing to follow the lead of the president and to use executive orders to address issues that seem too difficult to handle through the normal legislative or administrative processes.

CONCLUSION

It should be clear by now that there is a wide variety of motivations that prompt presidents to use executive orders to accomplish directly what they might otherwise do through legislation or other administrative actions. It is equally obvious why chief executives are attracted to the use of these tools. Indeed, they have not only been used to meet challenges that simply would not wait for more traditional policymaking; but have also been employed in some daring cases of presidential leadership, as in Truman's desegregation of the military. What is often not so obvious, particularly to inexperienced White House staffers desperate to please the boss, is that there are many complexities associated with the use of executive orders and more than a few significant downsides. The difficulties can range from practical short-term conflicts with other branches and levels of government to much longer-term and broader issues of legitimacy.

That having been said, executive orders are not the only tools of presidential direct action. Indeed, they are often used in connection with other such instruments. Chapter 4 addresses one of the least understood of these, the presidential memorandum.

FOUR

PRESIDENTIAL MEMORANDA: EXECUTIVE ORDERS BY ANOTHER NAME AND YET UNIQUE

If Bill Clinton chose to make his first official act the issuance of an executive order, Ronald Reagan made his the signing of a presidential memorandum. As it happens, it was a freeze in federal hiring, clearly a symbolic response to his campaign against government.[1] After all, this memorandum signing came moments after the new president had pronounced in his Inaugural Address that government was not the solution but the problem. He chose to dramatize this assertion by signing the memorandum even before leaving the Capitol.

Clinton learned a number of lessons from Reagan about showmanship and the use of presidential mandates. He repeated Reagan's flourish, also taking his first official action while still at the Capitol in his opening moments in office. And though Clinton elected to make his first move with an executive order, he quickly followed with a spate of presidential memoranda addressing a variety of important and extremely controversial topics.

Clinton took office on Wednesday, January 20, 1993. Two days later he issued significant policy changes in several controversial areas. He did so not by introducing legislation or even by signing executive orders, but by promulgating presidential memoranda. By Friday the new president had issued a memorandum to the secretary of health and human services (HHS), directing her to suspend the abortion Gag Rule imposed by the Bush administration and to promulgate proposed new regulations within thirty days.[2] Secretary Donna Shalala promptly published notice of the proposed rulemaking in the Federal Register. That same Friday Clinton ordered the HHS secretary to lift the moratorium on funding of fetal tissue experimentation.[3] On that same busy day, Clinton issued a memorandum to the secretary of defense, ordering him to reverse the existing ban on abortions in military hospitals so long as they were not paid for with Department of Defense (DOD) funds.[4]

Also on that Friday, he issued a memorandum to the acting administrator of the U.S. Agency for International Development (AID), directing that he end the so-called Mexico City Policy issued by President Reagan. That policy had required aid to be withheld from nongovernmental organizations "providing advice, counseling, or information regarding abortion, or lobbying a foreign government to legalize or make abortion available" and to remove the sanctions and conditions imposed by U.S. assistance pursuant to that policy.[5]

In a related action, Clinton issued a memorandum to HHS that directed the Food and Drug Administration (FDA) to reexamine its Import Alert 66-47, which effectively blocked importation of RU-486, the so-called abortion pill, and simultaneously called upon the secretary to take steps to support efforts to approve and support production of the drug domestically. The FDA ultimately completed that decision process in the final months of Clinton's administration. (That the issue had lost none of its controversial character over the years was demonstrated by the *New York Times* headline announcing the decision, "Joy and Outrage."[6])

Clinton's actions were not limited to debates over federal abortion policy. The following Wednesday, he issued what was to be one of the most controversial of his early policy decisions, the Memorandum on Ending Discrimination in the Armed Forces, better known as the gays in the military policy.[7] Unlike his directions to HHS to begin a public rulemaking process under an existing statute, this memorandum required the secretary of defense to draft an executive order "ending discrimination on the basis of sexual orientation to determine who may serve in the Armed Forces of the United States."

Also in his first week in office the president issued a memorandum to the director of the Office of Management and Budget, ordering a review by Clinton appointees at the top-agency levels before an agency would be permitted to send new regulations forward to the OMB for review under the existing Reagan regulatory restraint orders.[8] Interestingly, it effectively continued and reinforced the very Reagan executive orders constraining regulation that Clinton and Gore had campaigned against in 1992. This was the first of a set of what the administration termed "presidential directives," consisting of some twenty-five presidential memoranda and eighteen executive orders, that formed the basis for taking control of administrative agencies and ultimately implementing the administration's reinventing government initiatives.

Each administration seems to learn from its predecessors about how presidential power tools can be used, and each then seems to adapt the tools, applying those lessons, to new uses. Just as the Reagan administration learned new uses of the executive order from the Carter years, so Clinton employed lessons learned from the use of presidential memoranda by his Republican predecessors, Reagan and Bush. As with Reagan's use of executive orders, the Clinton administration took the lessons and ran with them, using the memorandum even more extensively than Reagan and Bush.

George W. Bush, in turn, learned the lessons from his predecessors, taking his first high-visibility actions in the form of presidential memoranda. Like Clinton, he made his first official action the issuance of a directive on ethics, though he chose a presidential memorandum for the task instead of an executive order.[9] Also on his first day in office and taking a cue from his father's administration, Bush issued his memorandum, Regulatory Review Plan, which was, at a minimum, a sixty-day moratorium on new rules, even those already submitted to the *Federal Register* for publication.[10] Other rulemaking proceedings were frozen indefinitely, pending a review by the new administration. Bush issued a third memorandum on his inauguration day that froze government hiring and made any hiring decisions that were to be taken subject to political appointees in the department involved.[11] The memorandum also directed agency heads to establish their own hiring processes and permitted them to delegate the operation of that plan to subordinates. Two days later, Bush issued his memorandum reversing Clinton's elimination of the Mexico City Policy and reinstating it as it was originally articulated by President Reagan.[12]

Given its evolving uses by contemporary presidencies, it is interesting and important to consider the use and abuses of the presidential memorandum. A new administration will do well to understand these devices and to address the same kinds of questions already raised regarding executive orders. Because the expanded use of these tools is relatively recent, the chapter will pay particular attention to the Reagan, Bush, and Clinton administrations.

WHAT ARE PRESIDENTIAL MEMORANDA?

As with other tools of presidential direct action, the precise definition of the presidential memorandum is unclear and evolving. In general, it is a pronouncement by the chief executive nominally directed at executive branch officials and labeled as a memorandum by the White House. In earlier times, it was sometimes known as a presidential letter.[13] As a practical matter, the memorandum is being used as the equivalent of an executive order but without fitting into its existing legal requirements.

In recent years memoranda have been lumped together with executive orders, with both referred to by the White House as presidential directives. And since there is no legal significance to the form of a presidential directive, the situation can be quite confusing. Even President Clinton was known to be confused about just exactly what he was doing when issuing these memoranda—and Clinton was a lawyer. He gave a speech in October 1994 at Carlmont High School in Belmont, California, discussing an executive order that he was going to sign, instructing the secretary of education to withhold funds from states that had not implemented a policy that actively attacked guns in the schools.[14] What he actually signed was a memorandum to the secretary concerning the implementation of the Gun-Free Schools Act and the Safe and Drug-Free Schools and Community Act.[15] He made the same mistake when he signed a memorandum on the Earned-Income Tax Credit, announcing, "I'm going to sign this Executive order and then ask Secretary Bentsen and our IRE Commissioner, Peggy Richardson, to talk about what they're going to do."[16]

The Clinton administration used both executive orders and memoranda broadly. For example, in presenting its policies designed to implement the reports of Vice President Gore's National Performance Review, the White House issued a list of directives:

PRESIDENTIAL DIRECTIVES IMPLEMENTING RECOMMENDATIONS OF THE NATIONAL PERFORMANCE REVIEW

Executive Orders

13048	Improving Administrative Management in the Executive Branch
12999	Computers for Education
12861	Elimination of Exec. Branch Regs
12862	Setting Customer Service Stds
12863	President's Foreign Intel. Advisory Board
12864	Advisory Council on the NII
12866	Regulatory Planning and Review
12871	Labor-Management Partnerships
12873	Fed. Acquisition, Recycling and Waste Reduction
12875	Enhancing Intergovernmental Partnership
12878	Commission on Entitlement Reform
12881	National Sci. and Tech. Council
12882	Presidential Commission on Science and Technology
12898	Env. Justice for Minority Populations
12902	Energy and Water Conservation
12906	Coordinating Geographic Data Access
12931	Federal Procurement Reform
13011	Federal Information Technology

Presidential Memoranda

12/17/99	Memorandum for the Heads of Executive Departments and Agencies on Electronic Government
1/12/99	Memorandum on Using Technology To Improve Training Opportunities for Federal Government Employees
6/1/98	Memorandum on Plain English in Government Writing

5/26/98	Memorandum on Actions to Further Improve Financial Management
5/14/98	Presidential Memorandum, on Privacy and Personal Information in Federal Records
5/01/98	Presidential Memorandum, Interagency Committees on Use of Alternate Means of Dispute Resolution and Negotiated Rulemaking
4/22/98	Presidential Memorandum on Strengthening Our Commitment to Service
4/21/98	Presidential Memorandum on Streamlining the Granting of Waivers
3/03/98	Conducting "Conversations with America" to Further Improve Customer Service
	Electronic Commerce
	Government Employment for Welfare Recipients
	Heads of Performance Measurement Pilot Projects
	Administration of Freedom of Information Act
	Agency Rulemaking Procedures
	Env. Justice for Minority Populations
	Env. Practices on Fed. Grounds
	Federal Procurement
	Implementing Management Reform
	Improving Customer Service
	Negotiated Rulemaking
	Report of Regulations Reviewed
	Streamlining Procurement Through EC
	Streamlining the Federal Workforce
	The President's Com. Enterprise Board
	Regulatory Reinvention Initiative

Vice Presidential Memorandum, Announcing Phase II of NPR[17]

But there are significant differences between orders and memoranda, starting with the fact that there is no stated process for developing memoranda and no requirement that they be published in the *Federal Register*, or anywhere else, for that matter. For their own purposes, presidents sometimes direct that particular memoranda be published in the *Register*. Most, though not all, memoranda are published in the *Weekly Compilation of Presidential Documents* and *The Public Papers of the President*. The memoranda are not numbered or indexed. Presidential determinations which are foreign policy actions are generally numbered chronologically based on the fiscal year; however, there are exceptions even among these. Other differences will be made clear, but the fact that memoranda are even simpler to issue and that they need not be published makes them both attractive to recent administrations and problematic as well. That is particularly true if they are used to modify significantly or even override policies issued through more standard devices, like executive orders or agency rules. Few members of Congress are even aware of this presidential direct action tool, which adds to its attractiveness. While it has a number of traditional uses, such as the presidential determination, it is an entirely flexible device that can be used alone or in combination with other presidential policy tools in a host of ways.

HOW ARE PRESIDENTIAL MEMORANDA USED?

Until relatively recently, presidents issued few memoranda, and most of these fit into three categories: presidential determinations, memoranda of disapproval, and hortatory declarations.

Presidential Determinations: A Standard Foreign Policy Tool

For the most part, presidential determinations stem from statutes that require the president to make findings concerning the status of a country or some activity in the foreign policy field. (For examples from the first year of the Clinton administration, see Table 4.1.) Once made, these findings then trigger such actions under the statutes as development assistance or sanctions. In some instances, presidents make findings and decide to act even though there may be limitations in the statute. At the same time, though, these determinations are required to be provided to the Congress so that the legislature can be aware of the administration's actions and respond appropriately. That might include oversight activities, such as hearings or other investigations, it might entail enacting appropriations changes or even result in new subject matter legislation. Though many of these determinations and actions are routine matters prepared and implemented by the State Department, some, like trade sanctions against Japan, special trade status for the People's Republic of China, or military sales or cooperation, can be highly controversial.

These presidential determinations issued as presidential memoranda are distinct from national security directives (NSDs) (see chapter 6). However, in some cases presidential determinations are not issued in standard presidential memoranda but as NSDs, which are often classified.[18]

Memoranda of Disapproval

Presidents have also issued memoranda of disapproval, which are public veto statements. For example, President Bush issued a memorandum of disapproval for the bill providing for Emergency Chinese Immigration Relief in November 1989, which reads in part:

Table 4.1. Clinton's Presidential Determinations, 1993

No.	Title	Authority	Action
93-18	Narcotics-producing countries	Foreign Assistance Act	Countries cooperating and in compliance
93-19	Trade with the PRC	Ex-Import Bank Act	Approval of Ex-Im loan to China for purchase of equipment
93-20	Funding sanctions re Serbia, Montenegro	Foreign Assistance Act	Authorized $5 million to support sanctions enforcement
93-22	Assistance to refugees in Bosnia, Croatia	Migration and Refugee Act	Authorized $30 million for support of victims and refugees
93-23	MFN status for the PRC	Trade Act	Extends waiver regarding MFN for China
93-24	Withdrawal of Russian troops from the Baltics	P.L. 102-391	Certifies withdrawal of Russian troops from Baltic countries
93-25	Trade with Albania, Romania, other republics	Trade Act	Extends waiver for trade with republics of former USSR
93-26	Trade with Bulgaria	Trade Act	Certifies Bulgaria not in violation of the act
93-27	Trade with Mauritania	Trade Act	Examines reviews on expropriation of private property
93-28	Assistance to Haiti	Foreign Assistance Act	Triggers development assistance processes for Haiti
93-29	Delegation of authority on trade with Japan	Delegation Act	Delegates authority to trade representative to determine Japanese compliance
93-30	Trade with Romania	Trade Act	Certifies trade relations with Romania
93-31	Sales of depleted uranium ammunition to Sweden	P.L. 102-391	Declares action notwithstanding section 551 of P.L. 102-391

Table 4.1, *continued*

No.	Title	Authority	Action
93-32	Elections in Angola	P.L. 102-484	Certifies free, fair, and democratic elections in Angola
93-33	Assistance to African refugees	Migration and Refugee Act	Designates returning African refugees for reintegration aid
93-34	Assistance to Mozambican refugees	Migration and Refugee Act	Provides $6.3 million to assist refugees and returnees in Mozambique
93-35	Defense assistance to Guyana	Foreign Assistance Act	Authorizes sale or lease of military equipment to Guyana
93-36	Nuclear exports to Romania	Atomic Energy Act	Finds Romania in violation of IAEA agreements but waives penalty
93-37	Bulgaria–United States nuclear cooperation	Atomic Energy Act	Approves nuclear cooperation agreement with Bulgaria
93-39	Assistance to Jordan	Foreign Assistance Act	Authorizes $6 million in aid notwithstanding provisions of P.L. 102-391
93-41	Funding for peacekeeping in Liberia	Foreign Assistance Act	Authorizes additional support for Liberian peacekeeping force
93-43	Somalia	Foreign Assistance Act	Authorizes $27 million in assistance to Somalia
94-1	Refugee admissions	Migration and Refugee Act	Sets 121,000 refugees for FY1994 with 3,000 unallocated
94-3	Trade with Japan	Delegation Act	Delegates authority to trade representative as to sanctions against Japan

Source: Weekly Compilation of Presidential Documents, 1993.

MEMORANDUM OF DISAPPROVAL FOR THE BILL PROVIDING FOR EMERGENCY CHINESE IMMIGRATION RELIEF, NOVEMBER 30, 1989

In light of the actions I have taken in June and again today, I am withholding my approval of H.R. 2712, the "Emergency Chinese Immigration Relief Act of 1989." These actions make H.R. 2712 wholly unnecessary.

I share the objectives of the overwhelming majority in the Congress who passed this legislation. Within hours of the events of Tiananmen Square in June, I ordered the Attorney General to ensure that no nationals from the People's Republic of China be deported against their will, and no such nationals have been deported. Since June, my Administration has taken numerous additional and substantive actions to further guarantee this objective.

Today I am extending and broadening these measures to provide the same protections as H.R. 2712. I am directing the Attorney General and the Secretary of State to provide additional protections to persons covered by the Attorney General's June 6th order deferring the enforced departure for nationals of China. These protections will include: (1) irrevocable waiver of the 2-year home country residence requirement which may be exercised until January 1, 1994; (2) assurance of continued lawful immigration status for individuals who were lawfully in the United States on June 5, 1989; (3) authorization for employment of Chinese nationals present in the United States on June 5, 1989; and (4) notice of expiration of nonimmigrant status, rather than institution of deportation proceedings, for individuals eligible for deferral of enforced departure whose nonimmigrant status has expired. . . .

These further actions will provide effectively the same protection as would H.R. 2712 as presented to me on November 21, 1989. Indeed, last June I exercised my authority to provide opportunity for employment to a wider class of Chinese aliens than the statute would have required. My action today provides complete assurance that the United States will provide to Chinese nationals here the protection they deserve. . . .

I have under current law sufficient authority to provide the necessary relief for Chinese students and others who fear returning to China in the near future. I will continue to exercise vigorously this authority. Waivers granted under this authority will not be revoked. . . .

My actions today accomplish the laudable objectives of the Congress in passing H.R. 2712 while preserving my ability to manage foreign relations. I would note that, with respect to individuals expressing a fear of persecution related to their country's coercive family policies, my actions today provide greater protection than would H.R. 2712 by extending such protection worldwide rather than just to Chinese nationals. Despite my strong support for the basic principles of international family planning, the United States cannot condone any policy involving forced abortion or coercive sterilization. . . .

The adjournment of the Congress has prevented my return of H.R. 2712 within the meaning of Article I, section 7, clause 2 of the Constitution. Accordingly, my withholding of approval from the bill precludes its becoming law. The Pocket Veto Case, 279 U.S. 655 (1929). Because of the questions raised in opinions issued by the United States Court of Appeals for the District of Columbia Circuit, I am sending H.R. 2712 with my objections to the Clerk of the House of Representatives.[19]

In this case, Bush effectively rewrote the legislation by issuing directives to accomplish the purposes of the statute that he thought appropriate but using the veto to dispose of the rest. The use of a memorandum of disapproval is not a new idea. It has been used in one way or another by virtually all postwar presidents. The first President Bush used it sixteen times during his term.

Hortatory Memoranda

Hortatory declarations have sometimes been the equivalent of presidential proclamations but are directed to executive branch agencies instead of the general public. Examples include encouragement to participate in charity drives such as the Red Cross appeals or the Community Chest (later the Combined Federal Campaign).[20] Others were essentially reminders of previously issued administration policies (often executive orders) such as civil rights commitments, or reminders that previous executive orders required notice to and consultation with tribal governments.[21] Still others have been, in the president's words, efforts to "get the word out" on some policy. In early 1994 President Clinton formally announced an effort by the administration to publicize the availability of the advance payment option on the earned income tax credit "as an important symbol of the core commitment of this administration to promote the values of work and family and community and to help people who work hard and play by the rules. . . . So today I am sending a memorandum to all Cabinet Secretaries and agency heads, instructing them to get that word out, to get their personnel and payroll offices on board so that Government employees know about the advance payment option for this earned-income tax credit."[22]

Apart from the foreign policy determinations, presidential memoranda were generally of limited importance and infrequently used until the Reagan years. During their entire terms Eisenhower issued forty-three, Kennedy twenty-two, Johnson ninety-three, Nixon sixty, Ford fifty-four, and Carter ninety-three. The Reagan and Bush administrations discovered a number of uses for the memorandum and the Clinton administration transformed them. In contrast to his early predecessors, Clinton issued many more memoranda.[23]

Year	Memoranda
1993	53
1994	65
1995	50
1996	50
1997	59
1998	85
1999	95
2000	79
Total	536

Indeed, during the Clinton years the memorandum came to be used more or less interchangeably with executive orders under the general rubric of presidential directives.

To Accomplish the Same Purposes as Executive Orders

Given these changes, it might not be surprising to find that presidential memoranda have come to be used for all of the purposes of executive orders. They often contain binding pronouncements directed at various units of the executive branch, make policy in fields generally conceded to the president, delegate authority granted to the president to various agencies or offices of the executive branch, create new organizations or modify the obligations of existing offices, control military and foreign affairs units, manage the civil service, and reallocate assets. In addition to these traditional applications of executive orders, recent presidents have found additional uses for the memorandum.

In Conjunction with Other Presidential Tools as Part of a Policy Mix

When, for example, the president issues a determination in the form of a memorandum, he or she may then take action on the basis of that determination in a number of ways. The White House may employ an executive order, a national security directive, a proclamation, or even call upon an executive branch department to undertake action through rulemaking or adjudication. Moreover, the administration may, and often does, employ several of these tools at the same time. In such settings these devices are mutually reinforcing, allowing an administration to have both scope and intensity in a particular area of policymaking.

For example, the United States in late 1993 and early 1994 found itself in the midst of a complex international situation involving highly enriched uranium. The complexity developed as international journalists made it clear that (1) Russia had a substantial amount of spent nuclear fuel; (2) its ability to secure it, handle it, and store it were completely inadequate; and (3) there were dangers that it would be stolen or sold.[24] The press kept the spotlight on several aspects of the nuclear issue. Besides the obvious safety issues, there was fear that the uranium might be dumped on the world market, depressing prices. While these public disclosures concerning the vulnerability of the Russian nuclear materials emerged, there was under way a delicate three-way negotiation involving the Ukraine, Russia, and the United States for nuclear disarmament in Russia and the Ukraine.[25] Success in that effort necessitated steps to ensure that weapons-grade nuclear materials were disposed of properly. Moreover, North Korea was said to be watching the European negotiations to inform its own interactions with the United States, which was seeking to end North Korea's nuclear research and development efforts. The United States engineered an agreement with Russia to address the problem by using a government corporation, the United States Enrichment Corporation, designed to become private over time. It was to enter into a contract for the purchase of a large quantity of the highly enriched uranium from Russia, a move that would not only address the dangerous nuclear materials problem but also provide cash-strapped Russia with badly needed hard currency.[26] Clinton employed a memorandum, Presidential Determination 94-19, to advance payments under the contract, using an exception to federal law that normally precludes advance payments to contractors.[27] This one policy action required a range of policy tools, including the presidential memorandum.

Initiating a Policy Process

Clinton's initial memoranda regarding the Gag Rule, gays in the military, and RU-486, among others, did not take any final policy action. Instead, they initiated more formal policymaking processes. In the case of the Gag Rule, the Department of Health and Human Services launched a rulemaking process aimed at reversing the Bush administration's revision of policy concerning federally funded family planning clinics. In the case of the military, the DOD was required by memorandum to examine its own practices and to prepare a draft executive order for the president's signature at the end of that process. The Food and Drug Administration was directed to (1) examine, by rulemaking, its policies affecting the importation and marketing of the controversial abortion drug RU-486; (2) reevaluate the process by which it certified imported drugs of this sort (a reconsideration of its licensure processes); (3) work on the importation controls that might interfere with access to the drug; and (4) determine whether the agency could encourage its production and marketing in the United States.

To Direct Agencies to Suspend Action or Impose Moratoriums

Several of Clinton's early memoranda launched new policymaking processes, but they also suspended existing policy, pending the final decisions. As in so many areas, however, the Clinton administration did not pioneer the use of memoranda to impose a moratorium. The use by presidents Reagan and Bush of memoranda and executive orders in their battles against administrative rulemaking is an obvious example. Briefly, it should be recalled that President Reagan, upon entering office, issued executive order 12291, which gave dramatic powers to the Office of Management and Budget to intervene in rulemaking by administrative agencies.[28] That order was the basis for battles in Congress and in the courts for the next four years.[29] Just days before taking the oath of office for the second time, Reagan issued Executive Order 12498, expanding the OMB's powers over agency rulemaking.[30] On its face, the order appeared only to require the development of a regulatory calendar and to allow the OMB to monitor what were termed prerulemaking activities. However, the true meaning of the order became clear only when one read the presidential memorandum issued on the same day.[31] When supplemented by the memorandum, the order gave the OMB power to prevent agencies from expending funds to study whether a rulemaking proceeding was necessary. Still, the battle against regulations continued. Although the Reagan orders announced that they only applied as permitted by law, it became clear that these processes were intended to discourage and delay not only rules that agencies themselves originated but also rules required by Congress.[32]

President Bush, who came to office in 1989, continued Reagan's orders in force and pushed the matter still further. The stage was already set for conflict, since key legislators were angry over the behavior of the Office of Information and Regulatory Affairs in the OMB. Originally created by the Paperwork Reduction Act, OIRA was the vehicle employed by the Reagan administration to administer its antirulemaking orders. Congress was also frustrated by its inability to obtain information about whether and how regulated groups were working with OIRA in a kind of back-door political appeal to the White House, outside the normal rulemaking process required by the Administrative Procedure Act and away from the view of oversight committees in the legislature. This led to threats from Congress that the PRA would not be reauthorized until this dispute was resolved.

In negotiations between the OMB and senior Democrats on the Hill, an agreement was reached, informally known as the "side bar agreement" but formally entitled "Administrative Agreement: Procedures Governing OIRA Review of Regulations Under Executive Order Nos. 12291 and 12498." Under the deal, Congress would move forward to reauthorize the PRA, and the OMB would ensure that the Office of Information and Regulatory Affairs would provide information to Congress about contacts with outside groups as well as any important communications between OIRA and other executive branch agencies. However, C. Boyden Gray, then White House Counsel, rejected the deal that had already been approved by the OMB director Richard Darman. Gray threatened to assert executive privilege, denying Congress even the kinds of information that it had been receiving to that point.[33] A deal was not struck with Congress, and the PRA was not reauthorized until well into Clinton's term.[34]

The clash between Congress and the White House on regulatory matters intensified during the Bush years for another significant reason. In April 1989, using a press release rather than either an executive order or a memorandum, Bush created Vice President Quayle's Council on Competitiveness. The action drew little attention at the time. Dan Quayle was not being taken seriously in many circles, and it was a time when new advisory bodies were being installed by the new administration. Executive branch agencies did not receive their direction on working with the Quayle Council until the cabinet secretary issued a memorandum on the subject in June 1990,[35] and it soon became clear that the council would have serious impact.

The Quayle Council turned out to be an aggressive antiregulatory body willing to prevail upon agencies, even though it had no statutory or executive order authority. The council participated in OIRA meetings and made decisions about pending rulemaking proposals totally outside the public eye.[36] Quayle demanded that agencies offer deregulation proposals.[37] The council defined its scope of authority broadly, claiming that it could review agency materials even beyond those covered by Executive Order 12291. Quayle asserted that the council could review "strategy statements, guidelines, policy manuals, grant and loan procedures, Advance Notices of Proposed Rulemaking, press releases, and other documents announcing or implementing regulatory policy that affects the public."[38] Members of Congress were outraged by the power grab, the methods, the secrecy, and the substantive policy changes of the council. Congressman David Skaggs (D-Colo.) asserted, "The Council has become an off-the-record, no-fingerprints operation for subverting necessary and appropriate regulatory activity of the Federal Government."[39] Henry Waxman (D-Calif.) issued a dramatic indictment: "There is unmistakable evidence that White House officials, spearheaded by Vice President Dan Quayle . . . are working with industry to undermine implementation of the new clean air law. . . . This is not only horrible policy, it is clearly illegal."[40]

The Bush administration asserted executive privilege over the information sought by Congress about the operation of the council,[41] but information about the kinds of impacts that it had on rulemaking in the environmental and health areas were leaked to reporters, including Quayle's role in the embarrassing fumbles by the United States at the Rio Earth Summit in 1992. That same year Bush decided to push the matter even further, making the attack on regulation one of the centerpieces of his reelection effort. It began with the State of the Union Address in January, where he announced that he was instituting a ninety-day moratorium on the issuance of new regulations. On that day, he had issued his presidential memorandum calling for the moratorium that made it clear that agencies were to report to the Quayle Council.[42] Interestingly, Bush also directed his memorandum to the chairs of independent regulatory commissions, agencies over which the president does not have direct authority. These agencies were made independent precisely to prevent political control by the White House. During the moratorium, the agencies were to "work with the public, other interested agencies, the Office of Information and Regulatory Affairs, and the Council on Competitiveness to (i) identify each of your agency's regulations and programs that impose a substantial cost on the economy and (ii) determine whether each such regulation or program adheres" to the administration's regulatory policies. It also required agencies to "designate, in consultation with the Council on Competitiveness, a senior official to serve as your agency's permanent regulatory oversight official." Bush left no doubt that this move was a deliberate attack on congressional criticisms of the administration's approach to regulation. In a second memorandum issued on the same day, Bush wrote, "Although the Congress has created the regulatory schemes within which we must operate, I am confident that, with your help, the executive branch can do much to create conditions conducive to a healthy and robust economy."[43]

The president extended the moratorium for another 120 days in a memo-randum issued in late April.[44] He reemphasized that the Quayle Council was at the center of the effort, beginning his remarks on signing the memorandum by issuing a "salute [to] the three generals in the war for regulatory reforms: our Vice President, Dan Quayle, Boyden Gray, and Dr. Michael Boskin," of the Council on Competitiveness.[45] He called for additional efforts at reduc-ing regulatory burdens and directed "the Competitiveness Council to take the lead in implementing these reforms." Bush continued throughout the cam-paign to laud the work of the council just as vigorously as candidates Clinton and Gore attacked the administration for the council's abuse of power and interference with rulemaking lawfully required by the Congress in such critical areas as the environment, health, and safety.

Bush put his moratorium center stage in his campaign, but he was not the first president to impose a moratorium. Actually, he borrowed the idea from the Reagan administration's early efforts. Reagan had imposed a sixty-day delay for rulemaking in January 1981.[46] At that time, the administra-tion was concerned enough about the controversial nature of this action to request an opinion from the attorney general, who supported the move.[47] Even so, the Bush administration pushed the moratorium tactic much fur-ther than its predecessor.

WHY ARE PRESIDENTIAL MEMORANDA EMPLOYED?

Recent presidents, particularly the Clinton administration, have found not only a wide range of possible uses for memoranda, but also have been drawn to this particular device. There is a variety of reasons why they are attractive options, many of which are similar to the factors that made executive orders a popular vehicle for contemporary White House action. However, memo-randa offer some additional attractions: (1) they have proven to be vehicles that generate favorable publicity; (2) they are a flexible way to address emer-gencies or to manage public responses to hot problems (including transitions into or out of emergencies); (3) they are devices the access to which and knowledge of can be controlled; (4) they are useful mechanisms with which to circumvent or even to confront the Congress; (5) they offer a tool for re-versing previous policies, including their use during transitions; (6) they present an accepted way to take rapid and significant action in foreign policy; (7) and they are a means to pay debts, reward supporters, answer critics, and send signals.

To Generate Favorable Publicity

The Clinton administration generated a steady stream of memoranda on a wide range of issues as the basis for news events, showing the president focusing on particular issues. In some instances, the topics were particular themes. Thus, for example, the administration issued a variety of memoranda, often with accompanying exchanges with reporters, on crime or crime-related issues, including

Memorandum on Federal Arrestee Drug Testing, December 18, 1995
Memorandum on the "One Strike and You're Out" Guidelines, March 28, 1996
Memorandum on the Development of a National Sexual Offender Registration System, June 25, 1996
Memorandum on Crime Victims' Rights, June 27, 1996
Memorandum on the Youth Crime Gun Interdiction Initiative, July 8, 1996
Memorandum on the Work Requirements Initiative, July 16, 1996
Memorandum on Ending Drug Use and Drug Availability for Offenders, January 12, 1998
Memorandum on Standards to Prevent Drinking and Driving, March 3, 1998
Memorandum on Steps to Combat Violence Against Women and Trafficking in Women and Girls, March 11, 1998
Memorandum on Prevention of Prison Inmates Inappropriately Receiving Federal Benefits, April 25, 1998
Memorandum on a Guidebook for Victims of Domestic Violence, November 4, 1998
Memorandum on Deterring and Reducing Gun Crime, March 20, 1999
Memorandum on Hate Crimes in Schools and College Campuses, April 6, 1999
Memorandum on Establishment of the Interagency Commission on Crime and Security in U.S. Seaports, April 27, 1999
Memorandum on the White House Council on Youth Violence, October 15, 1999
Memorandum on Improving Hate Crimes Reporting, September 13, 2000

This was an area in which the administration took considerable criticism, but the memoranda presented the picture of a White House actively generating policy aimed at law enforcement and victim assistance. Such actions can be taken virtually without cost because, in many instances, they are little more than declarations of policies and directives to agencies to pay attention to issues and to cooperate with other organizations rather than serious political or resource commitments.

Many of the presentations concerning directives on reinventing government fit into the same category. They were often long on rhetoric and relatively limited in terms of commitment of dollars or action but commonly issued at some public event with great fanfare. On September 11, 1993, President Clinton went to Texas to laud the state's efforts at reinventing government and to sign two executive orders and one directive (memorandum) implementing the report of the National Performance Review. In so doing, he said:

> Now, what I've tried to do is to determine what I can do by Executive order or directive and what I have to have the Congress' help on. And I'm going to do everything I can possibly do by Executive orders.
>
> Today, basically as a thank-you to Texas, I'm going to issue the first Executive orders here. . . . And I want to tell you what they are. The first order directs the Federal Government to do what successful businesses already do: Set customer service standards, and put the people that are paying the bills first. . . .
>
> Now, the second order will respond to what you saw when we announced this report. Do you remember when the Vice President gave me the report, we had the two forklifts full of paper? Almost all those regulations were regulations of the Government regulating itself. . . . Now, today, the Executive order I'm signing on that will make the Federal agencies cut those regulations on Government employees in half within 3 years.
>
> And, finally, I'm going to sign a directive today that tells everybody in my Cabinet that they have to take responsibility for making the personnel cut that I've outlined, and more than half of the personnel cut has to come from people who are basically in middle management, handing down rules and pushing up paperwork.[48]

The personnel cuts had already been announced. That was the substantive matter on the table, but the issuance of the directive in this case lent itself to the public event that the White House was staging.

To be sure, one of the key themes associated with the reinventing government campaign was the advocacy for what has come to be called "e-government," the expanded use of the Internet for enhancing government services, with particular attention to education. This effort, not surprisingly, elicited a number of presidential memoranda to keep the issue front and center.[49]

Another example involved two memoranda signed by the president at a public session held in conjunction with a conference on Native American issues at the White House, the Memorandum on Distribution of Eagle Feathers for Native American Religious Purposes and the Memorandum on Government-to-Government Relations with Native American Tribal Governments. In truth, neither of these really set any new course. They largely repeated policies previously expressed in executive orders (including 12876 and 12866). They provided no new resources and made no new commitments, but they offered a picture of a concerned administration issuing presumably important policy directives and, in conjunction with the conference, suggested that the conference had serious policy consequences.

That is not to say that there was anything inappropriate with such steps. It is merely to recognize that the administration had learned how to use memoranda effectively as a public relations tool. Thus, whether the memoranda at issue are substantively important or largely symbolic, the mere signing of the directive helps the White House generate news coverage and, in so doing, credits the administration with decisive movement on a particular subject.

A Convenient Way to Address Emergencies or to Manage Public Responses to Hot Problems

In addition to areas in which a president might want to establish a presence, there are some matters that are either real emergencies or problems that call for some kind of administrative action because public opinion seems to demand it. Given that the issuance of memoranda, in the form of presidential determinations, is a traditional tool of foreign policy, it has often been employed to address such emergencies abroad. For example, the disaster that was Kosovo produced five such pronouncements between January and September 1999 on issues ranging from assistance to Kosovo refugees to support for the UN interim administrative mission.[50] Though the U.S. involvement was far less, the brutality in East Timor also elicited a number of memoranda.[51] Like executive orders, memoranda can be a flexible and useful part of an effort to transition into or out of an emergency. For example, President Bush issued the Memorandum on the Return of Desert Shield/Desert Storm Participants to Federal Civilian Employment in March 1991 and the Memorandum Delegating Authority to Report on the Rebuilding of Kuwait early in 1992.

Natural disasters such as the terrible floods in Central America have also prompted the use of memoranda to mobilize assistance.[52] Natural disasters on the domestic front lead to requests for assistance. While virtually everyone is aware of the president's ability to declare a state of disaster and to make possible a range of assistance to states and local governments, businesses, and home owners, that is not the only possible response. Memoranda can be used either to provide real assistance or at least to demonstrate an administration's concern for a difficult situation. Thus, the Clinton administration responded to growing electrical power difficulties, first when a dramatic power outage struck the West Coast during summer 1996[53] and again four years later when it became apparent that California was facing an ongoing challenge to ensure adequate supplies of electricity at rates that could be paid by residential customers.[54]

There are other times, however, when issues rise to such a high level of public attention that an administration is expected to take some kind of action. These issues are often complex and policies to address them take a considerable period of study and debate to develop fully. The memorandum is a tempting tool in such circumstances, since it permits an administration to present a position on the problem in a flexible manner and to appear to be responsive to public concern while continuing the longer-term, less immediately gratifying work of producing full-blown policies. There are a number of contemporary examples. Early 1994 saw a stream of news media revelations, more than three hundred newspaper articles, of alleged abuses concerning experimentation with human subjects by Veterans Administration facilities, other government laboratories, and academic laboratories receiving federal grants.[55] They ranged from allegations of deliberate exposure to excessive amounts of radiation to experiments involving hallucinogenic drugs without informed consent and relatively dangerous or at best uncertain testing on subjects who were unaware of the true nature of the experiments or their possible consequences. In the midst of this activity, the Clinton White House issued its Memorandum on Research Involving Human Subjects.[56] When in late 1996 and early 1997 stories increased about possible human cloning, the administration responded with the Memorandum on the Prohibition on Federal Funding for Cloning of Human Beings.[57] And later that same month, it issued another admonition concerning experimentation in the Memorandum on Protections for Human Subjects of Classified Research.[58] A similar approach was used during concerns over food safety prompted by illnesses and even some deaths, following incidents involving tainted meat, with half-a-dozen memoranda issued between 1997 and 1999.[59]

To Circumvent or Even to Confront the Congress

Various presidents have employed executive orders to circumvent Congress (see chapter 3). The Reagan, Bush, and Clinton administrations have used memoranda not only to make end runs around Congress but also to take it on directly, effectively daring the legislature to take action against administration policy. The end run could sometimes be fairly sophisticated. The Reagan White House battled Congress directly over regulation during the first term, using Executive Order 12291 as a centerpiece of the attack. Following his reelection, Reagan issued another order to supplement the earlier directive, Executive Order 12498. Although the order appeared only to require work on regulatory planning, in a memorandum issued the same day the White House defined its terms in such a way as to give the Office of Management and Budget even more tools than before with which to battle regulatory agencies. President Bush then made clear his intention to take the more overtly aggressive approach in his memoranda issued on the regulatory moratorium. He also underscored his belief that more aggressive administrative efforts to attack regulation were necessary because of the recalcitrance of the Congress and that the administration intended to succeed despite the legislature if it could not do so in cooperation with it.

President Clinton, already inclined to use memoranda broadly, elected to use them in his conflicts with Congress as well. Having failed in its efforts to get broad reform of health care, the White House pressed the need for a patient's bill of rights as part of a counterattack against the increasing power of health maintenance organizations (HMOs) and other insurance and health care firms. Unable to get even this program through Congress—controlled after 1994 by the opposition Republicans—Clinton called for a patient's bill of rights in federal health programs through memoranda and took the occasion of their issuance to challenge Congress to act.[60]

Another example came with the ongoing battle between the Clinton White House and the Congress over gun control. On one side of the debate, Clinton issued a stream of memoranda (see p. 97) aimed at demonstrating that he was, contrary to right-wing criticism, tough on crime. At the same time, he issued a number of memoranda that sought by presidential directive to initiate some of the types of gun control that he could not move through the Congress. On August 11, 1993, Clinton held a Rose Garden signing ceremony to announce the administration's initiative to provide temporary grants to communities for additional police officers and signed two memoranda (which the news media incorrectly reported as executive orders). In the first, he directed the Department of the Treasury to reexamine the process by which the Bureau of Alcohol, Tobacco, and Firearms (ATF) assesses weapons to determine whether they fall under the ban on importation of assault weapons. The president also announced that the

ATF was suspending importation of weapons that arguably should be classified by the factoring system as banned and that it was publishing a notice of proposed rulemaking to reexamine the regulations covering the entire process.[61] The issue of which weapons classified as banned assault weapons had been a matter of contention, with the Bush administration taking a far narrower definition than the Clinton administration wanted and with arms manufacturers actively campaigning among legislators against any further restrictions. The second memorandum concerned closer regulation of gun dealers, particularly those who held federal dealers' licenses but who did not operate out of regular stores that could be readily observed and controlled. These orders came in the wake of a shooting in a San Francisco law firm when a gunmen opened fire with assault pistols, killing nine.[62]

It was also a period in which there were battles breaking out around the country about gun-related policies at the state and local level. Part of the turmoil was addressed by the *Los Angeles Times*'s recognition of the increasing use of assault weapons by gangs and the fact that these weapons were being used on campuses and in affluent communities.[63] Then, in October 1994, Clinton went to California to sign his memorandum (improperly reported as an executive order) on implementation of the Safe Schools legislation, under which schools could lose funding if they failed to enforce policies against guns on campus.[64] While Clinton was seeking to bolster his own anticrime credentials and to continue to press for more gun control legislation, this ceremony and its memorandum were part of an effort to help Senator Dianne Feinstein in her hotly contested reelection bid. Feinstein had been one of the sponsors of the legislation.

Thereafter, Clinton issued a memorandum in 1996 on gun supply interdiction aimed at suppliers of weapons in cases of youth crime in 1996;[65] another on child safety locks on guns issued by federal agencies in 1997,[66] a Memorandum on Enforcement of the Youth Handgun Safety Act in 1997;[67] another on importation of assault rifles;[68] and another in November of 1998 aimed at regulation of gun show sales of weapons.[69] In virtually all these cases, Clinton lauded his administration's gun control campaign and alternately encouraged and criticized Congress for failing to move White House legislative proposals.

Paying Debts, Rewarding Supporters, Answering Critics, and Sending Signals

Memoranda are attractive devices to pay debts, respond to constituencies or critics, and to send signals. They often attract little excitement or attention, but they are received by the target groups as significant. They convey the sense of action even if they are in truth essentially symbolic. Symbolic memoranda typically provide little substantive commitment but often contain cautions for awareness within agencies, consultation and information sharing among federal government units, data gathering, development of plans, and creation of interagency working groups or task forces. Despite a tendency to use grandiose rhetoric, memoranda often only really require agencies to show that they are giving consideration to some problem or group in their decisionmaking processes. Such directives usually commit no new resources or simply reallocate existing resources. They also make it a point to say that they are not intended to create any new entitlements. This is not to suggest that all memoranda issued to address particular constituencies are purely symbolic. Indeed, one of the difficulties for White House observers is to avoid being lulled into such complacency that truly important memoranda will be ignored.

Neither does this suggest that issuing memoranda directed to particular constituencies is simply a cynical exercise in superficial politics. It may be the case that an administration can both address constituents and press what the president considers to be an important policy theme. For example, the Reagan and Bush administrations used memoranda attacking regulation for obvious political reasons, but these directives also played significant roles in ongoing efforts by both administrations not only to block new regulatory efforts but also to trim existing practices. Similarly, the Clinton White House issued numerous memoranda on civil rights issues, environmental concerns, and Internet-related developments.

One of the more consistent examples of the use of memoranda in this mode during the Clinton years came in the area of what might be termed family and children policies. The many directives issued on this subject included those on

Missing Persons and Missing Children, January 19, 1996
Welfare Initiative for Teen Parents, May 10, 1996
Child Support Initiative, June 18, 1996 [two were issued with this title on
    the same day, with one directed to HHS and the other to the secretary
    of labor]
Family Friendly Work Arrangements, June 21, 1996
Criminal Child Support Enforcement, July 21, 1996
Guidelines to States for Implementing the Family Violence Provisions,
    October 3, 1996

Adoption and Alternative Permanent Placement of Children in the Public
  Child Welfare System, December 14, 1996
Federal Policies Targeted to Children in Their Earliest Years, February 24,
  1997
Expanded Family and Medical Leave Policies, April 11, 1997
Improving the Quality of Child Care in the United States, April 17, 1997
Children's Health Insurance Outreach, February 18, 1998
Steps to Improve Federally Sponsored Child Care, March 10, 1998
Actions to Improve Children's Health Insurance Outreach, June 22, 1998
Using the Internet to Increase Adoptions, November 24, 1998
New Tools to Help Parents Balance Work and Family, May 24, 1999
School-Based Health Insurance Outreach for Children, October 12, 1999
International Family Planning Waiver, November 29, 1999
Joint Guidelines for Supporting Responsible Fatherhood, June 23, 2000
Second Chance Homes for Pregnant Teens, August 21, 2000

These uses of memoranda can be particularly interesting when an administration is attempting to maintain a centrist image, which can be difficult if the issues involved are polarized. Thus, the Clinton White House issued a number of memoranda supporting its commitments to affirmative action and other civil rights concerns,[70] but it nodded to the right with its memoranda supporting religious expression and practices in schools and in the federal workplace.[71] Similarly, the administration issued memoranda supporting its claim to open government but sought to counter criticisms that it had little concern for security issues with another one.[72]

WHAT BENEFITS DO MEMORANDA OFFER AND WHAT PROBLEMS DO THEY POSE?

As with any policy tool, there are advantages to the use of memoranda and potential dangers as well. Some of those difficulties are even more troublesome precisely because the tool itself is so little understood by those who use it, by White House watchers in the media, by academics on whom citizens depend for information, and even by many of those directly affected by it.

The Advantages of Memoranda

Flexibility and ease of use top the list of positive attributes. Since there is no stated process for using memoranda and no legal obligations to publish or disseminate them in any way, they are the simplest of tools to use. Among other things, there is no particular reason why they need to state any legal authority unless they purport to add new binding policies that extend beyond the president's presumed constitutional authority. And indeed, with the exception of presidential determinations, which are generally grounded in statutory obligations or programs, memoranda commonly do not state any particular authority. When they do, the legal foundation for action is often tangentially mentioned rather than asserted as specific authority for the directive. To the degree that there is reference to authority at all in the memorandum, it is often to an executive order or an earlier directive that may itself be a memorandum.

If particular memoranda do present truly substantive policy choices, they can be handy devices precisely because they are read by the agencies responsible for their implementation but rarely really examined by the media or those outside government. Indeed, they often go unnoticed unless the White House really seeks to gain publicity for them and, if they are discovered, it may be years after they were issued and had their effects.

Memoranda are therefore particularly easy devices to use and lose. Since most are not published in the *Federal Register,* are not codified, and are not even indexed in status tables, as are executive orders, they can be created quickly to address temporary situations and then forgotten when the media move their attention to the next crisis on the horizon. The fact that some academic may eventually discover them when searching in the *Weekly Compilation of Presidential Documents* years later is of no consequence to the White House, where it is often said that two weeks is a political generation.

Further, because of their nature and their manner of promulgation, these directives are even more difficult to challenge than executive orders, notwithstanding the fact that they can have precisely the same kinds of effects. Since the memoranda often claim to add nothing new as policy but to build on existing policy and are directed not to outside organizations or citizens but to executive branch agencies, legal challenges are all but nonexistent.

The Downsides of a Seemingly Harmless Device

Given these characteristics, the memorandum would seem to be an extremely good tool for a new administration, at least from the perspective of new staffers who are seeking convenient tools to accomplish their agenda. Nevertheless, the use and abuse of memoranda pose a number of significant dangers. While some of the difficulties are based in the substantive policies announced in particular memoranda, others are broader and more generic in character. Many of these dangers are similar to those described for executive orders, but there are some additional concerns.

This discussion of dangers relies on the memoranda considered already, but it is instructive to examine yet another example from the Clinton years. A memorandum was issued by President Clinton in 1994 on environmental justice, a subject that would seem to be something so fair and reasonable that a presidential action in this area should be received positively and without controversy. However, the situation turned out to be far from that simple.

The administration came to office with strongly stated commitments to the environment and to civil rights. These issues came together as a growing advocacy movement emerged demanding environmental justice. One of the best known early voices charging that minority residents were being victimized by siting decisions that located environmentally dangerous or undesirable businesses near residential areas was Professor Robert D. Bullard. Bullard became involved when he worked with his students at Texas Southern University on research for a case being brought by his attorney wife on behalf of residents in a predominantly African-American Houston suburb.[73] The case, alleging racial discrimination in the siting decision for a solid-waste facility, failed, but it launched Bullard on a path of scholarship and political activity that took him a long way from Houston.[74] He ultimately published a number of studies arguing that decisions about where undesirable businesses were located were to be explained primarily as racial discrimination and not solely or primarily as an issue of social class.[75] He joined a growing chorus of academics, civil rights activists, and concerned citizens, challenging what Benjamin Chavis termed "environmental racism"[76] and demanding what is now broadly called "environmental justice."[77] While many largely white, middle-class communities were increasingly joining the Not in My Back Yard (NIMBY) chorus, African Americans, Latinos, and Native Americans were responding with their own refrain, Why Always in My Backyard (WAMBY)?[78] Indeed, the protests gained national visibility with demonstrations in Warren County, North Carolina, in fall 1982 that led to more than five hundred arrests.[79]

The following year, the movement received support from the U.S. General Accounting Office (GAO) when it issued a report supporting the charges of environmental discrimination.[80] The United Church of Christ Commission for Racial Justice issued its own report in 1987 that rejected the claim that the disproportionate injury to minority communities was a function of social class rather than race.[81] Moving into the early 1990s, the movement organized conferences to bring more formal research and analysis to its calls for federal action, culminating in a 1992 special issue on environmental justice published by the *National Law Journal* that criticized the government for a general failure to respond to the concerns of minority communities and for doing far less there when it did take action than it did in white areas.[82]

It was not at all clear what, if anything, the newly arrived Clinton administration was going to do about the environmental justice movement, even though Bullard participated in the transition process. However, pressures increased on the administration as longtime civil rights advocate Don Edwards (D-Calif.) took the lead in demanding that the EPA had an obligation under Title VI of the Civil Rights Act to move against recipients of federal funds who were engaged in environmental racism.[83] That demand was supported by the U.S. Commission on Civil Rights, which based its claims on studies done in the infamous "cancer alley" region of Louisiana, home to dozens of petrochemical industries.[84] The report called on the commission to demand action. Chairman Arthur Fletcher obliged, writing to the EPA administrator and calling for the use of civil rights statutes and regulations to attack the problem.[85]

President Clinton issued Executive Order 12898, Environmental Justice for Minority Populations, February 11, 1994.[86] It engendered relatively little excitement or attention outside the groups most immediately involved in the effort. It appeared to be limited to cautions for awareness within agencies, requirements for consultation and information sharing among federal agencies, and calls for data gathering. However, it lacked any mandate for any particular actions, and there was a specific statement that agencies were expected to accept these obligations with no new resources. It simply required agencies to show that they were considering environmental justice implications when they made decisions—though which decisions the order did not say—and to make plans to improve their record on environmental justice. Another provision of the order called for creation of an interagency committee to allow for improved communications across the executive branch and to evaluate agency proposals. These were, of course, precisely the kinds of provisions that are most commonly used in symbolic orders.

Moreover, the president asserted no specific statutory authority for the order, stating only that it was issued "by the authority vested in me as President by the Constitution and the laws of the United States of America." The order made no mention of Title VI of the Civil Rights Act. Of even greater interest was a limiting statement in Section 6-6 on judicial review:

> This order is intended only to improve the internal management of the executive branch and is not intended to, nor does it create any right, benefit, or trust responsibility, substantive or procedural, enforceable at law or equity by a party against the United States, its agencies, its officers, or any person. This order shall not be construed to create any right to judicial review involving the compliance or noncompliance of the United States, its agencies, its officers, or any other person with this order.

Indeed, the tone and language emphasized its focus on policymaking by federal agencies and the ability of affected groups to have their interests considered when Washington-based agencies made important policy decisions. It made no reference to state or local governments, which would have been unusual if the order was intended to focus on those units. After all, the Clinton administration made much of its concern about the impact of federal actions on state and local governments and often addressed those units directly in its executive orders when they were to be significantly involved.[87] More than that, the order said nothing about industrial siting decisions, land use, or any of the specific kinds of actions that had been at the heart of the environmental justice movement from the beginning.

Yet, on that same day, the president also issued a memorandum, Executive Order on Federal Actions to Address Environmental Justice in Minority Populations and Low-Income Populations.[88] The stated "purpose of this separate memorandum is to underscore certain provision [*sic*] of existing law that can help ensure that all communities and persons across this Nation live in a safe and healthful environment." Unlike the tone and language of the executive order, the memorandum clearly focused on the community and the federal government's responsibility to assist actively in achieving environmental justice goals at that level. The memorandum began by stating that the purpose of Executive Order 12898 was to "focus Federal attention on the environmental and human health conditions in minority communities and low-income communities with the goal of achieving environmental justice"—language quite different from that contained in the executive order itself.

Most important was the fact that the memorandum specifically invoked the civil rights laws as a tool required to be used by federal agencies. "Environmental and civil rights statutes provide many opportunities to address environmental hazards in minority communities and low-income communities. Application of these existing statutory provisions is an important part of this Administration's efforts to prevent those minority communities and low-income communities from being subject to disproportionately high and adverse environmental effects." The memo then directs that "in accordance with Title VI of the Civil Rights Act of 1964, each Federal agency shall ensure that all programs or activities receiving Federal financial assistance that affect human health or the environment do not directly, or through contractual or other arrangement, use criteria, methods, or practices that discriminate on the basis of race, color, or national origin."

The memorandum still did not specifically mention siting decisions or actions by state or local governments, but the specific invocation of Title VI made all the difference, and the tone of it made clear that the locus of action was the community, not Washington. By invoking Title VI, and by referring specifically to federal action against decisions that would have disproportionate effects, the memorandum was a far stronger statement of intentions, with language that carried important legal implications.

Indeed, those implications were apparently not clear to EPA administrator Carol M. Browner or to Attorney General Janet Reno, who participated in the press briefing when the order was announced. Asked by one reporter whether the nation would see environmental racism cases brought within the following year, Reno answered, "I don't know how you describe environmental racism, but what we want to do is make sure that we look at the people most at risk and that we make sure our environmental laws, our civil rights laws, are used as vigorously as possible to correct injustice."[89] No mention was made of state and local governments in that discussion and, insofar as any mention was made of enforcement actions, the discussion centered on corporations, individuals, government contractors, and federal agencies.

The EPA was at the center of a growing debate over environmental justice, even as it generated a controversial policy ultimately announced in 1998 by quite controversial means. The administration was committed to the broad policy of environmental justice; and civil rights groups, joined by some environmental activists, pressed for real action to back up the rhetoric. There were also citizens' groups forming and bringing their own litigation against communities and states on environmental justice claims. In 1996 the Chester Residents Concerned for Quality Living launched a challenge to the permitting processes in Chester and in the Pennsylvania Department of Environmental Protection on Title VI grounds.[90] It was at that point unclear whether a citizens' group could bring this kind of Title VI challenge, but the U.S. Court of Appeals for the Third Circuit concluded that they could do so.[91]

However, there were conflicts within the movement, between civil rights advocates and traditional environmentalists[92] and between different ethnocultural communities.[93] There were differences of opinion among African-American groups and even within communities about how to balance the concerns for environmental protection and the need for economic development and jobs.[94] Some local civil rights leaders called national environmental justice leaders outsiders who should respect the wishes of local residents who wanted the promised jobs, training programs, and health care programs that would come with the new facility. There was a variety of other critics emerging, as various academic writers and even some government studies challenged the methodology and data supporting some of the environmental justice claims.[95]

It was against this backdrop that the EPA announced its guidelines, the "Interim Guidance for Investigating Title VI Administrative Complaints Challenging Permits" in February 1998.[96] The proposal was published on the Internet, though not in the *Federal Register*. Although the term was not specifically used, the document was presented as what is known in administrative law as a policy statement. That permitted the EPA to use a provision of the Administrative Procedure Act that exempts policy statements, interpretive rules, and procedural rules from the standard rulemaking procedures under statute.[97] Given that provision, the proposal concluded, "EPA may decide to follow the guidance provided in this document, or to act at variance with the guidance, based on its analysis of the specific facts presented. This guidance may be revised without public notice to reflect changes in EPA's approach to implementing the Small Business Regulatory Enforcement Fairness Act of the Regulatory Flexibility Act, or to clarify and update text."

The agency began by taking both the executive order and the memorandum as authority. The focus was on permit-granting agencies at the state and local level: "Therefore, unless expressly exempted from Title VI by Federal statute, all programs and activities of a department or agency that receives EPA funds are subject to Title VI, including those programs and activities that are not EPA–funded."[98] That these guidelines clearly targeted state and local governments—and not industries or individuals, as the EPA administrator and attorney general had indicated in their previous public statements—was confirmed in August 1998 in testimony by Ann E. Goode, director of the EPA Office of Civil Rights.[99]

The EPA guidance asserted that "individuals may file a private right of action in court to enforce the nondiscrimination requirements in Title VI or EPA's implementing regulations without exhausting administrative remedies."[100] This aspect allowed groups to avoid administrative processes and exhaustion of remedies. They could go directly to court using an implied private right of action recognized by the relevant federal agency. The EPA guidance explicitly recognized claims against permitting agencies based on either discriminatory intent or effect.[101]

When the interim guidance was released there were numerous explosions so serious that the EPA had to execute a dramatic retreat. Although some of the responses were substantive, there was underlying frustration with the means that had been used to take this dramatic action. That anger was only intensified when the *Detroit News* reported, "State regulators were deliberately shut out of the plans, EPA documents obtained by The News show, because they 'might slow down the process.'"[102] This problem was not aided by the revelation that the EPA had created a task force to work on the guidance as far back as late 1996,[103] and still no effort had been made to include obviously important stakeholders.

Adding fuel to the fire was the strong feeling that the EPA had employed the interim guidance as a mechanism to permit the agency to avoid the normally required rulemaking proceedings that would have ensured more notice and opportunity for participation and that, under the existing Clinton Executive Order 12866 would have required a good deal of cost-benefit and other analyses for support. While the EPA never formally denied having closed out state and local stakeholders in the development of the process, Ann Goode did deny that the interim guidance approach had been used to evade cost-benefit analysis requirements. Yet when asked by Congressman Dingell (D-Mich.) whether she could point to any other instances when this particular means of policymaking had been employed by the agency, she could offer no examples.[104] Her attempts to insist that the "guidance" was merely an internal document for her office were roundly rejected, since it was clear that it was to be used to decide actual cases as well as to support private suits.[105]

Some thirty-four state environmental protection agency directors sent a protest letter to the EPA, and their organization, Environmental Council of the States (ECOS) led the charge to stop the EPA's action. The U.S. Conference of Mayors, the National Association of Counties, the National Governors' Association, and the Western Governors' Association joined the protest, insisting that land use regulation was a state and local function and that any federal agency that intended to take action in that field had to work closely with the states. African-American groups such as the National Association of Black County Officials and the National Chamber of Commerce joined the attack, along with leading African-American mayors. The claim was that there was a total failure to address the economic development side of the equation along with the effort to clean up the environment. There was broad concern that economic development efforts in cities and other old and inactive industrial areas would be stymied by federal delays and litigation by outside organizations. State and local officials supported the need to protect minority residents and the poor from bearing unfair environmental burdens in development efforts but insisted that the EPA's approach to crafting a policy was arrogant and predictably resulted in a bad product.

In Congress, the House Appropriations Committee moved to block spending for implementation of the interim guidance statement. The Subcommittee on Oversight and Investigations of the House Commerce Committee held hearings at which the EPA Civil Rights director Goode was roundly chastised.[106] In the end, the EPA had to pull back for some two years before once again proposing a policy, the status of which was still not clear as the Clinton administration left office.[107]

It is extremely interesting and complex to address the question of just where the policy is in all this and how the three important efforts to state a policy—the executive order, the presidential memorandum, and the EPA interim guidance statement—relate. The ways in which these devices were designed and employed in the environmental justice policy case clearly produced dramatic political and legal difficulties along the way, from both political parties and across racial, regional, and organizational lines. Those difficulties were in many ways substantive disagreements about the content of the policy, but it is clear that much of the controversy had to do with the instruments that were used to construct it and the process by which these tools were developed and used.

Memoranda Used or Perceived as Efforts to Switch Legal Foundations for Actions Mandated by Executive Order

Clearly, there was a significant change in character and approach on environmental justice policy from the executive order to the memorandum to the EPA interim guidance statement in the preceding example. The order clearly stated that it was focused internally on actions by federal agencies, and it made no direct reference to Title VI. The stated authority for the order was simply a claim to "the authority vested in me as President by the Constitution and laws of the United States of America." This is the kind of vague language commonly used by presidents since Carter in orders that are regarded as internal executive branch management orders. It does not identify the particular portion of the Constitution or the specific laws that the president considered supported the action. It is not good practice to use such blanket assertions of power, even in orders that are truly internal management action and that are not expected to have wide-reaching external effect, but it is a particularly problematic practice if the order is expected to have such broad and significant effect that legal challenges can be expected and the challengers are likely to be able to obtain standing to bring such suits. The order sought to reinforce its purely internal character, specifically asserting that "it is intended only to improve the internal management of the executive branch and is not intended to, nor does it create any right, benefit, or trust responsibility." This, too, has become boilerplate language intended to block judicial review or liability actions.

The memorandum issued the same day, however, plainly had a different function and pointed to a number of specific statutes, beginning with Title VI. The administration had not cited Title VI as authority in the order. Although the EPA interim guidance published in 1998 referenced the executive order, it clearly relied on the memorandum and its claim of Title VI authority as the basis for its actions. And though the EPA policy claimed to be only for internal guidance, its stated purpose was "to provide a framework for processing . . . of complaints filed under Title VI." As Goode testified, its target was state and local governments. And the policy claimed the broadest possible coverage of state and local decisions.[108] Moreover, the EPA guidance clearly intended to support a private right of action for environmental justice advocates to sue state and local officials and to provide the kind of federal agency rules that would reduce the burdens on those private litigants by removing the need to prove intentional discrimination.

If a president's order is the basis for action, it must state the authority on which it is issued.[109] And given that the ultimate target turned out to be federal regulation of state and local land use decisions, federal courts, particularly the contemporary Supreme Court, could be expected to demand much greater clarity and specificity of federal authority.[110] It can be, and in this case was, quite confusing to one who read the executive order when it was issued to see how it provided an authority to support the action ultimately taken by the EPA. Indeed, it appears that the nature of the authority claimed changed significantly from executive order, to presidential memorandum (as explained by the attorney general and the EPA administrator when it was issued), and to the EPA Interim Guidance. It is tempting for those affected and who seek to understand what is happening to them to regard such practices as a shell game.

Memoranda May Lead to the Perception of Hidden Intentions

The kind of shifting claims of purpose and authority demonstrated by the Clinton environmental justice case can convey the sense that the White House is deliberately attempting to hide its intentions. That is a particularly tempting conclusion when a presidential memorandum issued at the same time as the order appears to trump the order by significantly altering its nature and importance. After all, the Federal Register Act does not require publication of memoranda. Relatively few people are aware of and have ready access to the *Weekly Compilation of Presidential Documents* (though current editions are now being published on the Internet), and fewer still would expect that there would be something significantly different in the memorandum from that which was contained in the order. Memoranda are often not indexed or published in a way that would attract attention unless the White House wishes it. The executive order disposition tables provided on the Internet by the National Archives, which indicate the status of particular executive orders, make no mention of the existence of the memoranda issued with orders.[111]

The Reagan memorandum issued along with Executive Order 12498 provides a classic example. In that instance, organizations already in conflict with the White House over its uses of the OMB publicized the memorandum, but even that effort reached a limited audience.

Where there is already concern that a particular administration is using devices such as executive orders and memoranda outside the normal administrative rulemaking or legislative processes, the danger of creating even more controversy than might otherwise develop is clear. That is particularly true if it appears that the memorandum is a strong trump card played over a less controversial order.

The Substitution of Memoranda for Executive Orders

Some administrations have gone so far as to use memoranda as substitutes for executive orders. The Bush administration's attack on rulemaking is an obvious example. The president's imposition of a moratorium on rulemaking was plainly an action that he clearly intended to be binding. Moreover, he delegated authority to control the process to the Council on Competitiveness and also established a coordinating group made up of the Quayle Council, the Council of Economic Advisers, and the White House Chief of Staff, to which agencies would be accountable. This was a war on rulemaking, and officials in agencies responsible for rulemaking knew it, notwithstanding the inclusion of saving language such as "to the extent permitted by law" as boilerplate. The memorandum extending the moratorium reinforced the president's purpose.

Even so, at no point in any of the memoranda issued on the moratorium did Bush cite legal authority of any kind for his actions. Indeed, he went further, stating as the primary reason for his actions that "the Congress has thus far failed to pass most of the Administration's regulatory reform proposals."[112] He reiterated that point in his remarks on extending the moratorium and added the following threat, "I'm putting Congress on notice: I will veto any bill that attempts to put excessive new burdens of regulation on the backs of our families, our consumers, our workers, and our businesses. There will be no, and I repeat, no return to business-as-usual."[113] It is one thing for a president to take such dramatic action on the basis of legislative authority or even sometimes under conditions of apparent congressional acquiescence,[114] but quite another, as Truman learned, to act without specific authority in the face of congressional refusal to adopt presidential policies.[115]

The Unstructured Use of Quasi-Memos: Where Is the Real Action?

The Bush administration went further, however, using what might be termed quasi-memoranda to accomplish tasks of the sort generally considered grist for an executive order. The obvious example is the use of a press release as the vehicle to create the Quayle Council on Competitiveness. A year later a memorandum was issued by the White House chief of staff outlining its operations, and later still a vice presidential memorandum was issued asserting a broad scope of jurisdiction and authority. The latter devices were communicated in ways that made clear that the memoranda were to be understood as carrying the imprimatur of the president. That was confirmed with the memoranda and press remarks at the time of the moratorium on rules.

This was not the only such example, however. In May 1992, President Bush issued Executive Order 12807, intended to cause the Coast Guard to return Haitian immigrants to their country.[116] Yet the order did not mention Haitian refugees. As the Supreme Court found, "Although the Executive Order itself does not mention Haiti, the press release issued contemporaneously explained: 'President Bush has issued an executive order which will permit the U.S. Coast Guard to begin returning Haitians picked up at sea directly to Haiti.'"[117] The Court helped the administration justify its actions by acknowledging the press release as part of the policy.

Such policies are too important to be addressed by such quasi-memoranda. They are often the kinds of steps that should be taken by legislation or at least through the use of executive orders. Given these practices, it often seems that the policies are emerging as patchworks that can be difficult to understand and explain, even for those close to the process. Even the president himself has sometimes been confused as to the type of action he was taking and the instrument he was using.

CONCLUSION

Ultimately, it is likely that future administrations will continue to make significant use of presidential memoranda. As they have with executive orders and other tools of presidential direct action, recent administrations have tended to learn from their predecessors and even to discover new uses for such devices. Moreover, there are a number of attractive features to presidential memoranda.

Even so, a new administration would do well to think about the problems posed by the use of memoranda other than for presidential determinations or for largely hortatory purposes. There is little real advantage to their use over executive orders. If there is no intention to deceive or to game others in the policy arena, there is little reason to publish a separate memorandum on the same day as an executive order, when in each case considered here the material in the former could easily have been incorporated into the latter. And since the use of these memoranda came at considerable cost, it would seem a wiser strategy to avoid the troublesome practices. This admonition applies with particular force where existing practices confuse the legal authority for presidential action, cause the appearance of attempts to hide the true nature and purpose of administration policy, substitute memos for executive orders, or apply even more exotic techniques to craft policy that is in truth in the nature of an executive order. In terms of potential legal and political reactions, such practices lend themselves to accusations of patchwork policymaking, the inappropriate use of trump cards, and a willingness to employ shell games. As the reactions of state and local governments in the environmental justice case indicated, the excessive or problematic use of memoranda can present large targets and produce relatively little gain. After all, if an opponent wants to do so, it is relatively easy to use an administration's memoranda as evidence of presidential arrogance and abuse of power to attack truly substantive directives. And it is equally easy to charge cynical efforts at manipulation of public opinion with no real action for those memoranda that are little more than symbolic statements.

FIVE
PRESIDENTIAL PROCLAMATIONS: RULE BY DECREE

In an era when most knowledgeable Americans regard presidential proclamations as ceremonial exercises of little import, it might come as a surprise
to discover that they have been very controversial on several occasions in our
history. Indeed, a presidential proclamation was at the heart of the first major
challenge to the very nature and extent of presidential power. It seems like a
long time since the pitched battle over President Washington's Neutrality
Proclamation rocked the nation, but it is only a brief time since conservative
westerners seethed with anger over President Clinton's use of proclamations
to declare more lands to be protected federal reserves and his pardons
prompted protests from Republicans and Democrats alike.

Even in those situations in which a proclamation is largely hortatory, it
may be of serious significance. Harry Truman's first act as president was to
issue the proclamation announcing the death of Franklin Delano Roosevelt.
Coming as it did with the nation in the midst of World War II, the formal
announcement of the passing of the commander in chief, the only president
many people of military age could remember, was no mere ceremonial event.
It stunned the nation, shook the confidence of allies, and encouraged adversaries. Truman was not a well-known public figure outside the Congress and
his midwestern home state of Missouri. His performance in the issuance of
the proclamation and his behavior in the ceremonial events of his first week
in office had much to do with a rapid rise of confidence in the new administration at a time when it was sorely needed.

Like executive orders and presidential memoranda, the presidential
proclamation is an important tool of presidential direct action with its own
uses and limitations. Although it has changed over time, both in its nature
and uses relative to other policy tools, it should not be underestimated by a
new administration.

WHAT IS IT? THE NATURE OF PRESIDENTIAL PROCLAMATIONS

A proclamation is an instrument that states a condition, declares the law and
requires obedience, recognizes an event, or triggers the implementation of a
law (by recognizing that the circumstances in law have been realized). It may

call upon citizens outside government but within the United States or upon other countries or citizens of other countries to acknowledge the proclamation and bring themselves into compliance with it. As with executive orders, the processes for promulgating proclamations are governed by the Federal Register Act and by Executive Order 11030, issued by President Kennedy and amended by his successors over the years.

Proclamations are published in the *Federal Register,* but that does not mean they are widely known or understood. If the news accounts of reactions to President Clinton's western lands proclamations are to be believed, it still seems to come as a shock to many Americans, and even many officials, that the president can issue a proclamation with real and broad impact. Of course, some of the shock expressed by political figures in these situations has the flavor of the French prefect who was "shocked" to find that gambling was taking place at Rick's Café Americain in the memorable scene from *Casablanca.*

Despite the fact that proclamations are published, they still present some of the difficulties of access and organization that exist for executive orders. There are at the time of this writing 7,404 such proclamations. They have not been codified since 1989.[1] That is not a small matter, since although most are ceremonial, others are substantive, and they carry force in the same sense as executive orders. The Supreme Court has held that the authority of a presidential edict is not narrowly dependent, whether it is promulgated in the form of a proclamation or an order.[2] In fact, the historical catalogs of executive orders and proclamations record some presidential actions as executive orders in the form of a proclamation.[3] The form of a proclamation traditionally has been that it begins with a statement of conditions leading to the president's action, often as a series of "whereas" clauses, followed by a statement of the action to be taken, as in George Washington's proclamation of March 24, 1794:[4]

PROCLAMATION OF MARCH 24, 1794 BY THE PRESIDENT OF THE UNITED STATES OF AMERICA

Whereas I have received information that certain persons, in violation of the laws, have presumed, under color of a foreign authority, to enlist citizens of the United States and others within the State of Kentucky, and have there assembled an armed force for the purpose of invading and plundering the territories of a nation at peace with the said United States; and

Whereas such unwarrantable measures, being contrary to the laws of nations and to the duties incumbent on every citizen of the United States, tend to disturb the tranquillity of the same, and to involve them in the calamities of war; and

Whereas it is the duty of the Executive to take care that such criminal proceedings should be suppressed, the offenders brought to justice, and all good citizens cautioned against measures likely to prove so pernicious to their country and themselves, should they be seduced into similar infractions of the laws:

I have therefore thought proper to issue this proclamation, hereby solemnly warning every person, not authorized by the laws, against enlisting any citizen or citizens of the United States, or levying troops, or assembling any persons within the United States for the purposes aforesaid, or proceeding in any manner to the execution thereof, as they will answer for the same at their peril; and I do also admonish and require all citizens to refrain from enlisting, enrolling, or assembling themselves for such unlawful purposes and from being in anywise concerned, aiding, or abetting therein, as they tender their own welfare, inasmuch as all lawful means will be strictly put in execution for securing obedience to the laws and for punishing such dangerous and daring violations thereof.

And I do moreover charge and require all courts, magistrates, and other officers whom it may concern, according to their respective duties, to exert the powers in them severally vested to prevent and suppress all such unlawful assemblages and proceedings, and to bring to condign punishment those who may have been guilty thereof, as they regard the due authority of Government and the peace and welfare of the United States.

In testimony whereof I have caused the seal of the United States of America to be affixed to these presents, and signed the same with my hand. Done at the city of Philadelphia, the 24th day of March, 1794, and of the Independence of the United States of America the eighteenth.

G° WASHINGTON.

The commonly understood significant difference between executive orders and proclamations is that orders are directed to officials within the government while proclamations are aimed at those outside government.[5] A widely publicized example of this direct impact was President Carter's 1980 Proclamation 4771, requiring draft registration.[6] In that regard, it comes as a surprise to many people to learn that such proclamations as this decree have been the basis for criminal prosecutions. A man who refused on principle to register for the draft as required by the proclamation was indicted in a process in which the Reagan White House and Justice Department targeted known opponents of the program. David Alan Wayte, an active public opponent of the requirement, was indicted for failing to register. He challenged the validity of the proclamation, claiming, among other things, that the president had failed to follow procedural requirements for a thirty-days' notice before it could take effect and that Selective Service officials had failed to provide sixty-days' notice of its regulations as required by Executive Order 12044. The district court ruled in Wayte's favor, sharply attacking what it saw as blatant evidence of discriminatory prosecution and completely unacceptable conduct by the government during the case.[7] However, the U.S. Court of Appeals for the Ninth Circuit reversed, finding that no such procedural restrictions applied to this presidential proclamation[8] and that enforcement of the executive order against the Selective Service was a matter for the president to decide, not the courts.

On the way to its ruling against Wayte, the Ninth Circuit noted, "Absent the Proclamation, there is no basis for criminal prosecution for nonregistration."[9] This is by no means a recent development.[10] Judge James Wilson charged a grand jury that it could indict a violator of Washington's Neutrality Proclamation (see p. 123) even though there was no statute authorizing such an indictment.[11]

As we have seen, this internal versus external distinction can sometimes be unclear. Moreover, these days it is not uncommon for presidents to use several instruments together as a policy mix with which to address a particularly complex situation. Thus, for example, Presidents Ford and Carter issued proclamations first establishing the clemency program and then granting pardons.[12] They also directed the Justice Department to implement the policy by which eligibility for the pardons would be determined in conjunction with the Commission of Selective Service. When Presidents Bush and later Clinton sought to address the issue of boatloads of Haitian refugees, they employed both executive orders—to the Coast Guard concerning interdiction, processing, and return of the refugees—and proclamations—declaring the law and policy of the United States to American citizens who might seek to assist those would-be refugees.[13]

Yet precisely because proclamations are aimed at those outside government, the president's authority to issue them is more limited than it is with executive orders or other directives addressed to persons in the executive branch. The chief executive cannot, as in executive orders, merely assert general authority to control the executive branch under Article 2 of the Constitution as a basis for issuing a proclamation affecting those outside government. Moreover, it is much easier to mount a challenge to a proclamation than to an executive order, since those affected can more readily gain standing to sue.

At the same time, proclamations are usually upheld since they are often specifically authorized by statute. That is particularly true in the area of trade and foreign policy, where a statute or a ratified treaty specifically authorizes the president to take action by proclamation if specified events occur.[14] This kind of activity is often accomplished today through the use of presidential determinations in the form of presidential memoranda. In other situations, the president may claim statutory support based on the White House reading of legislation even where it is not at all clear that the statute really provides authority for his or her actions. Thus, President Nixon's now famous wage-price freeze was implemented in 1971 by proclamations he claimed were authorized by the Trade Expansion Act of 1962 and the Economic Stabilization Act of 1970.[15] In addition to imposing the freeze on wages and prices, Proclamation 4047 placed a surcharge on imported goods and imposed a set of financial constraints on domestic and international spending. Nixon's action was upheld because the court found the legislation extremely broad in its grant of emergency powers to the president even though it considered the legislation "incredibly broad, possibly unwise, and even potentially dangerous." By contrast, President Carter did not fare as well when he attempted to impose a surcharge on imported oil.[16] The same kinds of methods are used in judicial review to evaluate both proclamations and executive orders.

HOW ARE THEY USED?

The proclamation was a very different type of instrument in the early years of the Republic and has evolved over time. In the early days, the president had little in the way of an executive branch to implement policies, and those agencies that did exist did not have any systematic methods in place to issue the kinds of rules needed to implement policies across a large and rapidly growing nation. There was little in the way of a body of statutes that set forth national policy, and the evolving tensions over the relationship between the recently constructed national authority and the states were only beginning to be addressed. Even the president's own policy instruments were in their infancy. Presidential memoranda as vehicles for presidential determinations were years in the future. However, proclamations were devices that had been in existence for centuries and were well understood. Hence, they were accepted as the chief formal statements of U.S. foreign policy and published as such in the *United States Statutes-at-Large,* from its very earliest volumes. They were also understood domestically as orders from the president to the people in the tradition of royal proclamations issued in other times and places. Yet, that very heritage, and the abiding fear of a president who would be king, meant that substantive proclamations sometimes were met with suspicion or even outright conflict.

Presidential proclamations are of essentially three varieties that by their nature suggest their common uses. First, and by far the most numerous, are the hortatory proclamations that single out particular individuals, groups, or occasions for recognition and celebration. Second are those proclamations that are like presidential determinations and their domestic equivalent. These are used to invoke particular statutory or constitutional powers and can result in very significant actions. Third, there are policy pronouncements issued to those outside government that have the force of law, often issued in conjunction with another policy instrument, such as an executive order or an executive agreement.

Developing and Managing Foreign Policy

The role of proclamations was established early in our national history, partly because it was a well-understood device both domestically and internationally. Sovereign nations, and whoever spoke for them, be it king or president, were understood to be able to declare their policies with respect to other nations and to both bind their own citizens and warn others about the potential consequences of their behavior in light of those policies. It was obvious that the newly created United States of America was born into a turbulent world and was for a variety of reasons promptly thrust into the midst of what might today be termed superpower politics. President Washington launched efforts to negotiate some kind of new and acceptable relationship with the country against which it had fought a revolutionary war. Spain was operating at the very southern doors to the United States. And then there was the ongoing warfare between France and England.

The issue of how to build the new nation while avoiding getting caught in the middle of those European issues vexed Washington, divided the nation's leaders, fractured the cabinet, helped bring about the two-party political system, and ultimately could not prevent a war with Britain. It is difficult for contemporary Americans to understand how pervasively controversial it was for the United States to determine a position that would not tear the new country apart or plunge a weak and evolving nation into ongoing wars that it could not afford and did not want to fight. To that must be added several more specific challenges. For many Americans, there was abiding antipathy toward England for the behaviors that had led to the Revolution and for the hardships that war had brought. There was also an appreciation for the assistance provided by the French during the American Revolution and the fact that they had only recently launched their new republic, following their own revolution. Still, there were many people in the United States with an affinity for England who were horrified by the violent excesses of the French Revolution.

The behavior of the French and the British fanned the flames in the United States. While these battles raged, partisans within Washington's cabinet vied to influence the president. Alexander Hamilton argued for the British cause and Thomas Jefferson took the French side, but Washington ultimately adopted a compromise offered by Edmond Randolph.[17] Washington issued a proclamation on April 22, 1793, that, although entitled a Proclamation of Neutrality did not actually mention neutrality in its body. It announced that the United States intended to remain "friendly and impartial" toward the belligerents and called upon American citizens to do nothing that violated that spirit:

THE PROCLAMATION OF NEUTRALITY 1793

Whereas it appears that a state of war exists between Austria, Prussia, Sardinia, Great Britain, and the United Netherlands, of the one part, and France on the other; and the duty and interest of the United States require, that they should with sincerity and good faith adopt and pursue a conduct friendly and impartial toward the belligerant Powers;

I have therefore thought fit by these presents to declare the disposition of the United States to observe the conduct aforesaid towards those Powers respectfully; and to exhort and warn the citizens of the United States carefully to avoid all acts and proceedings whatsoever, which may in any manner tend to contravene such disposition.

And I do hereby also make known, that whatsoever of the citizens of the United States shall render himself liable to punishment or forfeiture under the law of nations, by committing, aiding, or abetting hostilities against any of the said Powers, or by carrying to any of them those articles which are deemed contraband by the modern usage of nations, will not receive the protection of the United States, against such punishment or forfeiture; and further, that I have given instructions to those officers, to whom it belongs, to cause prosecutions to be instituted against all persons, who shall, within the cognizance of the courts of the United States, violate the law of nations, with respect to the Powers at war, or any of them.

In testimony whereof, I have caused the seal of the United States of America to be affixed to these presents, and signed the same with my hand. Done at the city of Philadelphia, the twenty-second day of April, one thousand seven hundred and ninety-three, and of the Independence of the United States of America the seventeenth.

George Washington
April 22, 1793

Washington later issued executive orders to enforce that neutrality and to punish citizens who engaged in behavior that violated it.[18] He issued the proclamation on the very day that the new French consul general, Citizen Edmond Genet, arrived in the United States. Although Jefferson and the other pro-French leaders did their best to defend him, Genet set about a pattern of embarrassing behavior that was fast making America's professed neutrality a joke. When efforts were made to curb his activities, Genet threatened to take his case over Washington's head to the American people. Apart from the fact that such threats indicated a woeful ignorance of the American people, it meant that even his staunchest defenders came to support his removal. Washington eventually sent him packing.

The Neutrality Proclamation gave no specific statement of authority; however, it was ultimately ratified by Congress but only after a heated and protracted battle in both houses. The argument was about whether the president had the power to issue such a proclamation. This debate engendered the famous newspaper battle conducted under the pseudonyms Pacificus and Helvidius.[19] Jefferson, upon reading the first of the pro-proclamation pieces, wrote James Madison, imploring him, "For God's sake my dear sir, take up your pen and cut the worst of his heresies to pieces." A most reluctant Madison agreed, and the battle was joined.[20] This clash, along with the so-called removal debate—concerning whether the president had the power to remove appointed officials without congressional approval—provided the primary context for the debate over the nature and powers of the presidency in our early history. And, not incidentally, these two debates had much to do with the development of the Jeffersonian Republican party and Adams's Federalists, a framework that was firmly established by the election of 1800. Washington ultimately prevailed in the Neutrality Proclamation battle, and an important political precedent was established for the president's use of the proclamation in foreign affairs to state strong and binding positions for the nation.[21] Congressional scholars would argue, however, that it really represented no precedent, political or otherwise, since the president was forced in a most dramatic fashion to recognize the obligation to go to the Senate for its support.

The judicial support for the president's use of broad powers in foreign affairs today is most often traced to another case involving a proclamation. In 1934 Franklin Delano Roosevelt issued a proclamation, blocking the sale of arms and ammunition to Bolivia and Paraguay, parties involved in the Chaco conflict. Unlike Washington, though, Roosevelt was acting not on his own but enforcing a joint resolution issued by the Congress to take the action he proclaimed. Writing for the Supreme Court in *U.S. v. Curtiss-Wright Exporting Co.,*[22] Justice George Sutherland issued a series of sweeping statements about the president's foreign affairs powers. He announced the "plenary and exclusive power of the President as the sole organ of the federal government in the field of international relations."[23] Sutherland's dramatic pronouncements were clearly *obiter dictum* (statements not essential to the holding or reasoning in the case), given that the president was implementing a congressional enactment. His recitation of constitutional history supporting those assertions was clearly inaccurate law office history. Despite all this, and notwithstanding his failure to recognize the historical congressional role in foreign policy, Sutherland's statements have nevertheless been treated as the standard assumptions about presidential power ever since.[24]

Much of the heavy lifting in the foreign policy arena that was usually done by proclamations is now accomplished by memoranda and other presidential instruments. Nevertheless, proclamations are still used in conjunction with other devices like executive orders to instruct Americans or others on permissible behavior in the foreign policy arena (see the discussion of the Haitian refugee actions in chapter 4),[25] including with respect to matters of international trade. And they are still employed as a device for a president to announce the existence of a set of conditions that requires further action.

Making Formal Statements Recognizing Conditions or Problems

In an age when people watch wars fought live on cable news television and in which both leaders and citizens demand rapid-fire, seemingly almost instantaneous, decisions even on matters of great moment, there is little patience for subtlety or symbols, however important they may be. But important they often are, with consequences stretching far into the future. Thus, as the brief reference to Truman's proclamation announcing the death of Roosevelt indicated, this was not a mere ceremony but a firm statement that life and governance in the United States had changed and that there would be no going back.

A far more dramatic and fundamentally important example was Lincoln's Emancipation Proclamation:[26]

Whereas on the 22nd day of September, A.D. 1862, a proclamation was issued by the President of the United States, containing, among other things, the following, to wit:

"That on the 1st day of January, A.D. 1863, all persons held as slaves within any State or designated part of a State the people whereof shall then be in rebellion against the United States shall be then, thenceforward, and forever free; and the executive government of the United States, including the military and naval authority thereof, will recognize and maintain the freedom of such persons and will do no act or acts to repress such persons, or any of them, in any efforts they may make for their actual freedom.

"That the executive will on the 1st day of January aforesaid, by proclamation, designate the States and parts of States, if any, in which the people thereof, respectively, shall then be in rebellion against the United States; and the fact that any State or the people thereof shall on that day be in good faith represented in the Congress of the United States by members chosen thereto at elections wherein a majority of the qualified voters of such States shall have participated shall, in the absence of strong countervailing testimony, be deemed conclusive evidence that such State and the people thereof are not then in rebellion against the United States."

Now, therefore, I, Abraham Lincoln, President of the United States, by virtue of the power in me vested as Commander-In-Chief of the Army and Navy of the United States in time of actual armed rebellion against the authority and government of the United States, and as a fit and necessary war measure for supressing said rebellion, do, on this 1st day of January, A.D. 1863, and in accordance with my purpose so to do, publicly proclaimed for the full period of one hundred days from the first day above mentioned, order and designate as the States and parts of States wherein the people thereof, respectively, are this day in rebellion against the United States the following, to wit:

Arkansas, Texas, Louisiana (except the parishes of St. Bernard, Plaquemines, Jefferson, St. John, St. Charles, St. James, Ascension, Assumption, Terrebone, Lafourche, St. Mary, St. Martin, and Orleans, including the city of New Orleans), Mississippi, Alabama, Florida, Georgia, South Carolina, North Carolina, and Virginia (except the forty-eight counties designated as West Virginia, and also the counties of Berkeley, Accomac, Northhampton, Elizabeth City, York, Princess Anne, and Norfolk, including the cities of Norfolk and Portsmouth), and which excepted parts are for the present left precisely as if this proclamation were not issued.

And by virtue of the power and for the purpose aforesaid, I do order and declare that all persons held as slaves within said designated States and parts of States are, and henceforward shall be, free; and that the Executive Government of the United States, including the military and naval authorities thereof, will recognize and maintain the freedom of said persons.

And I hereby enjoin upon the people so declared to be free to abstain from all violence, unless in necessary self-defence; and I recommend to them that, in all cases when allowed, they labor faithfully for reasonable wages.

And I further declare and make known that such persons of suitable condition will be received into the armed service of the United States to garrison forts, positions, stations, and other places, and to man vessels of all sorts in said service.

And upon this act, sincerely believed to be an act of justice, warranted by the Constitution upon military necessity, I invoke the considerate judgment of mankind and the gracious favor of Almighty God.

It did not change reality for most of those held in slavery since it covered only the areas then under the control of the Confederacy. Yet it is difficult to overestimate the importance of this declaration in American history. When that decree was added to the proclamations announcing the ratification of the Civil War Amendments, the United States was in many important respects a new nation. That is not, of course, to minimize the history of Jim Crow and other kinds of racism that followed or to deny that there are huge differences between any pronouncements on civil rights and their realization. Even so, by any reasonable estimate, the nation was changed forever after these proclamations.

Presidential proclamations announcing changed conditions often carry two kinds of significance. First, they inform the people and the world of important changes and admonish them to come to grips with the new reality. They may also signal, as in the case of announcement of ratification of constitutional amendments or admission of new states, the culmination of a process.[27] Second, such a statement of a state of affairs often triggers statutory obligations on the part of the president to take further action. Most people are aware, for example, of the consequences of a declaration of emergency following a natural disaster, which mobilizes federal agencies and triggers various forms of financial assistance.

To Invoke Special Powers and Establish Emergency Actions

Indeed, proclamations are best known for their use in various kinds of emergencies. These are generally of three types, including war or insurrection, economic crises, or natural disasters. The first two have occasioned considerable controversy over time.

George Washington found it necessary to put down the Whiskey Rebellion in Pennsylvania. He declared the miscreants to be in a state of insurrection and moved to suppress the rebellion using his now famous proclamation:[28]

BY THE PRESIDENT OF THE UNITED STATES OF AMERICA
Whereas, combinations to defeat the execution of the laws laying duties upon spirits distilled within the United States and upon stills have from the time of the commencement of those laws existed in some of the western parts of Pennsylvania.

And whereas, the said combinations, proceeding in a manner subversive equally of the just authority of government and of the rights of individuals, have hitherto effected their dangerous and criminal purpose by the influence of certain irregular meetings whose proceedings have tended to encourage and uphold the spirit of opposition by misrepresentations of the laws calculated to render them odious; by endeavors to deter those who might be so disposed from accepting offices under them through fear of public resentment and of injury to person and property, and to compel those who had accepted such offices by actual violence to surrender or forbear the execution of them; by circulation vindictive menaces against all those who should otherwise, directly or indirectly, aid in the execution of the said laws, or who, yielding to the dictates of conscience and to a sense of obligation, should themselves comply therewith; by actually injuring and destroying the property of persons who were understood to have so complied; by inflicting cruel and humiliating punishments upon private citizens for no other cause than that of appearing to be the friends of the laws; by intercepting the public officers on the highways, abusing, assaulting, and otherwise ill treating them; by going into their houses in the night, gaining admittance by force, taking away their papers, and committing other outrages, employing for these unwarrantable purposes the agency of armed banditti disguised in such manner as for the most part to escape discovery;

And whereas, the endeavors of the legislature to obviate objections to the said laws by lowering the duties and by other alterations conducive to the convenience of those whom they immediately affect (though they have given satisfaction in other quarters), and the endeavors of the executive officers to conciliate a compliance with the laws by explanations, by forbearance, and even by particular accommodations founded on the suggestion of local considerations, have been disappointed of their effect by the machinations of persons whose industry to excite resistance has increased with every appearance of a disposition among the people to relax in their opposition and to acquiesce in the laws, insomuch that many persons in the said western parts of Pennsylvania have at length been hardy enough to perpetrate acts, which I am advised amount to treason, being overt acts of levying war against the United States, the said persons having on the 16th and 17th of July last past proceeded in arms (on the second day amounting to several hundreds) to the house of John Neville, inspector of the revenue for the fourth survey of the district of Pennsylvania; having repeatedly attacked the said house with the persons therein, wounding some of them; having seized David Lenox, marshal of the district of Pennsylvania, who previous thereto had been fired upon while in the execution of his duty by a party of armed men, detaining him for some time prisoner, till, for the preservation of his life and the obtaining of his liberty, he found it necessary to enter into stipulations to forbear the execution of certain official duties touching processes issuing out of a court of the United States; and having finally obliged the said inspector of the revenue and the said marshal from considerations of personal safety to fly from that part of the country, in order, by a circuitous route, to proceed to the seat of government, avowing as the motives of these outrageous proceedings an intention to prevent by force of arms the execution of the said laws, to oblige the said inspector of the revenue to renounce his said office, to withstand by open violence the lawful authority of the government of the United States, and to compel thereby an alteration in the measures of the legislature and a repeal of the laws aforesaid;

And whereas, by a law of the United States entitled "An act to provide for calling forth the militia to execute the laws of the Union, suppress insurrections, and repel invasions," it is enacted that whenever the laws of the United States shall be opposed or the execution thereof obstructed in any state by combinations too powerful to be suppressed by the ordinary course of judicial proceedings or by the powers vested in the marshals by that act, the same being notified by an associate justice or the district judge, it shall be lawful for the President of the United States to call forth the militia of such state to suppress such combinations and to cause the laws to be duly executed. And if the militia of a state, when such combinations may happen, shall refuse or be insufficient to suppress the same, it shall be lawful for the President, if the legislature of the United States shall not be in session, to call forth and employ such numbers of the militia of any other state or states most convenient thereto as may be necessary; and the use of the militia so to be called forth may be continued, if necessary, until the expiration of thirty days after the commencement of the ensuing session; Provided always, that, whenever it may be necessary in the judgment of the President to use the military force hereby directed to be called forth, the President shall forthwith, and previous thereto, by proclamation, command such insurgents to disperse and retire peaceably to their respective abodes within a limited time;

And whereas, James Wilson, an associate justice, on the 4th instant, by writing under his hand, did from evidence which had been laid before him notify to me that "in the counties of Washington and Allegany, in Pennsylvania, laws of the United States are opposed and the execution thereof obstructed by combinations too powerful to be suppressed by the ordinary course of judicial proceedings or by the powers vested in the marshal of that district";

And whereas, it is in my judgment necessary under the circumstances of the case to take measures for calling forth the militia in order to suppress the combinations aforesaid, and to cause the laws to be duly executed; and I have accordingly determined so to do, feeling the deepest regret for the occasion, but withal the most solemn conviction that the essential interests of the Union demand it, that the very existence of government and the fundamental principles of social order are materially involved in the issue, and that the patriotism and firmness of all good citizens are seriously called upon, as occasions may require, to aid in the effectual suppression of so fatal a spirit;

Therefore, and in pursuance of the proviso above recited, I, George Washington, President of the United States, do hereby command all persons, being insurgents, as aforesaid, and all others whom it may concern, on or before the 1st day of September next to disperse and retire peaceably to their respective abodes. And I do moreover warn all persons whomsoever against aiding, abetting, or comforting the perpetrators of the aforesaid treasonable acts; and do require all officers and other citizens, according to their respective duties and the laws of the land, to exert their utmost endeavors to prevent and suppress such dangerous proceedings.

In testimony whereof I have caused the seal of the United States of America to be affixed to these presents, and signed the same with my hand. Done at the city of Philadelphia the seventh day of August, one thousand seven hundred and ninety-four, and of the independence of the United States of America the nineteenth.

G. Washington

He was not acting alone in this matter but in concert with both Congress and the federal courts. Although this is one of the best-known such proclamations, there have been others. Washington, for example, issued proclamations warning various groups around the nation about violations of the treaties established with various Indian nations and in some cases ordering action against those who attacked the Indians or sought to steal their lands.[29]

Andrew Jackson issued one of the most dramatically worded presidential proclamations, responding to the Nullification Crisis brought about in 1832 when South Carolina nullified federal tax laws and declared its right to secede. Jackson issued his proclamation on December 10, making the case against nullification and secession, but also warning:

> This, then, is the position in which we stand. A small majority of the citizens of one State in the Union have elected delegates to a State convention; that convention has ordained that all the revenue laws of the United States must be repealed, or that they are no longer a member of the Union. The governor of that State has recommended to the legislature the raising of an army to carry the secession into effect, and that he may be empowered to give clearances to vessels in the name of the State. No act of violent opposition to the laws has yet been committed, but such a state of things is hourly apprehended, and it is the intent of this instrument to PROCLAIM, not only that the duty imposed on me by the Constitution, "to take care that the laws be faithfully executed," shall be performed to the extent of the powers already vested in me by law or of such others as the wisdom of Congress shall devise and Entrust to me for that purpose; but to warn the citizens of South Carolina, who have been deluded into an opposition to the laws, of the danger they will incur by obedience to the illegal and disorganizing ordinance of the convention—to exhort those who have refused to support it to persevere in their determination to uphold the Constitution and laws of their country, and to point out to all the perilous situation into which the good people of that State have been led, and that the course they are urged to pursue is one of ruin and disgrace to the very State whose rights they affect to support.

Fellow-citizens of my native States! The threat of unhallowed disunion—the names of those, once respected, by whom it is uttered—the array of military force to support it—denote the approach of a crisis in our affairs on which the continuance of our unexampled prosperity, our political existence, and perhaps that of all free governments, may depend. The conjuncture demanded a free, a full, and explicit enunciation, not only of my intentions, but of my principles of action, and as the claim was asserted of a right by a State to annul the laws of the Union, and even to secede from it at pleasure, a frank exposition of my opinions in relation to the origin and form of our government, and the construction I give to the instrument by which it was created, seemed to be proper. Having the fullest confidence in the justness of the legal and constitutional opinion of my duties which has been expressed, I rely with equal confidence on your undivided support in my determination to execute the laws—to preserve the Union by all constitutional means—to arrest, if possible, by moderate but firm measures, the necessity of a recourse to force; and, if it be the will of Heaven that the recurrence of its primeval curse on man for the shedding of a brother's blood should fall upon our land, that it be not called down by any offensive act on the part of the United States.

It fell to Abraham Lincoln actually to confront secession and to respond to the taking up of arms by the Confederate States. He did that by proclamation, and that proclamation and other actions he took to respond to the rebellion were later ratified by Congress and upheld by the Supreme Court.[30] Lincoln then employed a full variety of presidential direct action tools to govern during the war, affecting everything from the creation of military courts to the regulation of trade.

However, as the Whiskey Rebellion case demonstrated, it was not necessary to have anything quite so dramatic as a civil war to employ presidential powers in cases of civil unrest. In more contemporary times, President Kennedy invoked these powers by proclamation to address the refusal by Southern legislatures and governors to enforce civil rights. In 1962, Mississippi governor Ross Barnett sought by a variety of means to stop the desegregation of the University of Mississippi by blocking the registration of James Meredith. On September 30, Kennedy issued a proclamation to all involved parties, including members of the public who were attempting to frustrate the desegregation process by both peaceful and violent means, to "cease and desist therefrom and to disperse and retire peaceably forthwith."[31] He also issued an executive order that brought federal marshals and troops to the campus to bring an end to the violence and to protect Meredith. Ultimately, Barnett was cited for criminal contempt of court for his pains.[32] Concerns surfaced during the Nixon administration that the White House might invoke extraordinary powers to deal with Vietnam protesters and others considered by the administration to be subversives. These concerns were heightened by the president's reinvigoration by executive order of the Subversive Activities Control Board. Revelations of domestic surveillance and sharing of various lists took the fears from the realm of paranoia to the very real, very quickly.[33]

Well beyond these situations, however, is the use of proclamations in war. When the president proclaims a state of war, a wide range of powers and processes are triggered, from censorship to the commandeering of private ships for public use.[34] World War I provided numerous dramatic examples of these consequences. It also provided evidence that the action taken once hostilities are proclaimed will most likely produce consequences and problems to be resolved after the fighting has ended, which will also be declared with a proclamation.

With the approach of World War II, however, President Roosevelt did not wait for a declaration of war before using proclamations to begin mobilizing for hostilities. On September 8, 1939, FDR issued a proclamation declaring a limited national emergency to begin mobilization. On May 27, 1941, the president went beyond that to proclaim "that an unlimited national emergency confronts this country, which requires that its military, naval, air and civilian defenses be put on the basis of readiness to repel any and all acts or threats of aggression directed toward any part of the Western Hemisphere," and he called for priority to be given to diversion of resources to preparation for war.[35] He had learned a great deal about the use of presidential decrees from his experiences in the Wilson administration.

President Roosevelt had put those lessons to work long before Hitler's rise in Germany, as he waged war against the Great Depression, beginning in 1933. As Arthur Schlesinger has explained: "He had already settled on the main lines of his attack. Before arriving in Washington, he had rough drafts of two presidential proclamations: one calling a special session of Congress; the other declaring a bank holiday and controlling the export of gold by invoking forgotten provisions of the wartime Trading with the Enemy Act."[36] Roosevelt relied on legislation from 1917 to support his Bank Holiday proclamation.[37]

Later presidents learned from FDR; and Nixon and Carter, in particular, followed his lead—or tried to do so. Nixon used both executive orders and related presidential proclamations to shape and implement the wage-price guidelines that he imposed.[38] The wage-price controls were part of a wider effort to effect what Nixon termed the "stabilization of the economy,"[39] which was ultimately governed through a series of orders issued in spring and summer 1974.[40] Carter used Proclamations 4744, 4748, and 4751 in 1980 in his Petroleum Import Adjustment Program.

The Mechanism for Granting Pardons

Proclamations have been the device used to grant presidential pardons. As the Constitution provides in Article 2, section 2, "The President shall . . . have power to grant reprieves and pardons for offenses against the United States, except in cases of impeachment." That power has been interpreted broadly by the U.S. Supreme Court. It has found that the pardon power is complete and cannot be limited by legislation. That power may be granted, withheld, or granted with any conditions that the president wishes to require and "which do not in themselves offend the Constitution."[41]

Presidents have employed proclamations to issue different types of pardons over our history. As Alexander Hamilton contended in *Federalist* no. 74, "The principal argument for reposing the power of pardoning . . . [in] the Chief Magistrate is this: in seasons of insurrection or rebellion, there are often critical moments, when a well-timed offer of pardon to the insurgents or rebels may restore the tranquillity of the commonwealth; and which, if suffered to pass unimproved, it may never be possible afterwards to recall."[42] George Washington sought to use the power for just that purpose, offering pardons to those who had become involved in the developing Whiskey Rebellion as an incentive to abandon their behavior.[43] Other presidents have historically issued pardon proclamations at the end of wars in the form of an amnesty as part of an effort to heal the nation's wounds. Thus, President Ford sought to address some of the deep divisions in the nation at the end of the divisive Vietnam experience by providing amnesty for draft evaders. He issued a proclamation and an executive order on September 16, 1974, barely a month after taking office, creating the clemency program.

The beginning of the Ford administration came with the resignation of Richard Nixon, and one of Ford's first actions was to issue a pardon to the disgraced former leader (Proclamation 4311):[44]

BY THE PRESIDENT OF THE UNITED STATES OF AMERICA:
A PROCLAMATION
Richard Nixon became the thirty-seventh President of the United States on January 20, 1969, and was reelected in 1972 for a second term by the electors of forty-nine of the fifty states. His term in office continued until his resignation on August 9, 1974.

Pursuant to resolutions of the House of Representatives, its Committee on the Judiciary conducted an inquiry and investigation on the impeachment of the President extending over more than eight months. The hearings of the Committee and its deliberations, which received wide national publicity over television, radio, and in printed media, resulted in votes adverse to Richard Nixon on recommended Articles of Impeachment.

As a result of certain acts or omissions occurring before his resignation from the Office of President, Richard Nixon has become liable to possible indictment and trial for offenses against the United States. Whether or not he shall be so prosecuted depends on findings of the appropriate grand jury and on the discretion of the authorized prosecutor. Should an indictment ensue, the accused shall then be entitled to a fair trial by an impartial jury, as guaranteed to every individual by the Constitution.

It is believed that a trial of Richard Nixon, if it became necessary, could not fairly begin until a year or more has elapsed. In the meantime, the tranquility to which this nation has been restored by the events of recent weeks could be irreparably lost by the prospects of bringing to trial a former President of the United States. The prospects of such trial will cause prolonged and divisive debate over the propriety of exposing to further punishment and degradation a man who has already paid the unprecedented penalty of relinquishing the highest elective office of the United States.

Now, THEREFORE, I, GERALD R. FORD, President of the United States, pursuant to the pardon power conferred upon me by Article II, Section 2, of the Constitution, have granted and by these presents do grant a full, free, and absolute pardon unto Richard Nixon for all offenses against the United States which he, Richard Nixon, has committed or may have committed or taken part in during the period from January 20, 1969, through August 9, 1974.

IN WITNESS WHEREOF, I have hereunto set my hand this eighth day of September, in the year of our Lord nineteen hundred and seventy-four, and of the Independence of the United States of America the one hundred and ninety-ninth.

Gerald R. Ford

In upholding the Nixon pardon against legal challenge, Judge Fox likened it to the early idea of addressing those engaged in insurrections, as Washington had done.

Evidence now available suggests a strong probability that the Nixon Administration was conducting a covert assault on American liberty and an insurrection and rebellion against constitutional government itself, an insurrection and rebellion which might have succeeded but for timely intervention by a courageous free press, an enlightened Congress, and a diligent Judiciary dedicated to preserving the rule of law. . . . By pardoning Richard Nixon, who many believed was the leader of a conspiratorial insurrection and rebellion against American liberty and constitutional government, President Ford was taking steps, in the words of Alexander Hamilton in The Federalist, to "restore the tranquillity of the commonwealth" by a "well-timed offer of pardon" to the putative rebel leader. President Ford's pardon of Richard M. Nixon was thus within the letter and the spirit of the Presidential Pardoning Power granted by the Constitution. It was a prudent public policy judgment.[45]

President Bush later employed a proclamation to pardon a group of officials in his administration for their part in the Iran-Contra debacle. As he left office, President Clinton issued more than one hundred pardons to a wide variety of individuals, including Susan McDougal, who was jailed for extended periods and faced multiple prosecutions by the White Water special counsel. She was jailed primarily for refusing to testify against Clinton. Interestingly, the most controversial of his many pardons was for Marc Rich, one of the nation's most wanted international fugitives. There is little doubt that the Bush and Clinton pardons went well beyond the applications of the pardon power used by previous presidents.

WHY ARE PROCLAMATIONS USED?

Although presidents can use proclamations for various purposes, they may or may not choose to do so. The answers to why a president may elect to use them are generally much like the reasons for employing presidential memoranda. Indeed, memoranda have in some ways displaced proclamations, though the future of the latter very much depends on how presidents to come will want to use them. Having said that, there are a few reasons that prompt various administrations to employ this particular instrument.

One of the reasons is that a variety of statutes stipulate that a proclamation is the way a president is to issue a statement that conditions exist to trigger particular statutory actions. In the contemporary environment, a number of statutes dealing with foreign policy that at one time called for proclamations now require "presidential determinations," which are generally made by memoranda. However, the legislation varies, depending in part on when it was enacted. Other statutes, such as those dealing with recovery from natural disasters, specifically call for a proclamation. The same applies more generally with respect to emergencies; however, such proclamations are now also covered by the National Emergencies Act.

Beyond the issue of mandates, though, proclamations are easy to use and lend themselves to a variety of applications. Because they are the traditional way that presidents designate holidays, special days of observance, or citations of honor for individuals or groups, they are widely used to respond to constituents. Hortatory proclamations generally cost nothing, require no follow-up, and, perhaps most important, rarely provide a reason for anyone to be upset. In Washington, those are strong reasons indeed for selecting the proclamation. It is no surprise, then, to find administrations issuing literally dozens of such proclamations each year.

They can also be employed to build and maintain morale, to provide a formal context for a president to engage in moral suasion, and sometimes even as a way to encourage the public to accept sacrifices or constraints. President Truman's proclamation following VE Day is a classic example of the first of these reasons:

> The Allied armies, through sacrifice and devotion and with God's help, have wrung from Germany a final and unconditional surrender. The western world has been freed of the evil forces which for five years and longer have imprisoned the bodies and broken the lives of millions upon millions of freeborn men. They have violated their churches, destroyed their homes, corrupted their children, and murdered their loved ones. Our Armies of Liberation have restored freedom to these suffering peoples, whose spirit and will the oppressors could never enslave.
>
> Much remains to be done. The victory won in the West must now be won in the East. The whole world must be cleansed of the evil from which half the world has been freed. United, the peace-loving nations have demonstrated in the West that their arms are stronger by far than the might of dictators or the tyranny of military cliques that once called us soft and weak. The power of our peoples to defend themselves against all enemies will be proved in the Pacific as it has been proved in Europe.[46]

Washington's proclamations encouraging respect of Indian treaties, Jackson's on nullification, and Lincoln's regarding the Civil War are other examples.

Franklin Roosevelt's 1941 declaration of emergency, well before Pearl Harbor, called upon citizens to be prepared for sacrifice:

> I call upon all the loyal citizens engaged in production for defense to give precedence to the needs of the nation to the end that a system of government that makes private enterprise possible may survive.
>
> I call upon all our loyal workmen as well as employers to merge their lesser differences in the larger effort to insure the survival of the only kind of government which recognizes the rights of labor or of capital.
>
> I call upon loyal state and local leaders and officials to cooperate with the civilian defense agencies of the United States to assure our internal security against foreign directed subversion and to put every community in

order for maximum productive effort and minimum of waste and unnecessary frictions.

I call upon all loyal citizens to place the nation's needs first in mind and in action to the end that we may mobilize and have ready for instant defensive use all of the physical powers, all of the moral strength and all of the material resources of this nation.

Clearly, a president could elect many different means, from simple speeches to press releases, to accomplish these goals, but the very character of the proclamation adds a tone of seriousness and formality. It conveys the message that the president is here speaking not for a particular administration or even for the executive branch but formally and on behalf of all the people.

Proclamations afford a president a tool that can be used to round out a policy mix. As should be clear by now, contemporary presidents, particularly those since Nixon, have repeatedly used a combination of executive orders, proclamations, and memoranda to construct policy responses to issues on the public agenda. The examples of the draft-evader amnesty, the Nixon wage-price freeze, the Carter fuel policy, and the Bush and Clinton Haitian refugee programs indicate that it is not uncommon today to have one set of directives go to the public from the White House and another issued to the executive branch agencies given the active responsibility for implementation of the policy.

THE RELATIVE STRENGTHS AND WEAKNESSES OF PROCLAMATIONS AS PRESIDENTIAL TOOLS

Clearly, then, proclamations are useful presidential policy tools, and they do offer several beneficial features. Like any tool, though, they have limitations and can be used in ways that present difficulties.

The Upsides of Proclamations

Here again, the pluses offered by memoranda are generally applicable to proclamations. More specifically, there are few negatives to the use of hortatorical or celebratory proclamations. Apart from the fact that modern presidents have used presidential proclamations, citizen medals, military decorations, and other recognitions so often and with such obvious political purpose that they have devalued the currency, it is still a matter of considerable distinction to be publicly recognized in a proclamation. If one's group or cause is so lauded, there is clearly a measure of legitimacy conveyed in the process—legitimacy that can translate into contributions or other forms of support. Such groups or individuals will never forget the president's support.

Proclamations may be challenged, but like the other tools of presidential direct action, the odds of surviving a legal challenge are in most instances quite good. That is particularly true when the president is issuing a proclamation that makes a finding as to circumstances. For one thing, such proclamations are commonly issued in response to a legislative command. In instances where the president is asserting his or her own authority and is carrying out the will of the Congress, the White House action is at its strongest legal posture.

Even Proclamations Can Present Difficulties

Nevertheless, when the two more substantive types of proclamations are employed, there can be both positive and negative consequences, as was true with executive orders and memoranda, and for many of the same reasons. The idea of the president directly ordering private citizens or businesses to take or to avoid some action can cause some degree of frustration. There is a faint sense of royal prerogative that lurks in the background when the chief executive commands the citizenry. The reaction against such moves can make the White House, as compared with some other agency of government or even the Congress, the target of considerable criticism. That was certainly the case, for example, with Nixon's wage-price freeze and Carter's fuels proclamations. And when the proclamations affect such angry citizens directly, it is easier for them to obtain legal standing to sue when compared with executive orders or memoranda, which actually are aimed at executive branch agencies. Though it is true that presidents tend to do reasonably well under challenge, there have been some notable losses.

Related to this last point, the use of proclamations as parts of a policy mix can produce more difficulties than the use of the proclamation alone, since it poses all the potential liabilities of each of the individual policy tools plus the special issues that arise by virtue of their being combined. An example is provided by Ford's draft-amnesty program. The proclamation on amnesty was really conditioned on a set of decisions to be made by U.S. attorneys in each case concerning whether the individual file had "prosecutive merit." However, the process to be used to determine how the amnesty would work was the executive order issued at the same time as the proclamation and directed to the Justice Department. The U.S. attorneys around the country were given a relatively limited period and little guidance to determine which cases did have prosecutive merit. Those individuals could qualify for the amnesty, but only if they came forward and accepted a period of alternative service. Those men whose cases did not have prosecutive merit would be cleared and would not be required to do anything further to avoid legal action. One such U.S. attorney, William Lockhart, found the situation dangerous because it allowed and even encouraged arbitrary behavior. He concluded that under the program as constructed, he possessed "an unreviewed power to impose a sentence, in the form of a period of two years' alternative service, without trial or other adequate processes for establishing the facts, and without any understandable or meaningful standards, either for determining the kind of violation or circumstances constituting 'prosecutive merit,' or for determining appropriate periods of alternative service."[47] Indeed, he found that, given the way the executive order worked, individuals were open to more punishment than they were likely to have faced had the amnesty program never been created. In the end, Lockhart decided not to find prosecutive merit in any of the cases in his district, but he knew very well that he was an exception and that other U.S. attorneys took a different approach. The promise of the proclamation, then, seemed far less when the policy mix was viewed as a whole than it had been when viewed by itself. An additional lesson from this example is that the use of the pardon power through proclamations may be best used either specifically, and aimed at a particular individual, or broadly, to encompass a class of people that can be easily and nonarbitrarily defined. Previous presidents have done exactly that in an effort to help the nation heal its wounds following a major conflict.

But then, proclamations granting pardons have been controversial for other reasons as well. Ford's pardon of Richard Nixon and George Bush's pardons of the Iran-Contra co-conspirators are examples, and Bill Clinton's broad use of it is a third. It is one thing for a president to issue a pardon proclamation for individuals or groups with whom he or she has no direct personal connection, but when that power, plenary though it may be in legal terms, is invoked for political friends or allies, it can take on quite different dimensions.

The Nixon pardon came about in a difficult and, to many people, an unpalatable set of negotiations.[48] While a broad portion of the public accepted the idea of a pardon proclamation for Nixon to avoid further damage to the nation, the word of the negotiations was distasteful and unseemly. The process seemed to send a message to those who are justifiably in jeopardy that a precedent has been established under which presidents would grant a pardon but that the White House could be leveraged into negotiating its terms.

Then there was Proclamation 6518, issued by George Bush, pardoning administrative officials involved in Iran-Contra. The United States had been actively involved during the 1980s in conflict in Central America.[49] The United States supported right-wing regimes in El Salvador, Guatemala, and Honduras and, as part of that effort, supplied and trained Contra insurgents seeking to overturn the Sandinista government in Nicaragua. In the process, the United States violated the neutrality of allies like Costa Rica and engaged in a range of nefarious activities to support the Contras. The infamous Iran-Contra affair in which U.S. weapons were promised in exchange for assistance in money laundering in the attempt to get resources to the Contras was part of that effort.[50] Among other conclusions, the special counsel investigating Iran-Contra found:

- the sale of arms to Iran contravened United States Government policy and may have violated the Arms Export Control Act;
- the provision and coordination of support to the Contras violated the Boland Amendment ban on aid to military activities in Nicaragua;
- the policies behind both the Iran and contra operations were fully reviewed and developed at the highest levels of the Reagan Administration;
- although there was little evidence of National Security Council level knowledge of most of the actual contra-support operations, there was no evidence that any NSC member dissented from the underlying policy—keeping the contras alive despite congressional limitations on contra support;
- the Iran operations were carried out with the knowledge of, among others, President Ronald Reagan, Vice President George Bush, Secretary of State George P. Shultz, Secretary of Defense Caspar W. Weinberger, Director of Central Intelligence William J. Casey, and national security advisers Robert C. McFarlane and John M. Poindexter; of these officials, only Weinberger and Shultz dissented from the policy decision, and Weinberger eventually acquiesced by ordering the Department of Defense to provide the necessary arms; and
- large volumes of highly relevant, contemporaneously created documents were systematically and willfully withheld from investigation by several Reagan Administration officials.
- Following the revelation of these operations in October and November 1986, Reagan Administration officials deliberately deceived the Congress and the public about the level and extent of official knowledge of and support for these operations.[51]

The dirty little war in Central America and the financial abuses associated with it were not small matters to many in Latin America. Death squads killed many, and thousands more were driven into exile.[52] The Senate Judiciary Committee concluded in 1987 that "an estimated 62,000 innocent civilians have been killed since the start of the current civil war in El Salvador."[53]

The 1992 pardon by President Bush of a number of officials accused in the Iran-Contra matter was clearly seen to be an effort not to solve a national problem but to erase a stain on the Reagan and Bush administrations and to aid a group of political allies and others who had plainly faced prosecution and possible jail sentences for violating a variety of provisions of federal law. The fact that the pardon proclamation was issued only a month before Bush left office, and shortly before he would very likely have been called to testify and reveal his own part in the scandal, only underscored the distasteful nature of the act itself.

There seems little doubt that future presidents will rely on the Bush precedent. Certainly, Clinton took a cue from his actions. Clinton's pardon of Marc Rich ignited a firestorm of criticism from both Republicans and Democrats. Rich, a fugitive financier, was represented by Jack Quinn, Clinton's former White House counsel. Quinn approached Clinton for the pardon, claiming that Rich had been wrongly indicted for tax law violations and that he was prepared to address the matter in civil proceedings. Clinton granted the pardon, as part of the large number of dispensations that he granted on his way out of the White House. The pardon blew up in the headlines, however, when it was learned that not only was Rich's lawyer using his White House access to influence the president but also that Rich's former wife had made substantial financial contributions to both the Clinton Library Foundation and Hillary Clinton's senatorial campaign. Quinn appeared before the House Government Reform Committee in February 2001, but the testimony seemed to open more questions than it resolved. Indeed, the best that most of the committee's Democrats could do for Clinton was to find that his conduct showed poor judgment.

Thus there are dangers that pardon proclamations, once seen as compassionate mechanisms to bind the nation's wounds, will be regarded as a tool for the protection of political cronies. And if that perception exists within an administration, then unsavory behaviors may be encouraged, along with expectations that deals can be arranged to save the miscreants.

Such pardons can engender conflict with Congress, as they certainly did in the Iran-Contra example. Other uses of proclamations have also had that effect. President Clinton's decision to use a variety of proclamations during 1999 and 2000 to set aside federal lands in the West clearly was a deliberate use of proclamations to accomplish ends that he knew Congress would not support and that would drive western members of the legislature over the edge.[54] Clinton gambled, apparently successfully, that although Congress would react strongly, it would be unlikely to undo conservation measures, however unpopular they might be in the region. His actions, though, were a deliberate challenge to Congress of the sort that can have consequences far down the road with respect to other environmentally related legislation, even if the legislature did not react by amending the Antiquities Act in the short term.

Further, as was true of the other presidential power tools, incoming presidents can in many cases quickly dispose of policies issued as decrees by their predecessors. For instance, in the last days of his presidency, President Carter issued Proclamation 4813,[55] extending energy conservation measures established in the wake of the Arab oil embargo, but his decree lasted less than a month before it was revoked by President Reagan's Proclamation 4820.[56]

CONCLUSION

Ultimately, the presidential proclamation, usually regarded as a relatively trivial and often meaningless presidential edict, turns out to have a more significant and complex nature than it might appear. Indeed, history has found proclamations at the center of important controversies, from the first presidency to the most recent ones. Like the other tools of presidential direct action, they have a variety of legitimate uses. The evolving uses of presidential memoranda have placed some of the traditional applications of proclamations in doubt, but this tool as yet has not been completely relegated to ceremonial uses. Ironically, this seemingly innocuous device, like the other tools, can pose its own set of potential problems as well, suggesting that this too is a tool to be carefully and appropriately used by new administrations.

To this point, the discussion has focused on devices that are used relatively openly and that are fairly easily understood as techniques for making and implementing policy. There are, however, other presidential direct action tools that are far less well known and even less public than orders, proclamations, and memoranda, yet they have been important mechanisms for presidential action. They are national security directives (NSD) and presidential signing statements. The shadowy world of the NSD will be explored next.

SIX

NATIONAL SECURITY DIRECTIVES:
SECRET ORDERS, FOREIGN AND DOMESTIC

In previous chapters we have seen which tools contemporary presidents have often used first and with great fanfare. This chapter highlights some important actions that presidential administrations often put near the top of their priority list—sometimes even as one of the items of business on their first day in office—but that they rarely if ever discuss in public. The focus here is on the use, and abuse, of another tool of presidential direct action, the national security directive (NSD).

Few Americans really understand the negative impressions that people in other countries have about the United States. In some parts of the world, particularly in developing countries that were the battlegrounds of the cold war as the United States and the Soviet Union fought to control ever larger spheres of influence, that attitude today has something to do with how little Americans know about the way we have conducted ourselves over time. Is there some particular reason why many Iranians react so badly to anything American? Why is it that Latin Americans have little or no trust in America's pious pronouncements? How is it that the United States could find itself so often in difficulty in Asia? One element involved in answering those questions is simply that many Americans do not know, and have not been truthfully or fully informed, about U.S. policy in a particular part of the world and by what means that policy was carried out. Nor are many Americans aware that what may seem to be laudable purposes in the abstract have sometimes been pursued by means that do not fit the purposes. Frequently, the mechanisms by which those activities have been undertaken have been NSDs. When Americans come to understand how these directives have been involved in the Iran-Contra debacle, the U.S.–sponsored coup d'etat in 1953 in Iran that put the Shah back on the throne, the bloody U.S. coup that ousted the Arbenz government in Guatemala, and the real decisionmaking behind the prosecution of the Vietnam War, it becomes more obvious that NSDs have been tools for destruction as well as for the straightforward implementation of foreign policy. What may come as far more of a surprise, perhaps even as a shock, is that some administrations have employed national security directives not only to best foreign adversaries but also for domestic purposes. Sometimes such practices have even led members of the president's own cabinet to rebel.

The purpose here, however, is not merely to criticize the use of national security directives but more generally to explain how this little understood device is used. The analysis begins from the premise that presidents must have secure means to design, implement, and coordinate foreign and military policy. Thus, the basic idea behind the NSD is sound. However, like all tools, when improperly used, it can be not just a dangerous implement but a deadly weapon. The misuse of this device can be destructive not only for those it specifies as targets but also for the transparency, accountability, and legitimacy of the presidency, and even for the safety of our citizens.

WHAT IS A NATIONAL SECURITY DIRECTIVE?

The best definition of an NSD is probably the one used by President Johnson (though in his day the same instrument was referred to as a National Security Action Memorandum [NSAM]): "A National Security Action Memorandum was a formal notification to the head of a department or other government agency informing him of a presidential decision in the field of national security affairs and generally requiring follow-up action by the department or agency addressed."[1] In general, NSDs are presidential directives that establish policy through the National Security Council (NSC) and that are intended to implement and coordinate military policy, foreign policy, or anything else that is defined within the rubric of national security. As President Johnson's definition suggests, NSDs have been called by different names at different times. Originally designed as NSC Policy Papers during the Truman and Eisenhower years, these decisions came to be known as National Security Action Memoranda during the Kennedy and Johnson years. The Nixon administration renamed them National Security Decision Memoranda (NSDMs) and Ford kept that name, but President Carter later termed them Presidential Directives (PDs). Reagan labeled them National Security Decision Directives (NSDDs), but President Bush changed the name again, this time to National Security Directives (NSDs). The Clinton administration used Presidential Decision Directives (PDDs). George W. Bush called his National Security Presidential Directives (NSPDs). For most purposes, this discussion will simply use national security directive or NSD, except when referring to a particular directive issued by a specific president.

The NSDs clearly have many of the same effects as executive orders, but they are not defined as such and therefore are not covered by the Federal

Register Act. The vast majority of these directives are classified, though there has often been a debate about whether the use of the secret stamp has been excessive and intended primarily to conceal policy for political reasons or to protect the flanks of those involved in what they know to be troublesome decisionmaking.[2] Although most NSDs are clearly aimed at foreign policy and military affairs, some of the limited studies that have been done to date indicate that others have significant domestic impact.[3] Most administrations to date have refused to notify Congress of the existence of NSDs, to provide copies if they are specifically requested by Congress, or to send witnesses to testify at hearings on the subject.[4] When Colin Powell was national security adviser, he refused even to testify about NSDs during a congressional investigation.[5] The Clinton administration used its PDDs flexibly, with some published and others classified.

The NSC and the Development of NSDs

Because NSDs and the process by which they are created by the National Security Council are very much shaped by each individual president, as Robert Cutler, Eisenhower's national security adviser, has explained,[6] they are best understood by a brief sketch of their history. It became clear after Pearl Harbor that there needed to be a White House mechanism to coordinate communications, decisionmaking, implementation, and accountability for foreign and military action.[7] Although there had long been bureaucratic and interservice rivalries, the situation had not been improved by FDR's habit of pitting officials and agencies against one another in a kind of competition model of public policymaking. The Jackson Committee, which later studied the development of the NSC and its directives, concluded: "However, it was the deficiencies exposed by the pre–Pearl Harbor period of diplomatic and military maneuver, the handling of wartime problems involving relationships between foreign, military, and domestic policies, and the development of policies for the postwar period that demonstrated to many individuals, in and out of government, the need for better machinery for relating our foreign and our military policies."[8] General George C. Marshall was one of the leading advocates of coordination and control for national security issues during World War II.[9] Indeed, a State–War–Navy Coordinating Committee was established in 1944, but it was only a partial solution to the problem.

After the war, Ferdinand Eberstadt provided a report to Secretary of the Navy James Forrestal calling for a "national security council."[10] Truman eventually did create an agency he called the Central Intelligence Group, which was the precursor to the Central Intelligence Agency, and what he termed the National Intelligence Authority, which consisted of representatives of the State, War, and Navy Departments.[11]

However, it was the National Security Act of 1947 that ultimately created the National Security Council.[12] The act also produced the Central Intelligence Agency and the National Security Resources Board. The NSC was to be chaired by the president and included the secretaries of state, defense, army, navy, air force, and the chairman of the National Security Resources Board. Under the 1947 legislation, the CIA was to work for the NSC. It was later amended to remove the secretaries of the individual services, and the vice president was added. Later presidents each included various other officials as their priorities or the circumstances dictated.

The actual origins of the national security directive came from policy papers prepared for the NSC to guide discussions of the council. The papers presented a problem, analyzed it, and then provided a set of recommended conclusions. If President Truman accepted the conclusions, that part of the paper would be signed, and "it became the national security policy on the subject."[13] Since then, the tendency has been to have the NSC staff prepare a report with recommendations and to have those issued as the national security directive. In more recent years, NSDs have been preceded by study memoranda prepared by NSC staff on the topic at issue. In theory, these memoranda and their recommendations would form the basis for discussion at the meetings of the NSC, and their recommendations would be the basis for any NSD issued after that discussion. In practice, of course, different presidents have organized and operated their National Security Councils in different ways and labeled and used their NSDs in a variety of ways.

Variations on the Theme: Different Presidents and Varied National Security Policymaking

In its early years, the NSC evolved slowly. Although Truman presided at the first meeting, he rarely attended thereafter until the outbreak of the Korean conflict.[14] Indeed, he attended only twelve of fifty-seven meetings between 1947 and 1950. There has been speculation that Truman simply was not paying much attention to the NSC or that he was "keeping it at arm's length,"[15] but Sidney Souers, the first executive secretary of the NSC, argued that the president deliberately chose not to attend in order to avoid interfering with full and open discussions among the other members of the council. He would then have both the benefit of those debates and his own "freedom of action" to decide what to do with the recommendations.[16] At that time, the position that is now known as the national security adviser did not exist, and the executive secretary was the chief staff officer of the NSC. The draft NSC papers often originated in the State or Defense Departments. However, it became clear that the president's absence actually meant more conflict and little in the way of prompt resolution of issues. His absence also encouraged individual NSC members to lobby him. With the onset of the Korean conflict, there was the additional impetus of the war to command the president's direct involvement, and he attended 87 percent of the meetings from summer 1950 until he left office in 1953.[17]

But it was ultimately an NSD that made clear that the NSC had become an important force in national security policy. Paul Nitze drafted what has simply come to be known as NSC 68. Ostensibly a paper designed to explain the relationship between the United States and the USSR in the postwar world, it sounded an alarm, announcing the advent of the cold war, and provided the initial military and political doctrine by which that conflict was to be waged. Truman had directed "the Secretary of State and the Secretary of Defense to undertake a reexamination of our objectives in peace and war and of the effect of these objectives on our strategic plans, in the light of the probable fission bomb capability and possible thermonuclear bomb capability of the Soviet Union." In response, NSC 68 announced in April 1950:

Within the past thirty-five years the world has experienced two global wars of tremendous violence. It has witnessed two revolutions—the Russian and the Chinese—of extreme scope and intensity. It has also seen the collapse of five empires—the Ottoman, the Austro-Hungarian, German, Italian, and Japanese—and the drastic decline of two major imperial systems, the British and the French. During the span of one generation, the international distribution of power has been fundamentally altered. For several centuries it had proved impossible for any one nation to gain such preponderant strength that a coalition of other nations could not in time face it with greater strength. The international scene was marked by recurring periods of violence and war, but a system of sovereign and independent states was maintained, over which no state was able to achieve hegemony.

Two complex sets of factors have now basically altered this historic distribution of power. First, the defeat of Germany and Japan and the decline of the British and French Empires have interacted with the development of the United States and the Soviet Union in such a way that power increasingly gravitated to these two centers. Second, the Soviet Union, unlike previous aspirants to hegemony, is animated by a new fanatic faith, antithetical to our own, and seeks to impose its absolute authority over the rest of the world. Conflict has, therefore, become endemic and is waged, on the part of the Soviet Union, by violent or non-violent methods in accordance with the dictates of expediency. With the development of increasingly terrifying weapons of mass destruction, every individual faces the ever-present possibility of annihilation should the conflict enter the phase of total war.

On the one hand, the people of the world yearn for relief from the anxiety arising from the risk of atomic war. On the other hand, any substantial further extension of the area under the domination of the Kremlin would raise the possibility that no coalition adequate to confront the Kremlin with greater strength could be assembled. It is in this context that this Republic and its citizens in the ascendancy of their strength stand in their deepest peril.

The issues that face us are momentous, involving the fulfillment or destruction not only of this Republic but of civilization itself. They are issues which will not await our deliberations. With conscience and resolution this Government and the people it represents must now take new and fateful decisions.[18]

After calling for a program based on massive military buildup and an aggressive political approach, NSC 68 concluded, "The whole success of the proposed program hangs ultimately on recognition by this Government, the American people, and all free peoples, that the cold war is in fact a real war in which the survival of the free world is at stake."[19] Although the NSC discussed the paper on April 25, Truman did not act immediately but put it away for a time. There is speculation whether he would have accepted the recommendations put forth in NSC 68 if the situation had continued as it was,[20] but that discussion was rendered largely academic by the outbreak of war in Korea in June. Truman ultimately accepted the prescription, and, coupled with the costs of the Korean War, the defense budget skyrocketed.

Indeed, when Dwight Eisenhower came to office, one of his early actions was to reject NSC 68 as a guiding doctrine and to cut back on Truman's budget proposals by some $10 billion, with $5.2 billion of that taken from national security expenditures.[21] When his cuts sparked loud protests, he is reported to have replied, "Perhaps the [National Security] Council should have a report as to whether national bankruptcy or national destruction would get us first."[22] His reaction did not mean a rejection of the NSC, however—quite the contrary.

Eisenhower made the NSC operation a central element in his presidency, appointing Robert Cutler as the first special assistant to the president for National Security Affairs (now known as the national security adviser). Cutler came to the job with strong views. He began work quickly and energetically during the transition, allowing the new administration to reorganize the NSC and regularize its operations.[23] (It is worth noting in passing that Eisenhower accomplished a number of NSC organizational changes over the years using executive orders.[24]) In many respects, the NSC was perfectly suited to a president with Eisenhower's background as a commanding general used to working through groups of senior staff officers. And there was no doubt that he saw its regular and routine operation as a strength, chairing more than 90 percent of its 366 meetings during his years in the White House.[25] The NSC and its staff grew over the Eisenhower years, which ultimately attracted the criticism that the president was becoming the captive of the institutionalized NSC in foreign policy matters.

On the substantive policy side, the new administration moved quickly to replace NSC 68, under the banner of Project Solarium. The Solarium report was written by George G. Kennan, the author of the containment policy criticized by NSC 68. There was a battle during the Solarium phase between the forces of the military and the State Department, who argued for more investment to follow up on the NSC 68 security concerns, and those on the fiscal side, who argued that the country had at least as much to fear from the excessive spending as from arms. Eisenhower went with the economic forces laid out in NSC 162/2, Basic National Security Policy, known as the New Look policy. While making clear his willingness to use nuclear weapons, he made it equally clear that he intended to pay attention to the economics, not merely in terms of budget deficit but also in the sense of seeing trade and international economic policy as important weapons to counteract the Soviets.[26]

Eisenhower tried to communicate to his successor just how useful and important the NSC could be, but John F. Kennedy, with the encouragement of his transition adviser Richard Neustadt, was having none of it. Eisenhower recommended getting a national security adviser quickly, but Neustadt advised that this "should be avoided by all means until you have sized up your needs and get a feel for your new Secretaries of State and Defense."[27] Indeed, Kennedy was inclined to move rather dramatically away from standing organizations like NSC in favor of ad hoc task forces and committees. Nevertheless, after the Bay of Pigs debacle, it was clear that a properly operating NSC was important, and McGeorge Bundy supervised the effort as national security adviser. The same reticence to have a strong NSC also characterized Lyndon Johnson's administration. The president developed the Tuesday lunch group, which considered much of what the NSC would ordinarily have on its agenda. Still, both Kennedy and Johnson made considerable use of NSDs.

One of the continuing issues among administrations since the creation of the NSC has been the tension between the council and the Department of State, as some presidents have been frustrated by a State Department that they perceived to be a slow-moving, antagonistic bureaucracy with its own interests and a penchant for leaking sensitive information to the press when it seemed useful. For their part, secretaries of state did not want their control over foreign affairs snatched by a national security adviser or the NSC staff. During the Carter and the Reagan years such tensions were responsible, in part at least, for resignations by key administration players. During portions of the Nixon and Ford years, Henry Kissinger was both secretary of state and national security adviser. When he was asked to relinquish the latter position, the working relationship between State and the NSC remained relatively positive, with General Brent Scowcroft, as the new national security adviser, quite content to follow Kissinger's lead. Tensions emerged again during the Carter years when the president's heavy reliance on National Security Adviser Zbigniew Brezinski led to frustration for Secretary of State Cyrus Vance. Reagan's secretary of state, Alexander Haig, tried to preempt a significant role for the NSC at the beginning of the administration, but the White House power triumvirate blocked the effort. The key roles in White House decisionmaking played by Edwin Meese, James A. Baker, and Michael Deaver meant that neither Haig nor National Security Adviser Richard Allen was fully dominant. The NSC, however, came into far more prominence when William Clark came to replace Allen. Although Haig's successor, George Shultz, was a strong force at State, the NSC continued to be active under newly appointed National Security Adviser Robert McFarlane, until the Iran-Contra scandal broke. General Scowcroft was one of the members of the Tower Commission that investigated the Iran-Contra debacle, and that role, along with his previous experience and his relationship with the new chief executive, made him an obvious choice by President Bush for national security adviser. Scowcroft was able to work with Secretary of State James Baker as he had with Kissinger earlier. Clinton also selected a person with substantial NSC experience, W. Anthony Lake, as his first national security adviser, and Lake sought to work with Warren Christopher at State so as to avoid repeating past conflicts between the two organizations.[28] George W. Bush chose former national security adviser Colin Powell as his secretary of state and former staffer Condeleeza Rice to be his national security adviser, two people who have known and worked with each other before. While Rice was a personal foreign policy adviser during Bush's campaign, it seemed likely at the outset at least that Powell would take the lead in foreign policy and national security affairs and that Rice would seek to work with Powell at State. However, the situation became more complex as the administration took shape. At the time of this writing it is not clear how Rice and Powell will resolve the natural tensions between State and the White House.

While all of these dynamics have affected the organization and operation of the NSC over the years, national security directives continued to be important policy documents with far-reaching consequences. At the same time, they have been used in quite different ways, with significant changes in focus and emphasis by various administrations over time. In part, those differences were driven by the priorities of individual chief executives and by events on the world stage. Thus, for example, thirty-three of seventy-five NSC meetings during the Johnson years involved discussions of Southeast Asia. But whatever the subject, these directives remained important mechanisms for addressing it.

HOW ARE NSDs USED?

Even though the NSC and the national security directives that it produces vary dramatically from one administration to another, there is a variety of uses for them that have been common over time. Indeed, they have become increasingly attractive tools. Not surprisingly, this set of purposes has tended to evolve over the years as new kinds of national security issues have found their way onto the White House agenda.

National Security Organization for Decisionmaking and Coordination

Whatever the style and personality of the administration or the items pressing on the president's agenda, one of the first orders of business in most administrations is to organize the NSC, define the administration's preferred processes for developing national security directives, and determine their form and mechanisms for disposition. For most administrations, these decisions are set forth in NSD 1 and 2, often issued on the president's first day in office. That was the practice for the George W. Bush, Clinton, Bush, Carter, and Ford administrations.

Some administrations note the designations of the key reports and decision documents right away but may take longer to get around to a complete organization of the national security operation. Though Alexander Haig offered a draft National Security Decision Directive 1 on President

Reagan's inauguration day designed to afford the secretary of state primary control, internal political battles meant that the administration did not get around to issuing its organizational and operational plan for a year. That design was set out in NSDD 2, issued in January 1982. Indeed, the Reagan White House did not even formally establish its organization for crisis management until December 1981, in NSDD 3. The warfare within the administration went public relatively early on and posed significant problems. Reagan's key White House players, Meese, Deaver, and Baker, had not only killed Haig's draft, but they also managed to stop his effort to take the lead in national security crisis management. Haig's public and White House rhetoric gave rise to concern that he was dramatically overreaching. In March 1981 the Reagan insiders persuaded the president to announce publicly that Vice President Bush would be the crisis manager for the administration, which was a blow to the secretary of state. The next day the president issued a statement of confidence in Haig and reaffirmed his leadership role in foreign policy, but it was apparent to everyone in the United States and abroad that Haig was wounded and perhaps on the brink of resignation.[29] This was more than a bit ironic in light of Reagan's criticism during the campaign of Carter's foreign policy operation. The mess got worse a week later, when Haig responded to the attempted assassination of the president on March 30 by announcing from the White House that he was in charge and that he was the lead person in crisis situations. That was, of course, incorrect. Vice President George Bush hurried back from a Texas speaking engagement to take up his role as crisis manager and potential substitute for Reagan, should that be required.[30]

The moral of that story is that precisely because of the importance of the NSC and the policy instruments it employs—and since those matters are so completely within the discretion of the president—a newly arriving administration should have those directives ready as it takes office. At least as a temporary measure, there should be some formally stated design for national security operations. The issue is not simply that there may be political embarrassment for the administration. A public appearance of a lack of clear organization and management can create uncertainty among allies and contribute to instability. Coming as it did on the heels of the Iran Hostage crisis, the problems of the Reagan White House were troublesome to many observers.

At the end of another crisis, the resignation of Richard Nixon, Gerald Ford responded to this kind of problem, immediately issuing National Security Decision Memoranda 265, confirming that "the provisions of NSDM 1 and

NSDM 2, dated January 20, 1969, as amended and extended by subsequent National Security Decision Memoranda, which set forth the organization and procedures of the National Security Council System, are reaffirmed and remain in effect."

When the Reagan White House got around to issuing its long-awaited organizational plan, it announced the action publicly. The Reagan NSDD 2 set forth the responsibilities of the National Security Council, the secretary of state, the secretary of defense, and the director of Central Intelligence (DCI). It was clear from this directive that the DCI had gained authority in the national security apparatus of this administration.[31] The directive established Senior Interagency Groups (SIGs) on foreign policy, defense policy, and intelligence. It also created Regional and Functional Interagency Groups intended to assist the SIGs.

On the same day as it announced its new NSC setup, the White House also declared that it was clearing the decks of existing NSDs left over from the Carter years and served notice that it was taking actions to get control of sensitive information that had previously tended to leak and to find its way to the media.[32] The NSDD 4 issued that day rescinded thirty-two Carter presidential directives, retained eighteen, and slated an additional thirteen to be reviewed.

The George W. Bush administration, with Dick Cheney, Powell, Rice, and others on hand who recalled earlier problems and practice, moved quickly. National Security Presidential Directive 1 was issued on February 13, 2001, laying out the basic organization and operation for the NSC.

Coordination, Management, and Control

President Reagan's second national security adviser, William Clark, issued a statement about the NSDD overturning the Carter directives and seeking to control information leaks. It did not set out the terms of NSDD 19, Protection of Classified National Security Council and Intelligence Information, but Clark warned:

> We fully recognize the paradox inherent in our system, in which a free press is encouraged to collect and print whatever it believes to be in the public interest while the government has the responsibility to protect certain categories of sensitive information. The measures to be taken under this Directive should not be construed as criticism of the press. The press has been doing its job—collecting information—better than the government had been doing its job—protecting national security information. These limited measures are designed to restore a balance that has been lost.

The administration's frustration with the inability to stop leaks and get control was not new, to be sure, but the series of directives and its Executive Order 12356, significantly expanding administration control and uses of security classification as well as the processes it used to develop and enforce its security control policies, eventually created difficulties both within the administration and with the Congress.[33]

This effort to control people and information is only one dimension in an ongoing set of concerns addressed by NSDs from one administration to the next. There are numerous issues of coordination, management, and control that presidents must face. Some of these can be quite broad, as in President Kennedy's NSAM 55, Relations of the Joint Chiefs of Staff to the President in Cold War Operations, while others can be more focused, concerning the way in which specific agencies are to work together on a particular issue.

Often the challenges are both to coordinate and manage across agencies, not only during the initial policymaking process but also during implementation or field operations. Thus, in 1962, Kennedy indicated, "I feel that there is a need for accelerating our programs for underdeveloped countries and for affecting a closer tie between the Country Team planning in these areas and the Washington departments which participate in these programs. . . . To this end, I would like to have organized a program of field visits by senior interdepartmental teams, under State Department chairmanship, to a number of selected countries, with particular attention to Latin America."[34] Lyndon Johnson issued NSAM 341, The Direction, Coordination and Supervision of Interdepartmental Activities Overseas, in which he assigned the State Department the responsibility for coordination and directed his NSC Senior Interdepartmental Group and also Regional Interdepartmental Groups to participate in the effort.[35]

These challenges also extend to the management of U.S. intelligence operators and assets abroad. President Kennedy, for example, issued NSAM 13 in early 1963, in which he said, "I would like to get a memorandum on our exchange of persons programs behind the Iron Curtain, particularly with Poland and with Russia. What we could do to step them up." For obvious reasons, such operations are complex, and secrecy is a critical element.

Given the scope of national security issues, the strong personalities operating at the highest levels in the White House, and that each president has a personalized style of operations, these management challenges and responses vary significantly from one administration to the next, as do the policies generated as NSDs to address them.

General Assessments of National Security Issues and Development of Basic Policy and Doctrine

The organizational and management efforts are means to the end of developing and operating foreign and military policy. In carrying out those tasks, presidents face a mind-boggling set of challenges that involve operating at many levels. Effective national security policymaking requires broad strategic thinking, but it is also a highly contingent matter, which was true long before the fall of the Soviet Union brought an end to the bipolar cold war contest. And every president since the rise of the national security establishment in the Truman years has employed NSDs as a tool for the development of basic foreign affairs doctrine and policy. First there was NSC 68, launching the cold war, later replaced by Eisenhower's NSC 162/2, Basic National Security Policy, and then Kennedy articulated his Counterinsurgency Doctrine in NSAM 182, issued in 1962.

Some thirty-two years after NSC 68, President Reagan signed NSDD 32, U.S. National Security Strategy. It was a cold warrior's dream document, bringing back memories of the Truman-era directive. It saw the world situation as a contest between the Soviet Union and the United States, with the Soviets having taken the lead in a number of critical areas and going about the business of exploiting the weaknesses of the United States and its allies, not only in strategic military terms but also in efforts to expand its sphere of influence:

> Unstable governments, weak political institutions, inefficient economies, and the persistence of traditional conflicts create opportunities for Soviet expansion in many parts of the developing world. The growing scarcity of resources, such as oil, increasing terrorism, the dangers of nuclear proliferation, uncertainties in Soviet political succession, reticence on the part of a number of Western countries, and the growing assertiveness of Soviet foreign policy all contribute to the unstable international environment. For these reasons, the decade of the eighties will likely pose the greatest challenge to our survival and well-being since World War II and our response could result in a fundamentally different East-West relationship by the end of this decade.[36]

The Reagan NSDD focused heavily on "the modernization of our strategic nuclear forces and the achievement of parity with the Soviet Union" as the critical need for rebuilding the military, but it also called for greater development of conventional forces and enlistment of support from regional allies.

Shaping Intelligence Assignments—Research Requirements

Such broad statements of policy often come from major studies carried out by NSC staff or various task groups set up for that purpose by the White House. In the case of NSDD 32, the basis was National Security Study Directive (NSSD) 1-82, a directive that launched the study. Administrations through the Johnson years used NSDs as the vehicle to request such studies as well as for more specific intelligence tasking. Beginning with Nixon, however, each administration has developed a separate series of documents that outline requests for research on particular topics to be used to support NSDs. These have been called National Security Study Memoranda in the Nixon and Ford years, Presidential Review Memoranda during the Carter administration, National Security Study Directives under Reagan, National Security Reviews under Bush, and Presidential Review Directives during the Clinton years. President Ford, for example, called for studies on Thailand, Korea, Turkey, the Persian Gulf, Southern Africa, Italy, and Ethiopia. In addition to these country or regional studies, he also called for functional analyses with respect to arms transfer, export-import policy, security classification management, energy policy, military assistance advisory groups, civil defense policy, and defense policy and force posture.

Such studies are frequently employed as the basis for a course of action expected to continue over time as an important initiative. For example, President Nixon issued National Security Study Memorandum 124 in April 1971 seeking recommendations for "a study of diplomatic initiatives which the United States might take toward the People's Republic of China (PRC) with the objective of furthering the improvement of relations." Such studies are often requested on a rapid turnaround basis. Thus Nixon wanted the China results returned for high-level discussion in less than a month.

There is also the continuing challenge of assigning intelligence work so as to provide a wide range of essential coverage and yet be responsive to particular priority concerns. President Clinton sought to address this problem in PDD 35, issued in 1995.[37] His directive laid out a system of priorities from zero through four to guide assignment.[38] However, as in any discussion of the use of scarce resources, there have been debates both as to the president's priorities and whether the very existence of the PDD setting forth the priorities drives out other important intelligence needs. The House Permanent Select Committee on Intelligence launched a staff study that was ultimately published in spring 1996, *IC21: The Intelligence Community in the 21st Century,* that raised precisely those concerns.[39]

As crises develop, there are immediate needs for intelligence on the problems involved. It is common for administrations to indicate by NSD just where the intelligence-tasking authority will lie in such circumstances. Thus, President Reagan provided the director of Central Intelligence with broad authority not only to take action abroad but also to act domestically through counterintelligence actions or assignments to the FBI.[40]

Setting or Reviewing Regional or Country Policy

Although there is usually a desire to integrate policies across topics, regions, and circumstances, many NSDs are concerned with setting policy region by region or country by country. For samples from the Kennedy and Reagan eras of such policies and for a thumbnail sketch of the range of country or regional concerns faced by an administration, see Table 6.1.

Of course, there is throughout the Cold War period a continuing theme that runs through many directives concerning U.S. policy toward the Soviet Union. On the other hand, while the sub-text of the Cold War had an enduring presence across many years of presidential action, it had not been the only continuing country or regional focus. Certainly the Middle East, Europe, Central America, and Southeast Asia have been the subject of many directives through administrations going at least as far back as the Eisenhower. In a number of instances, administrations have issued wide-ranging directives that seek both to deal with each country specifically but within the context of an overall regional strategy. Thus, President Reagan issued NSDD 57 in 1982 aimed at establishing policy in the Horn of Africa, but laying out particular goals in Somalia, Sudan, Djibouti, Kenya, and Ethiopia.[41] Reagan also issued a number of such directives on Central America that were the foundations for U.S. support for the Nicaraguan Contras against the left wing Sandinistas and in support of the right wing regimes in El Salvador and Guatemala.[42]

Not surprisingly, individual countries can and do position themselves on the international security agenda in relatively dramatic ways, virtually demanding the attention even of the superpowers. For example, by mid-1966, President Johnson had become convinced that India's efforts to develop nuclear weapons represented an important development, particularly in light of recent Chinese nuclear tests and issued a directive ordering a serious study

Table 6.1. NSDs on Regional or Country Policy During the Kennedy and Reagan Administrations

	NSD No.	Topic	Date
Kennedy	17	Questions about the relationship between Cuba and Dominican Republic	02/13/61
	25	What should the president do with respect to Iran?	03/01/61
	33	Review of U.S. policy toward South Africa	03/22/61
	60	U.S. actions in relation to Portuguese territories in Africa	07/14/61
	73	Saudi Arabian arms request	08/20/61
	95	Renegotiation of Panama Canal treaty	09/15/61
	105	Policy toward Egypt and Syria	10/16/61
	123	Policy toward Yugoslavia	01/15/62
	179	Policy toward Indonesia	08/16/62
	206	Military assistance for internal security in Latin America	12/04/62
	211	U.S. policy toward Algeria	12/14/62
	212	U.S. policy toward Yugoslavia	12/14/62
	223	Appraisal of the Sino-Indian situation	02/26/63
	228	Review of the Iranian situation	03/14/63
	231	Middle Eastern nuclear capabilities	03/26/63
	243	Survey mission for the U.S. trust territory of the Pacific Islands	05/09/63
	251	Estimate of Greek political outlook	07/08/63
	262	Yemen disengagement	10/10/63
	265	New action program for Cyprus	10/17/63
Reagan	0[a]	South Africa policy	Summer 1981[b]
	17	Policy on Cuba, Nicaragua, Honduras, and El Salvador	11/16/81
	27	Further economic sanctions against Libya	03/09/82
	34	U.S. actions in the South Atlantic crisis	05/14/82
	37, 37a	Cuba and Central America	05/28/82
	54	U.S. policy toward Eastern Europe	09/02/82
	57	U.S. policy toward Somalia, Sudan, Djibouti, Kenya, and Ethiopia	09/17/82
	59	Cuba and Central America	10/05/82
	62	United States–Japan Relations	10/25/82

Table 6.1, *continued*

	NSD No.	Topic	Date
(Reagan)	64	Next steps in Lebanon	10/28/82
	75	U.S. policy on the USSR	01/17/83
	76	Nuclear cooperation with China	01/18/83
	82	U.S. initiatives in El Salvador	02/24/83
	100	U.S. military actions in Central America	07/28/83
	103	Lebanon	09/11/83
	105	U.S. security policy in the Eastern Caribbean–Grenada	10/04/83
	109	Lebanon	10/23/83
	110	Grenada	10/23/83
	111	Lebanon	10/28/83
	112	Exploitation of captured records—Grenada	11/15/83
	117	Lebanon	12/05/83
	124	U.S. policy in Central America and relations with Mexico	02/07/84
	133	U.S. policy toward Yugoslavia	03/14/84
	158	U.S. policy in Southeast Asia (the Kampuchea problem)	01/09/85
	163	U.S. policy toward the Philippines	02/20/85
	168	U.S. policy toward North Africa	04/30/85
	185	Private-sector cooperation in the Pacific Basin	09/04/85
	187	U.S. policy toward South Africa	09/07/85
	205	Sanctions against Libya	01/08/86
	212	U.S. policy toward Angola	02/10/86
	215	Philippines	02/23/86
	264	Central America	02/27/87
	272	U.S. objectives in Southern Africa	05/07/87
	273	U.S. policy toward South Africa	05/07/87
	274	U.S. policy toward Angola	05/07/87
	319	U.S. policy toward Indochina	11/14/88

[a]Unnumbered NSD. Christopher Simpson, *National Security Directives of the Reagan and Bush Administrations* (Boulder, Colo.: Westview Press, 1995), 12.
[b]Date unavailable.

of the situation and appropriate responses to it.[43] By August, the White House was calling for implementation of the recommendations that had been generated.[44] India's program as well as its relationship with Pakistan have been continuing themes over time in NSDs.

A Vehicle to Establish Positions on International Issues

To be sure, there are also cross-cutting issues that require emphasis. For example, President Ford used National Security Decision Memoranda in fall 1974 to establish "International Restraints on Environmental Warfare." In October he staked out the position that "It is in the United States' interests to consider with the USSR restraints on the use of environmental modification techniques for military purposes and, to this end, to enter into discussions with the Soviet Union to explore the possibility of such restraints."[45] A few weeks later, he issued another directive, this time rejecting "first use of herbicides in war" and "first use of riot control agents as an offensive weapon of war to facilitate or increase casualties."[46] Finally, in December he announced the ratification of the Geneva Protocol of 1925 on Gas Warfare.[47] However, in 1982 the Reagan administration took the position that in order to achieve its negotiation objectives with the Soviet Union, it would "ensure that modernization of short- and long-range chemical weapons systems proceeds so that the United States has a credible and effective deterrent retaliatory capability, in the area of chemical weapons arms control."[48]

Providing Guidance for Negotiations

Clearly, these directives on international issues can establish foundations within an administration on which to develop strategies and tactics for addressing particular negotiations, both bilateral and multilateral. National security directives have been issued to provide instructions to American negotiators involved in a host of settings. For a sampling of such directives across a number of administrations, see Table 6.2.

These directives vary. Some merely define overarching themes that are to guide U.S. negotiators, such as deep seabed development options and rights to freedom of navigation in Law of the Sea discussions. And others, such as the Strategic Arms Reduction Treaty (START) talks, are extremely detailed. The START negotiations instructions, for example, provide instructions on subjects from treatment of mobile Intercontinental Ballistic Missiles (ICBMS) to air-launched cruise missiles, to missile flight-test data, to air defenses and basing modes. It is also possible for current administrations to look back in

Table 6.2. NSDs Providing Negotiation Instructions

	NSD No.	Topic
Kennedy	32	U.S.–USSR commercial air transport agreement
	34	Moroccan bases
	152	Panama Canal policy and relations with Panama
Johnson	275	Exception of items from trade negotiations
	322	Guidelines for discussions on the nuclear defense of the Atlantic alliance
	323	Policy toward present and future of the Panama Canal
Ford	271	Instructions for the SALT (Strategic Arms Limitation) talks, Geneva
	273	Instructions for U.S. delegation to the PNE (Peaceful Uses of Nuclear Energy) negotiations
	288	Instructions for the U.S. delegation to the Geneva session of the third United Nations conference on the Law of the Sea
	302	Panama Canal treaty negotiations
Reagan	33	START (Strategic Arms Reduction Treaty) negotiations I
	36	START negotiations II
	44	START negotiations III
	53	START negotiations IV
	56	Intermediate-range Nuclear Forces (INF) negotiations I
	20	U.S. Law of the Sea policy
	153	Instructions for the Shultz–Gromyko meeting in Geneva

time through negotiating instructions to clarify patterns on types of negotiations, as in the case of disarmament, or with respect to particular issues, such as the long-term efforts to negotiate new Panama Canal agreements.

It comes as no surprise that these instructions can be the basis for considerable debate within the national security establishment in any given administration. Christopher Simpson, for example, points to President Reagan's NSDD 56, issued in September 1982, concerning Paul Nitze's famous "walk in the woods" conversation with his Intermediate-Range Nuclear Forces (INF) negotiating partner Yuli Kvitsinsky. The two negotiators discussed a formula that might result in an agreement, but hard-line Reagan officials, led by Richard Perle, reacted sharply against Nitze's actions. Simpson concluded, "This directive, prepared largely at Richard Perle's initiative, formalized President Reagan's rejection of Nitze's 'private' proposal."[49] The directive reads:

PRIVATE INF EXCHANGE

With respect to the private INF exchange which took place at the close of the last session, I have decided the following:

- The U.S. should continue to press for the zero/zero approach.
- No actions should be taken to close the private channel. If the Soviets respond in that channel, the following points should be made:
  - The U.S. believes the zero/zero proposal is the best approach to reduce the risk of nuclear conflict and to ensure effective verification.
  - The U.S. cannot accept a position in which the Soviets retain short time-of-flight SS-20 ballistic missiles while the U.S. foregoes Pershing II ballistic missiles (and retains only the slower, air-breathing GLCMs).
  - If the Soviets continue to be adamantly opposed to zero/zero, we should place the responsibility on them to propose alternatives for equitably reducing the total missile force structures.

In preparing for the possibility of a Soviet response to the exchange, an NSPG working group should prepare, on a close-hold basis, talking points which outline the specific military and other reasons why the U.S. cannot accept it.

A Vehicle for the Development and Implementation of Economic Policy

The economic aspects of national security policy have not always been recognized as central to national security, but they have come to play a critical role. In the contemporary context, NSDs control, and are affected by, a range of economic policy and financial realities in this country and abroad. Originally, the NSC had no representation from any financial or economically focused agency. It emerged from wartime experience, and there was for many years an ongoing debate whether NSC issues should be focused more on military affairs or on foreign policy as defined by the secretary of state. Eisenhower's secretary of states, John Foster Dulles, objected to the participation of the secretary of the treasury in NSC deliberations, a practice that had been initiated by Truman in 1949.[50] Even so, President Eisenhower did include his special assistant for economic policy in some NSC discussions.

It became increasingly clear over the years, however, that the financial issues, including financial management of national security policy, was a subject that had to be addressed. For one thing, the costs of policies announced in NSDs were substantial. Whether it was Truman's NSC 68 or Reagan's Strategic Defense Initiative (SDI), national security issues have often resulted in policies with large price tags. The issue has often not been simply an issue of cost but also a matter of deciding what mechanisms could legitimately be used to finance national security policy at home as well as in the field. As Congress sought to use spending limitations to ensure accountability, administrations increasingly have tried to be creative in finding ways to finance operations. The Iran-Contra debacle is an extreme example of the practice. Most financial issues are far more prosaic and involve such issues as President Kennedy's NSAM 1, Separate Budgeting of Spending Abroad,[51] and NSAM 171, designed to reduce Department of Defense overseas expenditures.[52] President Ford issued an NSD in 1975 that allowed wider discretion by recipients of U.S. financial assistance abroad to contract for goods or services locally.[53]

Further, economic policies per se have become policy tools of choice for a number of administrations. In some instances they have been relatively trivial, as in Kennedy's NSD that asked, "What exactly is the effect of our reduction from 500 to 100 dollars on the amount a tourist can bring in Duty Free. How much money is involved in these purchases and how much will it save abroad?"[54] In other instances, many economic policies are for much higher stakes. Thus, Kennedy issued another NSD later in 1961 that raised issues about the "economic effect upon the United States if England joins the common market."[55] Later presidents have issued NSDs concerning U.S. positions, in preparation for economic summits.[56]

The cold war, both in its early and more recent manifestations, saw the use of assistance to developing countries as a weapon. For example, the Reagan administration issued NSDs on the operation of the Food for Progress program that tied assistance to a willingness to move toward market-based economies and economic cooperation with the United States.[57] And in an age of globalization, it is not unusual to find that the Reagan administration incorporated private-sector partnerships into its development-assistance plans, such as in the administration's NSDD 185, providing government backing for "private-sector initiatives in the Pacific Basin."[58]

Trade has increasingly come to be seen as both an essential resource for national security concerns and also a weapon, particularly where military options are unrealistic. Although NSDs have been used to fashion trade policies with respect to particular countries or regions, they have also been employed more broadly. Decisions about U.S. influence on the coffee[59] and sugar markets,[60] as well as its gold position,[61] have all been subjects of NSDs. Even so, the use or the threatened use of trade sanctions has become an increasingly important tool but one that is also, potentially at least, politically sensitive. That has been particularly true where the trading partner in question is an ally, such as Japan. Thus, President Reagan, in his NSDD 154, describing his position in the forthcoming talks with Prime Minister Nakasone, noted that Japan's "extremely low ratio of manufactured goods imports to GNP" has led to "the buildup of protectionist pressures in the U.S."[62] Reagan indicated that he intended to warn Nakasone about that and to press for opening the markets in the "telecommunications, electronics, forest products, and medical equipment and pharmaceuticals" sectors. "During the discussions, I will caution the Prime Minister that, should there be insufficient progress on the Japanese side within a reasonably short time, we in the Administration will likely face severe domestic political pressures for discriminatory measures against Japan—pressures which we may find it difficult to resist."[63]

More often, NSDs have concerned either the management of trade sanctions or the integration of trade sanctions into larger national security policy mixes. Countries such as Cuba, Libya, Nicaragua, South Africa, Iraq, and others have long been the focus of NSDs on sanctions. Other countries have also been subject to such sanctions, although few Americans understood that there existed national security directives imposing a range of economic pressures. While the United States announced its general support for England in the Falklands/Malvinas War in 1982, the popular view was that the country would remain officially neutral. However, NSDD 34, issued by President Reagan, went further than most Americans realized. It provided for a suspension of "all military exports to Argentina" and suspended licenses for munitions, withheld "new Export-Import Bank credits, insurance, or guarantees," withheld any "new Commodity Credit Corporation guarantees," and withheld "any required U.S. consent for third-country transfers of U.S. origin items the export of which from the U.S. would not be approved under the above decisions."[64]

Most people regard trade decisions as relatively limited actions about interactions with another country's economy, but they have long been understood in the national security policy community in terms of economic warfare. As long ago as 1954, the CIA was preparing such reports as "Soviet Bloc Economic Warfare Capabilities and Courses of Action": "Economic warfare is defined in this estimate as the use of economic measures to alter the relative power positions and alignments of opposing nations or groups of nations. This can be done by affecting either the relative economic strength of the nations in the two groups or reducing the size and effectiveness of the opposing group by causing political defections or, what is more likely, dissensions."[65] In fact, during World War II, the Justice Department operated an Economic Warfare Section. The United States had been engaged in economic warfare, using the instruments of international trade as weapons, against Cuba for years before the Reagan administration launched its economic warfare strategy against the Soviet Union in 1982. In December 1963 the CIA praised the anti-Castro efforts and encouraged further steps: "These measures have been largely responsible for Castro's current economic distress, but additional effective economic warfare measures could be taken."[66]

But it was the Reagan administration that expanded the concept in dramatic terms in 1982. Roger W. Robinson Jr. was senior director of international economic affairs in Reagan's National Security Council and one of the principal architects, along with William Clark and CIA director William Casey, of NSDs that laid out the strategy for the battle. The opening salvo was fired in NSDD 54, United States Policy Toward Eastern Europe, issued in September 1982. This NSD laid out a set of incentives designed to pull Eastern European countries away from the USSR. These included most-favored-nation status, credits, International Monetary Fund (IMF) membership, and debt restructuring, in addition to such other encouragements as cultural and educational exchanges, scientific exchanges, high-level visits, supports in international organizations, and relaxation of restrictions on Eastern European diplomats and consular personnel.[67] The primary assault, though, came with NSDD 66, issued in November, which has been referred to as the Plan for Economic Warfare Against the USSR.[68] Actually entitled East-West Economic Relations and Poland-Related Sanctions, it set out to organize trade restraints by "the Allies" against the USSR. Although the summary of conclusions on which the allies agreed stated that "it is not their purpose to engage in economic warfare against the Soviet Union," it was in fact the U.S. purpose.[69] The core of NSD 66 was an effort to persuade the allies to halt natural gas purchases from the USSR, seek alternative sources of supply, stop sales of energy technology to the Soviets, and increase trade costs to the USSR by increasing interest rates for loans and placing restraints on trade credits.[70] Less than two months later, the Reagan White House issued its broad-based anti-Soviet strategy document, NSD 75,[71] which stated the U.S. economic objectives:

- Above all, to ensure that East-West economic relations do not facilitate the Soviet military buildup. This requires prevention of the transfer of technology and equipment that would make a substantial contribution directly or indirectly to Soviet military power.
- To avoid subsidizing the Soviet economy or unduly easing the burden of Soviet resource allocation decisions, so as not to dilute pressure for structural change in the Soviet system.

- To seek to minimize the potential for Soviet exercise of reverse leverage on Western countries based on trade, energy supply, and financial relationships.
- To permit mutual beneficial trade—without Western subsidization or the creation of Western dependence—with the USSR in non-strategic areas, such as grains.[72]

One of the strategically, and even tactically, important types of trade for U.S. national security policymakers has been in weapons and other types of military equipment.

To Plan and Execute Arms Sales and Transfers

The NSDs that lay out U.S. policy for various countries, regions, or situations have often combined military, economic, and political factors, though some administrations, like that of Jimmy Carter, sought to limit arms sales.[73] However, one of the early NSDs issued by President Reagan rescinded Carter's directive and replaced it with a new policy that advocated an active policy of conventional arms sales.[74] Moreover, it ordered that "United States Government representatives overseas will be expected to provide the same courtesies and assistance to firms that have obtained licenses to market items on the United States Munitions List as they would to those marketing other American products."[75] When the Clinton administration came to office, there was widespread speculation that the president would reverse that policy and limit arms sales, particularly since the cold war had ended and in light of Iran-Contra revelations. However, after an extended administration review process, Clinton issued PDD 34 in February 1995, essentially maintaining the policy in existence, though the White House sought to couch its actions in terms of a set of criteria to be used in making individual decisions about arms sales. In truth, though, there was little difference in Clinton's policy. Indeed, administration officials admitted publicly what had generally been understood in the Reagan and Bush years but not publicly stated, that is, that one of the considerations in approving sales would be the economic well-being of U.S. arms manufacturers. The policy, the treatment of arms as another element of U.S. economic development, and word about possible sales of aircraft and armored vehicles to newly independent states of Eastern Europe brought about widespread criticism.[76]

Most Americans expect that the United States will provide various types of military assistance to friendly nations, and that has certainly been common practice. For example, NSDs concerning arms sales to Israel have been a fixture in several administrations over time.[77] However, many people were not as aware of the other uses of arms sales, such as the effort to stabilize the India-Pakistan tensions by assuring both sides that their legitimate defense needs would be supported.[78] It came as a surprise to many when they learned that the United States had not only sold arms but also provided them at U.S. expense through covert means. For example, the Reagan administration provided arms and training to Sudan and Egypt by taking the military equipment to the countries in a military exercise called Operation Bright Star[79] and then left the equipment behind. It also provided support to the Contra rebels in Nicaragua by the same tactic in an exercise known as AHAUS TARA II (also known as Big Pine II).[80] Even the White House has been concerned when U.S.–supplied arms ended up in the hands of people who turned out to be brutal dictators or when they fell into the hands of adversaries.[81]

It is one thing when arms sales are public and backed by a policy statement from the administration, for which it may be called to answer by Congress or in the court of public opinion. However, the use of covert arms transfers has engendered very different reactions in both arenas. The Iran-Contra investigation produced not only evidence of NSDs calling for military assistance to the Contras[82] but also copies of findings in which President Reagan authorized sales of weapons to Iran and to the Contras. For example, with respect to Iran, Reagan's finding said in part:

> The USG will act to facilitate efforts by third parties and third countries to establish contact with moderate elements within and outside the Government of Iran by providing these elements with arms, equipment and related material in order to enhance the credibility of these elements in their effort to achieve a more pro–U.S. government in Iran by demonstrating their ability to obtain requisite resources to defend their country against Iraq and intervention by the Soviet Union.[83]

The finding makes clear that this action was taken "for the purposes of: (1) establishing a more moderate government in Iran, (2) obtaining from them significant intelligence not otherwise obtainable, to determine the current Iranian Government's intentions with respect to its neighbors and with respect to terrorist acts, and (3) furthering the release of the American hostages held in Beirut and preventing additional terrorist acts by these groups." As to the Contras, Reagan's finding concluded that it was essential to "provide support, equipment and training assistance to Nicaraguan paramilitary resistance groups as a means to induce the Sandinistas and Cubans and their allies to cease their support for the insurgencies in the region."[84] Some administrations have seen arms transfers as a way to obtain the assistance of allies to carry out what might otherwise require U.S. military assets.

Military Doctrine, Deployment, and Warfare Coordination

National security directives, not surprisingly, have also been used to establish military doctrine and to coordinate such concerns as force posture with foreign policy positions. But there is often a reflexive relationship between broad-based strategic policy decisions and the constantly changing context of global security challenges. National security directives have been used to address the strategic challenges, the policies on deployment of troops and equipment, and the initiation and conduct of warfare.

The broad strategic policies in contemporary administrations have been focused largely on debates over the development and deployment of weapons systems, despite the practice of presidents to pay lip service to the human resources side of the equation. The political and economic factors that support that tendency are obvious, beginning with the lobbying power of weapons manufacturers. Thus, the Reagan administration built much of its military strategy around its Strategic Forces Modernization policy. The administration's opening directive on this program was NSD 12, which began from the position that Reagan had staked out in the presidential campaign. The directive began by indicating that "the modernization program outlined by this directive will guide the long-term development of our strategic forces. It will help redress the deteriorated strategic balance with the Soviet Union. . . . This should, in turn, create better incentives for the Soviets to negotiate genuine arms reductions."[85] The directive then set out its "five mutually reinforcing parts":

1. Making our strategic communications and command systems more survivable, so that we can communicate over survivable networks without nuclear forces, even after an attack.
2. Modernizing the strategic bomber force by the addition of two new types of bombers.
3. Increasing the accuracy and payload of our submarine-launched ballistic missiles (SLBM) [additional line excised in declassification].
4. Improving strategic defenses.
5. Deploying a new, larger, and more accurate land-based ballistic missile.

To implement portions of this strategy, NSDD 12 called for the deployment of the B-1 bomber, arming of B-52 bombers with cruise missiles, development of Advanced Technology Bombers (now known as the B-2), and development and deployment of MX missiles in hardened silos. Reagan later issued a number of additional NSDs on his modernization program, primarily focused on the basing mode for the MX missile and driven by congressional and international concern that the United States might violate the Anti-Ballistic Missile treaty.[86] In fall 1982 Congress blocked deployment of the MX and demanded more information. Reagan issued NSDD 73, which created the Commission on Strategic Forces (better known as the Scowcroft Commission) to persuade Congress and directed that work continue on the MX and the planned dense-pack basing mode.[87] Not quite a year after creating the Scowcroft Commission, Reagan formally launched his lobbying and public relations effort to gain approval for the Strategic Defense Initiative, better known as Star Wars, in NSDD 116.[88]

The Reagan years, to be sure, were dramatic examples of the use of NSDs on defense issues, but most other presidents before him in the modern era issued their fair share of military directives. Thus, Ford issued his NSDM 344, calling for the construction of 157 new ships just before leaving office[89] and NSDM 348, Defense Policy and Military Posture, on the very day he left the White House.[90]

Of course, many presidents face issues that are broad and important but not as dramatic as broad-based military strategy and force posture. For example, President Kennedy issued an NSD calling on the secretary of defense to develop "counter-guerrilla forces," which we have since come to know as the Green Berets.[91] The more intensive use of special forces units over time in the so-called unconventional warfare role and the changing face of political and military conflict led the Reagan administration to develop an NSD setting out his approach to "Low-Intensity Warfare."[92]

> Low Intensity Conflict is a political-military confrontation between contending states or groups below conventional war and above the routine, peaceful competition among states. It involves protracted struggles of competing principles and ideologies. Low Intensity Conflict ranges from subversion to the use of armed force. It is waged by a combination of means employing political, economic, informational, and military instruments.[93]

President Johnson issued NSAM 292 in 1964, considering the issues associated with the deployment in Europe of the controversial aircraft then known as the TFX, later designated the FB-111.[94]

The deployment of troops has presented presidents with a range of political and military issues that involve measures from sending troops into harm's way in existing conflicts to low-intensity wars that had the potential to grow.[95] More often, the administrations worked with various constellations of positioning troops and their equipment in strategically important or tactically advantageous locations. Such deployments have also been used to project force as well as to prepare for possible action, as in the case of President Kennedy's buildup of troops in Europe as conflict with the USSR over Berlin grew.[96] As a number of recent presidents have learned, one of the more complex aspects of deployment can be extricating the troops from difficult situations. Thus, President Reagan's NSDD 123 laid out the plan for withdrawal of U.S. forces from Lebanon in the midst of continued fighting.[97]

National security directives have also been used both to launch military action and to direct combat operations. One of the more significant examples of such action was President Bush's NSD 54 that launched the Desert Storm attack on Iraq in 1991:[98]

> Pursuant to my responsibilities and authority under the Constitution as President and Commander in Chief, and under the laws and treaties of the United States, and pursuant to H.J. Res. 77 (1991), and in accordance with the rights and obligations of the United States under international law, including UN Security Council Resolutions 660, 661, 662, 664, 666, 667, 670, 674, 677, and 678, and consistent with the inherent right of the collective self-defense affirmed in Article 51 of the United Nations Charter, I hereby authorize military actions designed to bring about Iraq's withdrawal from Kuwait. These actions are to be conducted against Iraq and Iraqi forces in Kuwait by U.S. air, sea and land conventional military forces, in coordination with the forces of our coalition partners, at a date and time I shall determine and communicate through the National Command Authority channels.[99]

The next day, Desert Storm was launched. The order defines the purposes of the attack and the cautions to be observed during the battle. Interestingly, President Bush reserved the right to escalate hostilities and to target Saddam Hussein directly if Iraq should seek to destroy Kuwait's oil fields. In such a case, the NSD announces, "it shall become an explicit objective of the United States to replace the current leadership of Iraq. I also want to preserve the option of authorizing additional punitive actions against Iraq."[100] Iraq did set the fields on fire, and the United States did not "replace the current leadership of Iraq." Bush knew that his authority was limited both domestically, in terms of his dealings with the Congress, and internationally, in terms of holding the coalition together. To be sure, this was not the first time that NSDs had been used for such a purpose. President Reagan had issued NSDD 110 in fall 1983, setting in motion the invasion of Grenada.[101]

Notwithstanding Panama, Grenada, and Iraq, full-scale military attacks are the exception rather than the rule. However, there are other contexts in which combat is waged, often on a limited scale or where troops are placed in positions in which the likelihood of hostilities is high. In such situations, the White House has often sought, in the contemporary period, to be directly involved with the management of those forces because of the political volatility of the situation. One of the more common ways in which this has been done using NSDs is by the issuance of rules of engagement. Though many people have heard debates in the media over whether the rules of engagement were sufficiently robust to protect American forces or were too loose, permitting politically unintended clashes, few have actually seen such orders. President Reagan issued these rules of engagement to U.S. forces in Lebanon in early 1984:

> The Rules of Engagement (ROE) governing the defense of the official American presence in Lebanon will remain in effect. Specifically, U.S. Naval and tactical air power will be employed to destroy sources of hostile fire directed at the American Embassy compound, the Ambassador's residence and other U.S. personnel or facilities in Lebanon. As in previous practice, fire will be returned at organizationally associated targets if response to the source of fire is precluded. In view of the sudden and proximate threat to the Ambassador's residence which would be posed by a breakthrough at Suk al Gharb, the ROE for support to the LAF at that point is reaffirmed.
>   To permit effective and timely responses to hostile fire in the situations described above, the Secretary of Defense will ensure that adequate technical means are available so as to determine the source of hostile fire directed at American personnel in greater Beirut.[102]

The establishment of rules of engagement can also be important in instances where the U.S. assigns military advisers or trainers, as in the Bush administration's Andean Initiative in 1989 intended to help address threats from the Sendero Luminoso (Shining Path) rebels and to suppress the drug trade.[103]

The continuing debates over such issues has expanded as the United States has become increasingly involved in what are called peacekeeping forces but that are often actually peacemaking forces. There have been many debates over a range of issues, from mission to command and control to preparation for possible hostilities, that have been high visibility issues in the years since the attack on the Marine barracks in Lebanon, exacerbated by the debacle in Somalia. In response to the Somalia experience, the Clinton administration issued PDD 25 in May 1994:

1. Making disciplined and coherent choices about which peace operations to support;
2. Reducing U.S. costs for UN peace operations;
3. Defining clearly our policy regarding the command and control of American military forces in UN peace operations;
4. Reforming and improving the UN's capacity to manage peace operations;
5. Improving the way the U.S. government manages and funds peace operations;
6. Creating better forms of cooperation between the Executive, the Congress and the American public on peace operations.[104]

Management and Control of Nuclear Weapons and Power

Although attention has been focused in recent years on such activities as peacekeeping operations and what the Reagan White House dubbed "low-intensity conflict," the specter of nuclear weapons has loomed over the domestic and international scene throughout the life of the NSC. Certainly, the management and control of nuclear weapons and nuclear power as well as other peaceful uses of nuclear energy have been directed by presidential use of NSDs. As strange as it may seem, much of this activity has been treated as relatively routine work. It is usually carried on under the strictest security rules, but significant portions of enough of these orders have been declassified over the years to demonstrate the patterns. Primarily, NSDs are used to (1) control nuclear stockpiles and develop or update procedures for their use;[105] (2) deploy weapons and delivery systems;[106] (3) manage the development and testing of nuclear weapons;[107] and (4) make policy for and manage nuclear technology assistance to other countries, with a simultaneous concern for nonproliferation.[108]

Propaganda and Psychological Warfare

At the other end of the spectrum, several administrations have used NSDs in domestic and international conflict as part of the effort in carrying on propaganda or psychological warfare. Often termed "public diplomacy," propaganda efforts have long been regarded as essential in national security operations even if, as in the case of the Vietnam War, they have often failed to achieve White House goals. Indeed, President Johnson became so upset with the way information was getting to the media and through them to the public that he issued NSAM 308 in June 1964 to launch a propaganda effort: "I have therefore designated Mr. Robert J. Manning, Assistant Secretary of

State for Public Affairs, to generate and to coordinate a broad program to bring to the American people a complete and accurate picture of the United States involvement in Southeast Asia, and to show why this involvement is essential."[109] Later that same month, the White House expressed frustration with the nature and possible sources of news stories appearing in Washington media. In NSAM 313, Johnson reminded agency heads to ensure that Vietnam stories were filtered through Manning, as required by NSAM 308.[110] This effort is even more interesting, given that both of these NSDs were issued more than a month before the Gulf of Tonkin incident and the congressional resolution that followed.

If any administration understood the value of both propaganda and psychological warfare, it was the Reagan White House. Public diplomacy was especially important to Reagan, precisely because his administration was deliberately making dramatic, some might say radical, policy decisions, both domestically and internationally. Indeed, President Reagan issued NSDD 77 in early 1983, Management of Public Diplomacy Relative to National Security,[111] aimed at shaping public opinion with respect to the renewed cold war policies directed at the Soviet Union. Simpson discussed Oliver North's operation of the public diplomacy effort in Latin America and pointed out that between that operation and similar efforts concerning Afghanistan, parts of Africa, the USSR, and Eastern Europe, the administration was spending as much as $65 million annually on public diplomacy by fiscal year (FY) 1984.[112]

Following the invasion of Grenada, in late 1983 the White House issued NSDD 112, providing directions on how documents seized by U.S. forces during the invasion were to be used in propaganda efforts. The directive established an "interagency committee for public disclosure and information" under the secretary of state, with the responsibility to "develop plans for the short and long term exploitation [of seized documents] for public information and political action."[113] Also in late 1983, Reagan issued NSDD 116.[114] Although the title of the document referred to "consultation," it plainly launched a campaign to convince members of Congress and friendly nations to support, or at least not to actively oppose, the administration's SDI program. Reagan directed the Defense Department, the State Department, and the CIA to prepare presentations for that purpose:

> This presentation should highlight the potential that the strategic defense initiative offers for providing the basis for a policy of deterrence which utilizes the contribution of an effective defense rather than depending solely upon the threat of effective nuclear retaliation. It should also make clear

the risks that the U.S. and its allies face from the vigorous Soviet ballistic missile defense program. The emphasis in the technology plan on development and demonstration, as opposed to early deployment, should be underlined. The relationship between the strategic defense initiative and current deterrence doctrine, the strategic modernization program, existing arms control agreements, and our long-term commitments to our allies should be addressed. Finally, the presentations should stress the continued U.S. commitment to current deterrence doctrine and force planning as well as to existing alliance commitments and arms control initiatives.[115]

In May 1985 Reagan issued another and more detailed directive, NSDD 172, Presenting the Strategic Defense Initiative. It insisted that all publications, commentary, or statements of any kind on SDI were to be precleared by the assistant to the president for national security affairs, laid out a set of twelve talking points that all statements were to stress, and warned that undisciplined statements were dangerous as well as unacceptable, playing into the Soviet's side in the propaganda war. "Failing to [follow the directive] will create misunderstanding and suspicion of our intentions. This undermines the support that we seek, provides the Soviets additional propaganda opportunities, and adds to the difficulty of the task that our negotiators face in Geneva."

The administration's efforts were not limited to the USSR or to Latin American operations. In September 1985 the Reagan White House launched a public diplomacy effort aimed at criticism of its policy toward the apartheid regime in South Africa. In August President Reagan had insisted in an interview that racial segregation had ended in South Africa under the government of P. W. Botha, saying this during one of the most violent years in the country's recent history. The statement came at a time when authorities had closed the schools in Cape Town because of the level of violence following police shootings of demonstrators. Reagan publicly apologized, but the administration was fighting to head off congressional efforts to require stiff sanctions. The directive noted "growing Congressional and public criticism of our policy" and set out steps to be taken "to broaden both domestic and international support for them."[116]

It is difficult for many Americans to accept that their government has regularly engaged in psychological warfare, but it is a fact. Indeed, there is nothing new in that approach even in peacetime. During the Truman administration, the White House created the Psychological Strategy Board as part of the anti-Soviet cold war strategy. Although the board was later dissolved, psychological warfare has been employed by many presidents. Public attention was drawn to it during the Vietnam War. President Johnson was a strong supporter of the effort, writing in NSAM 325, "I am sending the Ambassador a private message to indicate my own interest in the strongest possible information and psychological warfare program."[117] Johnson ordered the secretaries of defense and state as well as the director of Central Intelligence and the Agency for International Development to "give all possible support to an intensified information and psychological warfare program." He underscored his commitment by adding, "Meanwhile, you are directed to proceed with all necessary actions on the firm understanding that it is my fixed policy that *no worthwhile undertaking shall be inhibited or delayed in any way by financial restrictions. We can and will find the resources we need for all good programs in Vietnam.*"

The Reagan administration, to reinvigorate psychological warfare capability, directed the Department of Defense to rebuild its psychological operations (PSYOP) assets *not only for use in wartime, but "with appropriate interagency coordination and in accordance with national law and policy, to participate in overt PSYOP programs in peacetime."*[118] One of the more controversial psychological warfare/propaganda efforts during the Reagan years was the support in NSDD 170 for Radio Martí, intended to maintain a steady attack on Cuba's Fidel Castro.[119]

Covert, Low-Intensity, and Hybrid Operations

Psychological warfare techniques have been built into most major covert operations, which have been one of the areas where presidents have designed and operated programs with NSDs. They have clearly been among the most controversial of White House uses of such directives. Sufficient quantities of material have now been declassified that a number of books could easily be written on the use of these techniques, just in the postwar era.

There seems to be a tendency to regard covert actions as completely distinct from other kinds of national security operations, but the evidence shows that there are many hybrid policies and projects. They consist not of one policy but are policy mixes that may involve combinations of covert and overt steps. These may include warfare involving foreign intelligence assets, support for indigenous operations in other countries, surreptitious involvement of U.S. forces, economic warfare, and psychological warfare as well as (or in some cases escalating to) overt diplomatic moves and limited, or even large-scale, military action.

The first such NSD was NSC 1/1 issued by Harry Truman, which was the basis for a covert effort to influence the Italian elections, a country whose strong Communist party was worrisome to Truman for years. Two later directives, issued in 1947 and 1948, provided an institutional foundation for covert action decisions outside the NSC.[120] President Eisenhower was a leading practitioner in the use of covert action, and in 1954 he established the 5412 Committee within the NSC to oversee such operations. The name, though not the functions of that group, was changed by President Johnson to the 303 Committee, the name taken from its redesignation by NSAM 303, issued in June 1964. The name was changed several more times over the years. In 1985 President Reagan moved to reinvigorate and reorganize covert operations in NSDD 150, "Covert Action Policy Approval and Coordination Procedures":[121]

> When the President determines that it is appropriate, he must have at his disposal appropriate means to assist allies and friends and to influence the actions of foreign countries, including the means to affect the behavior both when the US wishes to acknowledge its role, and to do this covertly when the revelation of US sponsorship, support, or assistance would adversely affect US interests. These tools include overt and covert diplomatic information channels, political actions, and covert action including paramilitary and intelligence support programs.[122]

Interestingly, the directive claimed, "Moreover, while the Constitution and the National Security Act of 1947 sanction the use of covert action, subsequent authorizations impose special reporting requirements." Just where in the Constitution the administration thought there was a basis for covert action is not indicated. The directive sets out requirements for covert action that integrate this NSDD with the requirements of Executive Order 12333. In addition to setting up processes for approval of covert action, the directive created a National Security Planning Group and a Planning and Coordination Group, the latter chaired by a representative of the vice president. Finally, it created a new level of security classification within Top Secret known as VEIL: "All information concerning covert action policies and review and approval procedures (i.e., Presidential Findings and Memoranda of Notifications and related correspondence) shall be protected under a separate, specially compartmented control and access system identified by the unclassified codeword 'VEIL.'"[123] Following the Iran-Contra affair, the president appointed the Tower Commission; and, in early 1987, in NSDD 266, Reagan issued instructions to implement its recommendations. In truth, most of the provisions are limited and come down to five specific points:

- Proposed covert actions will be coordinated with NSC participants, including the Attorney General, and their respective recommendations communicated to the President.
- All requirements of law concerning covert activities, including those requirements relating to presidential authorization and congressional notification, will be addressed in a timely manner and complied with fully.
- Consistent with the foregoing, covert activities will be subject to tightly restricted consideration, and measures to protect the security of all information concerning such activities will be enhanced.
- The NSC staff itself will not undertake the conduct of covert activities.
- The use of private individuals and organizations as intermediates to conduct covert activities will be appropriately limited and subject in every case to close observation and supervision by appropriate Executive departments and agencies.[124]

It also required a review of existing covert procedures and operations. At the completion of that review, the president issued NSDD 276, announcing limited changes in NSC organization and rescinding his NSDD 2 that had set forth the original Reagan administration's organization of the NSC. Only four months after that, the White House issued another NSDD, this time less concerned with formal organizational responses to criticism and more with bolstering the president's operational tools for authorizing and directing "special activities."[125] While setting forth requirements for prior notification of Congress, the directive also provided that the president could delay notification and move forward with the operation if he or she "determines that it is necessary."

The president who championed covert operations and laid the foundation for much of what has happened since was Dwight Eisenhower. Even before his new national security adviser had concluded his work on organizing the Eisenhower NSC, the new administration was well and truly on its way in covert activities. In its first two years in office, the Eisenhower administration undertook covert actions that eventually brought down the governments of two nations, Iran and Guatemala. And in both cases the effort was largely driven by anti-Communist cold war fervor, with a number of serious long-term problems as a result. The British sent MI6 officers to meet with CIA officials in November 1952, seeking U.S. participation in a coup intended to overthrow the government of Prime Minister Mohammad Mosaddeq of Iran and restoring the Shah to real control. Mosaddeq was no Communist, but his government, with broad popular support, had nationalized British oil company interests.[126] It was true that Mosaddeq's government was supported by the Tudeh (Communist party), but they were clearly not a major force in that government.[127] The British had undertaken an embargo and had previously launched their own unsuccessful covert efforts to unseat Mosaddeq but now sought U.S. involvement. The Truman administration refused. However, on February 3, 1953, only two weeks after coming to office, senior Eisenhower officials met with British representatives and agreed to move forward on a covert plot.[128] General Bedell Smith, the undersecretary of state, indicated that the Mosaddeq government was no longer acceptable. Planning work went on over the following months, and Eisenhower approved it on July 11. Launched on August 15, the plot, code-named Operation Ajax, very nearly failed. Indeed, many of those involved were ready to abandon the effort by August 18, but a shift in fortunes the following day produced success. Donald Wilber recalls the euphoria at the CIA on August 19: "It was a day that should never have ended, for it carried with it such a sense of excitement, of satisfaction, and of jubilation that it is doubtful whether any other can come up to it."[129] That success built the CIA into a larger-than-life force with a reputation for being able to bring down countries.

Indeed, the NSC approved its next coup on August 12, 1953, just days before the Iran action was scheduled to begin.[130] So confident was the national security establishment, that in less than a month, on September 11, the CIA had produced its General Plan of Action, outlining the overthrow of the government headed by Jacobo Arbenz Guzmán in Guatemala, an operation called PB Success.[131] Actually, steps toward the Guatemala coup had begun with President Eisenhower's NSC 144/1, issued in March 1953, which set out U.S. policy on Latin America and expressed concern with what it saw as a movement "toward radical and nationalistic regimes." Though it recognized the need for economic development, it saw significant foreign aid as unnecessary but relied instead on the market to meet that need. Neither did it address the serious and obvious human rights abuses in a number of Latin American governments. Overall, it saw Latin America more as a battleground for the cold war.[132]

The Arbenz government was elected in a free and fair election. Clearly no Communist, Arbenz was committed to land reform and other social reform measures, including a new labor code that permitted employees to organize for collective bargaining. The land reform took land that was not under cultivation for redistribution. The U.S.–based United Fruit Company complained that four hundred thousand acres were taken with compensation of three dollars per acre, the amount incidentally, that the company had used to value the land for Guatemalan tax purposes. Even so, the United Fruit Company launched a major public relations effort in Washington to convince American officials that it was a Communist government that would threaten the rest of the region.[133] It was true that four of the sixty-one votes in Arbenz's coalition were Communists, but none was a minister.[134] Communists were also barred from posts in a number of ministries.[135] Indeed, one of Eisenhower's friends observed at the time that there were more Communists in San Francisco than in Guatemala.[136] Nonetheless, the coup engineered by the Eisenhower administration ultimately overturned the Guatemalan government in June 1954, leaving a regime in power that was a ruthless abuser of human rights and ensuring a legacy of soundly based distrust and anger toward the United States that extends to this day.

Following these seemingly successful covert efforts, and given the events in Cuba that ultimately brought Fidel Castro to power, it was not surprising that the national security establishment was moving toward similar action in the Caribbean by the time John F. Kennedy came to office. In truth, neither Operation Ajax nor PB Success was really successful. According to the CIA's own assessments, both were botched operations that succeeded as much by luck as anything else. Although there were important lessons from both, that opportunity to learn was ignored. The after-action report by Donald N. Wilber was critical of a variety of aspects of the covert effort. Wilber, who had been the lead planner for the CIA on the effort, wrote, "If this history had been read by the planners of the Bay of Pigs, there would have been no such operation. . . . From time to time, I gave talks on the operation to various groups within the agency, and, in hindsight, one might wonder why no one from the Cuban desk ever came or read the history."[137] After laying out the many failures provided by the CIA's documents and experience in Guatemala, Nick Cullather noted that not only were the lessons not learned but also that the same people and tactics were used to develop later operations, including the Bay of Pigs. Afterwards, many of those involved in the two operations linked the success in Guatemala with the failure of the Bay of Pigs. "If the Agency had not had Guatemala," E. Howard Hunt, a case officer who served in both PB Success and JMARC later observed, "it probably would not have had Cuba."[138]

In the years following the Iran and Guatemala operations, Eisenhower issued a number of NSDs to address follow-on problems and to provide support for U.S.–backed regimes.[139] John F. Kennedy, like Eisenhower before him, plunged into covert action almost immediately after arriving in office. On February 6, 1961, Kennedy issued NSAM 10, asking, "Has the policy for Cuba been coordinated between Defense, CIA [Bissell], Mann and Berle? Have we determined what we are going to do about Cuba? What approaches are we going to make to the Latin American governments on this matter. If there is a difference of opinion between the agencies I think they should be brought to my attention." Indeed, Kennedy ultimately approved the Bay of Pigs operation only seventy-seven days after becoming president.[140] Even while he was working with the Bay of Pigs planners and deciding whether to launch the operation, he issued an NSD calling for a study of the possible effects of an embargo on Cuba, suggested by Senator George Smathers.

By March 11, Kennedy had more or less decided to move on the Bay of Pigs and issued NSAM 31:

> 1. Every effort should be made to assist patriotic Cubans in forming a new and strong political organization, and in conjunction with this effort a maximum amount of publicity buildup should be sought for the emerging political leaders of this organization, especially those who may be active participants in a military campaign of liberation. Action: Central Intelligence Agency.
> 2. The United States Government must have ready a white paper on Cuba, and should also be ready to give appropriate assistance to Cuban patriots in a similar effort. Action: Arthur Schlesinger in cooperation with the Department of State.
> 3. The Department of State will present recommendations with respect to a demarche in the Organization of American States, looking toward a united demand for prompt free elections in Cuba, with appropriate safeguards and opportunity for all patriotic Cubans. Action: Department of State.
> 4. The President expects to authorize U.S. support for an appropriate number of patriotic Cubans to return to their homeland. He believes that the best possible plan, from the point of view of combined military, political and psychological considerations, has not yet been presented, and new proposals are to be concerted promptly. Action: Central Intelligence Agency, with appropriate consultation.

On April 25, soon after the failed invasion was launched in mid-April, Kennedy found himself issuing a string of NSDs to address the Cuban issues in the wake of the Bay of Pigs.[141] He was then promptly plunged into what became the Berlin crisis, which was the basis for a number of NSDs over the next several months.

Cuba, as was true of Iran-Contra and other covert efforts, involved a hybrid policy mix, consisting of some very public actions and others that were covert. As its predecessors in Iran, Guatemala, Cuba, and Vietnam had done, the Reagan White House plunged into the world of covert operations almost immediately after taking office. By March 1981 the Reagan administration was on its way in Latin America with Director of Central Intelligence William Casey's creation of a Central American Task Force. In December Reagan issued a presidential finding to authorize covert CIA action, including paramilitary action, with $19 million to support Nicaraguan groups opposing the Sandinista government.[142] In 1982 Congress reacted against administration policy and passed the first Boland Amendment, limiting the use of U.S. funds in support of the Contras.[143] Eventually, the effort to circumvent congressional constraints became the basis for the Iran-Contra scandal. The Reagan White House developed NSDD 17, Policy on Cuba, Nicaragua, Honduras, and El Salvador, in November 1986 as its blueprint for action:[144] "U.S. policy is therefore to assist in defeating the insurgency in El Salvador, and to oppose actions by Cuba, Nicaragua, or others to introduce into Central America heavy weapons, troops from outside the region, trained subversives, or arms and military supplies for insurgents." The directive set out certain requirements for officials:

1. Create a public information task force to inform the public and Congress of the critical situation in the areas.
2. Economic support for a number of Central American and Caribbean countries (estimate $250 to $300 million FY 1982 supplemental).
3. Agreement to use most of the $50 million Section 506 authority to increase military assistance to El Salvador and Honduras. Reprogram additional funds as necessary.
4. Provide military training for indigenous units and leaders both in and out of country.
5. DELETED FOR SECURITY REASONS
6. Maintain trade and credit to Nicaragua as long as the government permits the private sector to operate effectively.
7. DELETED FOR SECURITY REASONS
8. Encourage cooperative efforts to defeat externally-supported insurgency by pursuing a multilateral step-by-step approach.
9. Support democratic forces in Nicaragua.
10. DELETED FOR SECURITY REASONS
11. DELETED FOR SECURITY REASONS

The Reagan administration's battle against the Sandinistas was fought with both overt and covert methods. The same had been true of other programs, including Vietnam. President Eisenhower had pressed support for the South Vietnamese government in a variety of forms, and Kennedy continued and expanded that effort. Less than a month after the failed Bay of Pigs invasion, Kennedy issued NSAM 52, laying out a series of decisions intended to support President Diem, including military support and preparations for possible commitment of U.S. troops. Kennedy served notice: "The U.S. objective and concept of operations stated in the report are approved: to prevent Communist domination of South Vietnam; to create in that country a viable and increasingly democratic society; and to initiate, on an accelerated basis, a series of mutually supporting actions of a military, political, economic, and psychological and covert character designed to achieve this objective."[145] Over the next year and a half, Kennedy issued an additional eight NSDs on Vietnam and Laos.[146] Throughout the Johnson years and into the Nixon era, the hybrid covert/overt effort in Southeast Asia was waged, with NSDs playing a significant part. Even while he was dealing with Vietnam, Nixon issued directives that eventually shaped U.S. involvement in efforts first to block the election and inauguration of Salvador Allende in Chile and later to support the coup that overturned that government in 1973.[147]

WHY ARE THEY USED?

Thus, national security directives have been applied in a variety of ways over time. Indeed, their usefulness in a wide array of circumstances is one of the most important reasons why presidents have employed them, but there are several other explanations as well.

A Secure, Structured, but Flexible Device for National Security Decisionmaking and Action

Every president since Truman has learned that it was important to organize the national security players, both organizations and individuals, within the administration and to provide some structure for decisionmaking. Those like Kennedy and Johnson, who tried to avoid the use of NSDs and the structures and processes for developing them, found themselves drifting back toward their use. They are flexible and therefore provide a decision framework that is loose enough to allow for the complexity and variability of national security policy issues, but they do provide some structure.

They also create a paper trail that permits an administration to move many participants in a variety of issues in varied parts of the world consistently through decisions. Just as important, they establish a foundation for later follow-up. Presidents often build on previous NSDs, as had been true in the case of instructions for negotiators in ongoing complex international diplomacy and for decisions in covert action arenas. These patterns often indicate where there are intelligence gaps. In such cases, administrations can then use a National Security Study Memoranda (or whatever a particular administration chooses to call its version of the same document) or an NSD to set intelligence tasks or analytic assignments for particular agencies or even for the entire NSC.

To Set New Policy and Change Course from a Previous Administration

NSDs that accumulate over time with respect to a given policy provide a continuity and momentum even across very different administrations, but they are also used as devices to make rapid changes. As Bromley Smith explained the situation confronting John Kennedy, "One of the first problems faced by the new president was how to deal with the existing national security policies of his predecessor."[148] Kennedy faced an eight-year history of NSC actions, a record of significant levels of covert activity, pending covert efforts in Southeast Asia and Cuba, and a range of other involvements. Eisenhower had earlier rejected outright the basic national security doctrine of the Truman administration and reshaped not only the policy but also the nature of the national security policymaking process itself. In later years, the Reagan administration found itself in a similar position in its response to the Carter administration. As was true in a variety of other areas, the new national security team and the chief executive had committed themselves to dramatic shifts in foreign and military policy. They sought to change policies in particular parts of the world, from the Middle East, to the USSR, to Latin America. It was clear that presidents also wished to establish a number of fundamental national security policy frameworks and strategies on which to build those country- or region-specific efforts. National security directives were used in order to accomplish both sets of objectives simultaneously.

Reagan's use of NSDs for altering national security policy extended beyond the policies and operational strategies to the structure and operation of national security decisionmaking. The fact that the administration did not get those pieces into place quickly brought not only internal difficulties but also public embarrassments, as questions such as the lack of clarity in decisionmaking for crisis management were debated in the media.

Contingency Planning and Crisis Management

Indeed, the management of crises and the planning for contingencies have prompted most presidents to issue NSDs. The broader contingency directives include orders such as Reagan's NSDD 3, which put the vice president in charge of a crisis management group to deal with potential nuclear confrontations along with a wide range of situations. It is now fairly common to issue orders to establish contingency operations.[149]

Quite apart from the broad idea of structuring the administration for contingencies, most presidents have faced particular crises. The horror of nuclear war, the fear of accidental detonation, and the possibility of nuclear attack by terrorists have meant that presidents have issued NSDs that seek to plan for a wide range of contingencies and to manage those that develop. Such actions as President Kennedy's NSAM 255, setting forth the use and operational control of the HOTLINE direct communications link between Washington and Moscow, following the Cuban Missile crisis, marked one of many contingency planning efforts, the need for which was learned the hard way. Yet the purpose of contingency planning is to anticipate possible actions. Many contingency NSDs address situations either looming in the near future or seek to anticipate longer-term challenges. Thus, the Kennedy administration issued NSDs aimed at preparing for action as the Berlin crisis evolved.[150] Johnson found the NSD a convenient way to acquire current thinking from outside the NSC on how to deal with a looming food crisis in India.[151] Once crises are realities, presidents sometimes find NSDs a relatively convenient device with which to address problems that flow from the situation.[152]

Managing Political Damage Control Efforts

Sometimes the need to deal with difficult situations is, in truth, a pressure to respond to problems created by the administration itself, as in the NSDs issued by Eisenhower after the U.S.–supported coup in Iran and by Kennedy after the failed Bay of Pigs operation. Similarly, the Reagan administration found itself attempting to push a large amount of money to support its strategic modernization policies and other military spending through an inadequate federal contracting operation. It should have come as no surprise when news reports began to surface of outrageous expenses, such as $659 ashtrays[153] and $7,622 coffee pots[154] in defense contracts. This Pentagon spending debate was even more controversial because Attorney General Edwin Meese had taken the position in summer 1985 that the administration could not constitutionally be bound by defense spending limits enacted by Congress in 1984. He backed down from that position when his action was met with a storm of protest.[155] Two weeks after that the White House issued the unclassified NSDD 175, establishing the Blue Ribbon Commission on Defense Spending, better known as the Packard Commission, to recommend management improvements. Following initial reports from the commission, the president issued NSDD 219 in early 1986, attempting to head off further congressional spending restraints.[156] The creation in 1982 of the Scowcroft Commission by NSD was an effort to convince Congress to allow progress on MX missile development and deployment.

Presidents can also be tempted to use NSDs for damage control for another reason. The Clinton White House, Reagan, and other administrations have used what are termed "fact sheets" or press releases to announce action taken by the president in the form of an NSD while keeping the directive itself classified. This practice permits the administration to assert that it has taken corrective action or launched an initiative, to put its preferred spin on the story, and still not reveal the actual details of the president's action. By the time the directive itself is declassified, years will have passed and little attention is likely to be paid to whether the real executive action matched the spin.

To Control Leaks and Information Releases that Might Be Used by Political Opponents

Presidents have long been tempted to use NSDs to try to head off public embarrassments by plugging leaks in the executive branch. References to Johnson's frustrations with leaks and resulting news stories on Vietnam provide some of the better-known examples, but virtually every modern administration has been frustrated by this practice. And when Reagan took office, the White House announced that, while it was certainly appropriate for the media to seek information, the new administration would do what it thought necessary to keep sensitive information secret. The president issued a string of NSDs intended to advance that purpose, some of which turned out to be among the most controversial actions of his administration, beginning with NSDD 19. The administration made the claim of constitutional authority, asserting, "The Constitution of the United States provides for the protection of individual rights and liberties, including freedom of speech and freedom of the press, but it also requires that government functions be discharged efficiently and effectively, especially where the national security is involved."

The attempt here was to put the administration's efforts to block information on the same footing as First Amendment freedoms of expression. This was very troubling, especially when it became clear just how far the administration was prepared to take that effort. The directive began by requiring advance approval by senior officials whenever materials concerned with subject matter that might touch on classified matters were discussed at all with the media. The core issue was that the administration had made clear its intention to reverse the previous approach to classification and dramatically to expand the scope and type of material that could and would be classified. The NSD then called for limiting the number of officials to the absolute minimum and warned even those that "the government's lack of success in identifying the sources of unauthorized disclosures of classified National Security Council information and documents of classified intelligence information must be remedied and appropriate disciplinary measures taken. Henceforth, in the event of unauthorized disclosure of such information, government employees who have had access to that information will be subject to investigation, to include the use of all legal methods."

If there had been any doubt as to just how far the administration was willing to go in its efforts, it was eliminated a year later when an increasingly frustrated White House issued NSDD 84.[157] The directive pressed agencies with people who had access to sensitive information to sign nondisclosure agreements and called upon agencies to generate rules governing media contacts as well as processes for investigating alleged leaks. It also called for FBI investigation, "even though administrative sanctions might be sought instead of criminal prosecution."[158] It also required the Office of Personnel Management, and any agencies with employees who had access to classified information, to generate policies that would provide for polygraph testing to be used in investigations of unauthorized disclosures and required that those policies must "at a minimum" provide that a refusal to cooperate in a polygraph result in adverse personnel actions. This directive could potentially have required large numbers of civil servants to sign contracts agreeing to prepublication review of anything they might write, even after their departure from office.[159] A number of leading Reagan administration officials refused to comply, Congress erupted with a storm of criticism, and the administration narrowed the applicability of the requirements to the CIA.[160] Almost a year after NSDD 84 was issued, the White House backed off, placing a moratorium on the nondisclosure agreements and polygraph portions of the directive.

However, the administration became more frustrated as criticism of it mounted. In fall 1985, two new directives, NSDD 196, Counterintelligence/Countermeasure Implementation Task Force,[161] and NSDD 197, Reporting Hostile Contacts and Security Awareness,[162] were issued. The counterintelligence directive once again imposed a polygraph requirement, which produced renewed reaction. The Hostile Contacts directive was even more expansive in some respects than NSDD 84. After dealing with the traditional agencies that handled highly classified material, NSDD 197 stipulated that they "are by no means the only agencies which are vulnerable to the loss of information or technology which may be critical to the ability of the United States to protect itself." It then required that "each department or agency of the US Government shall develop procedures which will" create programs to monitor and report employee contacts with foreign nationals or organizations. Though the language of the order indicated that the programs should fit the kind of work the employee did, it also included not merely employees with access to classified information but also added those who handled "sensitive information or technology" material, with neither of those terms defined. The section on reporting began by speaking of contacts with particular countries that appeared designed to get covered officials to reveal information but also included contacts by persons from any country designated by any agency. And it included not merely targeted contacts but also any circumstance in which there was "indicate[d] the possibility of continued professional or personal contacts."[163] It was even applied by organizations like the Department of Housing and Urban Development (HUD), despite the difficulty of understanding how any employee there could be coerced by a foreign agent into disclosing the secrets of HUD successes.[164]

Response to New or Evolving Threats

Though it is always possible and sometimes even tempting to push the envelope to the point where NSDs create political backlash, it remains true that new, different, and serious national security challenges are always developing. The national security directive is a vehicle that can begin to evaluate such threats and to organize responses to them. Contemporary presidents, for example, have experienced a developing need to shape space policy in a competitive international context, to face complex and sensitive border issues, to battle terrorism, and to address the many problems raised by changing technology and the security issues presented by its dissemination around the world.

Over time, as in the case of space policy, a rich body of NSDs may grow across several administrations.

A relatively recent example is the debate over NSDs concerning the control over and sale of leading-edge computers and telecommunications technology. The controversy can be traced to NSDD 145, on telecommunications and computer security, issued by President Reagan in fall 1984.[165] This directive sought (1) to provide a broad-based effort to create decisionmaking and coordinating mechanisms for oversight and advice; (2) to establish a broad concept of security for government information systems; (3) to designate a range of federal officials and assign them responsibilities for a variety of aspects of security for computer and telecommunications systems; (4) to provide a role for government in the industry's standard setting for critical systems design; and (5) to include all of these elements in the federal government's interactions with private-sector contractors. Several aspects raised concerns, but two were particularly controversial. First, expanding on an evolving practice in the Reagan years, the directive included not merely classified material but also "systems handling other sensitive, but unclassified, government or government-derived information, the loss of which could adversely affect the national security interest."[166] The other issue arose from concerns within the private sector that government would be intervening in the development and sale of technology in the United States and abroad. To these concerns were added others generated by NSDD 189 based on fears that university researchers were publishing information or disseminating it at international conferences in ways that would be used by other countries to advance their military capability.[167] This NSDD encouraged agencies through grants and contracts to examine the work to determine whether it should be classified and the researchers constrained in their ability to publicize it.

By the time the Clinton administration arrived on the scene, the technology, particularly computer technology, was much more sophisticated, more affordable, and therefore much more widely distributed. While the Clinton administration argued, on the one hand, for wide distribution and use of computers and the Internet, there was a growing concern about the use of this technology by terrorists and organized criminals. In particular, these concerns had to do with the increasingly effective encryption technology that permitted the senders of messages to communicate globally, instantly, and inexpensively in ways that could not be accessed by law enforcement or national security officials.

Not long after taking office, in April 1993 Clinton issued PDD 5, Public Encryption Management, calling for the installation of a technology known as the "clipper chip" in communications equipment. This device would have what were referred to as "key-escrow circuits" that could be used to decode encrypted messages. The two keys would be kept in separate data bases and could be accessed by law enforcement officials if they obtained a court order and provided it to the two agencies holding the software keys.[168] Clinton also issued presidential review directives in 1993 and 1994, seeking studies of the types of encryption technology and products available along with an assessment of the state of the market for them.[169] Over the next four years, Clinton used a combination of NSDs, memoranda, and executive orders to develop his administration's efforts to control exports of encryption technology and to provide support for law enforcement authorities. Throughout this time, he was challenged by the industry and by civil liberties groups worried that too much focus was being placed on balancing the economics of software and hardware sales with law enforcement concerns and that not enough attention was being given to the civil liberties aspects.

While the Clinton White House was engaged in that discussion, the administration was also addressing a related but different concern. There was increasing evidence that computer hackers had compromised government computer systems, government contractors' systems, and also large private-sector systems. All of this emerged as government was increasingly relying on Internet-based operations, contributing to a phenomenon now popularly known as e-government. Some of the invasions of systems were relatively harmless, if frustrating, but it was becoming increasingly apparent that hackers were creating a range of new national security threats. Beyond the individual hacker episodes, it was also becoming increasingly clear that the United States, along with the rest of the world, was entering an era of cyberterrorism and even cyberwarfare. The Clinton administration issued a series of NSDs in an effort to address these threats. In May 1998 Clinton released fact sheets describing PDD 62 and PDD 63. The first of these established the Office of the National Coordinator for Security, Infrastructure Protection, and Counter-Terrorism within the NSC to "oversee the broad variety of relevant policies and programs, including such areas as counter-terrorism, protection of critical infrastructure, preparedness and consequence management for weapons of mass destruction." Responding to recommendations provided by the President's Commission on Critical Infrastructure Protection, Clinton created the National Infrastructure Protection Center, the Information Sharing and

Analysis Center, a National Infrastructure Assurance Council, and a Critical Infrastructure Assurance Office. This directive "sets a goal of a reliable, interconnected, and secure information system infrastructure by the year 2003, and significantly increased security to government systems by the year 2000, by [among other things] immediately establishing a national center to warn of and respond to attacks [and] ensuring the capability to protect critical infrastructures from intentional acts by 2003." The directive also sought to establish a working relationship among the federal government, state and local governments, and the private sector.

WHAT ARE THEIR POTENTIAL STRENGTHS AND LIABILITIES?

For a new administration, the advantages of national security directives as policy tools often become quickly apparent. At the same time, the experiences of various presidents, as we have seen, indicate a number of potential dangers in their use.

A Variety of Attractive Features

On the positive side, NSDs have virtually all the benefits of presidential memoranda. Beyond that, they are generally classified, though a president may choose to publicize some directives in their entirety or generate fact sheets outlining some of their features. Most of the time, though, even the existence of NSDs is safeguarded, let alone their contents. And even when contents are declassified in later years, significant portions may remain under wraps.

In addition to these controls, participation in the development and implementation of NSDs can be limited to relatively small groups of people. Indeed, the ability of the White House to custom design its National Security Council, to modify the office and duties of national security adviser and the practice of convening small groups for special projects or advice provide extremely attractive opportunities to presidents concerned about losing control to large organizations like the State or Defense Departments or to other cabinet offices.

Even presidents like Kennedy and Johnson found NSDs useful tools to coordinate work across a wide range of issues that arose around the world. There are ongoing problems and, at the same time, unique crises to be addressed. The use of NSDs helps to manage multiple and diverse national security issues.

Although they do provide structure, NSDs are not constraining. They are extremely flexible instruments, partly because they are hidden from public view. That is one of the reasons that they can be so useful in addressing new national security–related threats.

The Risks of an Attractive Tool

Nevertheless, some of the very features that make NSDs attractive also present some of their most serious dangers. First, there is the new person on the job trap given the tendency for new administrations to plunge into important and potentially dangerous courses of action using NSDs in their first days in office. Indeed, several did so even before they had fully organized their NSC operations. Certainly that was true of Eisenhower and the decisions to move forward on the Guatemala and Iran operations. Kennedy fell into the same trap with the Bay of Pigs.[170]

The Bay of Pigs case provides an example of another problem: the danger of group think in a small, closed environment. Arthur Schlesinger, who was at that time a special assistant to the president, with particular responsibilities for Latin American issues, made the point cogently with respect to the Bay of Pigs decision:

> One's impulse to blow the whistle on this nonsense was simply undone by the circumstances of the discussion. . . . It is one thing for a special assistant to talk frankly in private to a president at his request, and another for a college professor, fresh to the government, to interpose his unassisted judgment in open meeting against that of such august figures as the Secretaries of State and Defense and the Joint Chiefs of Staff, each speaking with the full weight of his institution behind him. The members of the White House staff who sat in the Cabinet Room failed in their job of protecting the President.[171]

In addition to the question whether potential warning voices will be stilled because of the group dynamics in the NSC, there is another element in operation. That is, group think involving a small but dedicated set of players can lead to a mentality that holds that the end justifies the means. That was certainly part of the findings of virtually all the investigations of the Iran-Contra affair. The issue is not simply the particular actions that may be taken in any given case but also that such a mentality can shape a range of important policy determinations over time, as was true with a series of NSDs during the Reagan years on Latin America.

One of the results of these kinds of problems is the danger that there is an increased tendency toward covert action. The record shows that even supposedly successful covert actions can create more problems than they solve and can have long-standing consequences, as was true (even according to the

CIA's own assessment) in the Guatemalan and Iranian operations. Then there have often been, as in the cases of the U.S. covert actions in Guatemala, El Salvador, and Chile, dramatic violations of human rights that grew from the operations as well.

Though national security directives were not the only instruments involved in such operations, it is clear that their development and issuance play important roles in covert operations. They were also important parts of operations that may have begun through largely covert operations, such as Vietnam, but became full-blown military actions. Certainly, a reading of President Johnson's NSDs on Vietnam, even before the Gulf of Tonkin, gives an ominous sense of the dangers ahead.

The fact of the secrecy of NSDs in covert settings produces another problem, interestingly, one identified in a study done for the CIA on Operation PB Success in Guatemala. The awareness of covert actions that comes to light over time provides support for rumors that many more situations are the result of such actions. The need to maintain security prevents efforts to dispel misimpressions, and that unwillingness to address the situation directly only seems to confirm whatever rumors may exist.[172] The more the rumors feed on one another, the more they damage U.S. credibility around the world. Related to this is the tendency in many parts of the world to make assumptions about the involvement of various agencies of the U.S. government, as in the case of the Agency for International Development or the United States Information Agency (USIA), either directly in covert operations or as covers for covert action. Later, when information came to light from NSDs that these agencies were indeed involved to some extent in covert operations,[173] it confirmed the worst suspicions and has undermined the credibility of these agencies for years to come. The irony is that some of the information about these activities came initially not from early declassification of NSDs but often from the writings of people who were involved in the operations. This also raises a number of other issues that are beyond the scope of this study associated with the problems of the use, abuse, and limitations of security classifications.[174]

To identify these concerns is not to suggest that there are never circumstances in which some kinds of covert actions, or as more recent administrations have termed them, "low-intensity conflicts," are necessary. It is to suggest that the way that decisions are taken about them is important, as are the instruments used to craft the operations and execute them, including NSDs.

One of the sets of concerns presented by the use of NSDs to structure and operate national security policy is that they must be managed. Sometimes presidents take the trouble to modify or rescind prior NSDs, as in the case of Johnson's NSAM 323 on the Panama Canal, but in other cases they do not. The failure to attend carefully to the existing body of NSDs can create a number of unknowns for new administrations. Thus such careful attention is only one of the many dimensions of ensuring thorough and consistent administration of NSC operations and presidential decisionmaking.

Unfortunately, the evidence is that a number of administrations, particularly in their early years, have not paid attention to these issues; and some, as in the case of Kennedy and Johnson, deliberately sought to avoid careful structure and management of them in favor of informal and ad hoc arrangements. Whether the situation in a particular administration is one in which the end justifies the means or one in which a regularized process and reasonable levels of organization and management are simply rejected, serious problems can result. Indeed, the Tower Commission concluded that much of what took place in connection with Iran-Contra provided prime examples of what can happen when the concern for process and management is ignored or circumvented. According to the Tower Report,

> The arms transfer to Iran and the activities of the NSC staff in support of the Contras are case studies in the perils of policy pursued outside the constraints of orderly process
>
> The Iran initiative ran directly counter to the Administration's own policies on terrorism, the Iran/Iraq war, and military support to Iran. This inconsistency was never resolved, nor were the consequences of this inconsistency fully considered and provided for. The result taken as a whole was a U.S. policy that worked against itself.
>
> The Board believes that failure to deal adequately with these contradictions resulted in large part from the flaws in the manner in which decisions were made. Established procedures for making national security decisions were ignored. Reviews of the initiative by all the NSC principals were too infrequent. The initiatives were not adequately vetted below the Cabinet level. Intelligence resources were underutilized. Applicable legal constraints were not adequately addressed. The whole matter was handled too informally, without adequate written records of what had been considered, discussed, and decided.
>
> This pattern persisted in the implementation of the Iran initiative. The NSC staff assumed direct operational control. The initiative fell within the traditional jurisdictions of the Departments of State, Defense, and CIA. Yet these agencies were largely ignored. Great reliance was placed on a network of private operators and intermediaries. How the initiative was to be

carried out never received adequate attention from the NSC principals or a tough working-level review. No periodic evaluation of the progress of the initiative was ever conducted. The result was an unprofessional and, in substantial part, unsatisfactory operation.

In all of this process, Congress was never notified.[175]

This last point, that Congress has so often not been notified of NSC actions, and particularly of NSDs, is one of the serious problems inherent in their use. The discussion to this point has indicated a number of instances in which tensions between the White House and the Hill have been created or exacerbated because of an unwillingness to provide national security directives to the Congress, even in carefully controlled conditions. These tensions have increased as both Republican and Democratically controlled Congresses have been frustrated by failed attempts to get the White House even to acknowledge the existence of NSDs, much less to provide copies of them. Moreover, a number of officials have refused to testify at all before congressional committees concerning the use of such directives. While the frustrations of members of the legislature have increased in more recent times, they had expressed these concerns well before the Reagan administration came on the scene.[176]

Even so, the number and scope of NSDs issued by the Reagan White House led to a particularly revealing battle that took place in 1987 and 1988. In 1987, during hearings on NSDD 145, on technology transfers and telecommunication, Congressman Anthony Beilenson, who was at that time the chair of the Oversight Subcommittee of the Intelligence Committee, expressed his concern that his committee was unable to obtain or review NSDs. Congressman Jack Brooks, working with Speaker Jim Wright, launched an effort to obtain more information about NSDs and how they were managed in the White House. In a series of letters, Brooks and Wright pressed then National Security Assistant Frank Carlucci to provide a list of NSDs to Congress.[177] Carlucci responded with a list of twenty-five NSDs that had been declassified, twelve that had been partially declassified, and twenty-one others about which fact sheets or press releases had been provided. The full list was never delivered. When Brooks held hearings a year after the request on legislation he sponsored to address disclosure of NSDs, then National Security Adviser Colin Powell refused even to testify.[178] Congressman Lee Hamilton, chair of the Iran-Contra Committee, testified at the 1988 hearing regarding his frustration over the use of NSDs:

> I think all of us have had the experience of listening to testimony by executive branch officials who are articulating policy of the Federal Government, and have had those officials refer to an NSDD as the basis of that policy.

We don't know what that NSDD is and we cannot evaluate the official's comments without reference to it, but it is not available to us. . . .

The use of secret NSDDs to create policy infringes on Congress' constitutional prerogatives by inhibiting effective oversight and limiting Congress' policymaking role. NSDDs are revealed to Congress only under irregular, arbitrary, or even accidental, circumstances, if at all. Even the Intelligence Committees do not usually receive copies of NSDDs.[179]

It was against this background that Congressman Brooks expressed the concern of members of the legislature. "The usurpation of congressional power through the secret issuance of NSDDs undermines democracy, leaving Congress and the Nation in the dark as to just how our Government is being run. The mobilization of resources and formulation of policy affected through these directives without congressional oversight amounts to nothing more than the imposition of secret law. As such, I believe the unchecked use of NSDDs poses a serious threat to our Republic."[180] These concerns continued into the Bush administration, and the House Government Operations Committee continued to consider a revised version of the presidential directives legislation proposed by Brooks. However, then came Operation Desert Shield, followed by Desert Storm, and attention was turned to support for the troops in the field. Interestingly, as we now know, Operation Desert Storm was launched by an NSD.

However, one of the specific concerns expressed by legislators was that NSDs were also increasingly being developed that had significant domestic impact. The General Accounting Office undertook a study of NSDs, reported at the 1988 hearings. The study reviewed 247 NSDs (or their equivalents) from the Kennedy to the Reagan administrations that had been disclosed by one means or another. It found that 116 of the 247 set forth policy, ordered policy implementation, or committed resources. Of that 116, 70 percent established policy, 59 percent carried out policy, and 19 percent committed resources. (The fact that some orders did more than one explains the total in excess of 100 percent.) Moreover, the GAO evaluation found that 41 percent of those substantive directives dealt primarily with military policy, 63 percent with foreign policy, and 22 percent with domestic policy. Of the total 116 substantive directives, the GAO examined directives issued during the Reagan years and found that there were as many Reagan orders that had domestic impact as there were with military impact and more than that number with a foreign policy impact.[181] The fact that an NSD has a title or language that is framed in terms of a national security threat or as counterintelligence does not mean that it is without potentially broad domestic impact. That was certainly a problem that emerged with respect to NSDD 84 and later directives based on it. Orders that began with officials in national security agencies handling clearly classified materials ended up being applied to all agencies of the federal government that handled sensitive material, with that term left wide open. And then these broad directives were backed by threats of preclearance requirements for any kind of discussion of one's experience even after leaving office and by the use of polygraphs. It was the breadth and unnecessary application of these mechanisms to control people that led even a few staunch Reagan political appointees to object to the NSDs and in some cases even to refuse to obey them.

Similar concerns have been expressed with respect to Reagan's NSDD 189, seeking to constrain the sharing of scientific research. The concerns about the domestic effects of NSDs have been compounded because administrations use a combination of executive orders and NSDs in various ways that raise questions about the nature and scope of administrative action. An example is the Reagan administration's NSDD issued in 1986 on narcotics and national security, which defined narcotics trafficking as a national security threat and invoked Executive Order 12333, which in turn was used to prompt action by military and intelligence organizations in support of the war on drugs.[182] The controversial NSDD 84 that operated in concert with E.O. 12356 on security classification is another case in point. During the Clinton years, the evolution of infrastructure protection, particularly the NSDs, executive orders, and memoranda concerned with encryption and antihacker efforts, provides a more recent example.

The point is not that the policy goals that these administrations sought to pursue were inappropriate in themselves but that the use of tools designed primarily to address foreign policy, military affairs, and intelligence operations on the domestic side sends up warning signals for possible abuses of power and threats to civil liberties. The reality that such policies are based in significant part at least on classified NSDs only exacerbates those fears.

CONCLUSION

At the end of the day, the perception of Congress, the American people, our allies, and nonaligned countries is that the United States has moved toward policymaking by NSD to avoid transparency and democratic accountability, however worthy the policy goals might be, and that road is a dangerous and destructive one to travel. Christopher Simpson summarized the point well when he wrote that presidents, working through their national security staffs, have too often "operated far outside the usual checks and balances of the U.S. federal system."[183]

The issue is not whether to use national security directives. Neither is it a question of whether they are good or bad in themselves. Rather, the issue is how they are employed and when they are used. In a constitutional republic that purports to operate under the rule of law, it must always be remembered that ends and means are intimately interrelated. How something is done can often be as important as what is done. Indeed, the choice of means today places boundaries around the options available to chief executives in the future. This is not to make process more important than purpose. In an era when one is tempted to paraphrase a well-known corporate advertising slogan and lament the fact that in our contemporary world process is our most important product, it is easy to dismiss means. That is particularly true for several recent generations raised on the motto, "if it feels good, do it." But the presidency is not a shoe company, and the chief executive cannot "just do it."

Given the importance of NSDs (or whatever they may be called by the sitting administration), it also would appear to be important to provide a vehicle to ensure that Congress, through its intelligence committees, could at least be informed of the existence of the directives and that mechanisms be created for the exchange of information in ways consistent with other existing intelligence, military affairs, or foreign policy arrangements. It is also essential that there be a good fit between the use of this tool of presidential action and the essential values of the political system they are supposed to be intended to serve.

SEVEN

PRESIDENTIAL SIGNING STATEMENTS:
A DIFFERENT KIND OF LINE ITEM VETO

Secretary of Energy Bill Richardson sat before the Senate Armed Services Committee on June 21, 2000, to answer for the dramatic security lapses that had been discovered at Los Alamos National Laboratories. To be sure, the secretary expected to be raked over the coals by Senate Republicans, led by John Warner (R-Va.). What he may not have anticipated was that the elder statesman of the Senate and former majority leader Robert Byrd (D-W.Va.), would almost take him apart. Byrd's assault was not aimed at the details of the security problem but at what he called the "supreme arrogance" exhibited by Richardson and others in the executive branch in their attitude toward the Congress.

> I think you've been very contemptible of the Congress in which you served. . . . You know the Congress and you also should know the Constitution. . . . I think there is a mind-set in the Department, perhaps in you, that the Congress is to be treated like a lap dog; that those people up there don't know anything about what they're doing. We don't have to listen to them. We will appear before the committees when we decide that we want to go and there's not much that they can do about it. Well there is. I have been in this Congress a long time, forty-eight years, and I have voted upon several occasions for resolutions providing for contempt of Congress and I wouldn't have any hesitancy about voting for such a resolution concerning you. . . .
>
> You've shown a contempt of Congress that borders on a supreme arrogance of this institution. Let me tell you there are still people up here who work hard. There are still people up here who believe in the Constitution of the United States. There are people up here who believe in this Congress. . . . You have shown a supreme, a supreme contempt of the committees of this Congress. When you decided that you would go . . . before the Intelligence Committee when you were ready—you weren't ready yet—that was a supreme act of callous arrogance, and I resent it. . . . There should have been a subpoena of you. . . . It is not for you to decide when to appear. . . .
>
> This Congress and the heads of departments of this government ought to work together. We ought to have confidence in one another and what we have to say. And the fact [is] that you have really thrown away a treasure, that treasure being the confidence of the Congress. Some of the members of Congress, at least, don't have any faith in what you have to say. . . . I'm

sorry that you've lost that credibility at least with me. . . . I think it's a rather sad story because you have had a bright and brilliant career, but you would never, never again receive the support of the Senate of the United States for any office to which you might be appointed. It's gone. You've squandered your treasure and I'm sorry.

Senator Joseph Lieberman (D-Conn.), soon to be his party's nominee for vice president, pressed Byrd's critique. "We've got a crisis here and it is driven not by ideology or party. . . . In recent years, as one crisis after another has occurred, there's certainly a sense that we haven't been working on the same team. . . . As Senator Byrd just spoke so powerfully, there's been a concern that the Department and the Secretary have been battling with Congress about one or another of the remedies that have been proposed and, when they've been proposed, has not carried them out. I just want to say that has to stop and that has stopped this morning." Senator James Inhofe (R-Okla.) followed Lieberman and observed that when the members spoke of the captain of the ship being responsible, "It's the wrong guy that we're talking about here. . . . I suggest that the captain of the ship is not Bill Richardson but is Bill Clinton."

There was no doubt that Republicans enjoyed the opportunity to turn public attention to the failures of a Democratic administration, particularly in an area in which they had repeatedly warned and challenged the White House over the years, and in the midst of a presidential election year. However, as Democrats and Republicans made clear, there was more at issue than the partisan conflict that had come to typify Washington. There was real frustration by legislators of both parties with the sense that the White House had decided to do whatever it pleased, even if that meant repudiating the provisions of legislation that the president had signed. This particular confrontation can be traced back to a statement issued by the president in October 1999 when he signed the Defense Authorization Act for Fiscal Year 2000. His statement, to all intents and purposes, told the Congress that Clinton did not intend that his administration would implement the law as the Congress had written it. In general terms, the message was that the administration would do as it saw fit with respect to the creation and staffing of the National Nuclear Security Administration (NNSA), a semiautonomous agency within the Department of Energy mandated by the legislation and charged with oversight of security issues.

The use of a presidential signing statement in an effort to nullify or at a minimum to express a president's interpretation of a statute was not a practice invented by Bill Clinton. As has often been true of the tools of presidential direct administration, he had learned this from his predecessors, particularly from Ronald Reagan. It was the Reagan administration that had taken what had been a relatively benign and largely ceremonial practice of issuing a statement on signing of legislation and worked to make it a systematic and effective weapon to trump congressional action and to influence not only the implementation of law but also its legal interpretation.

The presidential signing statement as a presidential power tool is, at least in its contemporary manifestation, relatively new and still evolving. Therefore, the limited assessment here of its use will focus on the Reagan, Bush, and Clinton administrations.

WHAT ARE THEY?

Presidential signing statements (PSSs) are announcements made by the president, usually prepared by the Justice Department, that go beyond merely lauding passage of a statute to identify provisions of the legislation with which the president has concerns. They also provide the president's interpretation of the language of the law, announce constitutional limits on the implementation of some of its provisions, or indicate directions to executive branch officials as to how to administer the new law in an acceptable manner. So constituted, the signing statement has been used as a tool of presidential direct action since the Reagan administration.

Attorney General Edwin Meese III is the person generally credited with developing the signing statement into its current incarnation and establishing it firmly as a mechanism of presidential power. The Reagan administration, however, certainly was not the first to use this tool to object to legislation or to announce a concern with an interpretation of a particular provision.[1] In a Department of Justice (DOJ), Office of Legal Counsel memoranda prepared for White House Counsel, The Legal Significance of Presidential Signing Statements, Assistant Attorney General Walter Dellinger described some sixteen cases in thirteen different presidential administrations in which signing statements indicated concerns with portions of the legislation before the president for signature.[2] It was also true that the Carter administration began to look more carefully at possible expanded uses for the signing statement and its relationship to decisions not to enforce some portions of statutes considered by the president to be unconstitutional or to defend them in court if attacked.[3] Still, it was when Attorney General Meese moved from the White House to the DOJ that the signing statement was transformed into what it has become.

When the Reagan administration came to office, its leaders intended nothing less than a revolution in government and in the nation, from fundamental values to public policy to institutional operations. As they saw it, they were in for a battle. Meese, then one of Reagan's well-known troika, recalled, "We were up against the 'establishment'—a Congress whose senior members ranged from skeptical to overtly hostile, the media who considered the President's ideas strange, if not bizarre, and a vast array of groups who had a stake in keeping things the way they were."[4] He made that observation even though Republicans had control of the Senate at the time.

Part of the reason for that assessment was that the Reagan White House intended to challenge long-standing operating assumptions, and that meant legal challenges in addition to political battles. While some of those challenges would be focused on particular policies, others were more fundamental. For example, Meese argued, "Another major threat to constitutional government which the Reagan administration faced was the legislative opportunism that arose out of the Watergate controversy during the early 1970s. Congress had used this episode to expand its power in various ways vis-à-vis the executive branch."[5] The administration's frustration with Congress only grew after Republicans lost control of the Senate. The administration also concluded that the other principal problem as to the constitutional powers of the executive was the judiciary. "The conclusion that the President drew was obvious enough: if the problem we confronted had come about because of judges, then something had to be done about the judges."[6]

To be sure, the White House set about addressing the latter issue by a deliberate and careful screening of appointees for federal judgeships who would support the administration's ideas about the proper role of the judiciary in relation to the president and in its interpretations of the Constitution. However, the presidential signing statement promised to be a useful device for more specific battles and a way in which to play a more active and continuing role in judicial interpretation of statutes. The administration would establish a systematic process of preparing signing statements designed to defend executive branch authority. In addition to making the administration's views clear on the particular policies at issue, this process would provide directives to executive branch officials governing the implementation of new legislation to support those interpretations. It would present the president's views as a legitimate and authoritative part of the legislative history of new statutes. To accomplish the latter goal, the administration had to find a way to ensure regular presentation of the signing statements along with legislative history materials. Meese accomplished this in 1986 through an agreement with the West Publishing Company to include the statements in the *U.S. Code Congressional and Administrative News* legislative histories. This, he said, "will improve statutory interpretation by making clear the president's understanding of legislation at the time he signs a bill. This will recognize the importance of these Presidential signing statements as legislative history."[7] Moreover, it would ensure that "they will be more accessible to both the Bench and the Bar."[8] Whatever it was before the Reagan years, the presidential signing statement came of age in the 1980s as a tool and perhaps even a weapon of presidential direct action.

HOW ARE THEY USED?

The effort to enshrine the signing statement as part of the legally recognized legislative history has drawn the most attention and indeed the most controversy, spawning a significant body of law review literature. However, that is only one of several uses to which presidential signing statements have been put in recent administrations.

The Signing Statement as a Type of Fiscal Line Item Veto

Some of the earliest signing statements concerned efforts to alter spending legislation, such as Andrew Jackson's modification in 1830 of an appropriation for roads.[9] Louis Fisher has explained that some modern debates over presidential impoundment of funds can be traced to such presidential statements.[10] In more contemporary times, some presidents have been very direct in using signing statements to respond to congressional attempts to control administrative action through spending mandates, conditions, or prohibitions. For example, the Energy and Water Development Appropriations Act of 1992 prohibited the president from expending funds from the act to undertake certain types of studies concerning pricing for hydroelectric power. However, President Bush rejected the constraint, asserting, "Article II, section 3, of the Constitution grants the President authority to recommend to the Congress any legislative measures considered 'necessary and expedient.' Accordingly, in keeping with the well-settled obligation to construe ambiguous statutory provisions to avoid constitutional questions, I will interpret section 506 so as not to infringe on the Executive's authority to conduct studies that might assist in the evaluation and preparation of such measures."[11]

That is not to say that every president who took such a position was prepared to state that the action was based on an inherent line item veto authority. Fisher points out that Bush was tempted to make such a claim but ultimately did not,[12] partly because the Office of Legal Counsel (OLC) under Charles Cooper had issued an opinion during the Reagan administration concluding that the line item veto was not constitutional.[13] Although his successor, William P. Barr, reexamined that argument, he too concluded that such a presidential claim would be difficult to defend.[14]

It has long been tempting for presidents to seek a full-blown line item veto power, but it was not until the Clinton administration that legislation authorizing such action went into effect. Presidents who, like Reagan, had served as governors before coming to Washington particularly missed the kind of power they had possessed in the statehouse. However, even the limited line item veto authority eventually delegated to the president was ultimately short-lived, with the Supreme Court striking it down soon after the first significant uses of the power.[15]

Even so, presidents have used other provisions of law to support what is in effect a species of item veto, just as Bush did in the Energy and Water Development Act case. In this instance, Bush relied on the president's Article 2, section 3 authority to recommend legislation deemed "necessary and expedient." To develop recommendations that would fit that standard, Bush claimed, it would be necessary to do studies. He therefore asserted that he would expend funds for the study if he considered it necessary.

The Substantive Line Item Veto Statement

Presidents have gone well beyond line item vetoes of appropriations to substantive vetoes. These are cases in which chief executives have specifically rejected provisions of statutes even as they signed the legislation. These actions are usually based on broad-based claims to constitutional authority. The nondisclosure requirements that the Reagan administration imposed by national security directive created a wave of protest, not only from people within the executive branch but also from Congress. In signing legislation that included prohibitions on enforcement of those nondisclosure requirements, Reagan wrote:

> This provision raises profound constitutional concerns. Indeed, a provision in last year's omnibus continuing resolution (Public Law 100-202) identical to section 619 was recently declared unconstitutional by the United States District Court for the District of Columbia. The Court concluded that restrictions on the implementation or enforcement of nondisclosure agreements required of Government employees with access to

classified information impermissibly interfered with my ability to prevent unauthorized disclosures of our most sensitive diplomatic, military, and intelligence activities.

As President of the United States, I have the constitutional responsibility to ensure the secrecy of information whose disclosure would threaten our national security. Our Nation's security depends upon our success in diplomatic, military, and intelligence activities, and that success depends upon our ability to protect the Nation's secrets. The Supreme Court has recognized my authority in this area. In accordance with my sworn obligation to preserve, protect, and defend the Constitution, section 619 will be considered of no force or effect unless and until the ruling of the District Court is reversed by the Supreme Court.[16]

Reagan also nullified an amendment to the Central Intelligence Act that required reports prepared by the CIA Inspector General, including the recommendations to the head of the agency, be submitted to congressional intelligence committees. The president rejected that provision on grounds that it "would conflict with the constitutional protection accorded the integrity and confidentiality of the internal deliberations of the Executive branch."[17] Another such veto by Reagan declared a provision of the Veterans Benefits Bill of 1988 as unconstitutional on grounds that it required the budget request submitted by the Court of Veterans' Appeals to be incorporated into the White House budget proposal without presidential review. Reagan found that that provision interfered with his power to recommend legislation.[18]

In signing the Medical Waste Tracking Act, Reagan recognized that the statute permitted him to exempt, under special circumstances, a particular federal facility from the law, but he answered that there could be no legal enforcement by the EPA against another executive branch agency in any case. He asserted that such a suit would not be a legitimate "case or controversy" because both parties would be part of the executive branch.[19] What is interesting here is that the language the chief executive is purporting to interpret is, of course, not drawn from Article 2, describing the powers of the president, but from Article 3's definition of judicial powers. In another case, Reagan flatly pronounced that "one provision of the bill is unconstitutional." He concluded that the part of the bill that prevented the Federal Energy Regulatory Commission from approving operation of a hydroelectric plant without the approval of the local governing body was "unconstitutional because it authorizes officials who have not been selected in a manner consistent with the Appointments Clause . . . to perform significant authority pursuant to the laws of the United States."[20]

These were not mere warnings or calls for further negotiations with the legislature but determinations by the president that purported to be authoritative as to the validity of particular statutory provisions. Indeed, in the hydroelectric case, the president went on to rule that the offending section was severable from the other provisions of the statute, and he would treat it accordingly. This was quite a term of court, given that all these substantive vetoes were handed down in a two-month period.

As the Reagan examples indicate, these adjudications of invalidity are most often based on constitutional grounds. President Bush followed suit with a number of his statements. Bush signed a bill requiring affirmative action contracting for the Department of Energy in the building of the controversial Superconducting Super Collider in Texas. The Bush White House determined that there was no valid basis for an affirmative action program in this case, however, and concluded, "I therefore direct the Secretary . . . to administer the section in a constitutional manner." That is to say, he was to act without regard to the affirmative action requirement. At that time, the Supreme Court had already upheld the same kind of 10 percent federal contract set-aside program for minority business enterprises.[21] It had reaffirmed that decision just two years before the Bush signing statement.[22] Since then, the sharply divided Supreme Court has constrained such programs,[23] but that decision came four years after Bush's action and was not the law at the time of the president's signing statement. The bottom line was that the administration opposed affirmative action and made its own determination that the program was unconstitutional. The president underscored that position in signing the Civil Rights Act of 1991, in which he referred to what he termed "quotas or unfair preferences" and ordered that "incentives to engage in such illegal conduct" were to be banned.[24]

Fixing Outer Boundaries to Statutes

Often, when a president finds a provision of a bill to be unconstitutional, or even if the White House does not make quite so dramatic an assertion, it is common to announce an interpretation of the legislation that will put boundaries on the new law so that it does not create the constitutional conflict.[25] The responsible administrative officials are then directed to implement the new policy in that way. That is, of course, what Bush did in the affirmative action example.

The Office of Legal Counsel under the Reagan, Bush, and Clinton administrations argued that the president has the power to refuse to enforce a statute if he or she determines that the statute violates the Constitution.[26] Ironically, the constitutional basis for that assertion is the Article 2, section 3 requirement that the president "shall take Care that the Laws be faithfully executed." The logic runs as follows. The president has a duty to take care that the laws are faithfully executed. The Constitution is the supreme law of the land. Therefore, the president is duty-bound not to enforce a statute that violates the Constitution. Thus, when Congress enacted legislation designed to require President Bush to include members of a legislatively controlled group in U.S. negotiating delegations, the administration responded: "In our view, that was a clearly unconstitutional encroachment on the President's appointment authority as well as on his authority to administer the foreign relations of the United States. . . . We said that the President could sign the bill and at the same time announce that the provision would not be enforced. In fact, that is what was done, and no legislative members were appointed."[27]

Moreover, presidents take the position that the White House could save a constitutionally defective statute by interpreting it in such a way as to avoid the constitutional conflict and may instruct administrative officials to pursue that course. Another action by the Bush White House demonstrates the practice. The Congress reacted strongly when the Supreme Court in 1988 and 1989 issued a series of interpretations of Title VII of the Civil Rights Act of 1964 that significantly weakened its effectiveness. The White House negotiated with the Congress on amendments but ultimately vetoed what would have been the Civil Rights Act of 1990. The negotiations resumed, resulting in the passage of the Civil Rights Act of 1991. In signing the bill into law, Bush expressed his concern that the use of the "disparate impact" standard for determining the presence of discrimination might be unfairly applied to businesses. The White House move (1) established the administration's reading for the legislative history, (2) sought to influence future judicial interpretations, (3) set boundaries on the meaning of the relevant sections of the statute, and (4) controlled implementation. The signing statement recognized as authoritative the analysis prepared during the legislative process by Senator Robert Dole (R-Kans.) and the Bush administration. The president then announced, "These documents will be treated as authoritative interpretive guidance by all officials in the executive branch with respect to the law of disparate impact as well as the other matters covered in the document."[28]

This was not a new tactic. Reagan had used the same approach on a number of occasions before Bush and his successor applied the technique as well. Thus, Reagan announced that he was signing a statute that authorized the

Administrator of the General Services Administration to "assign to a State the authority of the United States to 'administer criminal laws and health and safety laws with respect to lands or interests in lands under the control of the Administrator' located in the State." The White House concluded that it would interpret that provision to apply only to state law because any wider interpretation would violate the president's appointment powers under Article 2, section 2, clause 2, since it would allow an official not appointed by the president to enforce federal law.[29]

President Clinton found himself in conflict with Congress over his handling of U.S. peacekeeping operations in Somalia. Among other things, Congress moved to prohibit the president from placing U.S. troops under commanders from other countries. Though Clinton signed the bill, he added, "I construe [this section] as not restricting my constitutional responsibility and authority as Commander in Chief, including my ability to place U.S. combat forces under the temporary tactical control of a foreign commander where to do otherwise would jeopardize the safety of U.S. combat forces in support of UNOSOM II. Such U.S. combat forces shall, however, remain under the operational command and control of U.S. commanders at all times."[30]

Clinton followed Bush in another technique commonly used in presidential signing statements: the practice of setting boundaries on legislation by interpreting provisions that were clearly intended to be mandatory as advisory only. Interestingly, Bush and Clinton used this same device on two versions of the same statute. In legislation on ocean fisheries, both the Bush administration, on original passage, and the Clinton White House, on reauthorization, warned that they were signing the legislation but with a clear boundary to be observed in implementation. That limit concerned when and whether the administration would undertake international negotiations. Later, the Federal District Court for the Middle District of Florida rejected a claim that the secretary of commerce was required by that law to negotiate with international organizations to address disputed issues. The court held that international negotiations are, under the Constitution, the province of the executive and agreed with contentions in the Bush and Clinton signing statements:

> In signing the bill . . . President George Bush stated: "Numerous provisions of the Act could be construed to encroach upon the President's authority under the Constitution to conduct foreign relations, including the unfettered conduct of negotiations with foreign nations. . . . To avoid constitutional questions that might otherwise arise, I will construe all these provisions to be advisory, not mandatory."

In signing the 1996 amendments to the Magnuson Act, President William J. Clinton reiterated that, "Under our Constitution, it is the President who articulates the Nation's foreign policy and who determines the timing and subject matter of our negotiations with foreign nations."[31]

Reagan, Bush, and Clinton have used this same approach in situations in which the executive branch was called upon to make recommendations to Congress for further legislation. The same was true when presidents were required in a bill to appoint officials to a body from lists submitted by the congressional leadership. Clinton argued in one such case, "The Constitution prohibits the Congress from sharing in the power to appoint officers of the United States other than through the Senate's confirmation role. As such, no statute may require an appointment to be made from a list submitted by a Member, committee, or other agency of the Congress. I therefore do not interpret [that section] as binding and direct the Secretary of Transportation to regard any lists submitted [to it] as advisory."[32]

Related to this advisory versus mandatory interpretation tactic is the practice of flatly pronouncing provisions unconstitutional, as in the case of legislative veto, but then transforming the provision into a notification and consultation requirement. Presidents at least as far back as Dwight Eisenhower issued signing statements criticizing Congress on such grounds,[33] as did the Kennedy, Johnson, Carter, and Reagan administrations.[34] Even former House minority leader Gerald Ford attacked a committee approval requirement in order to spend funds as he wished.[35] The Supreme Court ultimately struck down legislative vetoes in *Immigration and Naturalization Service v. Chadha*.[36] The *Chadha* ruling, along with two other opinions decided by the U.S. Circuit Court of Appeals for the D.C. Circuit[37] and later affirmed by the Supreme Court,[38] found unconstitutional committee or one-house vetoes of executive actions as violative of the principle of bicameralism that required both houses of Congress to act in order to adopt legally binding statements. However, the rulings went further to conclude that they violated the separation of powers by intruding on the Article 2 powers of the executive and the Article 3 powers of the judiciary. As Louis Fisher has pointed out, that did not stop the Congress from adopting additional legislative veto provisions, nor did it prevent committee chairs and legislative leaders from insisting that the executive branch comply with existing veto requirements.[39] Those battles continued over time, and in some instances, the Reagan, Bush, and Clinton administrations insisted in particular signing statements that they would ignore legislative veto requirements,[40] though in other instances they relented.[41]

One of the tactics used by the White House in these ongoing battles was to interpret requirements that agencies submit their actions to Congress for approval and read them instead as requirements for notification and consultation with Congress. Reagan asserted in one statement:

> In granting authority of making appropriations by law, the Congress may not reserve to its committees approval or veto power over the exercise of that authority or the expenditure of those appropriations. The reservation of such power to congressional committees clearly conflicts with the constitutional principles the Supreme Court enunciate in INS v. Chadha. . . . The Executive branch will continue to provide committees the notification and full consultation that interbranch comity requires in matters in which the Congress had indicated such a special interest.[42]

An Effort to Add the President's Opinion to the Legislative History

For the Reagan administration and its successors, one of the primary uses for signing statements was not to wage war with Congress but to influence the understanding that courts and other relevant political players would have of the legislative history behind a particular law. The issue of whether such statements should be regarded as part of the legislative history and what significance, if any, they should have in the use of legislative histories by judges in statutory interpretations continues to be hotly disputed in the pages of law reviews, as it has been since the Reagan era.[43] Attorney General Meese certainly thought that this was an important and legitimate opportunity for the president. Former attorney general William Barr and others have argued in favor of the proposition but have not been quite so obviously certain that such statements would be taken seriously. According to Barr, "The President has a constitutionally-mandated part in the legislating process. To the extent that legislative history is given effect, it may be that presidential signing statements should be viewed as part of legislative history."[44]

Part of the reason for Barr's qualified language is that, to this point at least, it is far from clear what level of significance courts will attribute to such signing statements. There are cases in which they have played a part in a judicial finding. In a case interpreting provisions of the Sentencing Reform Act, the U.S. Circuit Court of Appeals for the Second Circuit included such a statement as one of five factors supporting its interpretation: "Third, though in some circumstances there is room for doubt as to the weight to be accorded a presidential signing statement in illuminating congressional intent, President Reagan's views are significant here because the Executive Branch participated in the negotiation of the compromise legislation."[45] It is one thing for a court to include comments from signing statements as one factor in its interpretations, but it may be quite another in cases in which the president's interpretation is dramatically at odds with a significant body of more traditional legislative history documentation.

To Avoid Practical Problems Such as End of Session Vetoes or Vetoes of Large, Complex Statutes

Barr and Douglas Kmiec, who, like Barr, was formerly an assistant attorney general for the Office of Legal Counsel and charged with advising the White House and preparing signing statements, have noted that in addition to these broad uses of the statement, there are a number of pragmatic applications. These include an effort to provide an option to a full-blown presidential veto in difficult circumstances in which the veto might create an untenable situation. Both men cite as examples legislation adopted by Congress just before it goes into recess and large complex bills that cannot as a practical matter be completely blocked. As Barr explains, "At the very end of its session, Congress frequently passes large bills and then leaves town. The only choice we have is to veto the bill and, say, shut down the foreign operations of the United States altogether for six months, or to sign the bill and note exception to some provision we think is unconstitutional. Thus, in some instances, signing statements have directed subordinate officials to disregard provisions of a bill that are thought to be clearly unconstitutional and severable."[46]

Quite apart from end-of-session situations, Kmiec has explained the problem posed by complex and essential bills. He has referred to "Congress' practice of lumping together numerous unrelated provisions in omnibus bills, often inserting the most controversial provisions in emergency appropriations measures passed at, or after, fiscal deadlines."[47] In such circumstances, he argues, while a veto of the entire bill may theoretically be an option, in practical terms it simply is not a viable alternative. Kmiec points to the example of Franklin Roosevelt, who signed the Lend-Lease Act because it was necessary to meet a global crisis. Roosevelt took it upon himself to prepare a legal opinion justifying his action and conveyed it to his then attorney general (soon to be associate justice of the Supreme Court) Robert H. Jackson.[48] He ordered Jackson to file the opinion to block any effort to cite the fact that he had signed the bill "as a precedent for any future legislation comprising provisions of a similar nature."[49]

Structuring Implementation of a Statute

There is one other practical use of signing statements: to structure the implementation of a statute. When the administration has been unsuccessful in its negotiations with the Congress but is unwilling to employ a normal veto, the president may elect to issue a signing statement that provides conditions, limitations, or specific interpretations and then instruct the responsible executive branch officials to implement the new law in accordance with those directions.

These statements may have a section that expresses the president's disagreement with aspects of the statute that are considered so serious as to justify a directive to the agency head charged with implementation of the new law to ignore certain provisions or to administer them in ways that clearly depart from the language of the legislation. For example, when Clinton signed the reauthorization of the Merit System Protection Board and the Office of Special Counsel in October of 1994, he concluded, "I have been advised that one provision in this bill . . . which concerns the apparent authority of an arbitrator to discipline a Federal employee who was not a party to the original action, raises serious constitutional questions. Accordingly, I am directing the agencies to follow appropriate procedures to protect the constitutional rights of such Federal employees and to consider the need for remedial legislation."[50] The administrators had their marching orders, regardless of the language of the statute.

President Bush also had his difficulties with personnel-related legislation. Kmiec explained that his office recommended a veto of one version of the Whistle Blower Protection Act but also signaled a desire to reopen negotiations, with the hope that it might produce a more satisfactory statute. One of the issues had to do with the requirement that the special counsel submit information directly to Congress. The Congress produced a new version, which called for concurrent submission of information to a presidential designee and to Congress. However, in signing the bill, Bush stated, "I do not interpret these provisions to interfere with my ability to provide for appropriate prior review of transmittals by the Special Counsel to the Congress."[51] Assessing the process, Kmiec concluded, "OLC's legislative function had thus traveled the full executive route, from reviewer and disapproving critic to draftsman and implementing agent."[52]

If the president issues such instructions, affected administrators must respond or face the wrath of the White House. Moreover, they must be aware not only of the substantive directive that is being issued in the statement but also that a failure to follow White House policy means either outright opposition from the Justice Department or at least that it will not support the agency that goes off on its own. Once the implementation of a statute is undertaken, the early steps often shape the operation of the policy for years to come.

WHY ARE THEY USED?

Clearly then, presidents have found a variety of applications for this particular tool of presidential direct action. As with each of the other tools, there are a number of reasons that presidents choose to employ the device.

To Provide Recognition for Political Allies and Supporters

Historically, one of the most common reasons for issuing a signing statement is to express the president's appreciation to those who have provided support through the legislative process.[53] News coverage of legislation often obscures the fact that bills can literally take many years to work their way through Congress. In the process, the members who undertake their sponsorship and the party leaders who must often conduct negotiations required to move the work along incur political costs—sometimes career-ending costs—to accomplish the task.

Even in cases where the gratitude is merely for cooperation rather than for heroic efforts, it is still worth the president's energy. After all, the administration, in all likelihood, will need to call upon its friends as well as those on the other side of the aisle for support throughout its term in office.

Making Political Points

In this same vein, signing statements are often used to make political points. Credit taking and criticism for public consumption frequently occupy much of the page space in such presidential statements. Thus, President Clinton was quick to point to Vice President Al Gore's interest in information technology as he signed the Government Printing Office Electronic Information Access Enhancement Act of 1993.[54] In 1994, in signing legislation related to the Clinton administration's reinventing government initiatives, the president was quick to claim credit for his own efforts and for the National Performance Review headed by Gore. A prime example is Clinton's statement on signing the Federal Workforce Restructuring Act of 1994 that facilitated the administration's effort to cut the federal workforce by 273,000. The statement lauded the National Performance Review and pointed to the legislation as proof that the administration had demonstrated its commitment to action.[55]

Presidents are equally happy to employ signing statements to chastize legislators. Thus, Clinton expressed his disappointment that Congress had chosen to appropriate $300 million more for various water projects than he had requested at a time when resources were tight and deficit reduction efforts meant sacrifice in many areas.[56] Once control of the Congress passed into Republican hands, Clinton used his signing statements effectively to draw attention to congressional moves that partially shut down the federal government. The legislative efforts to intimidate the White House into adopting Republican budget priorities and various riders attached to those bills that would have significantly reshaped a wide variety of policies failed miserably. More to the point, on each occasion when it became necessary to adopt partial continuing resolutions to keep critical government functions operating, the president took the opportunity to employ his signing statements to provide the news media with running commentary on what he made clear was to be seen as a Republican problem:

> Although I welcome H.J. Res. 136, it is a poor substitute for what the Congress should do immediately—that is, send me an acceptable continuing resolution to reopen the departments and agencies that are at least partially shut down because they lack fiscal year 1996 appropriations. . . . To be sure, H.J. Res. 136 prevents the serious impact that the partial shutdown could have had on 3.3 million veterans and their survivors as well as nearly 9 million low-income children. But the shutdown continues to hurt millions of innocent Americans—from the 20,000 parents and students each day who cannot apply for student aid, to the 2,500 moderate- and low-income working families each day who cannot get their Federal Housing Administration (FHA) mortgage loans processed. The shutdown also has forced the affected departments and agencies to furlough a total of about 280,000 Federal employees, throwing their lives into disruption and raising their fears just as the holidays approach. . . . The congressional majority apparently wants to use a partial Government shutdown to force me into accepting their extreme budget plan. It did not work last month, when the majority prompted an earlier shutdown by not sending me an acceptable continuing resolution. And it will not work now.[57]

In all, he issued some thirteen such statements before a final resolution of the battle was achieved. The president's messages resonated well with the public and the Congress eventually capitulated, but with consequences for a long time to come.

Sometimes presidents may find that signing statements intended to score points may end up coming back to them. When Clinton signed the Independent Counsel Reauthorization Act of 1994, he criticized Republicans who opposed the legislation. "Regrettably, this statute was permitted to lapse when its reauthorization became mired in a partisan dispute in the Congress. Opponents called it a tool of partisan attack against Republican Presidents and a waste of taxpayer funds. It was neither. In fact, the independent counsel statute has been in the past and is today a force for Government integrity and public confidence."[58] That occurred before Clinton became intimately involved with the special counsel process. Both he and his Republican adversaries were happy to allow that statute to die quietly when next it came up for reauthorization.

Leveraging the Legislature

Clinton, like his Republican predecessors, had to deal with legislatures dominated by the opposition party. In part because of this, recent administrations have demonstrated a propensity to use signing statements to leverage the legislature. Although the Reagan and Bush administrations handled much of this effort with and through the Office of Legal Counsel, Kmiec pointed out that most of the impetus for challenges through signing statements during his tenure came not from legal concerns but from policy disputes and efforts to address them.[59] During the Clinton years, there was less frequent and systematic effort through the Justice Department channel and more overt and obvious political use of the signing statements. While he had a Democratic Congress, Clinton made little serious use of signing statements; but, as it had with other divided governments before him, that changed in early 1995 when the Newt Gingrich–led Republican victory changed the political landscape in Washington.

The White House has used signing statements as both carrots and sticks. At the end of round one of a battle with Congress, the president has sometimes employed signing statements to set out the administration's position and invite renewed negotiations. At other times, the possibility of a statement designed to win at that stage what the White House could not achieve by compromise is always present. Like most such deterrents, however, it is most effective when the threat is seen as present and credible but not necessarily frequently used.

An Effort to Prompt or Influence Judicial Action

Well beyond the obvious political reasons for using signing statements, there is a serious and longer-term factor that prompts chief executives to employ this tool with considerable care. There is often a desire to influence judicial decisions that might result from challenges to a statute and even in some instances to encourage such litigation. Clearly, a number of the uses of signing statements are designed to serve an administration's desire to have its interpretation of statutes be implemented and supported by the courts. That was the focus of a great deal of effort by Attorney General Meese to have signing statements incorporated into legislative history.

During the Reagan administration, the president interpreted sections of the Safe Drinking Water Amendments of 1986 to permit enforcement discretion when the statute plainly used mandatory language.[60] The Supreme Court had recognized that Congress could place reviewable standards on enforcement discretion.[61] If, however, the Court accepted the statute as discretionary rather than mandatory, it would face a far more favorable standard of review. In another situation, the White House attempted to impose a higher standard of proof on enforcement actions that charge discrimination under the Immigration Reform and Control Act of 1986.[62] In these and many other examples, including Bush's interpretation of the Civil Rights Act of 1991, the White House, with the support of its Justice Department, was maneuvering for advantage in court by seeking to define the administration's implementation options in part by shifting levels and burdens of proof and by contributing its definitions of legislative standards. In 1999 the Clinton White House sought to interpret language in the Gramm-Leach-Bailey financial reform legislation as "providing States with a constitutionally permissible choice of whether to participate" in order to avoid a claim that the statute forced states to use their regulatory powers.[63] That was critical because in 1997 the Supreme Court prohibited that kind of mandate in the initial challenge to the Brady gun control legislation.[64] Indeed, in some cases these interpretations go further and are in reality efforts to do an end run around the courts by using signing statements as a kind of declaratory judgment to pronounce the law without waiting for judicial rulings.

Other situations are even more direct. Litigation may be imminent. It was clear that the Gramm-Rudman-Hollings deficit reduction legislation would be challenged because it called for a draconian process for limiting expenditures. Legislators agreed to permit final votes on the measure on the condition that a simple and expedited process was available to bring litigation and to get to the Supreme Court for review. Reagan played to that fact when, in his signing statement, he indicated that there were constitutional difficulties with the authority given by the act to the comptroller general with respect to directions to the president. The Supreme Court noted that fact in the *Bowsher v. Synar* decision: "In his signing statement, the President expressed his view that the Act was constitutionally defective because of the Comptroller General's ability to exercise supervisory authority over the President."[65] That point was at the heart of the Court's ruling striking down the legislation.[66]

In other situations, however, administrations have sought to prompt litigation with the hope that it would provide a victory in court that the White House could not win in Congress. This is also one way to attack the practice of hanging riders on critical and complex bills in settings in which a full veto of the bill seems infeasible. It is also a way to fight a statute without the risk of defying it.

A classic example of this use of signing statements came during the Clinton administration and concerned the National Defense Appropriations Act for FY1996. Clinton vetoed the first version of the legislation and managed to obtain several concessions from Congress in the negotiations on the second bill. However, while it was back, the ultraconservative congressman Robert Dornan (R-Calif.) added an amendment requiring the discharge of any member of the military who was HIV–positive, without regard to the person's actual fitness to serve.

Clinton signed the statute but concluded that that provision was unconstitutional and announced that he would support efforts in Congress to eliminate it.[67] In that statement, the president announced that he had directed the attorney general not to defend the HIV ban in Court if it was challenged. He also issued a presidential memorandum, instructing the secretaries of defense, transportation, and veterans affairs that they were to provide to any affected service members "the full benefits they are entitled to, including, among other things, disability retirement pay, health care coverage for their families, and transition benefits such as vocational education."[68]

At a press briefing on the administration's actions, White House Counsel Jack Quinn was asked, "Did the President have the opportunity to tell the Defense Department not to enforce the law if he finds it unconstitutional?" Quinn replied:

> There are ample reasons why we're not in a position to direct the Secretary of Defense not to enforce it. What it boils down to, frankly, is that we don't have the benefit of a prior judicial determination to the effect that this provision is unconstitutional, and in circumstances where you don't have the benefit of such a prior judicial holding, it's appropriate and necessary to

enforce it. Among other things, we will be setting in motion enforcement of this policy, that is how we will get a case moving, the ultimate result of which, of course, we believe firmly will be for the courts to strike this down as unconstitutional.[69]

Walter Dellinger, then assistant attorney general for the Office of Legal Counsel, supported Quinn:

> When the President's obligation to execute laws enacted by Congress is in tension with his responsibility to act in accordance with the Constitution, questions arise that really go to the very heart of the system. And the President can decline to comply with the law, in our view, only where there is a judgment that the Supreme Court has resolved the issue. And here the courts have not had an opportunity to resolve it, and the action the President is taking, if the leadership of the House and Senate choose to defend this provision, will ensure that the courts are presented with a full range of argument in making their determination.

Dellinger's position was interesting in part because it allowed far less latitude for the president to refuse to act than had his 1994 memorandum to the White House on that subject.[70] In that opinion, Dellinger had indicated that the president was not required to enforce unconstitutional provisions and not required to wait until the courts had pronounced them unconstitutional. "If the statute is unconstitutional, it is unconstitutional from the start."[71] This HIV dispute was clearly a situation in which the White House sought to encourage litigation rather than to bring about a political confrontation with Congress by simply refusing to comply.

It was also clear that the administration was announcing its hope and expectation that a suit would be brought promptly. Indeed, after noting that the statute permitted six months for the separation of the roughly one thousand people who would be affected, the attorneys indicated that "the Secretary will undertake to set in motion procedures to effectuate this provision. . . . That, we believe, will create the condition under which a lawsuit might appropriately be brought on behalf of the potentially affected military men and women." Asked if a case could be brought and resolved in the six-month period, Quinn replied that it would probably take longer but that it would be common in such a case for there to be an injunction issued against the government to freeze the situation in place. The attorneys also responded that the administration might file a brief in such a case in support of the plaintiffs and that, in any case, they had been directed formally to notify the Congress that Justice Department lawyers would not support the legislation in court.

The Tendency to Use Past Presidential Signing Statements to Establish Legitimacy of Current Actions

That same press briefing provides a view of another reason to use a signing statement: as precedent to support current positions. Indeed, in his signing statement on the HIV issue, Clinton observed, "As Franklin D. Roosevelt said in 1943, explaining his decision to sign an important appropriations bill notwithstanding the fact that it contained a provision that infringed upon individual rights, 'I cannot . . . yield without placing on record my view that this provision is not only unwise and discriminatory, but unconstitutional.'"[72] Reporters asked the White House lawyers whether there was precedent for such an action as refusing to defend. Dellinger was ready to elaborate on the Roosevelt precedent:

> In 1943, President Roosevelt signed the Urgent Efficiency Appropriations Act notwithstanding his reluctance because of a provision that in his view violated the Constitution by depriving named individuals who were singled out by Congress of the right to ever receive any pay from their government jobs. The President directed the Attorney General not to defend the constitutionality of the provision. The Senate, in fact, defended in the Court of Claims through counsel, and the court ruled in United States versus Lovett that the President was correct in his conclusion and held that provision of the Urgent Efficiency Appropriations Act unconstitutional.

Signing statements have been cited as precedent by others as well. Asked by Senator Jesse Helms (R-N.C.) about his views on the International Criminal Court Treaty, then Secretary of State Designate Colin Powell answered that he had serious reservations about the treaty and that the Congress should not be "standing on your tippy-toes waiting for the Bush administration to ask for any—any—movement toward ratification."[73] Powell then cited Clinton's signing statement for the proposition that there were difficulties with the treaty and that Clinton had made clear that he had signed it only to allow discussions to continue.

Even some lobbyists have seen utility in citing such precedents. During hearings on the plan for Everglades restoration, a lobbyist for Florida Citrus Growers sought to delay action on it on grounds that further studies were needed. In so doing, he cited Clinton's signing statement on the Water Resources Development Act of 1999, in which the White House had noted that many of the project's features were not yet ready for authorization because reviews had not been completed and that, until the reviews were done, there would be both technical and economic questions that would remain unanswered.[74]

Such uses of signing statements as precedent, and their use by an expanding group of participants in the legal and policy communities, exceed even former Attorney General Meese's original plans. As more players become aware of the statements, and as more attention is paid by the White House to the ways they can be used and the reasons for employing them, it is likely that this kind of practice will grow.

WHAT ARE THEIR POTENTIAL STRENGTHS AND LIABILITIES?

Signing statements share many of the attractive qualities common to the other tools of presidential direct action. Moreover, they have a variety of uses and meet a number of needs. Yet they also present a number of potential difficulties, particularly for administrations that seek to push the envelope.

The Special Pluses of Signing Statements

In addition to the particular uses and challenges already discussed, four more general positive factors recommend the use of signing statements. First, each administration can shape the instrument as it sees fit and use it according to its own priorities. Like NSDs, there is really no external control on the use of this tool. An administration may choose to use it with heavy involvement by the Office of Legal Counsel, with concern for a systematic effort to establish or to reclaim ground it feels has been lost to other institutions. Thus, the Reagan White House made a point of using such statements often, systematically, and with a recurring theme of redressing what it regarded as a growing intrusion of the Congress into the constitutional domain of the executive. The fact that such an approach meant frequent and direct conflict with the legislature was a given. The Reagan White House did not expect a positive working relationship with the Democratically dominated Congress and was more than prepared to engage in open conflict with it on a variety of fronts. The administration chose to use administrative strategies to accomplish many of the goals it was unlikely to achieve in Congress.[75] Reagan was also fully prepared to have his people litigate the administration's differences with the legislature.

When the Clinton administration came into office, the situation was quite different. Though his White House turned out to be quite willing to use a variety of executive tools to accomplish its goals, it hoped to be able to work with the Congress, including, for many purposes, members of the Republican minority. Indeed, some Democrats came to have serious concerns about whether Clinton was expending more efforts working with the Republicans on budget issues, the North American Free Trade Agreement, and the General Agreement on Tariffs and Trade than he was in addressing more traditional Democratic concerns. Until the right-wing revolution in Congress led by Newt Gingrich (R-Ga.) put very conservative Republicans in power in early 1995, Clinton used his signing statements largely for promoting his administration's accomplishments and lauding his allies. The real change in approach came as the budget battles of 1995 brought the government to a halt. Even then, though, the Clinton administration chose to use its signing statements more often in a political mode than in a legal vein, notwithstanding occasional battles on that front as well. Indeed, as the last vestiges of civil relations with the Republicans melted away with the advent of the drive for impeachment, the Clinton White House was increasingly prepared to take on Congress with whatever tools were available. Shortly after the battles reached a climax with Clinton's signing statement on the National Nuclear Security Agency in the Department of Energy in fall 1999, the *Christian Science Monitor* dubbed the president's increased willingness to use executive direct action tools against Congress "Project Podesta": "It's been a mark of the Clinton administration to rule by executive fiat, circumventing a hostile Congress. . . . With one year to go and a presidential legacy at stake, the White House plans to aggressively pursue this strategy, dubbing it "Project Podesta" after the chief of staff [John Podesta] who's spearheading it."[76] As Robert Byrd's diatribe against Bill Richardson indicated, by this point in his presidency Clinton's use of signing statements, and other tools, had frustrated Democrats as well as Republicans.

As a president elected under the most controversial of circumstances, working with a Congress controlled by the slimmest of margins by his own party, George W. Bush faced a very different situation. At the time of this writing, it is unclear how this Bush administration will shape its signing statement strategy, though it is likely that he may wish to frame his approach as one intended to facilitate ongoing negotiations in complex areas. At the end of the day, however, the choice of how to shape that strategy is strictly up to the president.

A second positive factor is that signing statements, depending on how they are used, can provide a way to work with Congress that can avoid broad pitched battles on essential legislation. As several examples indicate, the president can avoid a standoff on critical legislation while using the statement to preserve the administration's position on a particular issue and continue negotiations with respect to that problem. Managed with care, such an approach can sometimes be used to antagonize fewer potential enemies than would be the case with a full veto. That, in turn, may avoid the so-called train wrecks that can occur if the White House and Congress feel the need to play a high-stakes game of chicken with essential legislation. It can also mean the White House can focus its energies and expend less political capital to accomplish its ends than would be entailed in a wider approach.

Third, in using signing statements, particularly those that are institutionally and legally based, the president usually works from claims to Article 2 constitutional powers, which, as the various heads of the OLC have argued, is the strongest base for action that the White House can assert. Presidents of both parties have used their treaty, appointment, executive privilege, and general executive powers to manage that branch of government to challenge with considerable force legislative actions. The breadth of a variety of judicial rulings in these areas granting deference to presidential actions and a variety of significant separation of powers rulings in the 1970s, 1980s, and 1990s,[77] coupled with the difficulty of launching a challenge to a signing statement,[78] may very well provide a strong base for presidential assertions that certain legislative provisions are invalid.

And fourth, with respect to legal assertions, there is some evidence, limited though it may be, that Attorney General Meese may be achieving his goal of having various players and institutions treat signing statements as part of the legislative history of a statute. That does not mean that they will be treated as authoritative and binding, but there clearly is more awareness of them in the legal community and more reference to them than was true before the Reagan years.

The Dangers of Dramatic Uses of Signing Statements

All of these factors suggest that if an administration is willing to develop and work its signing statement strategy carefully and within reasonable limits, there are opportunities to be realized. However, there are certainly also downsides, and the more dramatic and confrontational their application, the more pronounced those liabilities may become.

The first issue arises from the fact that some of the more significant signing statements have been of doubtful legal validity, notwithstanding those presumptions in favor of the president.[79] There is no question that presidents throughout history have expressed their views as to the appropriateness or even the constitutionality of legislation.[80] The long-running debate over the line item veto had, as one of its major elements, the continuing presidential distaste for having to sign a piece of legislation on a take-it-or-leave-it basis. However, when the president takes the formal step of presenting a kind of declaratory judgment on the meaning of the law and then explicitly or implicitly instructs responsible officials in the government to ignore, or modify in operation, the terms of a statute, the matter takes on a somewhat greater significance than a mere expression of presidential displeasure with the Hill. In those circumstances, the president is exercising a form of line item veto. That is precisely what has happened in many of the cases previously cited.

The Supreme Court has already rejected the idea of a line item veto as a violation of Article 1 of the Constitution.[81] It did so even though in the situation before it in 1998, the Congress had delegated that power to the chief executive by statute and even though it was a very limited form of line item veto of appropriations. In so doing, the Court pointed out that while Article 1, section 7, authorizes the president to veto legislation sent to him by Congress before it can become law, there are two important ways in which the line item veto differs from that process. First, it permits the president to reach back into properly enacted law to veto a provision. Once he or she signs it, it is law. Second, it permits the president to veto not the whole legislation but pieces of it. The Court held that "in both legal and practical effect, the President had amended two Acts of Congress by repealing a portion of each. . . . There is no provision in the Constitution that authorizes the President to enact, to amend, or to repeal statutes."[82]

The line item veto is also different, the Court said, from legislation that requires the president to take action if new conditions arise as specified in the legislation. In that situation, the president, or an agency charged to issue administrative regulations, is carrying out the will of Congress as expressed concerning particular actions to be taken in the event of a specified set of conditions.[83] The line item veto, by contrast, does not carry out law but indeed substantially alters it and does so not under command but at the discretion of the president. The signing statement version of the line item veto is even less defensible than the type struck down by the Court in *Clinton v. New York,* because these actions fly in the face of congressional action rather than responding to a delegation of authority from that body.

It is somewhat ironic that President Reagan and his successors have often cited the case in which the Supreme Court struck down the legislative veto, *Immigration and Naturalization Service v. Chadha,*[84] in a number of their

signing statements to justify their conclusion that Congress had acted uncon-
stitutionally and to support their own actions under the signing statement. In
striking down the line item veto, the Court made clear that the Article 1 ruling
in *Chadha* applies just as much to the president as it does to the Congress.
Just as Congress may not reach inside the executive to control administrative agency actions once it has enacted a statute, neither may the executive
reach into enacted legislation to alter its provisions. The president has a check
on the Article 1 power of the Congress; but the enactment of legislation, including decisions as to its terms, remains a legislative power, not an Article 2
executive power.

The effort by the Justice Department to use *Myers v. United States,*[85] one
of the most extreme statements of presidential authority under Article 2, to
justify virtually any action a president wishes to take in the executive branch
has simply gone too far. That 1926 ruling was a sweeping statement of presidential authority under Article 2, but it cannot be read effectively to override all other parts of the Constitution, particularly the legislative and judicial
articles of the Constitution, Articles 1 and 3. In fact, the ruling in *Myers* has
been narrowed significantly since it was originally issued.[86] Moreover, the
importance of the *Myers* case is matched, and indeed trumped, by another
and even older precedent, *Kendall v. United States ex rel. Stokes,* which held
that the president's executive powers do not justify ordering an executive
branch official to violate properly established law.[87] Presidents from Truman
to Clinton found out the hard way that there are definite limits to their power
imposed by both Article 1 and 2 of the Constitution. That was true for Truman
even though he claimed to be acting in the steel seizure case on the basis of
his foreign affairs powers and his authority as commander in chief, two of
the most widely respected elements of Article executive power.[88] It was
equally true for Richard Nixon, who in the Watergate tapes case argued that
he was acting solely within the executive branch.[89]

The Nixon case highlights another important constitutional problem with
many signing statements: the attempt by presidents to issue what amount to
declaratory judgments intruding upon the Article 3 powers of the courts. The
fact that presidents, like other constitutional officers, should be concerned
about the constitutionality of their actions does not mean that they have a
definitive authority to pronounce on the constitutionality of the actions of other
institutions or to define the boundaries of their own authority. In *United States
v. Nixon,* a unanimous Supreme Court declared: "In the performance of assigned constitutional duties each branch of the Government must initially

interpret the Constitution, and the interpretation of its powers by any branch is due great respect from the others. . . . Many decisions of this Court, however, have unequivocally reaffirmed the holding of Marbury v. Madison . . . that '[it] is emphatically the province and duty of the judicial department to say what the law is.'"[90]

The U.S. Circuit Court of Appeals for the D.C. Circuit had made the same point in its rulings striking down the legislative veto. It found that an attempt by the Congress to make its own definitive and binding interpretation of a previously enacted statute intruded upon that Article 3 power of the judiciary. Such an action, the court held, "diminishes the role of the Judiciary and expands that of Congress. Accordingly, it violates the separation of powers doctrine."[91] That D.C. Circuit opinion was later affirmed without opinion by the Supreme Court.[92]

This concern with the attempt by the White House to preempt the judiciary as well as the legislative branch arose in a challenge to a signing statement during the Reagan administration. In *AMERON, Inc. v. U.S. Army Corps of Engineers,* the district court upheld the Competition in Contracting Act in the face of a signing statement that declared portions of it unconstitutional and that directed executive branch officials not to comply with the law.[93] After that initial ruling, Attorney General Meese wrote an open letter to the *New York Times* and later testified before Congress, indicating that the district court's ruling was not going to be obeyed. When the case came back to the district court at a later stage, Judge Ackerman not only quoted the *Marbury v. Madison* statement of the judicial power to Meese but also added, "The Executive Branch's position that they can say when a law is unconstitutional . . . flies in the face of the basic tenet laid out so long ago by the United States Supreme Court [that] 'no man in this country is so high that he is above the law. No officer of the law may set that law at defiance, with impunity. All the officers of the Government, from the highest to the lowest, are creatures of the law and are bound to obey it.'"[94] The district court's constitutional ruling against the administration was sustained on appeal, though Judge Ackerman's injunction was modified.[95] The U.S. Circuit Court of Appeals for the Ninth Circuit came to the same conclusions about Reagan's signing statement on the contracting statute and added:

> Art. §7 does not empower the President to revise a bill, either before or after signing. It does not empower the President to employ a so-called "line item veto" and excise or sever provisions of a bill with which he disagrees. The only constitutionally prescribed means for the President to effectuate his

objections to a bill is to veto it and to state those objections upon returning the bill to Congress. The "line item veto" does not exist in the federal Constitution, and the executive branch cannot bring a de facto "line item veto" into existence by promulgating orders to suspend parts of statutes which the President has signed into law.[96]

However, even if a significant signing statement is legally valid, it may have the potential to intensify conflict with the Congress dramatically, particularly if there is an ongoing pattern of such behavior. That conflict, once ignited, can burn out of control, with consequences not only for the current administration but for presidents yet to come.

For example, the *AMERON* controversy may have started with a simple dispute about the amount of a bond submitted by a company bidding on a federal contract to clean and repair sewers at West Point, but it rapidly grew in scope and intensity. After the president's signing statement, Budget Director David Stockman issued OMB Bulletin 85-8, commanding federal agencies not to cooperate with the GAO's efforts to implement the Competition in Contracting Act. Judge Ackerman issued his first ruling in *AMERON* in late March 1985. In that same month, Meese insisted in testimony before the House Government Operations Committee that the administration would not implement a statute it considered to be in violation of the president's constitutional power. In April, Attorney General Meese appeared before the House Judiciary Committee and informed its members that the administration would neither comply with the statute nor obey the decision of the district court. Members of the House and Senate then moved to intervene in the *AMERON* case. Meese persisted. However, the House Judiciary Committee then voted twenty-one to twelve to eliminate funds for the office of the attorney general in the pending budget process. The *New York Times* issued an editorial on May 13, "Civics Lesson for Mr. Meese," that referred to recent complaints by Education Secretary William Bennett that schoolchildren did not understand how a bill was enacted or that "a President can't declare a law unconstitutional. Now it appears that the problem extends as high as the White House. President Reagan has declared unconstitutional a key provision of a law he signed last year, and Attorney General Meese has instructed Government Agencies not to obey it."[97] The House Government Operations Committee, with strong Republican support, voted to condemn the administration's actions, which, by this point, had nothing to do with government contracting and everything to do with obedience to the rule of law and respect for coordinate branches of government.

Meese waded further into the fray on May 21, when he provided a letter to the editor of the *New York Times* in which he insisted on the administration's right to disobey the law.[98] A week later, Judge Ackerman ruled for the second time in the case and issued an injunction with his stinging rebuke to the attorney general and the president. On June 3 the administration capitulated in the face of the new injunction and growing congressional opposition. The last word on this battle belonged to Chairman Peter Rodino (D-N.J.) of the House Judiciary Committee, the man who had presided over the Nixon impeachment hearings. In an answer on the *New York Times* Op-Ed page to Meese, Rodino warned that this issue was far larger than a political dispute:

> The Attorney General seems to believe that the Administration's lawlessness has fostered a "constructive dialogue" between the executive branch and Congress. But it is hardly "constructive" when the bipartisan leadership of both the House and the Senate have no choice but to go to court to force the President to carry out his constitutional duty to enforce the law.
> Nor is it "constructive" when the House Judiciary Committee is compelled to take the drastic step of defending the office of the Attorney General because of the Administration's defiance of a statute. It is, rather, a confrontation—one in which Congress must take extraordinary measures to preserve the Constitution. . . .
> This Administration's radical assertion of unbridled executive authority violates the constitutional mandate of separation of powers. If a President, by executive fiat, can disregard laws with which he disagrees, then he usurps the power of Congress to write and repeal laws. And if he can prevent the enforcement of a law by unilaterally labeling it unconstitutional, then he usurps the authority of the courts to interpret the laws. . . .
> Congress has acted to protect the Constitution's framework of separation of powers and the principle of the rule of law. The President, no less than the average citizen, must comply with duly enacted statutes. No one, including the President, is above the law.[99]

It was precisely the same kind of concern that drove the harsh criticism of Secretary of Energy Richardson in the administration's signing statement battle with Congress over the National Nuclear Security Administration. To make matters worse, it quickly became clear that, although a brief reference was made to constitutional concerns in Clinton's signing statement, this was a policy and a political dispute and had little to do with constitutional matters. Moreover, the administration responded by taking action Congress had forbidden. This was the so-called "double-hatting" process under which existing Energy Department officials, including the secretary, would take over the duties that the Congress had demanded be handled by independent officials, who would not have conflicts of interest. As the president's statement directed,

> The responsibilities placed by S. 1059 in the National Nuclear Security Administration potentially are of the most significant breadth, and the extent of the Secretary of Energy's authority with respect to those responsibilities is placed in doubt by various provisions of the Act. Therefore, by this Statement I direct and state the following:
>
> 1. Until further notice, the Secretary of Energy shall perform all duties and functions of the Under Secretary for Nuclear Security.
> 2. The Secretary is instructed to guide and direct all personnel of the National Nuclear Security Administration by using his authority, to the extent permissible by law, to assign any Departmental officer or employee to a concurrent office within the NNSA.
> 3. The Secretary is further directed to carry out the foregoing instructions in a manner that assures the Act is not asserted as having altered the environmental compliance requirements, both procedural and substantive, previously imposed by Federal law on all the Department's activities.
> 4. In carrying out these instructions, the Secretary shall, to the extent permissible under law, mitigate the risks to clear chain of command presented by the Act's establishment of other redundant functions by the NNSA. He shall also carry out these instructions to enable research entities, other than those of the Department's nuclear defense complex that fund research by the weapons laboratories, to continue to govern conduct of the research they have commissioned.
> 5. I direct the Director of the Office of Personnel Management to work expeditiously with the Secretary of Energy to facilitate any administrative actions that may be necessary to enable the Secretary to carry out the instructions in this Statement.
>
> The expansive national security responsibilities now apparently contemplated by the Act for the new Under Secretary for Nuclear Security make selection of a nominee an especially weighty judgment. Legislative action by the Congress to remedy the deficiencies described above and to harmonize the Secretary of Energy's authorities with those of the new Under Secretary that will be in charge of the NNSA will help identify an appropriately qualified nominee. The actions directed in this Statement shall remain in force, to continue until further notice.

This was far more than a refusal to enforce the statute. It was an order to do that which the Congress had expressly rejected. Moreover, the last paragraph sent a clear message to Congress that the administration intended not to appoint anyone at any time soon to the new post of undersecretary for nuclear security, and perhaps not at all if the Congress did not relent.

Even worse, this battle came at a time when the administration had made its contempt for the Hill more than clear. To Democrats and moderate Republicans in Congress who fully understood the bad blood between zealots at both ends of the avenue and who had been around to see many interbranch clashes, the behavior being exhibited in the NNSA case was extreme and damaging. When Senator Byrd let loose his tirade against Secretary Richardson, he was speaking to more than a cabinet officer, and he was speaking for others besides himself.

Then there are the dangers of a number of administrative difficulties that may develop over time as a result of signing statements. These are low-visibility matters, but they can affect how policies are implemented or, for that matter, are not implemented over time. Although at least since the late 1980s signing statements have been published in a way that can be more easily located and used, they are not well understood. Few in the policy arena know enough to look for them or how to access their nature and role. Agencies do take cognizance of them, however, as they begin implementation of a piece of legislation and build the president's position into their actions. From that point on, though, the statement more or less disappears. It is important for any new administration to discover how previously issued signing statements shaped implementation of legislation in the various agencies and to determine how to amend or correct (depending on the president's point of view) current practices with origins not in statute but in the president's declarations.

In the midst of such ambiguity, it can be difficult for agencies to be forthright and yet comply with both the statute and the signing statement. That is particularly true when presidents have challenged the Congress or insisted on an interpretation that is at the very least controversial at the other end of the avenue. The agency that must administer the law is automatically in a cross fire.

The agency is potentially and very possibly in trouble in court as well. An agency in this type of situation effectively begins its administrative rulemaking processes and other responsibilities of program implementation with what amount to rules written by the president that may very well be contrary to the legislation. That makes the agency immediately subject to legal attack. Those White House statements that constrain agency action are also not always made with adequate expert opinion from the agencies to complement the legal opinions offered by the Office of Legal Counsel. Thus, the agency is open to the charge that its behavior is arbitrary and capricious, in violation of the Administrative Procedure Act. Given that the agency must begin with what amounts to a dispute over the statute between the White House and the Hill, it starts work with a recognition of this legal vulnerability.

Precisely because other implementation activities begin from the premise of the statute plus the signing statement, the agency's implementation efforts are shaped in ways that can be extremely difficult to determine later. It can therefore be difficult for a new administration to trace the ambiguities and even contradictory behaviors that are present in an agency's actions. Kmiec pointed to a difficulty of this type in describing the signing statement on the Whistle Blower statute: "Yet, OLC's words, adopted by the President in his message of approval, are not without their inconsistencies. How, after all, was executive branch material to be submitted [to Congress] 'concurrently but only following prior review'? At a minimum, this is a metaphysical challenge. Some in Congress would say it is the manipulation, even disregard, of the public law."[100] If the people who prepare signing statements in the Office of Legal Counsel cannot answer that question, just how is an administrator to respond to it?

CONCLUSION

Clearly, presidential signing statements have come to be a potent, and a potentially very dangerous, tool of presidential direct action, used alongside the other techniques. Although there is certainly a history behind such statements, like many of the other devices, they have been finding ready users in recent administrations willing to apply them in new and sometimes dramatic ways.

For their part, legislators are asking why it should be the case that a president can issue a signing statement that to all intents and purposes directs an agency not to implement a statute as it was enacted by the Congress. If presidents can do so, why does it come as a surprise that some then raise questions about compliance with judicial rulings? In any case, it is past time to address directly the nature, uses, and abuses of signing statements, at least where they contain specific directives to administrators responsible for implementation of the statute involved.

EIGHT

PRESIDENTIAL DIRECT ACTION
AND WASHINGTON RULES:
THE DANGERS OF POWER TOOLS

As a new administration comes to office, there is much to consider, not merely with respect to people and policy but also with regard to the means the White House will employ and the tools it will use to craft and direct implementation of the policies. How these devices are used matters. The use and abuse of tools of presidential direct action that we have considered reinforce the political reality that ends and means are intimately interrelated.

It is true that presidential executive orders, proclamations, memoranda, national security directives, and signing statements are devices that can be used in a variety of ways to achieve the president's goals. They offer a range of uses to respond to a variety of motives with a number of advantages. It should also be clear, however, that there are caveats to be considered in their use; for each of these tools, as history has demonstrated, can result in difficulties for the president, for the nation, and even for the global community. Some of these problems are relatively detailed concerns that would seem to be of more interest to political operatives, public administrators, and lawyers, but other issues, such as the basic argument about the relationship between the president and the rule of law, are broad indeed. The discussion of each of these presidential tools throughout the book presents both types of concerns and emphasizes how interconnected they are. As the analysis of the use of these tools demonstrates, in many important respects, democracy is in the details.

This concluding chapter considers briefly three themes that should be of concern to analysts, observers of the political scene, practitioners in the art of governing, and particularly to members of a new administration. These are the questions of how a new administration can frame and evaluate its use of these tools of presidential direct action, some basic principles about their use, and the importance of contemplating the consequences of their use for Washington rules.

PRESIDENTIAL DIRECT ACTION: FINDING A USEFUL LENS TO VIEW THE FULL PANORAMA

The longtime presidential adviser Bryce Harlow often warned that one of the greatest dangers for any president is the tendency to become overwhelmed with thousands of problems and actions that take the chief executive's attention away from the larger view of the office and its operation. It would be helpful if the new president could find a framework that would sustain a sense of the way the White House is using these powerful tools of direct action. One such approach is to think in terms of near-term and long-term factors as well as to pay attention to the internal utility, that is, within the executive branch, and the external consequences in contemplating the use of these tools. It is useful for a president to contemplate in any given situation in which of these areas the executive's primary purposes lie and what the possible consequences of action might be.

Power Management

A president who is focused on the short-term, internal view of a possible decision may elect a power management approach. The emphasis is on efficient, effective, prompt, and controlled action within the executive branch. This is an increasingly common approach employed by new administrations; certainly it has been by Reagan and his successors.

Whether spoken or unspoken, the tendency to adopt a power management perspective as the base for the use of presidential direct action tools may grow from an assumption that alternative approaches will simply not work or not work rapidly enough because of recalcitrant administrative agencies or opposition by other institutional players inside or outside the Beltway. The executive orders on rulemaking issued by presidents Carter, Reagan, Bush, and Clinton and the Bush memoranda on the rulemaking moratorium are clear examples of this approach.

The tendency to use this approach may also stem from the idea that the situation confronting the White House is a real or a perceived emergency in which the executive branch must be mobilized for action. Another tendency is to use this type of approach in national security matters where the White House holds the view that time is of the essence and a particular window of opportunity exists that must be seized. This kind of action is common in the use of national security directives. Control of sensitive materials, personnel practices, or communications is often the focus of this kind of activity.

Another feature of the power management approach is the attempt to use the policies of the executive branch to make a wider political point. Certainly the Reagan administration's Drug Free Workplace order is an example, as are many of the Clinton-era orders and memoranda associated with the reinventing government initiative.

Still, the power management approach presents many of the dangers and challenges of the various types of instruments. The costs can be high, and the damage both within government and to people outside it can be significant. The rulemaking orders have tied administrative agencies up in knots for years and have trapped them in a cross fire between the Congress that adopted statutes requiring regulations to be issued and presidents who tried to measure their success by the number of rulemaking processes they could block. Reagan's NSD 84 and other related directives seeking to impose dramatically intensified controls on access to information and control over communication during and after government employment incited a minirebellion even among a number of cabinet-level officials and conveyed a sense of the tenor of leadership being exercised in the executive branch that drew fire from many sources. The Clinton ethics order was meant to make a very public and political point, but it was one of the factors contributing to the administration's inability to staff many of its key positions for months.

The Governance Approach

A different perspective arises when the president takes an internal but longer-term strategy. It can be termed a governance approach. In contrast to power management, the president can and does make use of tools of direct action to manage the executive branch. In this mode, the White House's management efforts are not in competition with those of the Congress or administrative agencies but are intended to work with them. Executive orders or national security directives may be issued to supplement other traditional techniques of administrative law or to implement legislation. The combination of these policy instruments is then used to govern the executive branch. One example of such a use was the Carter administration's open development of the security classification order.

Historically, for example, security classification orders, personnel practices orders, hortatory proclamations, or memoranda used to render congressionally mandated determinations (sometimes called findings) are used together. National security directives have been used to structure and chronicle the decisionmaking and oversight of national security activities by every administration since Truman. Often, the president who employs the governance approach to direct action instruments is carrying out statutes that call for the various types of White House actions under given conditions. These are constructive and useful. Another aspect of this approach is the use of these devices for traditional management concerns within the executive branch and the military.

This is not to suggest that there are not difficulties that can arise in the process of more or less standard management of the executive branch using various types of directives. The Reagan administration's handling of the employees' contributions issue and a number of other efforts to address private conduct by public employees generated a great deal of heat, both within the executive branch and outside it, as well as major litigation. In general, however, when presidents act within this governance approach, their legal authority and political legitimacy are at their high point.

The Power Policy Action

The use of presidential decrees outside the executive branch that seek impact in the near term is more in the nature of a power policy action. New administrations are increasingly sensitive to the tendency of the so-called honeymoon period for new presidents to become shorter over time. The twenty-four-hour news cycle and the changes in journalistic norms have only intensified the feeling that the new president needs to strike hard and fast. Other presidents come into office amid promises of cooperation and consultation but quickly become frustrated by the many veto points that can be targeted by opponents to block action. Foot-dragging by those who claim to be administration allies can be equally maddening. Presidents who face a Congress dominated by the other political party can easily be tempted to seek direct action by using these tools as the only way to accomplish their goals.

There is also the interesting question whether we have come to what Arthur Schlesinger worried about three decades ago—the advent of the "plebiscitary presidency." With the Reagan, Bush, and Clinton administrations behind us, it is interesting to consider how he thought that plebiscitary presidency would look: "The President, instead of being accountable every day to Congress and public opinion, would be accountable every four years to the electorate. Between elections, the President would be accountable only through impeachment and would govern, as much as he could, by decree."[1]

Whatever presidents' general inclinations might be, it is clearly the case that various types of emergencies cause them to move to a power policy mode. That has certainly been true in periods of war or insurrection, but it has also been true in financial emergencies and foreign policy crises. Indeed, there are times when circumstances seem not only to tolerate rapid direct action but even to demand it. Even the courts have been willing to recognize the president's authority to act in such circumstances, dating back to Washington and Lincoln. On the other hand, the question of what constitutes a legitimate emergency and how far emergencies other than war will support which kinds of presidential direct action is a matter of continuing debate.

The power policy approach, and the attitudes that drive it, can create major difficulties even for actions taken under security classification in foreign affairs. Several administrations, starting at least with Eisenhower, upon taking office, promptly took the power approach and launched covert or hybrid foreign policy actions with national security directives that ultimately blew up—in the long run, if not in the short term. The discussion of the national security directives has provided a number of examples indicating that covert operations created difficulties far beyond the country or the situation that prompted the initial actions. Moreover, the Iran-Contra scandal provides an obvious example of the tendency of the secret stamp and the power approach to feed on each other.

Many of the presidents' uses of these power tools have not come in military or foreign affairs but in domestic matters. Often, the way the president executed the power policy strategy was at least as controversial as the substance of the policy. In some instances, the basic idea of a policy was one that could command considerable agreement, but the mode of action jeopardized the desired end. One example was Clinton's environmental justice executive order and memorandum as well as the Environmental Protection Agency's interim guidance document that flowed from them. The decision by the White House to proceed by a power policy approach placed limits on real opportunities for discussion and participation by states and localities. This less than forthright policymaking process ultimately enmeshed the administration, the EPA, and the policy itself in a hard battle characterized by recriminations and threats. In the end, a worthy policy goal suffered. States and local officials and members of Congress, not to mention various civil rights groups, were alienated in the process.

The Institutional Lens

In areas where the long term is an important consideration and the scope of the effort is broad, the concerns are often institutional. For a chief executive who adopts this approach, the long-term well being, integrity, and efficacy of the presidency are the critical issues. Such an approach is neither narrow nor short term.

The institutional perspective begins from the premise that in this constitutional Republic, institutions matter. Process democracy alone is not enough under the Constitution. A president operating in this mode would most likely agree with Michael Sandel's observation that "political institutions are not simply instruments that implement ideas independently conceived; they are themselves embodiments of ideas."[2] That is not to suggest that the presidency stands alone. When the president acts from an institutional perspective, he or she necessarily comprehends the impact of the constitutional dialogue on the institution of the presidency, to use Louis Fisher's terms, and of the presidency on the nation's other critical institutions.

Yet, there have been times when presidents push so hard that Congress feels the need to react though they have seemed somewhat reluctant to do so. For example, the push by the Reagan White House on several fronts in its use of these power tools led to efforts in 1988 to enact a Presidential Directives and Records Accountability Act.[3] Another effort was launched by John Conyers (D-Mich.) in mid-1990, but it collapsed when Desert Shield was launched and Desert Storm followed. Clinton's often dramatic use of several of these devices virtually dared the Congress to act. Indeed, it seemed as if his signing statement on the Energy Department security issue was a slap in the face as no less a figure than Senator Byrd made clear. Not long thereafter, the Rules Committee in the House took testimony on the use and abuse of White House direct action instruments. The next day hearings were held before the Subcommittee on Commercial and Administrative Law of the House Judiciary Committee. The subcommittee was acting in response to legislation introduced by Congressmen Bob Barr (R-Ga.), Ron Paul (R-Tex.), and Jack Metcalf (R-Wash.). These efforts contained a number of dramatic statements about constraints on presidential powers and provisions that would most likely have engendered constitutional challenges themselves. However, the common elements that could find their way into future legislation included constraints on funding in some circumstances (a standard legislative option), report-and-wait provisions that avoid the constitutional constraints on the legislative veto but provide Congress with an opportunity to be on notice and to respond, and efforts to restrict the effort of the White House to imply broad authority from legislation that does not specifically address direct presidential action. Given the politics of the upcoming election year and the apparent partisan division in this case as well as the scope of the legislation, no action resulted. However, there are steps Congress could take, such as requiring more publication of more types of materials and eliminating exemptions from the Federal Register Act. It could require codification in forms far more usable to the legislature and, for that matter, to the public. It could address notification issues with respect to national security directives that fit more closely with its current procedures for handling classified information. It could also address current constraints on standing to challenge White House actions and other issues related to judicial review. These would be both legally and politically feasible. Even without legislation, Congress could choose to organize oversight of presidential direct action in ways far more systematic and effective than it has to this point. Whether the Congress will act and what it will do clearly will be influenced by whether and how the president uses these instruments of direct action.

At the same time, this approach does not require that the president merely accept popular opinion or stand mute if strong opposition arises from key members of Congress. An example would be President Truman's order desegregating the armed forces.[4] His action was by no means precipitous, and he clearly understood the opposition that he faced, but he acted, nonetheless. Of course, hindsight may demonstrate that a president misperceived a situation or misapplied a particular directive. What was thought to be a legitimate institutional approach may be rejected, as in Truman's seizure of the steel mills.

This simple four-part framework is but one of many possible ways to place the use of these tools in a larger view. It is most important that there be a vision of the way in which the powers of the office are to be employed as well as a sensitivity to cautions about their application in particular circumstances.

SIMPLE RULES FOR THE USE OF PRESIDENTIAL POWER TOOLS

Some years ago, I advanced a number of simple suggestions for the use of presidential power tools. Although they may have been written with a bit of tongue in cheek, the substance is an accurate reflection of real problems that are evident in the past misuse of these devices by various presidents, particularly since the Reagan era.

First, know the tools, their uses, and the risks involved in applying each in a given setting. Just as the choice of organizational form should follow function, the choice of individual policy tools to perform a governance job matters. Once it is clear what tools are available and the character and constraints of each are fully understood, the problem is to choose the right tool for the right job. A number of administrations have run into trouble because they pulled the tools out of the box and started to play with them the moment they came in the door and well before they understood what they were playing with or what damage could result.

Second, do not attempt to use too many tools at the same time. Even for a president with great dexterity, this can present serious problems. Piling memoranda on executive orders used in conjunction with national security directives, and occasionally with a signing statement and proclamations as well, can create an ungainly mess. The policy action that results can rival any contraption pictured in the Rube Goldberg cartoons.

Third, never use power tools when not completely sober. It is tempting to regard situations as crises whether they are or not and to heed every call for emergency action. Emergencies and crises, real or imagined, clearly make the power tools particularly attractive. A sober second look is useful at precisely the time when it seems most tempting to move quickly. Moreover, when presidents have used proclamations, orders, or directives under conditions of emergency, it is often not clear, when normal conditions return, just how to employ more appropriate long-term tools to carry out whatever repair or reconstruction is necessary. Jerry-built structures erected during periods of stress have a way of lingering past their appropriate time. This admonition is not limited only to emergencies. It also applies to situations in which frustration with Congress or other institutional players, in or out of the executive branch and outside the Beltway, as well as within it, causes the administration to want simply to cut through the challenges and move decisively.

Fourth, always operate tools on a safely grounded power source. The temptation of recent administrations to make broad claims to act as president under the powers vested in them by the Constitution or to define the "duty to take care" clause so broadly that it swallows the rest of the Constitution is a dangerous way to proceed and a good way to find actions challenged on both political and legal grounds. This is what happened to President Clinton, for example, when he issued the controversial striker replacement order.

It is no small bit of irony that President George W. Bush ran afoul of almost precisely the same problem only eight months after taking office. The preceding chapters already noted that Bush reversed a number of Clinton's prolabor executive orders and added a few that ran in the opposite direction. One of these was Executive Order 13202, which moved to block the use of Project Labor Agreements on federally funded financial construction projects. The Bush order cited the same broad statement of authority as Clinton's ill-fated striker replacement order, but the U.S. District Court for the District of Columbia cited the opinion overturning the Clinton directive as it struck down the Bush order.[5]

The extra care and effort given to the proper identification and careful explication of the basis for authority and fit with other existing law need not be burdensome or disruptive and can pay important dividends as time passes.

For one thing, the effort to do so conveys a sense of respect for Congress, state and local governments, and the public. Great authority is vested by statute in the president, and careful use of that power is likely to engender more. An unwillingness to work with the other branches can have the opposite impact. Perhaps a more careful grounding of presidential action, rather than bold assertions, may help to rebuild an effective working relationship with Congress and restore the viability of Washington rules.

PRESIDENTIAL ACTION TOOLS AND WASHINGTON RULES

The discussions of the use and abuse of these presidential power tools, and particularly these practices by presidents since the 1980s, make it clear that they have contributed to the breakdown of the informal rules that have for so long permitted committed adversaries to address the nation's most controversial topics and yet to continue to work together. Anyone whose experience in the nation's capital predates this period will recognize these unwritten norms as Washington rules. In describing these rules, there is no expectation that there were not violations from time to time or that there have been some officials who had a habit of abusing the norms. Indeed, to some power players today, they may seem somewhat quaint. Having said that, perhaps only those who actually lived with these rules understand how important they really were in the lives of both professional staff and elected officials.

The rules are relatively few in number. First, a deal made is a deal done—commitment is not required but if it is undertaken fulfillment is expected. If for some overwhelming reason it becomes necessary to retract the commitment, the player involved owes an explanation to the other principal in the deal.

Second, we do not ask someone to act contrary to his or her political best interest, which usually means contrary to the interests of one's constituents or one's institutional integrity.

Third, a professional is expected to make his or her best case on the merits of a policy, but deliberate lies are not to be tolerated. This one could get stretched to near breaking point, but there has long been one telling line. If an advocate or a person in government presented false information that then put another player in jeopardy in a public debate or policy position, it used to be time to pack up and leave town.

Fourth, do not behave today in ways that will make it impossible to work with people of the other party or other institutions tomorrow. Although it may be possible to ram a policy or an institutional action through today, tomorrow it will be time to talk about future budgets or confirmation of officials.

The party in power today still needs at least to avoid obstruction by the other side. And when that party comes back to power, they will remember how they were treated.

Fifth, do not deliberately behave in a manner intended publicly to embarrass another stakeholder personally. Political positions are fair game. It is a tough town and a hard business with high stakes. Reciprocal character assassination is a no-win enterprise.

Sixth, respect the essential character of staff communications. Declarations of war between officials or institutions can make it impossible for knowledgeable and experienced staff members to conduct the communications needed to make things happen. That, in turn, means that top officials will have to negotiate with their counterparts on details, which eventually will interfere with their ability to attend to big questions. Pushed far enough, blocking staff communications can result in paralysis.

Seventh, staff understand the boundaries of confidentiality of their principals. There is a level of communication that is appropriate and open as well as a set of information that is provided in confidence and must remain that way. Trust matters. Once it is lost, it is difficult, if not impossible, to recover.

Eighth, staff understand the boundaries of commitment on behalf of their principals. Political players must work through their staff and must rely on their judgment in negotiations. That also means that staff members work diligently to be clear on their principals' positions and to know how far to commit them, if at all, in any given situation.

Ninth, absent a compelling reason, staff are obligated by deals previously done. If their organization or their political principal has established a position, it is a commitment to be honored.

Tenth, in general, personal lives are out of bounds unless the private conduct has a direct impact on performance in the public role. This is the famous rule that was to be honored by the press as well as other players in the government. Unfortunately, it began to fade rapidly after the reports of the extracurricular behavior of Wilbur Mills. There remained a longing for a restoration of this rule, but it could be observed by those in the system whether the press accepted it or not.

Eleventh, it is appropriate to challenge an opponent's cases as vigorously as possible but not to misrepresent that case deliberately. There are enough serious debates to be fought without cheap shots and straw-man arguments. This rule suffered mightily as ideology was used to justify going over the top in characterizing one's adversaries.

Finally, money is dangerous, and it should not be used in such a way as to make others vulnerable to cheap shots by the media or political opponents. Long before political action committees and soft money became issues, there was a concern with avoiding silly or awkward financial situations.

To the degree that presidential power tools are used to hide important actions, to deceive other players as to the true nature of an administration's decision, to make an end run around the other institutions, or to fabricate what purports to be real authority for important moves by piling one directive on top of another, these rules are dramatically undermined. Moreover, staff members who are asked to operate within that kind of environment cannot honor their obligations under the Washington rules. Beyond all that, the rules depend on a minimum level of trust, even of adversaries, and an acceptance of the principle of reciprocity. Therefore, once a decision by the White House is made to go it alone and to reject the need to maintain that minimum level of trust, a downward spiral is set in motion. This happened, for example, with respect to the Reagan administration's behavior on environmental protection issues, ultimately producing formal charges of contempt of Congress. It also happened in a fundamental way with respect to Iran-Contra. Another example of the downward spiral was the Meese assertion that the Reagan White House would ignore both Congress and the courts on the competition-in-contracting debate. It happened during the Clinton years as well, with the Department of Energy debacle providing a classic example.

It must be recognized clearly that the Congress bears some of the responsibility for the frustrations in the White House that have fueled the use and abuse of orders, memoranda, national security directives, and certainly presidential signing statements. For example, the fact that many members of Congress have felt the breakdown of Washington rules within their own institutions and in the media has prompted a number not to seek reelection. The change in status of staff and of members' attitude and behavior toward staff have also played a part in the erosion of the rules. The general attack on the professional civil service, including those professionals who serve in congressional staff agencies, is another factor. When it becomes clear that members are prepared to abandon professionalism and concern for the institutions of government on ideological grounds or to serve personal ambition as the highest value, the results can be devastating within and among the critical institutions of government.

Further, presidents have every right to ask why only the executive branch should be excoriated for violating institutional comity and undermining

Washington rules while the Congress is spared similar criticism. It is appropriate, for example, for the president who is chastised by the Congress for illegality because the White House directed executive branch officials to disregard provisions of enacted statutes to ask why it should be acceptable for the Congress to adopt legislative veto requirements and shared appointment controls legislation that has repeatedly been found unconstitutional in federal courts, including the U.S. Supreme Court. The congressional leadership must bear responsibility for failing to prevent the now epidemic practice of making every important piece of legislation a Christmas tree on which members are permitted to hang an assortment of provisions that are clearly bad laws. It is difficult to criticize the president for using various power tools against Congress instead of participating in good faith in the evolution of legislation if the Congress is prepared to suspend its own rules to write legislation on the floor without recourse to normal subcommittee and committee processes. Some of the same members of Congress who have blasted presidents for seeking to rewrite legislative history after the fact have themselves created post hoc reports to support legislation that never went through hearings to develop a full committee record in real time.

Nonetheless, the president is in a very different position from members of Congress, in no small part because he or she can unilaterally employ the tools of direct action. The chief executive is not just one member of a 435- or even a 100-member body. These tools are potent and can be used at the command of the president alone, should he or she decide to operate in that way.

The point is not that presidents should be weak or fail to use the instruments at their disposal to honor their constitutional oath and the commitments made to the voters who put them in office. Neither is it that concern for the dangers presented by abuse of power is somehow a naive view that must yield to political reality. In considering the vote he was about to cast on the nomination of Attorney General Designate John Ashcroft, Senator Joseph Biden (D-Del.) pointed out, in evaluating Ashcroft and the responsibilities he was being asked to undertake, that as a senator with many years in Washington he was not naive about politics and power. He recognized, as he put it, that "this is not Boys' State," but he went on to explain that it actually matters in the lives of many people how officials perform in office. In the same way, the degree to which the power players in the nation's capital, and particularly a new presidential administration, will accept or reject Washington rules will matter, too.

CONCLUSION

James L. Sundquist expressed a common lament among those individuals concerned about the changes in politics and in the way Washington operates. In seeking to address those concerns, he wrote: "Exhortation will not satisfy the souls of systems designers, but it is the only option that is practically available."[6] There is perhaps something more that can be presented than just exhortation. The analyses of the ways that presidents have employed executive orders, proclamations, memoranda, national security directives, and signing statements and the consequences that have resulted presented here suggest a variety of reasons to take care with their use. When Senator Byrd held forth in the Senate Armed Services Committee on the behavior by Secretary Richardson but in truth addressed the Clinton administration, he was seeking to convey the message that there are consequences resulting from the abuse of power. They are consequences that affect the democracy, the institutions of our constitutional Republic, and the future of the individuals who may ride high on waves of political power now but who will learn that such power truly is fleeting.

NOTES

A NOTE ON FINDING SOURCES

While there are many citations throughout the volume and some discussion of issues of access to material, it is useful to summarize briefly how to locate the kinds of presidential materials discussed in this book. While each of these items is found in particular sources, there are some general sources of great use with which the reader may not already be familiar. Not surprisingly, much of the material that one needs is now available on the World Wide Web. The University of Michigan has prepared one of the most useful overall finding aids entitled Federal Government Resources, President of the United States, *http://www.lib.umich.edu/govdocs/fedprs.html*. It is a broad-based site, containing perhaps the widest selection of presidential materials available on the Web. Related to that is POTUS, the Internet Public Library site for Presidents of the United States, *http://www.ipl.org/ref/POTUS/*. This site was a cooperative effort of the University of Michigan School of Information and Bell & Howell Information and Learning. It provides a wide range of information arrayed by president as well as quick and easy links to the presidential libraries. The libraries vary widely in terms of the amount and type of material that they make available online. The George W. Bush presidential library was the first to be created after the Internet had become a critically important research focus and it has already provided easily searchable access to many documents. Speaking of innovations, the cooperative relationship between the Lyndon Baines Johnson Presidential Library and C-SPAN to provide the tapes of presidential telephone conversations online has added a great deal. Since the tapes are searchable to a reasonable level of specificity, it is possible to gather previously unavailable contextual information.

There is one other point worth noting in the area of relatively recent developments. The Clinton Administration was the first presidency to operate quite intentionally on the Internet. While that raised a host of issues during the Clinton years, it produced even more complex questions when the administration left office. On its first day in office, the George W. Bush administration eliminated all of the Clinton White House Web pages. That was all the more problematic since the new administration also held up publication of the *Federal Register* while it decided how it would respond to a series of controversial executive orders and proclamations issued by Clinton in the final months of his administration. To many who had been seeking Clinton materials, the thought was that the Clinton Web materials were simply gone except for those that would ultimately appear in the *Register*. George W. Bush later issued Executive Order 13233 imposing greater control over the release of presidential papers from previous administrations. However, under the Presidential Records Act, 44 U.S.C. §2201 et seq., computer-based as well as paper records must be maintained and the Archivist of the United States has responsibility for that area. Thus, the Archives has established an online access to Clinton materials at *http://www.clinton.nara.gov*. With these general suggestions in mind, let us turn to each of the specific kinds of devices in turn.

As a general rule, executive orders are readily available since they must be published in the *Federal Register*. These are now available on the Internet through the Government Printing Office "GPO Access" page *http://www.access.gpo.gov/su_docs/db2.html.* However, these are limited to approximately the last ten years. The difficulty is to find them since they have not been fully codified since 1989. At that time, Office of the Federal Register published the *Codification of Presidential Proclamations and Executive Orders: April 13, 1945–January 20, 1989* (Washington, D.C.: Government Printing Office, 1989). At the time of this writing, the most easily accessible tool for obtaining executive orders is the National Archives Executive Order Disposition Tables on the World Wide Web at *http://www.nara.gov/fedreg/eo.html.*

For more historic orders, there are three generally available sources. A study was done for the U.S. House of Representatives, Committee on the Government Operations, in 1957, which reached back with at a least a general history and listing of orders. This is still a useful document and is *Executive Orders and Proclamations: A Study of the Use of Presidential Power,* 85th Cong., 1st Sess. (1957) (Committee Print). The two Works Projects Administration (WPA) volumes provide the most complete historical information available in single sources. The New York study is W.P.A. Historical Records Survey, *Presidential Executive Orders, Volume One* (New York: Hastings House Publishers, 1944). This volume focuses on numbered executive orders. However, there were many (just how many we do not know) unnumbered executive orders dating all the way back to George Washington. Descriptions of these orders are provided in Clifford L. Lord, ed., *List and Index of Presidential Executive Orders, Unnumbered Series—Historical Records Survey, N.J.* (Newark, NJ: Works Projects Administration, 1942).

Proclamations have been available in the United States *Statutes at Large* dating back to the third volume of that set. Contemporary proclamations are published in the *Federal Register* and the *Weekly Compilation of Presidential Documents.* Older editions of the Public Papers of the President series published by the Government Printing Office contain more orders and proclamations, but more contemporary volumes provide tables that reference where these materials can be found in the *Federal Register.*

The simplest way to access many of the oldest presidential proclamations is through the Avalon Project at the Yale Law School with a broad range of materials and effective indexing on its Internet site. That site is "Avalon Documents in Law, History, and Diplomacy," *http://www.yale.edu/lawweb/avalon/avalon.htm.*

Once one departs from orders and proclamations, the search process can be more complex. Presidents sometimes direct that memorandum be published in the *Federal Register,* though there is no specific requirement that they be published at all. Many memoranda are published in the *Weekly Compilation of Presidential Documents.* Some are published on the Internet site of the agency most directly concerned with the issue at hand. Thus, Clinton's environmental justice memorandum was not published in the *Register,* but was placed on the U.S. Environmental Protection Agency Web page. However, one had to be familiar with the agency's organization to navigate its site to find the materials. Similarly, when George W. Bush issued a memorandum, that actually went out over the signature of the Director of the Office of Management and Budget, the memorandum calling for an across-the-board cut was published on the OMB Internet site. Some memoranda are published in the *Public Papers of the President* series. Finally, the POTUS Internet site can be used to move to presidential library sites. Some, but by no means all, of the libraries have been increasing their online documents collections.

National security directives are, for what should be obvious reasons, among the most difficult presidential direct action tools to locate. Even here, though, much is available to one who knows where to look. The simplest method for locating materials is the Federation of American Scientists, Intelligence Resource Program, Presidential Directives and Executive Orders, *http://www.fas.org/irp/offdocs/direct.htm.* This site provides descriptions of NSDs by administrations back to the Truman years as well as links to those directives that are available on the Internet. There is a considerable body of material available since the Kennedy, Johnson, and Ford libraries have provided almost all of the NSDs from these administrations online. Most of the Reagan directives are available as well, largely because of investigations of Iran/Contra and other congressional investigations. Many of these materials can be found through the Federation of American Scientists site or through the National Archives online search capabilities. Another valuable resource for these directives and related documents is the National Security Archive, George Washington University, *http://www.gwu.edu/~nsarchiv/ NSAEBB/.* Many of these materials were made available as a result of a host of Freedom of Information Act disclosure requests over time. The same is true of the material available on the Central Intelligence Agency "Electronic Document Release" Internet site *http://www.foia.ucia.gov/.* These sites are searchable as well as providing sets of material relating to particularly famous or infamous international policies. It is also important not to overlook the series of international relations materials provided by the U.S. Department of State, Foreign Relations of the United States, *http://www.state.gov/ r/pa/ho/frus/.*

Finally, presidential signing statements are available, but not always easy to locate, particularly for administrations prior to Reagan. The *Weekly Compilation of Presidential Documents* is a basic source, both online for most of the past decade, but in hard copy beyond that. The *Public Papers of the President* series contains some of these materials but the way in which these materials are indexed changed over time. Since the Reagan era, and as a result of the efforts of Attorney General Meese, they have been published in the *U.S. Code Congressional and Administrative News* series. For older administrations, it is useful to work backwards from the date of the enactment of legislation to consult the presidential library Internet sites or the *Public Papers of the President* series.

When working with signing statements, as well as some of the other presidential tools, it is helpful to check the U.S. Department of Justice Office of Legal Counsel Internet site "Memoranda and Opinions by Year," *http://www.usdoj.gov/olc/opinionspage.htm.* As chapter 7 explains, the OLC plays a major role in the signing statement process and often produces opinions and supporting memoranda in conjunction with the issuance of such statements.

In sum, many of the key materials about presidential power tools can be located, and increasingly on the Internet. However, it is important to use a range of finding aids and sources such as those described. It is also necessary, in order to obtain the most complete picture of any given situation, to be aware of the interrelationships among the different tools. For example, it is good practice when locating a significant executive order to check to determine whether there has also been a presidential memorandum issued. Similarly, when media reports indicate that the White House has issued an executive order in some controversial area, it is important to determine whether the action at issue really involved an order or concerned a presidential memorandum or national security directive. As this book explains, it can be important which device is used, in addition to the fact that it is important to identify the kind of instrument in order to locate it.

I. THE TOOLS OF PRESIDENTIAL DIRECT ADMINISTRATION

1. See Irene S. Rubin, *The Politics of Public Budgeting: Getting and Spending, Borrowing and Balancing*, 3d ed. (Chatham, N.J.: Chatham House, 1997); Allen Schick, *The Federal Budget: Politics, Policy, Process* (Washington, D.C.: Brookings Institution, 1995); Louis Fisher, *Presidential Spending Power* (Princeton, N.J.: Princeton University Press, 1975).

2. See Robert F. Durant, *The Administrative Presidency Revisited: Public Lands, the BLM, and the Reagan Revolution* (Albany: State University of New York Press, 1992); Richard P. Nathan, *The Administrative Presidency* (New York: John Wiley and Sons, 1983); Richard P. Nathan, *The Plot That Failed: Nixon and the Administrative Presidency* (New York: John Wiley and Sons, 1975).

3. Counterstaffing is a process of deliberately appointing to agencies people who have very different policy views or management styles from others in the particular agency in an effort to force significant change, even at the cost of high levels of conflict. I have explored this concept in greater detail in *Public Law and Public Administration*, 3d ed. (Itasca, Ill.: F. E. Peacock, 2000), chap. 10. See also Durant, *Administrative Presidency Revisited.*

4. James P. Pfiffner, *The Strategic Presidency,* 2d ed., rev. (Lawrence: University Press of Kansas, 1996).

5. I began by examining the tables of contents of a relatively lengthy list of contemporary books on the presidency and found no mention whatever of these tools. What is more surprising is that almost none of the authors even addressed these tools as items in their indexes. There were only indirect references, in referring to a controversy in which they were central, and then the text references themselves said relatively little about the order or proclamation in question or how it was issued.

6. Although there is a common tendency from today's perspective to date this phenomenon from the 1980s, it reaches back further than that. See, e.g., James L. Sundquist, *The Decline and Resurgence of Congress* (Washington, D.C.: Brookings Institution, 1981).

7. "Remarks on Action to Preserve Privacy of Medical Records and an Exchange with Reporters," *Weekly Compilation of Presidential Documents* 35 (1999): 2125. President George Bush expressed similar frustrations on a number of occasions. See, e.g., Memoranda for the Secretary of the Interior, . . . Agriculture, Energy, Administrator of the Environmental Protection Agency, Chairman of the Federal Energy Regulatory

Commission, Chairman of the Nuclear Regulatory Commission, January 28, 1992, <*http://bushlibrary.tamu.edu*> August 20, 2001.

8. Christopher H. Pyle and Richard M. Pious, *The President, the Congress, and the Constitution* (New York: Free Press, 1984), 61–75.

9. Richard E. Neustadt, *Presidential Power: The Politics of Leadership with Reflections on Johnson and Nixon* (New York: John Wiley and Sons, 1976).

10. See Louis Fisher, *Constitutional Conflicts Between Congress and the President,* 4th ed., rev. (Lawrence: University Press of Kansas, 1997); Edward S. Corwin, *The President: Office and Powers, 1787–1984,* rev. Randall W. Bland, Theodore T. Hindson, and Jack W. Peltason (New York: New York University Press, 1984); James Hart, *The Ordinance Making Powers of the President of the United States* (Baltimore: Johns Hopkins University Press, 1925).

11. The usual source to which supporters of the prerogative point is chapter 14 of John Locke, *The Second Treatise of Government,* ed. Thomas P. Peardon (New York: Bobbs-Merrill, 1952).

12. Lord Hailsham of Marylebone, ed., *Halsbury's Laws of England* (London: Butterworths, 1973), §1099.

13. 12 Co. Rep. 74, 75 (1611).

14. See Bernard Bailyn, *The Ideological Origins of the American Revolution* (Cambridge: Harvard Belknap, 1963).

15. Corwin, *The President,* 5–6.

16. Ibid., and Hart, *Ordinance Making Powers,* 115–117.

17. Corwin, *The President,* 6.

18. See F. Glen Abney and Thomas P. Lauth, *The Politics of State and City Administration* (Albany: State University of New York Press, 1986).

19. Alexander Hamilton, James Madison, and John Jay, *The Federalist Papers* (New York: Mentor Books, 1961), 309. See also Raoul Berger, *Executive Privilege: A Constitutional Myth* (Cambridge: Harvard University Press, 1974), 49–56.

20. Max Farrand, ed., *Records of the Federal Convention of 1787,* 4 vols. (New Haven: Yale University Press, 1966), 1:66, and James Wilson, "Lectures on the Law," in *The Works of James Wilson,* ed. R. McCloskey (Cambridge: Harvard Belknap, 1967), 326–327.

21. Hamilton et al., *Federalist Papers,* 423.

22. See, e.g., Herbert Storing, ed., *The Anti-Federalist* (Chicago: University of Chicago Press, 1985), 308–311.

23. Hamilton et al., *Federalist Papers,* 415–423.

24. See ibid. and Joseph Story, *Commentaries on the Constitution of the United States, with a Preliminary Review of the Constitutional History of the Colonies and States Before the Adoption of the Constitution* (Boston: Charles C. Little and James Brown, 1851), §§1492, 1512, 1513.

25. Story, *Commentaries,* §1501.

26. Locke, *Second Treatise,* 93–94.

27. James Madison, *The Writings of James Madison,* ed. Gaillard Hunt, 9 vols. (New York: G. P. Putnam's Sons, 1906), 6:144.

28. See Louis Fisher, *Executive Orders and Proclamations, 1933–1999: Controversies with Congress and in the Courts* (Washington, D.C.: Congressional Research Service, 1999).

29. Louis Fisher, *Constitutional Dialogues: Interpretation as Political Process* (Princeton, N.J.: Princeton University Press, 1988).

30. James David Barber, *The Presidential Character* (Englewood Cliffs, N.J.: Prentice-Hall, 1972).

31. Michael Sandel, *Democracy's Discontent* (Cambridge: Harvard University Press, 1996), ix.

32. Colin Campbell, S.J., *Managing the Presidency: Carter, Reagan, and the Search for Executive Harmony* (Pittsburgh: University of Pittsburgh Press, 1986), 3.

33. 16 *Fed. Reg.* 3503 (1952).

34. *Youngstown Sheet & Tube v. Sawyer,* 343 U.S. 579 (1952).

35. *Dames & Moore v. Reagan,* 453 U.S. 654 (1981).

36. Executive Order (E.O.) 12044, 43 *Fed. Reg.* 12661 (1978).

37. This led to the Unfunded Mandates Reform Act of 1995, P.L. 104-4, 109 Stat. 48. See also Laurence J. O'Toole Jr., ed., *American Intergovernmental Relations,* 3d ed. (Washington, D.C.: Congressional Quarterly Press, 2000); David B. Walker, *The Rebirth of Federalism,* 2d ed. (New York: Chatham House, 2000).

38. Examples include responses to the Clinton administration order on federalism, E.O. 13083, 63 *Fed. Reg.* 27651 (1998), which was eventually withdrawn (subsequently suspended by E.O. 13095, 63 *Fed. Reg.* 42565 [1998]), and reactions to the EPA development of interim guidance on permitting processes affecting environmental justice developed under E.O. 12989, 59 *Fed. Reg.* 7629 (1994) and Memorandum on Environmental Justice, *Weekly Compilation of Presidential Documents* 30 (1994): 279.

39. See, e.g., E.O. 11246, 30 *Fed. Reg.* 12319 (1965) on affirmative action contracting.

40. See *Hodel v. Virginia Surface Mining and Reclamation Ass'n,* 452 U.S. 264 (1981).

41. See *Hirabayashi v. United States,* 320 U.S. 81 (1943); *Korematsu v. United States,* 319 U.S. 432 (1943).

42. *United States v. Curtiss-Wright Export Corp.,* 299 U.S. 304 (1936).

43. *The Prize Cases,* 67 U.S. (2 Black) 635 (1862).

44. See, e.g., *Ex parte Milligan,* 71 U.S. (4 Wall.) 2 (1866); *Ex parte Endo,* 323 U.S. 283 (1944).

45. See *Independent Gasoline Marketers Councils v. Duncan,* 492 F.Supp. 614 (D.D.C. 1980).

2. EXECUTIVE ORDERS

1. *Weekly Compilation of Presidential Documents* 29 (1993): 77.

2. E.O. 13198, Agency Responsibilities with Respect to Faith-Based and Community Initiatives, 66 *Fed. Reg.* 8497 (2001); E.O. 13199, Establishment of White House Office of Faith-Based and Community Initiatives, 66 *Fed. Reg.* 8499 (2001).

3. See the Administrative Procedure Act, 5 U.S.C. §551 et seq.

4. See Florida governor Jeb Bush, E.O. 99-281, <*http://www.state.fl.us/eog/executive_orders/1999/November/eo99-281*> July 30, 2001; California governor Pete

Wilson, E.O. W-136-95 and W-136-96; see *Coalition for Economic Equity v. Wilson,* 946 F.Supp. 148 (NDCA 1996), vacated and remanded, 122 F.3d 692 (9th Cir. 1997).

5. U.S. House of Representatives, Committee on Government Operations, *Executive Orders and Proclamations: A Study of the Use of Presidential Power,* 85th Cong., 1st sess., 1957, Committee Print, 1 (hereafter House, 1957 Study).

6. The cases of *Menotti v. Dillon,* 167 U.S. 703 (1897), and *United States v. Oregon and California Railroad,* 176 U.S. 28 (1900), are examples of situations in which executive orders directly affected the property of citizens and companies and were permissible.

7. U.S. Senate, Report of the Special Committee on National Emergencies and Delegated Emergency Powers, *Executive Orders in Times of War and National Emergency,* 93d Cong., 2d sess., 1974, Committee Print, 2 (hereafter Committee on National Emergencies).

8. Clifford L. Lord, ed., *List and Index of Presidential Executive Orders, Unnumbered Series—Historical Records Survey, N.J.* (Newark, N.J.: Works Projects Administration, 1942) (hereafter WPA, NJ).

9. W.P.A., *Historical Records Survey, Presidential Executive Orders* (New York: Hastings House Publishers, 1944), 1:vi (hereafter WPA, NY).

10. *United States v. Reynolds,* 250 U.S. 104, 110 (1919).

11. WPA, NY, 1:viii–ix.

12. E.O. 11354, 32 *Fed. Reg.* 7695 (1967), 12080 (1978), Jimmy Carter, *Public Papers of the President, 1978* (Washington, D.C.: Government Printing Office, 1979), book 2, and 12608, 3 C.F.R. (Comp. 1987): 245.

13. 5 U.S.C. §551 et seq.

14. *Dalton v. Specter,* 511 U.S. 462 (1994).

15. See Al Gore, *From Red Tape to Results: Creating a Government That Works Better and Costs Less,* Report of the National Performance Review (Washington, D.C.: Government Printing Office, 1993).

16. 49 Stat. 500, 44 U.S.C. §1501 et seq.

17. WPA, NY, 1:541.

18. Louis Fisher, *Executive Orders and Proclamations, 1933–1999: Controversies with Congress and in the Courts* (Washington, D.C.: Congressional Research Service, 1999), 1.

19. *Panama Refining Co. v. Ryan,* 293 U.S. 388, 412 (1935).

20. 44 U.S.C. §1511.

21. Office of the Federal Register, *Codification of Presidential Proclamations and Executive Orders: April 13, 1945–January 20, 1989* (Washington, D.C.: Government Printing Office, 1990).

22. "This section does not require codification of the text of Presidential documents published and periodically compiled in supplements to Title 3 of the Code of Federal Regulations" (44 U.S.C. §1510[g]).

23. See *The Grapeshot,* 76 U.S. (9 Wall.) 129 (1869).

24. WPA, NY.

25. U.S. Senate, Committee on National Emergencies, 2.

252 BY ORDER OF THE PRESIDENT

27. Executive Orders Disposition Tables, April 13, 1945–July 2, 2001, <http://www.nara.gov/fedreg/eo.html> July 30, 2001.

28. Robert Caro, *The Power Broker: Robert Moses and the Fall of New York* (New York: Knopf, 1974).

29. *Youngstown Sheet & Tube v. Sawyer,* 343 U.S. 579 (1952).

30. See, e.g., *Hynes v. Grimes Packing Co.,* 337 U.S. 86 (1949). See also *Haig v. Agee,* 453 U.S. 280 (1981).

31. *Amalgamated Meat Cutters and Butcher Workmen of North America, AFL–CIO v. Connolly,* 337 F.Supp. 737 (D.D.C. 1971); *Independent Gasoline Marketers Council v. Duncan,* 492 F.Supp. 614 (D.D.C. 1980).

32. 3 U.S.C.S. § 301 (2000).

33. *Yakus v. United States,* 321 U.S. 414, 424 (1944).

34. *Panama Refining Co. v. Ryan,* 293 U.S. 388, 415 (1935).

35. *A.L.A. Schechter Poultry Corp. v. United States,* 295 U.S. 495, 537–538 (1935).

36. There are some judges who have attempted to argue for a restoration of the nondelegation doctrine, led by Chief Justice William Rehnquist. See *Industrial Union AFL–CIO v. American Petroleum Institute,* 448 U.S. 607 (1980). A number of groups have sought to test whether the Supreme Court might be willing to use the nondelegation doctrine in a challenge to the Clean Air Act. However, the Supreme Court ultimately upheld the delegation; see *Whitman v. American Trucking Associations,* 531 U.S. 457 (2001).

37. *Dames & Moore v. Regan,* 453 U.S. 654, 668–669 (1981).

38. *In re Wilson,* 140 U.S. 575 (1891).

39. See, e.g., *Hirabayashi v. United States,* 320 U.S. 81, 91 (1943).

40. See *Isbrandtsen-Moller v. United States,* 300 U.S. 139 (1937); *Fleming v. Mohawk Wrecking & Lumber,* 331 U.S. 111 (1947); *Swayne v. Hoyt,* 300 U.S. 297, 300–301 (1937).

41. See *Dames & Moore v. Regan,* 668–669.

42. One of the most commonly cited sources for this point is, ironically enough, the Civil War era *Milligan* case. "The power to make the necessary laws is in Congress; the power to execute in the President. Both powers imply many subordinate and auxiliary powers. Each includes all authorities essential to its due exercise. But neither can the President, in war more than in peace, intrude upon the proper authority of Congress, nor can Congress upon the proper authority of the President" (*Ex parte Milligan,* 71 U.S. [4 Wall.] 2, 139 [1866]).

43. See *Cole v. Young,* 351 U.S. 536 (1956); *United States v. Symonds,* 120 U.S. 46 (1887); *Kendall v. United States,* 37 U.S. (12 Pet.) 524 (1838).

44. *Little v. Barreme,* 6 U.S. (2 Cranch) 170 (1804).

45. 74 F.3d 1322 (D.C.Cir. 1996).

46. *Minnesota v. Mille Lacs Band of Chippewa Indians,* 143 L.Ed.2d 270 (1999).

47. Harold Relyea, "The Evolution of Government Information Security Classification Policy: A Brief Overview (1773–1973)," in U.S. House of Representatives, Committee on Government Operations, *Executive Classification of Information,* H.Rept. 93-221, 93d Cong., 1st sess., 1973, 11.

48. U.S. House of Representatives, Committee on Government Operations, *Security Classification Policy and Executive Order 12356,* H.Rept. 97-731, 97th Cong., 2d sess., 1982, 5 (hereafter *Reagan Security Order Report*).

49. E.O. 8381, 5 *Fed. Reg.* 1145 (1940).

50. E.O. 10104, 15 *Fed. Reg.* 597 (1950), and E.O. 10290, 16 *Fed. Reg.* 9795 (1951).

51. E.O. 10501, 18 *Fed. Reg.* 7049 (1953).

52. See, generally, *Laird v. Tatum,* 408 U.S. 1 (1972).

53. 37 *Fed. Reg.* 5200 (1972).

54. 43 *Fed. Reg.* 28949 (1978).

55. 47 *Fed. Reg.* 14874 (1982).

56. 50 U.S.C. §435 (2000).

57. 60 *Fed. Reg.* 19825 (1995).

58. *Little v. Barreme.*

59. *Menotti v. Dillon,* 167 U.S. 703 (1897), and *United States v. Oregon and California Railroad,* 176 U.S. 28 (1900).

60. These included E.O. 5062 (1929), 5211 (1929), and 5067 (1929), WPA, NJ.

61. *Haig v. Agee,* 453 U.S. 280 (1981).

62. 36 *Fed. Reg.* 15727 (1971).

63. See *Amalgamated Meat Cutters and Butcher Workmen of North America v. Connally.*

64. Brownlow Commission, *Report of the President's Committee on Administrative Management* (Washington, D.C.: Government Printing Office, 1937).

65. Louis Fisher, *Constitutional Conflicts Between Congress and the President,* 4th ed., rev. (Lawrence: University Press of Kansas, 1997), 97.

66. 58 Stat. 387, §213 (1944).

67. Fisher, *Executive Orders,* 3, quoting (90 *Cong. Rev.* 6022 [1944]).

68. 26 *Fed. Reg.* 1789 (1961).

69. Issued February 17, 1981, 46 *Fed. Reg.* 13193 (1981).

70. 50 *Fed. Reg.* 11036 (1985).

71. Christine Triano and Nancy Watzman, *All the Vice President's Men* (Washington, D.C.: OMB Watch, 1991), i.

72. 58 *Fed. Reg.* 6189 (1983).

73. Bob Woodward, *The Agenda: Inside the Clinton White House* (New York: Simon and Schuster, 1994).

74. E.O. 12841, 58 *Fed. Reg.* 13529 (1993).

75. E.O. 12896, 59 *Fed. Reg.* 5515 (1994).

76. E.O. 12897, 59 *Fed. Reg.* 5517 (1994).

77. E.O. 12910, 59 *Fed. Reg.* 21915 (1994).

78. E.O. 19, May 31, 1983, <*http://www.goer.state.ny.us/MC/handbook/appdxg.html*> as of April 14, 2001.

79. Office of the Mayor, "Mayor Unveils Ethics Reform Aims to Strengthen Integrity of City Government," October 27, 1997, <*http://w5.ci.chi.il.us./Mayor/SpecialNotices/html/Ethics.97.10.27.html*> as of April 14, 2001.

80. See *Coalition for Economic Equity v. Wilson,* 122 F.3d 692 (9th Cir. 1997).

81. <*http://www.state.fl.us/eog/executive_orders/1999/November/eo99–281.html*> as of April 14, 2001.

82. *Rutan v. Republican Party of Illinois,* 497 U.S. 62 (1990).
83. E.O. 12886, 58 *Fed. Reg.* 68708 (1993).
84. E.O. 12888, 58 *Fed. Reg.* 69153 (1993).
85. E.O. 12908, 59 *Fed. Reg.* 21907 (1994).
86. See Carter's E.O. 12036, 43 *Fed. Reg.* 3674 (1977).
87. May 23, 1979, 44 *Fed. Reg.* 30311 (1979).
88. 453 U.S. 280 (1981).
89. Ibid., at 299.
90. *United States v. Curtiss-Wright Export Corp.,* 299 U.S. 304, 319 (1936).
91. 361 U.S., at 662.
92. *United States v. Sperry Corp.,* 493 U.S. 52 (1989).
93. 62 *Fed. Reg.* 28301 (1997).
94. *Crosby v. National Foreign Trade Council,* 147 L.Ed.2d 352 (2000).
95. Ibid., at 363.
96. 236 U.S. 459 (1915).
97. Ibid., at 469–471.

3. STRATEGIES, TACTICS, AND POLITICAL REALITIES OF EXECUTIVE ORDERS

1. See, e.g., *United States v. Reynolds,* 250 U.S. 104 (1919), describing the operations of the shipping board.
2. P.L. 94-412, 90 Stat. 1255, 50 U.S.C. §1621.
3. U.S. Senate, Special Committee on the Termination of the National Emergency, *Summary of Emergency Powers Statutes,* 93d Cong., 1st sess., 1973, iii.
4. Arthur S. Link and William B. Catton, *American Epoch,* vols. (New York: Knopf, 1973), 2:111.
5. Franklin D. Roosevelt, *The Public Papers and Addresses of Franklin D. Roosevelt* (New York: Random House, 1938), 2:15.
6. Frank Freidel, *Franklin D. Roosevelt: A Rendezvous with Destiny* (Boston: Little, Brown, 1990), 93.
7. U.S. Senate, Committee on National Emergencies, 43.
8. Resolution of March 9, 1933, c. 1, Title I, sec. 1, 48 Stat. 1, codified as 12 U.S.C. §95(b).
9. E.O. 6073, March 10, 1933, WPA, NY, 1:503.
10. E.O. 6102, April 5, 1933, WPA, NY, 1:506.
11. E.O. 6111, April 20, 1933, WPA, NY, 1:507.
12. *Norman v. Baltimore & Ohio Railroad,* 294 U.S. 240 (1935).
13. Arthur M. Schlesinger Jr., *The Coming of the New Deal* (Boston: Houghton Mifflin, 1958), 8.
14. U.S. Senate, Committee on National Emergencies, 33.
15. Ibid., 45.
16. David McCullough, *Truman* (New York: Simon and Schuster, 1992), 467–474.
17. Ibid., 469.
18. *Woods v. Cloyd W. Miller Co.,* 333 U.S. 138 (1948).
19. E.O. 9693, 3 C.F.R. (Cum. Supp. 1946): 503.

20. E.O. 9727, 3 C.F.R. (Cum. Supp. 1946): 539; E.O. 9758, 3 C.F.R. (Supp. 1946): 539.

21. E.O. 9727, 3 C.F.R. (Cum. Supp. 1946): 531; E.O. 9736, 3 C.F.R. (Cum. Supp. 1946): 543.

22. McCullough, *Truman,* 502–504.

23. Ibid., 528.

24. *United States v. United Mineworkers,* 330 U.S. 258, 304 (1947).

25. *United States Grain Corporation v. Phillips,* 261 U.S. 106 (1923).

26. See House, 1957 *Study.*

27. See E.O. 9672, December 31, 1945.

28. E.O. 9674, January 4, 1946.

29. E.O. 9699, February 21, 1946.

30. *Fleming v. Mohawk Wrecking and Lumber,* 331 U.S. 111, 116 (1947). See also *Woods v. Cloyd W. Miller,* 333 U.S. 138 (1948).

31. *United States v. Allied Oil Corp.,* 341 U.S. 1, 5 (1951).

32. Harold C. Relyea, "National Emergency Powers and Y2K Problems," *CRS Report for Congress,* July 22, 1999, 6.

33. 61 *Fed. Reg.* 37347 (1996).

34. 63 *Fed. Reg.* 6467 (1998).

35. *Immigration and Naturalization Service v. Chadha,* 462 U.S. 919 (1983).

36. Harold C. Relyea, "National Emergency Powers," *CRS Report for Congress,* July 22, 1999, 12.

37. 26 *Fed. Reg.* 1463 (1961).

38. 26 *Fed. Reg.* 1553 (1961).

39. E.O. 10922, 26 *Fed. Reg.* 1655 (1961).

40. E.O. 10923, 26 *Fed. Reg.* 1699 (1961).

41. E.O. 10929, 26 *Fed. Reg.* 2583 (1961).

42. 26 *Fed. Reg.* 5731 (1961).

43. E.O. 10944, 26 *Fed. Reg.* 4419 (1961).

44. E.O. 12834, 58 *Fed. Reg.* 5911 (1993).

45. E.O. 12839, 58 *Fed. Reg.* 8515 (1993).

46. E.O. 12861, 58 *Fed. Reg.* 48255 (1993).

47. See, generally, Bob Woodward, *The Agenda: Inside the Clinton White House* (New York: Simon and Schuster, 1994).

48. Helen Dewar and Frank Swoboda, "Republican-Led Filibuster Kills Striker Replacement Bill in Senate," *Washington Post,* July 14, 1994, p. A7.

49. *Midwest Motor Express, Inc. v. International Brotherhood of Teamsters, Chauffeurs, Warehousemen and Helpers of America, Local 120,* 512 N.W.2d 881 (Minn. 1994).

50. Frank Swoboda, "UAW Strikes Caterpillar Nationwide; Act Tests Labor's Ability to Bar Use of Permanent Replacement Workers," *Washington Post,* June 23, 1994, p. D12.

51. Roy Malone, "Doe Run Strikers Lose Jobs at Smerter, Replacement Workers Vote Out Teamsters Local," *St. Louis Post–Dispatch,* January 12, 1995, p. 1C.

52. E.O. 12954, 60 *Fed. Reg.* 13023 (1995).

53. Ibid., §1.

54. *Chamber of Commerce v. Reich,* 74 F.3d 1322 (D.C.Cir. 1996).

55. Ruth P. Morgan, *The President and Civil Rights* (New York: St. Martin's Press, 1970), 13–14.

56. U.S. House, 1957 Study, 72.

57. McCullough, *Truman,* 552–553.

58. Ibid., 551–553.

59. Ibid., 553.

60. *Cornelius v. NAACP Legal Defense and Education Fund,* 473 U.S. 788 (1985).

61. "Conversation with Joseph Alsop," *Washington Post* columnist, November 25, 1963, 10:40 A.M., LBJ White House Tapes, C-SPAN, <*http://www.c-span.org/lbj*> August 10, 2001.

62. 28 *Fed. Reg.* 12789.

63. "Conversation with Senator Thomas Kuchel" (R-Calif.), November 11, 1963, 5:26 P.M., LBJ White House Tapes, C-SPAN, <*http://www.c-span.org/lbj*> August 10, 2001.

64. "Conversation with Senator Richard Russell" (D-Ga.), November 29, 1963, 8:55 P.M., LBJ White House Tapes, C-SPAN, <*http://www.c-span.org/lbj*> August 10, 2001.

65. *California Department of Human Resources Development v. Java,* 402 U.S. 121, 130–131 (1971).

66. 32 *Fed. Reg.* 1111 (1967).

67. 44 *Fed. Reg.* 22027 (1979).

68. 51 *Fed. Reg.* 4475 (1986).

69. 51 *Fed. Reg.* 43718 (1986).

70. 59 *Fed. Reg.* 2935 (1994).

71. 30 *Fed. Reg.* 12319 (1965).

72. 26 *Fed. Reg.* 1977 (1961).

73. Vaughn Davis Bornet, *The Presidency of Lyndon B. Johnson* (Lawrence: University Press of Kansas, 1983), 53–54. See also Bruce J. Schulman, *Lyndon B. Johnson and American Liberalism* (Boston: Bedford Books, 1995), 106–117.

74. Lyndon B. Johnson, *Public Papers of the Presidents of the United States, 1965* (Washington, D.C.: Government Printing Office, 1966), 2:636.

75. Ibid., Memorandum on Reassignment of Civil Rights Functions, September 24, 1965, 2:1017–1019.

76. He also issued E.O. 11247 at the same time (30 *Fed. Reg.* 12327 [1965]). This order assigned responsibilities for action under Title VI of the 1964 act to the attorney general.

77. Legality of Revised Philadelphia Plan, 42 Op. Atty. Gen. 405 (1969).

78. U.S. Senate, Hearings Before the Subcommittee on Separation of Powers of the Committee on the Judiciary, *The Philadelphia Plan,* 91st Cong., 1st sess., 1969.

79. *Contractors Association of Eastern Pennsylvania v. Secretary of Labor,* 442 F.2d 159 (3d Cir. 1971).

80. 52 *Fed. Reg.* 34188 (1987).

81. 52 *Fed. Reg.* 41685 (1987).

82. 47 *Fed. Reg.* 30959 (1982).

83. 53 *Fed. Reg.* 8859 (1988).

84. See, generally, Cornelius M. Kerwin, *Rulemaking: How Government Agencies Write Law and Make Policy,* 2d ed. (Washington, D.C.: Congressional Quarterly Press, 1999).

85. The full story of how the order and the leases worked is provided in *Mammoth Oil Co. v. United States (Teapot Dome),* 275 U.S. 13 (1927). See also *Pan American Petroleum and Transport Co. v. United States,* 273 U.S. 456 (1927).

86. *Mammoth Oil v. United States,* 275 U.S., at 43.

87. Inaugural Address, January 20, 1981, Ronald Reagan, *Public Papers of the President of the United States, 1981* (Washington, D.C.: Government Printing Office, 1982), 1.

88. I have explained this phenomenon in detail in Phillip J. Cooper, *Public Law and Public Administration,* 3d ed. (Itasca, Ill.: F. E. Peacock, 2000).

89. The training was provided by the right-wing Heritage Foundation. See, generally, Stuart M. Butler, Michael Sanera, and W. Bruce Weinrod, *Mandate for Leadership II* (Washington, D.C.: Heritage Foundation, 1984).

90. Carolyn Ban and Patricia Ingraham, "Short-Timers: Political Appointee Mobility and Its Impact on Political/Career Relations in the Reagan Administration," *Administration and Society* 22 (1990): 106.

91. 46 *Fed. Reg.* 13193 (1981).

92. See *Environmental Defense Fund v. Thomas,* 627 F. Supp. 566 (D.D.C. 1986); *Natural Resources Defense Council v. Ruckelshaus,* 1984 U.S. Dist. LEXIS 23589 (D.D.C. 1984).

93. Testimony of James C. Miller III, in "The Role of OMB in Regulation": Hearing Before the Subcommittee on Oversight and Investigation of House Committee on Energy and Commerce, 97th Cong., 1st sess., 1981, 46, quoted in *Environmental Defense Fund v. Thomas,* 627 F.Supp., at 570.

94. Ibid., at 571.

95. 46 *Fed. Reg.* 9909 (1981).

96. E.O. 12288, 46 *Fed. Reg.* 10135 (1981).

97. 46 *Fed. Reg.* 12943 (1981).

98. 46 *Fed. Reg.* 13967 (1981).

99. 46 *Fed. Reg.* 13969 (1981).

100. E.O. 12333, 46 *Fed. Reg.* 59941 (1981); E.O. 12334, 46 *Fed. Reg.* 59955 (1981).

101. E.O. 12356, 47 *Fed. Reg.* 14874 (1982).

102. E.O. 12314, 46 *Fed. Reg.* 38329 (1981).

103. E.O. 12305, 46 *Fed. Reg.* 25421 (1981).

104. 46 *Fed. Reg.* 13193 (1981).

105. 43 *Fed. Reg.* 12661 (1978).

106. Executive Order 12866, 58 *Fed. Reg.* 51735 (1993).

107. 43 *Fed. Reg.* 51375 (1978).

108. *AFL–CIO v. Kahn,* 472 F.Supp. 88, 92 (D.D.C. 1979).

109. Ibid., at 94–95.

110. *Perkins v. Lukens Steel Co.,* 310 U.S. 113, 127 (1940).

111. 472 F.Supp., at 101.

112. 51 *Fed. Reg.* 32889 (1986).

113. Schlesinger, *Coming of the New Deal,* 11–12.

114. WPA, NY, 1:91.

115. See *Raines v. Byrd,* 521 U.S. 811 (1997).

116. U.S. Senate, Special Committee on National Emergencies and Delegated Emergency Powers, *Summary of Executive Orders in Times of War and National Emergencies,* 93d Cong., 2d sess., 1974, Committee Print, 5.

117. U.S. Senate, Special Committee on the Termination of the National Emergency, *Summary of Emergency Powers Statutes,* 93d Cong., 1st sess., 1973, 6.

118. WPA, NY, 1:218.

119. Ibid.

120. 63 *Fed. Reg.* 27651 (1998).

121. 63 *Fed. Reg.* 42565 (1998).

122. I am grateful to Louis Fisher for reminding me of the critical provisions in Section 623 of the Omnibus Consolidated and Emergency Supplemental Appropriations Act for FY 1999, 112 Stat. 2681.

123. See Louis Fisher, *Executive Orders and Proclamations, 1933–1999: Controversies with Congress and in the Courts* (Washington, D.C.: Congressional Research Service, 1999).

124. 64 *Fed. Reg.* 43255 (1999).

125. 59 *Fed. Reg.* 7629 (1994).

126. *Public Citizen v. Department of Justice,* 491 U.S. 440 (1989).

127. Ibid., at 464.

128. 74 F.3d 1322 (D.C.Cir. 1996).

129. 55 F.3d 732 (2d Cir. 1995).

130. See *Dalton v. Specter,* 511 U.S. 462 (1994).

131. *Little v. Barreme,* 6 U.S. (2 Cranch) 170 (1804 Term).

132. See, e.g., *United States ex rel. Skinner & Eddy Corporation v. McCarl,* 275 U.S. 1 (1927); *U.S. Shipping Board Merchant Fleet Corporation v. Harwood,* 281 U.S. 519 (1930).

133. *United States v. Pewee Coal Co.,* 341 U.S. 114 (1951).

134. 7 *Fed. Reg.* 1407 (1942).

135. 56 Stat. 173 (1942).

136. Freidel, *Franklin D. Roosevelt,* 407.

137. Proclamation 4417, 41 *Fed. Reg.* 7741 (1976).

138. 102 Stat. 903 (1988).

139. WPA, NY, 1:57.

140. 341 U.S. 123 (1951).

141. See also *Peters v. Hobby,* 349 U.S. 331 (1955).

142. *Cole v. Young,* 351 U.S. 536 (1956).

4. PRESIDENTIAL MEMORANDA

1. Memorandum Directing a Federal Employee Hiring Freeze, *Weekly Compilation of Presidential Documents* 17 (1981): 6–7.

2. Presidential Memorandum on the Title X "Gag Rule," *Weekly Compilation of Presidential Documents* 29 (1993): 87–88.

3. Presidential Memorandum on Fetal Tissue Transplantation Research, *Weekly Compilation of Presidential Documents* 29 (1993): 87.

4. Presidential Memorandum on Abortions in Military Hospitals, *Weekly Compilation of Presidential Documents* 29 (1993): 88.

5. Presidential Memorandum on the Mexico City Policy, *Weekly Compilation of Presidential Documents* 29 (1993): 88.

6. Robin Toner, "Joy and Outrage," *New York Times,* September 29, 2000, p. A1.

7. *Weekly Compilation of Presidential Documents* 29 (1993): 112.

8. Presidential Memorandum on Review of Regulations, *Weekly Compilation of Presidential Documents* 29 (1993): 93.

9. Presidential Memorandum on Standards of Official Conduct, *Weekly Compilation of Presidential Documents* 37 (2001): 211.

10. Presidential Memorandum on Regulatory Review Plan, 66 *Fed. Reg.* 7701 (2001).

11. Presidential Memorandum on Government Hiring Controls, White House Internet Site, *<http://www.whitehouse.gov/news/releases/20010123-3.html>* as of February 11, 2001.

12. Presidential Memorandum on Restoration of Mexico City Policy, *Weekly Compilation of Presidential Documents* 37 (2001): 216.

13. WPA, NY, 1:vi.

14. Remarks to the Students at Carlmont High School in Belmont, California, *Weekly Compilation of Presidential Documents* 30 (1994): 2099.

15. Implementation of the Gun-Free Schools Act of 1994, and the Safe and Drug-Free Schools and Communities Act, *Weekly Compilation of Presidential Documents* 30 (1994): 2150.

16. *Weekly Compilation of Presidential Documents* 30 (1994): 479.

17. National Partnership for Reinventing Government Library Internet Site *<http://govinfo.library.unt.edu/npr/library/direct.htp>* November 22, 2000.

18. See, e.g., National Security Action Memoranda 278: Presidential Determination re Aid to Indonesia, February 3, 1964, *<http://www.lbjlib.utexas.edu/johnson/archives.hom/NSAMs/nsam278.asp>* August 13, 2001.

19. *<http://bushlibrary.tamu.edu/papers/1989/89113002.html>* August 13, 2001.

20. See, e.g., Memorandum on the 1994 Combined Federal Campaign, *Weekly Compilation of Presidential Documents* 30 (1994): 1749.

21. *Weekly Compilation of Presidential Documents* 30 (1994): 893.

22. *Weekly Compilation of Presidential Documents* 30 (1994): 478.

23. *Weekly Compilation of Presidential Documents.*

24. See, e.g., Richard Boudreaux, "Russian Agency Reveals Crisis in Nuclear Power Safety: Report Cites 20,000 Violations Last Year." *Los Angeles Times,* February 16, 1994, p. A9.

25. Ann Devroy, "Pact Reached to Dismantle Ukraine's Nuclear Force: Detailed Plan to Be Signed Friday, Clinton Announces," *Washington Post,* January 11, 1994, p. A1; Selig S. Harrison, "'Package' Incentives for Forswearing Nuclear Arms," *Washington Post,* January 30, 1994, p. C7.

26. See, e.g., Agis Salpukas, "U.S. Bidding in Nuclear-Fuel Market," *New York Times,* January 18, 1994, p. D7.

27. Memorandum on the Purchase of Highly Enriched Uranium from Russia, *Weekly Compilation of Presidential Documents* 30 (1994): 640.

28. 46 *Fed. Reg.* 13193 (1981). See Morton Rosenberg, "Beyond the Limits of Executive Power—Presidential Control of Agency Rulemaking Under Executive Order 12291," *Michigan Law Review* 20 (1981): 193.

29. See, e.g., *Environmental Defense Fund v. Thomas,* 627 F.Supp. 556 (D.D.C. 1986); *American Pilots' Association v. Gracey,* 631 F.Supp. 828 (D.D.C. 1986).

30. 50 *Fed. Reg.* 1036 (1985).

31. *Weekly Compilation of Presidential Documents* 21 (1985): 13.

32. See *Environmental Defense Fund v. Thomas.*

33. C. Boyden Gray, counsel to the president, to John Conyers, chairman, Committee on Government Operations, April 30, 1990.

34. Paperwork Reduction Act of 1995, P.L. 104-13, 109 Stat. 163, 44 U.S.C. §3501 et. seq.

35. Christine Triano and Nancy Watzman, *All the Vice President's Men* (Washington, D.C.: OMB Watch, 1991), i.

36. See Malcolm D. Woolf, "Clean Air or Hot Air?: Lessons from the Quayle Competitiveness Council's Oversight of EPA," *Journal of Law and Public Policy* 10 (1993): 97.

37. This was done in an October 1990 memorandum to cabinet secretaries and agency heads. See Triano and Watzman, *All the Vice President's Men,* 7.

38. Ibid., memorandum from the vice president to all heads of executive departments and agencies, March 22, 1991, quoted at 7.

39. Congressman David E. Skaggs (D-Colo.), quoted in Keith Schneider, "Prominence Proves Perilous for Bush's Rule Slayer," *New York Times,* June 30, 1992.

40. Christine Triano, "Quayle and Co.," *Government Information Insider,* June 1991, p. 8.

41. Don R. Clay, assistant administrator, Environmental Protection Agency, to John D. Dingell, chair, Subcommittee on Oversight and Investigations, September 1991.

42. Memorandum for certain department and agency heads, "Memoranda on Reducing the Burden of Government Regulation," January 28, 1992, George Bush, *Public Papers of the Presidents of the United States, 1992–1993* (Washington, D.C.: Government Printing Office, 1993), book 1, 166.

43. Ibid., memorandum on Regulatory Coordination.

44. Memorandum on Implementing Regulatory Reforms, *Weekly Compilation of Presidential Documents* 28 (1992): 728.

45. "Remarks on Regulatory Reform," *Weekly Compilation of Presidential Documents* 28 (1992): 726.

46. The president's memorandum, "Postponement of Pending Regulations," was published on January 29, 1981 (46 *Fed. Reg.* 11227).

47. Opinion of the Office of Legal Counsel, Presidential Memorandum Delaying Proposed and Pending Regulations, 5 Op. O.L.C. 55 (1981).

48. *Weekly Compilation of Presidential Documents* 29 (1993): 1733–1734.

49. Memorandum on Electronic Government, December 17, 1999, *Weekly Compilation of Presidential Documents* 35 (1999): 2641; Memorandum on Expanding Access

to Internet-based Educational Resources for Children, Teachers, and Parents, April 18, 1997, *Weekly Compilation of Presidential Documents* 33 (1997): 551; Memorandum on Electronic Commerce, July 1, 1997, *Weekly Compilation of Presidential Documents* 33 (1997): 1006; Memorandum on Electronic Commerce, November 30, 1998, *Weekly Compilation of Presidential Documents* 34 (1998): 2396.

50. Memorandum on Assistance to Kosovo, January 25, 1999, *Weekly Compilation of Presidential Documents* 35 (1999): 125; Memorandum on Humanitarian Relief for Kosovar Refugees, April 21, 1999, *Weekly Compilation of Presidential Documents* 35 (1999): 690; Memorandum on Assistance to Refugees Fleeing Kosovo, April 29, 1999, *Weekly Compilation of Presidential Documents* 35 (1999): 767; Memorandum on Emergency Refugee Admissions Consultations Relating to Kosovars, April 30, 1999, *Weekly Compilation of Presidential Documents* 35 (1999): 769; Memorandum on the Drawdown of Commodities and Services for the United Nations Interim Administration Mission in Kosovo, September 21, 1999, *Weekly Compilation of Presidential Documents* 35 (1999): 1785.

51. Memorandum on Military Assistance for States Participating in the Multinational Force for East Timor, September 21, 1999, *Weekly Compilation of Presidential Documents* 35 (1999): 1785; Memorandum on Assistance for Refugees and Victims of the Timor and North Caucasus Crisis, November 10, 1999, *Weekly Compilation of Presidential Documents* 35 (1999): 2353.

52. Memorandum on Emergency Disaster Relief for Central America, November 6, 1998, *Weekly Compilation of Presidential Documents* 34 (1998): 2279.

53. Memorandum on Western Power Outage, July 3, 1996, *Weekly Compilation of Presidential Documents* 32 (1996): 1189.

54. Memorandum on Potential Electrical Shortages in California, August 3, 2000, *Weekly Compilation of Presidential Documents* 36 (2000): 1783.

55. Gustav Niebuhr, "Cold-War Tests Prompt an Ethics Debate; Experts Express Differing Opinions on Morality of Government Radiation Experiments," *Washington Post,* January 4, 1994, p. A6; Brian McGrory and Sean P. Murphy, "Inmates Used in '60s Drug Test," *Boston Globe,* January 1, 1994, Petro/Regional, p. 1; Scott Allen, "Kennedy Dropped Testing Probe; Taft's Anger Led to 1971 Decision," *Boston Globe,* February 12, 1994, National/Foreign, p. 5; Melissa Health, "Charity Patients Irradiated to Gauge Effect on Soldiers: Radiation Experiments on 82 People with Cancer Lasted Until 1972. Sixty Days After Exposure, 25 Had Died," *Los Angeles Times,* January 6, 1994, p. A1; Michael Ross, "Glenn Urges Probe for Toxic Experiments: Senator Says U.S. Should Disclose If Any Patients Were Unwittingly Exposed to Any Hazardous Substance in Tests Like Those for Radiation," *Los Angeles Times,* January 7, 1994, p. A20; "Experiments on Humans: It's Past Time to Unlock Those Laboratory Doors," *San Diego Union–Tribune,* January 5, 1994, p. B6; "VA Hospitals Included in Nuclear Experiments Probe," *Los Angeles Times,* January 1, 1994, p. A1.

56. *Weekly Compilation of Presidential Documents* 30 (1994): 323.

57. *Weekly Compilation of Presidential Documents* 33 (1997): 281.

58. *Weekly Compilation of Presidential Documents* 33 (1997): 422.

59. Memorandum on Privacy and Personal Information in Federal Records, May 14, 1998, *Weekly Compilation of Presidential Documents* 34 (1998): 870; Memorandum

on the Food Safety Initiative, October 2, 1997, *Weekly Compilation of Presidential Documents* 33 (1997): 1479; Memorandum on the Joint Institute for Food Safety Research, July 3, 1998, *Weekly Compilation of Presidential Documents* 34 (1998): 1326; Memorandum on the National Academy of Sciences Report on Food Safety, August 25, 1998, *Weekly Compilation of Presidential Documents* 34 (1998): 1654; Memorandum on the Safety of Imported Foods, July 3, 1999, *Weekly Compilation of Presidential Documents* 35 (1999): 1277; Memorandum on Imports of Lamb Meat, July 7, 1999, *Weekly Compilation of Presidential Documents* 35 (1999): 1310.

60. Patient Protection, November 13, 2000, Memorandum on the Health Care "Consumer Bill of Rights and Responsibilities," November 20, 1997, *Weekly Compilation of Presidential Documents* 33 (1997): 1872; Memorandum on Federal Agency Compliance with Patient Bill of Rights, February 20, 1998 (had previously issued a directive in November of 1997), *Weekly Compilation of Presidential Documents* 34 (1998): 298; Memorandum on Improving Health Care Quality and Ensuring Patient Safety, December 7, 1999, *Weekly Compilation of Presidential Documents* 35 (1999): 2530.

61. Memorandum on Importation of Assault Pistols, *Weekly Compilation of Presidential Documents* 29 (1993): 1605.

62. "On the Urban Battlefield," *St. Louis Post–Dispatch,* July 7, 1993, p. 2C; "They're Only Used to Kill People: Ban All Semiautomatic Guns in the State, Period," *Los Angeles Times,* July 12, 1993, p. B6.

63. Kevin Johnson, "Summit Called over Rise in Gang Crime: County Supervisors Urge City and Law Enforcement Officials to Join in a November Meeting to Address the Alarming Jump in Assaults with Weapons on Campuses and in Affluent Communities," *Los Angeles Times,* July 24, 1993, p. B1.

64. Memorandum on Implementation of Safe Schools Legislation, *Weekly Compilation of Presidential Documents* 30 (1994): 2150.

65. Memorandum on the Youth Crime Gun Interdiction Initiative, *Weekly Compilation of Presidential Documents* 32 (1996): 1205.

66. Memorandum on Child Safety Lock Devices for Handguns, *Weekly Compilation of Presidential Documents* 33 (1997): 287.

67. *Weekly Compilation of Presidential Documents* 33 (1997): 856.

68. Memorandum on Importation of Modified Semiautomatic Assault-Type Rifles, *Weekly Compilation of Presidential Documents* 33 (1997): 1825.

69. Memorandum on Preventing Firearms Sales to Prohibited Purchasers, *Weekly Compilation of Presidential Documents* 34 (1998): 2780.

70. Memorandum on Affirmative Action, July 19, 1995, *Weekly Compilation of Presidential Documents* 31 (1995): 1264.

71. Memorandum on Religious Expression in Public Schools, July 12, 1995, *Weekly Compilation of Presidential Documents* 31 (1995): 1227; Memorandum on Religious Exercise and Religious Expression in the Federal Workplace, August 14, 1997, *Weekly Compilation of Presidential Documents* 33 (1997): 1246.

72. Memorandum on Upgrading Security at Federal Facilities, June 28, 1995, *Weekly Compilation of Presidential Documents* 31 (1995): 1148.

73. Robert D. Bullard, *Dumping in Dixie: Race, Class, and Environmental Quality* (Boulder, Colo.: Westview Press, 1990), xiii.

74. *Bean v. Southwestern Waste Management Corp.,* 482 F.Supp. 673 (S.D.Tex. 1979).

75. Bullard, *Dumping in Dixie,* xiii; see also Robert D. Bullard, ed., *Confronting Environmental Racism* (Boston: South End Press, 1993).

76. Quoted in Louisiana Advisory Committee to the U.S. Commission on Civil Rights, *The Battle for Environmental Justice in Louisiana: Government, Industry, and the People* (Washington, D.C.: U.S. Commission on Civil Rights, 1993). See also "Testimony of Dr. Benjamin F. Chavis, Jr. on Behalf of the National Association for the Advancement of Colored People on Environmental Equity and Environmental Justice," in U.S. House of Representatives, Hearings Before the Legislation and National Security Subcommittee of the Committee on Government Operations, *Environmental Protection Agency Cabinet Elevation—Environmental Equity Issues,* 103d Cong., 1st sess., 1993, 28, n. 2.

77. See, e.g., Bunyan Bryant, ed., *Environmental Justice* (Washington, D.C.: Island Press, 1995).

78. Testimony of Congresswoman Nydia M. Velazquez, in *Environmental Protection Agency Cabinet Elevation,* 11–12.

79. "Carolineans See Governor in PCB Landfill Dispute," *New York Times,* October 10, 1982, p. 31.

80. U.S. General Accounting Office, *Siting of Hazardous Waste Landfills and Their Correlation with Racial and Economic Status of Surrounding Communities* (Washington, D.C.: GAO, 1983).

81. United Church of Christ, Commission for Racial Justice, *Toxic Wastes and Race in the United States: A National Report on the Racial and Socioeconomic Characteristics of Communities with Hazardous Waste Sites* (New York: United Church of Christ, 1987).

82. Marianne Lavelle and Marcia Coyle, "Unequal Protection," (special supplement) *National Law Journal,* September 21, 1992, reprinted in *Environmental Protection Agency Cabinet Elevation,* 169–177.

83. *Environmental Protection Agency Cabinet Elevation,* 100–101.

84. Memorandum on Upgrading Security at Federal Facilities, 1148.

85. Arthur A. Fletcher to Carol M. Browner, September 24, 1993, reprinted in *Environmental Protection Agency Cabinet Elevation,* 144.

86. 59 *Fed. Reg.* 7629 (1994).

87. See, e.g., E.O. 12866, 58 *Fed. Reg.* 51735 (1993).

88. *Weekly Compilation of Government Documents* 30 (1994): 279.

89. Transcript of press briefing, February 11, 1994, 3–4, White House, Office of Press Secretary *<http://clinton6.nara.gov/1994/02/1994-02-11-briefing-by-browner-and-reno-on-environmental-justice.html>* December 2, 2001.

90. See, generally, Sheila Foster, "Justice from the Ground Up: Distributive Inequities, Grassroots Resistance, and the Transformative Politics of the Environmental Justice Movement," *California Law Review* 86 (1998): 775.

91. *Chester Residents Concerned for Quality of Life v. Seif,* 132 F.3d 925 (3d Cir. 1997).

92. Bullard, ed., *Confronting Environmental Racism,* 22. See also Bryant, *Environmental Justice,* 9–15.

93. Jace Weaver, ed., *Defending Mother Earth* (Maryknoll, N.Y.: Orbis Books, 1996), xv.

94. See, e.g., Colin Crawford, *Uproar at Dancing Rabbit Creek: Battling Over Race, Class, and the Environment* (Reading, Mass.: Addison-Wesley, 1996).

95. Vicki L. Been, "Locally Undesirable Land Uses in Minority Neighborhoods: Disproportionate Siting or Market Dynamics," *Yale Law Journal* 103 (1994): 1406. Christopher H. Foreman of the Brookings Institution had become an ardent African-American critic of environmental justice advocates, capping his ongoing criticism with the publication of *The Promise and Peril of Environmental Justice* (Washington, D.C.: Brookings Institution, 1998); see also U.S. General Accounting Office, *Hazardous and Nonhazardous Waste: Demographics of People Living Near Waste Facilities* (Washington, D.C.: GAO, 1995).

96. Cited hereafter as "Interim Guidance" at *<http://es.epa.gov/oeca/oej>*. This material was later removed when the web sites were changed but should be available through the National Archives Clinton Project at *<http://www.clinton.nara.gov>*.

97. 5 U.S.C.§553(B)(3)(A).

98. "Interim Guidance," 3.

99. U.S. House of Representatives, Hearing Before the Subcommittee on Oversight and Investigations of the Committee on Commerce, *EPA's Title VI Interim Guidance and Alternative State Approaches,* 105th Cong., 2d sess., 1998, 77.

100. "Interim Guidance," 4.

101. Ibid.

102. David Mastio, "EPA Plan Risks Metro Growth: A New Push to Classify Inner-City Pollution as a Civil Rights Offense Draws Cries of Dismay," *Detroit News,* April 19, 1998, p. A1.

103. Testimony of Ann E. Goode, *EPA's Title VI Interim Guidance and Alternative State Approaches,* 76.

104. Ibid., 86.

105. Other efforts to use policy statements to avoid rulemaking requirements when it was clear that the agency intended to use its legal authority to impose sanctions in accordance with what purported to be only guidance had failed in federal court; see, e.g., *McLouth Steel Products Corporation v. Thomas,* 838 F.2d 1317, 1320 (D.C.Cir. 1988); see also *American Hospital Association v. Bowen,* 834 F.2d 1037, 1044 (D.C.Cir. 1987).

106. Goode, in *EPA's Title VI Interim Guidance and Alternative State Approaches,* 87.

107. 65 *Fed. Reg.* 39650 (2000).

108. "Interim Guidance," 3–4.

109. *Youngstown Sheet & Tube v. Sawyer,* 343 U.S. 579 (1952).

110. See *United States v. Morrison,* 146 L.Ed.2d 658 (2000); *United States v. Lopez,* 514 U.S. 549 (1995).

111. See, e.g., *<http://www.nara.gov/fedreg/eo1994.html>* August 14, 2001.

112. Memorandum for certain department and agency heads, "Memorandum on Reducing the Burden of Government Regulation," January 28, 1992, 1, *<http://bushlibrary.tamu.edu/papers/1992/92012805.htm>*, December 3, 2001.

113. "Remarks on Regulatory Reform," 726.

114. *Dames & Moore v. Regan,* 453 U.S. 654 (1981).
115. *Youngstown Sheet & Tube v. Sawyer.*
116. 57 *Fed. Reg.* 23133 (1992).
117. *Sale v. Haitian Centers Council,* 509 U.S. 155, 164 (1993).

5. PRESIDENTIAL PROCLAMATIONS

1. Office of the Federal Register, *Codification of Presidential Proclamations and Executive Orders, April 13, 1945–January 20, 1989* (Washington, D.C.: Government Printing Office, 1990).

2. *Wolsey v. Chapman,* 101 U.S. 755 (1879).

3. WPA, NJ, and WPA, NY. A number of the executive orders were issued "in the form of a proclamation" according to the WPA, NY Survey, as in the case of E.O. 6 in 1868 announcing the ratification of the Fourteenth Amendment and certified as valid; WPA, NY, E.O. 7 certified the Fourteenth amendment as in effect (1:1).

4. Avalon Project, Yale Law School, <*http://www.yale.edu/lawweb/avalon/presiden/proclamations/gwproc09.htm*> August 14, 2001.

5. House, 1957 Study, 1.

6. Proclamation 4771, 1980.

7. *United States of America v. Wayte,* 549 F.Supp. 1376 (D.C.Cal. 1982).

8. *United States v. Wayte,* 710 F.2d 1385 (9th Cir. 1983); see also *United States v. Martin,* 557 F.Supp. 681 (N.E.Dist. Iowa 1982).

9. *United States v. Wayte,* at 1388.

10. See *Hirabayashi v. United States,* 320 U.S. 81 (1943).

11. Charles Warren, *The Supreme Court in United States History,* 2 vols. (Boston: Little, Brown, 1923), 1:112–118.

12. 11803 39 Fed. Reg. 33297 created a clemency board to hear cases and 11804 39 Fed. Reg. 33299 (1974) authorized the director of Selective Service to develop and implement the alternative service program.

13. See *Sale v. Haitian Centers Council,* 509 U.S. 155 (1993).

14. See the discussion of the Chip Protection Act in Charles R. McManis, "International Protection for Semiconductor Chip Designs and the Standard of Judicial Review of Presidential Proclamations Issued Pursuant to the Semiconductor Chip Protection Act of 1984," *George Washington Journal of International Law and Economics* 22 (1988): 331.

15. See Stanley Friedelbaum, "The 1971 Wage-Price Freeze: Unchallenged Presidential Power," *Supreme Court Review* (1974): 33.

16. See Petroleum Import Adjustment Program Proclamations 4744 *Weekly Compilation of Presidential Documents* 16 (1980): 592 (establishes the oil import fee program); Petroleum Import Adjustment Program, *Weekly Compilation of Presidential Documents* 16 (1980): 657; Petroleum Import Adjustment Program Proclamation 4751 *Weekly Compilation of Presidential Documents* 16 (1980): 760; Imports of Petroleum and Petroleum Products Proclamation *Weekly Compilation of Presidential Documents* 16 (1980): 1140 (rescinds the oil import program).

17. See Ralph Ketcham, *James Madison* (New York: Macmillan, 1971), 341–345. For the Neutrality Proclamation, see Avalon Project, Yale Law School, <*http://www. yale.edu/lawweb/avalon/neutra93htm*>.

18. See *Little v. Barreme*, 6 U.S. (2 Cranch) 170 (1804).

19. House, 1957 Study.

20. Cited in Ketcham, *Madison*, 345.

21. Leonard D. White, *The Federalists* (New York: Macmillan, 1956), 63.

22. 299 U.S. 304 (1936).

23. Ibid., at 319–320.

24. See, e.g., *Dames & Moore v. Regan*, 453 U.S. 654 (1981).

25. See discussion of Haitian refugee actions in chapter 4 and also *Sale v. Haitian Centers Council*, 509 U.S. 155 (1993).

26. See Proclamation 17, January 1, 1863, 12 Stat. 1268 (1863).

27. See proclamation admitting the state of New Mexico to the Union, 37 Stat. 1723 (1912).

28. <*http://www.yale.edu/lawweb/avalon/presiden/proclamations/gwproc03.htm*> August 15, 2001.

29. See, e.g., George Washington, Proclamation of August 26, 1790, <*http://www.yale. edu/lawweb/avalon/presiden/proclamations/gwproc13.htm*> August 15, 2001; proclamation of March 19, 1791, <*http://www.yale.edu/lawweb/avalon/presiden/proclamations/ gwproc05.htm*> August 15, 2001; proclamation of December 12, 1792, <*http://www. yale.edu/lawweb/avalon/presiden/proclamations/gwproc07.htm*>.

30. *The Prize Cases*, 67 U.S. 635 (1863).

31. Proclamation of September 30, 1962, 76 Stat. 1506.

32. See *United States v. Barnett*, 376 U.S. 681 (1964).

33. See the debates surrounding *Laird v. Tatum*, 408 U.S. 1 (1972).

34. See, e.g., *The Lake Monroe*, 250 U.S. 246 (1919).

35. Proclamation of May 27, 1941, 55 Stat. 1647.

36. Arthur M. Schlesinger, *The Coming of the New Deal* (Boston: Houghton Mifflin, 1958), 4.

37. 40 Stat. 411, §5(b). See *Youngstown Sheet & Tube v. Sawyer*, 343 U.S. 579 (1952), Jackson, J., concurring.

38. See E.O. 11615, 36 *Fed. Reg.* 15727 (1971); Proclamation 4074, 3 C.F.R. (Comp. 1971–1975): 60 (amended by E.O. 11617, 36 *Fed. Reg.* 20139 [1971]).

39. See E.O. 11627, October 15, 1971, 36 *Fed. Reg.* 20139; 11630, October 30, 1971, 36 *Fed. Reg.* 21023; 11632, November 22, 1971, 36 *Fed. Reg.* 22221; 11640, January 26, 1972, 37 *Fed. Reg.* 1213; 11660, March 23, 1972, 37 *Fed. Reg.* 6175; 11674, June 29, 1972, 37 *Fed. Reg.* 12913; 11695, January 11, 1973, 38 *Fed. Reg.* 1473; 11723, June 13, 1973, 38 *Fed. Reg.* 15765; 11730, July 18, 1973, 38 *Fed. Reg.* 19345.

40. Nixon's E.O. 11781, May 1, 1974, 39 *Fed. Reg.* 15749, and E.O. 11788, June 18, 1974, 39 *Fed. Reg.* 22113.

41. *Schick v. Reed*, 419 U.S. 256, 264 (1974).

42. Alexander Hamilton, James Madison, and John Jay, *The Federalist Papers* (New York: Mentor Books, 1961), 449.

43. Proclamation of July 10, 1795, <*http://www.yale.edu/lawlib/avalon/presiden/ proclamations/gw12.htm*> August 15, 2001.

44. 3 C.F.R. (Comp. 1971–1975): 385.

45. *Murphy v. Ford,* 390 F.Supp. 1372, 1373–1374 (W.D.Mich. 1975).

46. Proclamation 2651, May 8, 1945, 3 C.F.R. (Comp. 1943–1948): 35.

47. William J. Lockhart, "Discretionary Clemency: Mercy at the Prosecutor's Option," *Utah Law Review* 1976 (1976): 55, 64.

48. See John Robert Greene, *The Presidency of Gerald R. Ford* (Lawrence: University Press of Kansas, 1995).

49. See, e.g., Martha Honey, *Hostile Acts: U.S. Policy in Costa Rica in the 1980s* (Gainesville: University Press of Florida, 1994).

50. See Lawrence E. Walsh, *Iran-Contra: The Final Report of the Independent Counsel* (New York: Random House, 1993).

51. Ibid., xiii–xiv.

52. See, e.g., U.S. Senate, Hearing Before the Subcommittee on Immigration and Refugee Affairs of the Committee on the Judiciary, *Central American Migration to the United States,* 101st Cong., 1st sess., 1989; U.S. House of Representatives, Hearing Before the Subcommittee on Immigration, Refugees, and International Law of the Committee on the Judiciary, *Central American Asylum-Seekers,* 101st Cong., 1st sess., 1989.

53. U.S. Senate, Report of the Committee on the Judiciary to Accompany S. 332 as Amended, *Providing for a GAO Study on Conditions of Displaced Salvadorans and Nicaraguans, and for Other Purposes,* 100th Cong., 1st sess., 1987, 3.

54. See, e.g., Proclamation 7263, *Weekly Compilation of Presidential Documents* 36 (2000): 27; 7266, *Weekly Compilation of Presidential Documents* 36 (2000): 27; 7317, *Weekly Compilation of Presidential Documents* 36 (2000): 1271; 7373, *Weekly Compilation of Presidential Documents* 36 (2000): 2819.

55. *Weekly Compilation of Presidential Documents* 17 (1981): 2878.

56. *Weekly Compilation of Presidential Documents* 17 (1981): 123.

6. NATIONAL SECURITY DIRECTIVES

1. Bromley K. Smith, *Organizational History of the National Security Council During the Kennedy and Johnson Administrations* (Washington, D.C.: National Security Council, 1988), 23.

2. See Christopher Simpson, *National Security Directives of the Reagan and Bush Administrations* (Boulder, Colo.: Westview Press, 1995) (hereafter *Reagan and Bush*).

3. See, e.g., U.S. House of Representatives, Hearing Before a Subcommittee of the Committee on Government Operations, *Presidential Directives and Records Accountability Act,* 100th Cong., 2d sess., 1988 (hereafter *Presidential Directives*).

4. Ibid. See also Harold Relyea, "The Coming of Secret Law," *Government Information Quarterly* 5 (1988): 97.

5. Colin L. Powell to Jack Brooks, August 3, 1988, in *Presidential Directives,* 25.

6. Robert Cutler, "The National Security Council under President Eisenhower," in *The National Security Council: Jackson Subcommittee Papers on Policy-Making at the*

Presidential Level, ed. Henry M. Jackson (New York: Frederick A. Praeger, 1965) (hereafter *Jackson Papers*).

7. U.S. Senate, Subcommittee on National Policy Machinery, *Organizational History of the National Security Council During the Truman and Eisenhower Administrations,* 86th Cong., 2d sess., 1960. Committee Print (hereafter, Jackson Report).

8. Ibid., 1.

9. Ibid.

10. Ibid., 2.

11. 11 *Fed. Reg.* 1337 (1946).

12. P.L. 80-253, 61 Stat. 495 (1947).

13. Jackson Report, 13. See also Sidney W. Souers, "Policy Formulation and National Security," *American Political Science Review* 43, no. 3 (June 1949): 536.

14. Jackson Report, 5.

15. U.S. Department of State, Office of the Historian, *History of the National Security Council 1947–1997,* August 1997, 4 <*http://www.fas.org/irp/offdocs/NSChistory.htm*> August 18, 2001 (hereafter *NSC History*).

16. Sidney W. Souers, "The National Security Council Under President Truman," in *Jackson Papers,* 108.

17. Jackson Report, 16, n. 29.

18. NSC 68, <*http://www.fas.org/irp/offdocs/nsc-68-1.htm*> August 18, 2001.

19. Ibid.

20. David McCulloch, *Truman* (New York: Simon and Schuster, 1992), 773.

21. Chester J. Pach Jr. and Elmo Richardson, *The Presidency of Dwight D. Eisenhower* (Lawrence: University Press of Kansas, 1991), 76–77.

22. Ibid.

23. See Cutler, "National Security Council under President Eisenhower."

24. See, e.g., 10483, September 2, 1953, 3 C.F.R. (Comp. 1949–1953): 968. See also E.O. 10598, February 29, 1955, 3 C.F.R. (Comp. 1954–1958): 245; E.O. 10610, 3 C.F.R. (Comp. 1954–1958): 250; E.O. 10700, 3 C.F.R. (Comp. 1954–1958): 360.

25. Pach and Richardson, *Eisenhower,* 78.

26. Ibid., 80.

27. Smith, *Organizational History,* 3.

28. *NSC History,* 19.

29. See Hedrick Smith, "Foreign Policy: Costly Feud," *New York Times,* March 26, 1981, p. A1.

30. Steven R. Weisman, "Bush Flies Back from Texas Set to Take Charge in Crisis," *New York Times,* March 31, 1981, p. A1.

31. See *Reagan and Bush,* 9.

32. Statement by William P. Clark, assistant to the president for National Security Affairs, White House press release, January 12, 1982.

33. See, e.g., *Presidential Directives.*

34. NSAM 173, July 18, 1962.

35. NSAM 341, March 2, 1966.

36. NSDD 32, "U.S. National Security Strategy," May 20, 1982, 3.

37. PDD 35, March 2, 1995.

38. Federation of American Scientists, "Intelligence Resource Program," PDD 35, <http://www.fas.org/irp/offdocs/pdd35.htm> August 18, 2001.

39. See U.S. House of Representatives, Staff Study for the Permanent Select Committee on Intelligence, *IC21: The Intelligence Community in the Twenty-first Century,* 104th Cong., 1st sess., 1996, <http://www.gpo.gov/congress/house/intel/ic21/ic21001. html> August 18, 2001.

40. NSDD 22, January 29, 1982.

41. Reagan NSDD 57, September 17, 1982, U.S. Policy Toward Somalia, Sudan, Djibouti, Kenya, and Ethiopia (see *Reagan and Bush,* 76).

42. NSDD 17, November 16, 1981; NSDD 124, February 7, 1984.

43. NSAM 351, June 10, 1966.

44. NSAM 355, August 1, 1966.

45. NSDM 277, October 15, 1974. The Ford NSDMs can be reached through the Federation of American Scientists' site, as can all the preceding references, but they can also be accessed through the Ford Administration National Security Study Memoranda and Decision Memoranda site, <http://www.ford.utexas.edu/library/document/ nsdmnssm.htm>.

46. NSDD 279, November 2, 1974.

47. NSDD 281, December 9, 1974.

48. NSDD 18, January 4, 1982.

49. *Reagan and Bush,* 75; for Reagan's directive, see E.O. 12866, 58 *Fed. Reg.* 51735 (1993).

50. *NSC History,* 7.

51. NSAM 1, February 3, 1961.

52. NSAM 171, July 16, 1962.

53. NSDM 294, May 12, 1975.

54. NSAM 18, February 15, 1961.

55. NSAM 76, August 20, 1961.

56. See, e.g., NSDD 25, February 12, 1982; NSDD 60, October 9, 1982; NSDD 118, December 5, 1983; NSDD 131, March 12, 1984; NSDD 152, December 20, 1984; NSDD 198, November 7, 1985; NSDD 241, September 26, 1986; NSDD 297, January 20, 1988.

57. See NSDD 156, January 3, 1985; NSDD 167, April 29, 1985; and Reagan's NSDD 156, January 3, 1985.

58. NSDD 185, September 4, 1985; *Reagan and Bush,* 582–583.

59. NSDM 317, February 23, 1976.

60. NSAM 244, May 15, 1963.

61. NSAM 81, August 28, 1961.

62. NSDD 154, January 1, 1985, 1; *Reagan and Bush,* 485.

63. NSDD 154, January 1, 1985, 2.

64. Reagan NSDD 34, May 14, 1982, 1–2; *Reagan and Bush,* 121–122.

65. Central Intelligence Agency, "Soviet Bloc Economic Warfare Capabilities and Courses of Action," NIE 10–54, March 9, 1954, 1.

66. Central Intelligence Agency, memorandum, "Current US Policy with Respect to Cuba," December 12, 1963, 4.

67. NSDD 54, September 2, 1982, 2–4.

68. *Reagan and Bush,* 80–81.

69. See Center for Security Policy, "Summary of the Proceedings of the Hoover Institute and Casey Institute Symposium on the Fall of the Berlin Wall: Reassessing the Causes and Consequences of the End of the Cold War," February 22, 1999, <*http://security-policy.org/papers/1999/99-R47at.html*> August 18, 2001. See also Peter Schweizer, *Victory* (New York: Atlantic Monthly Press, 1994).

70. NSDD 66, November 29, 1982, 1–2.

71. NSDD 75, January 17, 1983.

72. Ibid., 2.

73. PD 13, May 13, 1977; see *Reagan and Bush,* 11.

74. NSDD 5, July 8, 1981, 32–35.

75. Ibid., 3.

76. Norman Kempster, "Clinton Policy Backs U.S. Arms Sales Abroad: Military Health of American Industries Is Made an Explicit Objective of President's Stance on Weapons Trade," *Los Angeles Times,* February 18, 1995, p. A32; "The Arms Bazaar Expands Eastward," *New York Times,* March 9, 1995, p. A24; R. Jeffrey Smith, "Clinton Rejects Bid to Rein in Arms Sales; Weapons Export Policy to Stress Flexibility," *Washington Post,* February 17, 1995, p. A9.

77. See, e.g., NSAM 290, March 19, 1964; NSDM 270, September 24, 1974; NSDM 315, January 31, 1976.

78. See, e.g., NSDM 289, March 24, 1975.

79. *Reagan and Bush,* 16.

80. See, e.g., NSDD 100, July 28, 1983.

81. See, e.g., President Ford's NSDM 322, "American Equipment Captured in Indochina," March 31, 1976.

82. NSDD 100, July 28, 1983.

83. Finding Pursuant to Section 662 of the Foreign Assistance Act of 1961, as Amended, Concerning Operations Undertaken by the Central Intelligence Agency in Foreign Countries, Other Than Those Intended Solely for the Purpose of Intelligence Collection, January 17, 1986, in U.S. Congress, Joint Hearings Before the House Select Committee to Investigate Covert Arms Transactions with Iran and the Senate Select Committee on Secret Military Assistance to Iran and the Nicaraguan Opposition, *Iran-Contra Investigation,* 100th Cong., 1st sess., 1987, testimony of John M. Poindexter, 503 (hereafter Iran-Contra Hearings).

84. Finding Pursuant to Section 662 of the Foreign Assistance Act of 1961, as Amended, Concerning Operations Undertaken by the Central Intelligence Agency in Foreign Countries, Other Than Those Intended Solely for the Purpose of Intelligence Collection, January 17, 1986, testimony of George P. Schultz, Iran-Contra Hearings, 472–474.

85. NSDD 12, October 1, 1981, 1.

86. NSDD 35, May 17, 1982; NSDD 69, November 22, 1982; NSDD 91, April 19, 1983.

87. NSDD 73, January 3, 1983.

88. See also NSDD 172, May 30, 1985.

89. NSDM 344, January 18, 1977.

90. NSDM 348, January 20, 1977.

91. NSAM 2, February 3, 1961.

92. NSDD 277, June 15, 1987.

93. Ibid., 1.

94. NSDM 292, March 25, 1964.

95. See President Kennedy's NSAM 12, February 6, 1961, and NSAM 28, March 9, 1961.

96. NSAM 92, September 8, 1961; NSAM 93, September 12, 1961.

97. NSDD 123, February 1, 1984.

98. NSD 54, January 15, 1991.

99. Ibid., 1–2.

100. Ibid., 3.

101. NSDD 110, October 21, 1983.

102. NSDD 128, February 26, 1984, 2.

103. NSD 18, August 21, 1989, *Bush and Reagan,* 895.

104. U.S. Department of State, Bureau of International Organizational Affairs, "Clinton Administration Policy on Reforming Multilateral Peace Operations," February 22, 1996, <*http://www.fas.org/irp/offdocs/pdd25.htm*> 2.

105. See NSAM 37, April 6, 1961; NSAM 86, August 31, 1961; NSDM 276, October 15, 1974; NSDD 13, October 19, 1981; NSDD 28, March 17, 1982; NSDD 162, February 11, 1985; and PDD 15, October 5, 1993.

106. See NSAM 35, April 6, 1961; NSAM 36, April 6, 1961; NSAM 147, April 18, 1962; NSAM 305, June 16, 1964.

107. See NSAM 69, August 15, 1961; NSAM 87, September 12, 1961; NSAM 112, November 13, 1961; NSAM 113, November 13, 1961; NSAM 116, December 1, 1961; NSAM 210, December 12, 1961; NSAM 245, May 21, 1963; NSAM 307, June 19, 1964; NSDD 51, August 10, 1982.

108. See NSAM 148, April 18, 1962; NSAM 294, April 20, 1964; NSDM 299, June 23, 1975; NSDD 6, July 16, 1981.

109. NSAM 308, June 22, 1964.

110. NSAM 313, June 31, 1964.

111. NSDD 77, January 14, 1983.

112. *Reagan and Bush,* 229.

113. NSDD 112, November 12, 1983, 3.

114. NSDD 116, December 2, 1983.

115. Ibid., 2.

116. NSDD 187, September 7, 1985, 1–2.

117. NSAM 325, March 12, 1965, 1 (emphasis added).

118. NSDD 130, March 6, 1984, 3 (emphasis added).

119. NSDD 170, May 20, 1985.

120. NSC 4 and NSC 10/2 (see *NSC History,* 5).

121. NSDD 159, January 18, 1985.

122. Ibid., 1.

123. Ibid., 6.

124. NSDD 266, March 31, 1987, 7.

125. NSDD 286, October 15, 1987.

126. See, generally, James A. Bill, *The Eagle and the Lion: The Tragedy of American-Iranian Relations* (New Haven: Yale University Press, 1988), chaps. 2–3.

127. Mark J. Gasiorowski, "The 1953 Coup d'Etat in Iran," paper, Department of Political Science, Louisiana State University.

128. The detailed factual information on the Iran coup is taken from the CIA's own after-action report prepared by the agency's lead planner on the project. See Donald N. Wilber, "Clandestine Service History: Overthrow of Premier Mossadeq of Iran, November 1952–August 1953," March 1954, published on the *New York Times* Internet Site, <*http://www.nytimes.com/library/world/mideast/iran-cia-intro.pdf*> as of January 15, 2001.

129. Ibid., 77.

130. Nick Cullather, *Secret History: The CIA's Classified Account of Its Operations in Guatemala, 1952–1954* (Stanford, Calif.: Stanford University Press, 1999), 38.

131. Memorandum for the director of Central Intelligence, "Guatemala—General Plan of Action," September 11, 1953. See CIA, Electronic Document Release Center, <*http://www.foia.ucia.gov/frame2.htm*> August 18, 2001.

132. Pach and Richardson, *Eisenhower,* 89–90.

133. Cullather, *Secret History,* 15–17.

134. Ibid., 21.

135. Ibid., 90.

136. Ibid.

137. Quoted in James Risen, "Secrets of History: The CIA in Iran," *New York Times,* <*http://www.nytimes.com/library/world/mideast/041600iran-cia-intro.html*> as of January 15, 2001, introduction.

138. Cullather, *Secret History,* 110.

139. For example, on Iran, he issued NSC 5402, 5504, 5703/1, 5821/1, and 6010.

140. Smith, *Organizational History,* 35.

141. See, e.g., NSAM 42, April 25, 1961; NSAM 43, April 25, 1961; NSAM 45, April 25, 1961; NSAM 46, April 25, 1961; NSAM 47, April 25, 1961.

142. Iran-Contra Hearings, 31–32.

143. Defense Appropriations Act for Fiscal Year 1983, P.L. 97-377, §793, 96 Stat. 1833, 1865 (1982).

144. NSDD 17, January 4, 1982. Although it has a January date, the decisions for this directive were taken at an NSC meeting on November 16, 1981.

145. NSAM 52, May 11, 1961, 1.

146. NSAM 65, August 11, 1961; NSAM 104, October 13, 1961; NSAM 111, November 22, 1961; NSAM 115, November 30, 1961; NSAM 149, April 19, 1962; NSAM 189, September 28, 1962; NSAM 249, June 25, 1963; NSAM 259, August 20, 1963; NSAM 263, October 11, 1963.

147. See, e.g., NSDM 93, November 9, 1970, <*http://www.gwu.edu/~nsarchiv/NSAEBB8/ch09-01.htm*> August 18, 2001.

148. Smith, *Organizational History,* 27.

149. PDD 56, May 1997.

150. NSAM 41, April 25, 1961; NSAM 62, July 24, 1961; NSAM 70, August 15, 1961; NSAM 109, October 23, 1961; NSAM 117, November 29, 1961.

151. NSAM 339, December 17, 1965.

152. See, e.g., NSAM 227, February 27, 1963, "Decisions Taken at the President's Meeting on Yemen Crisis, 25 February 1963."

153. Bill Keller, "Admiral Says He Was Wronged in Removal over $659 Ashtrays," *New York Times,* June 1, 1985, sec. 1, p. 30.

154. "Special Bipartisan Panel to Study Pentagon Spending," *New York Times,* June 14, 1985, p. A17.

155. David Burnham, "Meese Says He Will Advise Obedience on Spending Rules," *New York Times,* June 4, 1985, p. A14.

156. NSDD 219, April 1, 1986.

157. NSDD 84, March 11, 1983.

158. Ibid., 2.

159. See U.S. Senate, Hearing Before the Committee on Governmental Affairs, *National Security Decision Directive 84—Safeguarding National Security Information,* 98th Cong., 1st sess., 1984; Julia K. Craig, "The Presidential Polygraph Order and the Fourth Amendment: Subjecting Federal Employees to Warrantless Searches," *Cornell Law Review* 69 (1984): 896; Note, "National Security Directive 84: An Unjustifiably Broad Approach to Intelligence Protection," *Brooklyn Law Review* 51 (1984): 147; Comment, "The Constitutionality of Expanding Prepublication Review of Government Employees' Speech," *California Law Review* 72 (1984): 962.

160. The director of the Information Security Oversight Office and the DCI developed forms to be signed by Foreign Service personnel, among others, in attempting to implement NSDD 84. That engendered litigation by the National Federation of Federal Employees, the American Federation of Government Employees, and the American Foreign Service Association. See *National Federation of Federal Employees v. U.S.,* 695 F.Supp. 1196 (D.D.C. 1988); *American Foreign Service Assn. v. Garfinkel,* 490 U.S. 153 (1989); *American Foreign Service Assn. v. Garfinkel,* 732 F.Supp. 13 (D.D.C. 1990).

161. NSDD 196, November 1, 1985.

162. NSDD 197, November 1, 1985.

163. Ibid., 2.

164. See A. M. Cunningham, "Secrets of the Presidents: Secret Directives on National Security," *Technology Review* 93 (1990): 14.

165. NSDD 145, September 17, 1984.

166. Ibid., 2.

167. NSDD 189, September 21, 1985.

168. PDD 5, April 16, 1993.

169. PRD 27, April 16, 1993; PRD 48, late 1994. The declassified version of the market study was later published as "U.S. Department of Commerce and National Security Agency, A Study of the International Market for Computer Software with Encryption," *<http://www.epic.org/crypto/export_controls/commerce_study_summary.html>* as of January 18, 2001.

170. See Smith, *Organizational History,* 35.

171. Quoted in Ibid.

172. See Cullather, *Secret History.*

173. An example is Kennedy's NSAM 132 issued in 1962, which called upon the Agency for International Development to participate in counterinsurgency efforts in Latin America by supporting local police forces in internal security and other counter-insurgency efforts. See also NSAM 150, April 20, 1962, calling for AID to require countries to use U.S. military engineers as contracting agents on AID–funded projects.

174. Whether one agrees or disagrees with his conclusions, Simpson provides an excellent discussion of some of these problems (*Reagan and Bush,* xx–xxi).

175. The President's Special Review Board, *The Tower Commission Report* (New York: Bantam Books, 1987), 62–63.

176. U.S. Senate, Committee on National Emergency and Delegated Emergency Powers, *National Emergencies and Delegated Emergency Powers,* 94th Cong., 2nd sess., 1976, 16.

177. Jack Brooks to Frank Carlucci, March 31, 1987, in *Presidential Directives,* 9–10.

178. Ibid., Colin E. Powell to Jack Brooks, August 3, 1988, 35.

179. Ibid., 29.

180. Ibid., 2.

181. Ibid., 80–83.

182. Note, "The Navy's Role in Interdicting Narcotics Traffic: War on Drugs or Ambush on the Constitution?" *Georgetown Law Journal* 75 (1987): 1947–1966.

183. *Reagan and Bush,* 2–3.

7. PRESIDENTIAL SIGNING STATEMENTS

1. Louis Fisher, *Constitutional Conflict Between Congress and the President,* 4th ed. (Lawrence: University Press of Kansas, 1997), 132–141.

2. Walter Dellinger, assistant attorney general, memorandum for Bernard N. Nussbaum, counsel to the president, "The Legal Significance of Presidential Signing Statements," November 3, 1993, <*http://www.usdoj.gov:/olc/signing.htm*> August 18, 2001.

3. *The Attorney General's Duty to Defend and Enforce Constitutionally Objectionable Legislation,* 4A Op. O.L.C. 55, 59 (1980) (Civiletti, A.G.); *Recommendation That the Department of Justice Not Defend the Constitutionality of Certain Provisions of the Bankruptcy Amendments and Federal Judgeship Act of 1984,* 8 Op. O.L.C. 183, 195 (1984).

4. Edwin Meese III, *With Reagan: The Inside Story* (Washington, D.C.: Regnery Gateway, 1992), 119.

5. Meese, *With Reagan,* 322.

6. Ibid., 316.

7. Edwin Meese III, *Major Policy Statements of the Attorney General: Edwin Meese III, 1985–1988* (Washington, D.C.: Government Printing Office, 1989), 78.

8. Ibid., 79.

9. Douglas W. Kmiec, "OLC's Opinion Writing Functions: The Legal Adhesive for a Unitary Executive," *Cardozo Law Review* 15 (1993): 337, 345.

10. Fisher, *Constitutional Conflict,* 132–136.

11. Statement on Signing the Energy and Water Development Appropriations Act, 1992, *Weekly Compilation of Presidential Documents* 27 (1991): 1143.

12. Fisher, *Constitutional Conflict,* 135–136.

13. 12 Op. O.L.C. 159 (1988).

14. William P. Barr, "Attorney General's Remarks, Benjamin N. Cardozo School of Law," *Cardozo Law Review* 15 (1993): 31, 35.

15. *Clinton v. New York,* 524 U.S. 417 (1998).

16. Statement on Signing the Treasury, Postal Service and General Government Appropriations Act, 1989, September 22, 1988, P.L. 100-440, Ronald Reagan, *Public Papers of the President, 1988–1989* (Washington, D.C.: Government Printing Office, 1990), book 2, 1204–1205.

17. Ibid., Statement on Signing the Intelligence Authorization Act, Fiscal Year 1989, book 2, 1249–1250.

18. Ibid., Statement on Signing a Veterans Benefits Bill, November 18, 1988, book 2, 1558.

19. Ibid., Statement on Signing the Medical Waste Tracking Act of 1988, November 2, 1988, P.L. 100-582, book 2, 1430–1431.

20. Ibid., Statement on Signing the Bill Prohibiting the Licensing or Construction of Facilities on the Salmon and Snake Rivers in Idaho, November 17, 1988, P.L. 100-677, book 2, 1525.

21. *Fullilove v. Klutznick,* 448 U.S. 448 (1980).

22. *Richmond v. J. A. Croson Co.,* 488 U.S. 469 (1989). While the Court overturned the Richmond, Virginia, program, it reaffirmed *Fullilove* and differentiated state affirmative action programs from federal programs.

23. *Adarand Constructors, Inc. v. Peña,* 515 U.S. 200 (1995).

24. *Weekly Compilation of Presidential Documents* 27 (1991): 1701.

25. Kmiec, "OLC's Functions," 346.

26. Ibid.; Barr, "Attorney General's Remarks"; 18 Op. O.L.C. 199 (1994). The Clinton-era opinion was written by Walter Dellinger and is published as "Legal Opinion from the Office of Legal Council to the Honorable Abner J. Mikva," *Arkansas Law Review* 48 (1995): 313.

27. Barr, "Attorney General's Remarks," 39.

28. *Weekly Compilation of Presidential Documents* 27 (1991): 1701.

29. Statement on Signing the Public Buildings Amendments of 1988, November 17, 1988, P.L. 100-678, Reagan, *Public Papers,* book 2, 1525.

30. *Weekly Compilation of Presidential Documents* 29 (1993): 2330.

31. *Southern Offshore Fishing Association v. Daley,* 995 F.Supp. 1411, 1427 n. 23 (M.D.Fla. 1998).

32. *Weekly Compilation of Presidential Documents* 30 (1994): 1422.

33. Dellinger, "Legal Opinion," 323.

34. Ibid., 323–325.

35. Ibid., 324.

36. 462 U.S. 919 (1983).

37. *Consumer Energy Council v. Federal Energy Regulatory Commission,* 673 F. 2d 425 (D.C.Cir. 1982); *Consumers Union v. FTC,* 691 F.2d 575 (D.C.Cir. 1982).

38. *Process Gas Consumers v. Consumer Energy Council,* 463 U.S. 1216 (1983); *United States Senate v. FTC,* 463 U.S. 1216 (1983).

39. Fisher, *Constitutional Conflict,* 152–159.

40. See, e.g., *Weekly Compilation of Presidential Documents* 30 (1994): 1422.

41. Fisher, *Constitutional Conflict,* 157–158.

42. Statement on Signing the Department of the Interior and Related Agencies Appropriations Act, Fiscal Year 1989, September 27, 1988, Reagan, *Public Papers,* book 2, 1228.

43. See, e.g., Marc N. Garber and Kurt A. Wimmer, "Presidential Signing Statements as Interpretations of Legislative Intent: An Executive Aggrandizement of Power," *Harvard Journal on Legislation* 24 (1989): 363.

44. Barr, "Attorney General's Remarks," 40.

45. *United States v. Story,* 891 F.2d 988, 994 (2d Cir. 1989).

46. Barr, "Attorney General's Remarks," 39.

47. Kmiec, "OLC's Functions," 347–348.

48. Robert H. Jackson, "A Presidential Legal Opinion," *Harvard Law Review* 66 (1953): 1353.

49. Ibid., 1358.

50. *Weekly Compilation of Presidential Documents* 30 (1994): 2202.

51. *Weekly Compilation of Presidential Documents* 25 (1989): 516.

52. Kmiec, "OLC's Functions," 344.

53. See, e.g., Clinton's statement on signing the Hazard Mitigation and Relocation Assistance Act in later 1993. *Weekly Compilation of Presidential Documents* 29 (1993): 2504.

54. *Weekly Compilation of Presidential Documents* 29 (1993): 1043.

55. *Weekly Compilation of Presidential Documents* 30 (1994): 651. See also Statement on Signing the Government Management Reform Act of 1994, *Weekly Compilation of Presidential Documents* 30 (1994): 2006, again claiming credit for the NPR.

56. *Weekly Compilation of Presidential Documents* 29 (1994): 2204.

57. *Weekly Compilation of Presidential Documents* 31 (1996): 2228.

58. *Weekly Compilation of Presidential Documents* 30 (1994): 1383.

59. Kmiec, "OLC's Functions," 345.

60. See William D. Popkin, "Judicial Use of Presidential Legislative History," *Indiana Law Journal* 66 (1991): 669, 705–706.

61. *Heckler v. Chaney,* 470 U.S. 821 (1985).

62. Popkin, "Judicial Use," 706–707.

63. *Weekly Compilation of Presidential Documents* 35 (1999): 2363, 2365.

64. *Printz v. United States,* 521 U.S. 898 (1997).

65. *Bowsher v. Synar,* 478 U.S. 714, 719 n. 1 (1986).

66. Ibid., at 758–759.

67. *Weekly Compilation of Presidential Documents* 32 (1996): 260.

68. Memorandum on Benefits for Military Personnel Subject to Involuntary Separation as a Result of HIV, William J. Clinton, *Public Papers of the President, 1996* (Washington, D.C.: U.S. Government Printing Office, 1997), book 1, 200.

69. Press briefing by Counsel to the President Jack Quinn and Assistant Attorney General Walter Dellinger, February 9, 1996, <*http://clinton6.nara.gov/1996/02/1996-02-09-Quinn-and-dellinger-briefing-on-HIV-provision.html*> August 18, 2001.

70. 18 Op. O.L.C. 199 (1994).

71. Dellinger, "Attorney General's Remarks," 317.

72. *Weekly Compilation of Presidential Documents* 32 (1996): 261.

73. Testimony of Secretary of State-Designate Colin Powell, Hearing of the Senate Foreign Relations Committee, Confirmation Hearing of General Colin Powell to be Secretary of State, January 17, 2001, Federal News Service. <*http://www.un.it/usa/01pow117.htm*> August 18, 2001.

74. Testimony of Ken Keck, director of Legislative and Regulatory Affairs, Florida Citrus Mutual, Hearing Before the Subcommittee on Transportation and Infrastructure of the Senate Environment and Public Works Committee, the Comprehensive Everglades Restoration Plan, 106th Cong., 2d sess., 2000, 232.

75. See, e.g., Robert F. Durant, *The Administrative Presidency Revisited* (Albany: State University of New York Press, 1992), and Richard P. Nathan, *The Administrative Presidency* (New York: John Wiley and Sons, 1983). I have dealt with this aspect of the Reagan years at greater length in Phillip J. Cooper, *Public Law and Public Administration,* 3d ed. (Itasca, Ill.: F. E. Peacock, 2000), chaps. 1 and 10.

76. Francine Kiefer, "Clintonian 'Tyranny' Rankles Hill," *Christian Science Monitor,* November 9, 1999, p. USA 1.

77. *Buckley v. Valeo,* 424 U.S. 1 (1976); *Immigration and Naturalization Service v. Chadha,* 462 U.S. 919 (1983); *Bowsher v. Synar,* 478 U.S. 714 (1986).

78. For example, the difficulties of standing can be substantial; see, e.g., *Raines v. Byrd,* 521 U.S. 811 (1997).

79. See, generally, Morton Rosenberg, "Assessment of Legal Issues Raised by the President's Directions to the Secretary of Energy with Respect to the Implementation of the National Nuclear Security Administration Act in His Signing Statement of October 5, 1999," American Law Division, Congressional Research Service, November 1, 1999.

80. Fisher, *Constitutional Conflict.*

81. *Clinton v. New York,* 524 U.S. 417 (1998).

82. Ibid., at 438.

83. Ibid., at 442–447.

84. Kiefer, "Clintonian 'Tyranny.'"

85. 272 U.S. 52 (1926).

86. See *AMERON, Inc. v. United States,* 787 F.2d 875, 883 (3d Cir. 1986).

87. 37 U.S. (12 Pet.) 524, 610 (1838).

88. *Youngstown Sheet & Tube v. Sawyer,* 343 U.S. 579 (1952).

89. *United States v. Nixon,* 418 U.S. 683 (1974).

90. Ibid., at 703.

91. *Consumer Energy Council of America v. Federal Energy Regulatory Commission,* 673 F.2d 425, 478 (D.C.Cir. 1982).

92. *Process Gas Consumers v. Consumer Energy Council,* 463 U.S. 1216 (1983).

93. 607 F.Supp. 962 (D.N.J. 1985).

94. *AMERON, Inc. v. U.S. Army Corps of Engineers,* 610 F.Supp. 750, 755 (D.N.J. 1985), citing *United States v. Lee,* 106 U.S. 196, 220 (1882).

95. *AMERON, Inc. v. United States Senate,* 787 F.2d 878 (3d Cir. 1986); reaffirmed after reargument *AMERON, Inc. v. United States Senate,* 809 F.2d 979 (3d Cir. 1986).

96. *Lear Siegler v. Lehman,* 842 F.2d 1102, 1124 (9th Cir. 1988).

97. *New York Times,* May 13, 1985, p. A18.

98. Ibid., May 21, 1985, p. A26.

99. Ibid., "Even the President Is Not Above the Law," June 7, 1985, p. A26.

100. Kmiec, "OLC's Functions," 344–345.

8. PRESIDENTIAL DIRECT ACTION AND WASHINGTON RULES

1. Arthur M. Schlesinger, *The Imperial Presidency* (Boston: Houghton Mifflin, 1973), 377.

2. Michael J. Sandel, *Democracy's Discontent* (Cambridge: Harvard University Press, 1996), ix.

3. *Presidential Directives.*

4. E.O. 9981, 3 C.F.R. (Comp. 1943–1948): 722.

5. *Building and Construction Trades Department, AFL–CIO v. Allbaugh,* 2001 U.S. Dist. LEXIS 17509 (2001).

6. James L. Sundquist, *The Decline and Resurgence of Congress* (Washington, D.C.: Brookings Institution, 1981), 479.

BIBLIOGRAPHY

Abney, F. Glen, and Thomas P. Lauth. *The Politics of State and City Administration.* Albany, N.Y.: State University of New York Press, 1986.

Bailyn, Bernard. *The Ideological Origins of the American Revolution.* Cambridge: Harvard Belknap, 1963.

Ban, Carolyn, and Patricia Ingraham. "Short-Timers: Political Appointee Mobility and Its Impact on Political/Career Relations in the Reagan Administration." *Administration and Society* 22 (1990): 106.

Barber, James David. *The Presidential Character.* Englewood Cliffs, N.J.: Prentice-Hall, 1972.

Barr, William P. "Attorney General's Remarks, Benjamin N. Cardozo School of Law." *Cardozo Law Review* 15 (1993): 31.

Been, Vicki L. "Locally Undesirable Land Uses in Minority Neighborhoods: Disproportionate Siting or Market Dynamics?" *Yale Law Journal* 103 (1994): 1406.

Berger, Raoul. *Executive Privilege: A Constitutional Myth.* Cambridge: Harvard University Press, 1974.

Bill, James A. *The Eagle and the Lion: The Tragedy of American-Iranian Relations.* New Haven: Yale University Press, 1988.

Bornet, Vaughn Davis. *The Presidency of Lyndon B. Johnson.* Lawrence: University Press of Kansas, 1983.

Brownlow Commission. *Report of the President's Committee on Administrative Management.* Washington, D.C.: Government Printing Office, 1937.

Bryant, Bunyan, ed., *Environmental Justice.* Washington, D.C.: Island Press, 1995.

Bullard, Robert D. *Dumping in Dixie: Race, Class, and Environmental Quality.* Boulder, Colo.: Westview Press, 1990.

———, ed. *Confronting Environmental Racism.* Boston: South End Press, 1993.

Butler, Stuart M., Michael Sanera, and W. Bruce Weinrod. *Mandate for Leadership II.* Washington, D.C.: Heritage Foundation, 1984.

Campbell, Colin, S.J. *Managing the Presidency: Carter, Reagan, and the Search for Executive Harmony.* Pittsburgh: University of Pittsburgh Press, 1986.

Cash, R. "Presidential Power: Use and Enforcement of Executive Orders." *Notre Dame Lawyer* 39 (1963): 44.

Comment: "The Constitutionality of Expanding Prepublication Review of Government Employee's Speech." *California Law Review* 72 (1984): 962.

———. "Executive Orders and the Development of Presidential Power," *Villanova Law Review* 17 (1972): 688.

Cooper, Phillip J. "By Order of the President: Administration by Executive Order and Proclamation." *Administration and Society* 18 (1986): 233.

———. *Public Law and Public Administration.* 3d ed. Itasca, Ill.: F. E. Peacock, 2000.

Corwin, Edward S. *The President: Office and Powers, 1787–1984.* Revision ed. Randall

W. Bland, Theordore T. Hindson, and Jack W. Peltason. New York: New York University Press, 1984.

Craig, Julia K. "The Presidential Polygraph Order and the Fourth Amendment: Subjecting Federal Employees to Warrantless Searches." *Cornell Law Review* 69 (1984): 896.

Crawford, Colin. *Uproar at Dancing Rabbit Creek: Battling over Race, Class, and the Environment.* Reading, Mass.: Addison-Wesley, 1996.

Cullather, Nick. *Secret History: The CIA's Classified Account of Its Operations in Guatemala, 1952–1954.* Stanford, Calif.: Stanford University Press, 1999.

Dellinger, Walter. "Legal Opinion from the Office of Legal Council to the Honorable Abner J. Mikva." *Arkansas Law Review* 48 (1995): 313.

Durant, Robert F. *The Administrative Presidency Revisited: Public Lands, the BLM, and the Reagan Revolution.* Albany: State University of New York Press, 1992.

Farrand, Max, ed. *Records of the Federal Convention of 1787.* 4 vols. New Haven: Yale University Press, 1966.

Fisher, Louis. *Constitutional Conflicts Between Congress and the President.* 4th ed., revised. Lawrence: University Press of Kansas, 1997.

———. *Constitutional Dialogues.* Princeton, N.J.: Princeton University Press, 1988.

———. *Executive Orders and Proclamations, 1933–1999: Controversies with Congress and in the Courts.* Washington, D.C.: Congressional Research Service, 1999.

———. "How to Avoid Iran Contras." *California Law Review* 76 (1988): 939.

———. *Presidential Spending Power.* Princeton, N.J.: Princeton University Press, 1975.

Foreman, Christopher H. *The Promise and Peril of Environmental Justice.* Washington, D.C.: Brookings Institution, 1998.

Foster, Sheila. "Justice from the Ground Up: Distributive Inequities, Grassroots Resistance, and the Transformative Politics of the Environmental Justice Movement." *California Law Review* 86 (1998): 775.

Freidel, Frank. *Franklin D. Roosevelt: A Rendezvous with Destiny.* Boston: Little, Brown, 1990.

Friedelbaum, Stanley H. "The 1971 Wage-Price Freeze: Unchallenged Presidential Power." *Supreme Court Review* 1974 (1974): 33.

Garber, Marc N., and Kurt A. Wimmer. "Presidential Signing Statements as Interpretations of Legislative Intent: An Executive Aggrandizement of Power." *Harvard Journal on Legislation* 24 (1989): 363.

Gilhooley, Margaret. "Executive Oversight of Administrative Rulemaking: Disclosing the Impact." *Indiana Law Review* 25 (1991): 299.

Gore, Al. *From Red Tape to Results: Creating a Government That Works Better and Costs Less.* Report of the the National Performance Review. Washington, D.C.: Government Printing Office, 1993.

Greene, John R. *The Presidency of Gerald R. Ford.* Lawrence: University Press of Kansas, 1995.

Hamilton, Alexander, James Madison, and John Jay. *The Federalist Papers.* New York: Mentor Books, 1961.

Hart, James. *The Ordinance Making Powers of the President of the United States.* Baltimore: Johns Hopkins University Press, 1925.

Heclo, Hugh. *A Government of Strangers.* Washington, D.C.: Brookings Institution, 1977.

Hess, Stephen. *Organizing the Presidency.* 2d ed. Washington, D.C.: Brookings Institution, 1988.

Honey, Martha. *Hostile Acts: U.S. Policy in Costa Rica in the 1980s.* Gainesville: University Press of Florida, 1994.

Jackson, Henry M., ed. *The National Security Council: Jackson Subcommittee Papers on Policy-Making at the Presidential Level.* New York: Frederick A. Praeger, 1965.

Jackson, Robert H. "A Presidential Legal Opinion." *Harvard Law Review* 66 (1953): 1353.

Kerwin, Cornelius M. *Rulemaking: How Government Agencies Write Law and Make Policy.* 2d ed. Washington, D.C.: Congressional Quarterly Press, 1999.

Ketcham, Ralph. *James Madison.* New York: Macmillan, 1971.

Kmiec, Douglas W. "OLC's Opinion Writing Functions: The Legal Adhesive for a Unitary Executive." *Cardozo Law Review* 15 (1993): 337.

Locke, John. *The Second Treatise of Government.* Ed. Thomas P. Peardon. New York: Bobbs-Merrill, 1952.

Lockhart, William J. "Discretionary Clemency: Mercy at the Prosecutor's Option." *Utah Law Review* 1976 (1976): 55.

Lord, Clifford L., ed. *List and Index of Presidential Executive Orders, Unnumbered Series—Historical Records Survey, N.J.* Newark, N.J.: Works Projects Administration, 1942.

Lord Hailsham of Marylebone, ed. *Halsbury's Laws of England.* London: Butterworths, 1973.

Louisiana Advisory Committee to the U.S. Commission on Civil Rights. *The Battle for Environmental Justice in Louisiana: Government, Industry, and the People.* Washington, D.C.: U.S. Commission on Civil Rights, 1993.

Madison, James. *The Writings of James Madison.* Ed. Gaillard Hunt. 9 vols. New York: G. P. Putnam's Sons, 1906.

Mayer, Kenneth R. *With the Stroke of a Pen: Executive Orders and Presidential Power.* Princeton: Princeton University Press, 2001.

McCloskey, R., ed. *The Works of James Wilson.* Cambridge: Harvard Belknap, 1967.

McCullough, David. *Truman.* New York: Simon and Schuster, 1992.

McManis, Charles R. "International Protection for Semiconductor Chip Designs and the Standard of Judicial Review of Presidential Proclamations Issued Pursuant to the Semiconductor Chip Protection Act of 1984." *George Washington Journal of International Law and Economics* 22 (1988): 331.

Meese, Edwin III. *Major Policy Statements of the Attorney General: Edwin Meese III, 1985–1988.* Washington, D.C.: Government Printing Office, 1989.

———. *With Reagan: The Inside Story.* Washington, D.C.: Regnery Gateway, 1992.

Milton, George F. *The Use of Presidential Power, 1789–1943.* New York: Octagon Books, 1965.

Moe, Ronald C. "Exploring the Limits of Privatization." *Public Administration Review* 47 (1987): 453.

Moe, Ronald C., and Thomas H. Stanton. "Government-Sponsored Enterprises as Federal Instrumentalities: Reconciling Private Management with Public Accountability." *Public Administration Review* 49 (1989): 321.

Morgan, Ruth. *The President and Civil Rights: Policy-Making by Executive Order.* New York: St. Martin's, 1970.
Mosher, Frederick C. "The Changing Responsibilities and Tactics of the Federal Government." *Public Administration Review* 40 (1980): 541.
Nathan, Richard, P. *The Administrative Presidency.* New York: Wiley, 1983.
———. *The Plot That Failed: Nixon and the Administrative Presidency.* New York: John Wiley and Sons, 1975.
Neustadt, Richard. *Presidential Power: The Politics of Leadership with Reflections on Johnson and Nixon.* New York: John Wiley and Sons, 1976.
Note: "Enforcing Executive Orders: Judicial Review of Agency Action Under the Administrative Procedure Act." *George Washington Law Review* 55 (1987): 659.
———. "The National Security Agency and Its Interference with Private Sector Computer Security." *Iowa Law Review* 72 (1987): 1015.
———. "National Security Directive 84: An Unjustifiably Broad Approach to Intelligence Protection." *Brooklyn Law Review* 51 (1984): 147.
———. "The Navy's Role in Interdicting Narcotics Traffic: War on Drugs or Ambush on the Constitution?" *Georgetown Law Journal* 75 (1987): 1947.
Office of the Federal Register. *Codification of Presidential Proclamations and Executive Orders, April 13, 1945–January 20, 1989.* Washington, D.C.: Government Printing Office, 1990.
O'Toole, Laurence J. Jr., ed. *American Intergovernmental Relations.* 3d ed. Washington, D.C.: Congressional Quarterly Press, 2000.
Pach, Chester J. Jr., and Elmo Richardson. *The Presidency of Dwight D. Eisenhower.* Rev. ed. Lawrence: University Press of Kansas, 1991.
Patterson, Bradley H. Jr. *The Ring of Power.* New York: Basic Books, 1988.
Pfiffner, James P. *The Strategic Presidency.* 2d ed., rev. Lawrence: University Press of Kansas, 1996.
Popkin, William D. "Judicial Use of Presidential Legislative History." *Indiana Law Journal* 66 (1991): 699.
President's Special Review Board. *The Tower Commission Report.* New York: Bantam Books, 1987.
Pyle, Christopher H., and Richard M. Pious. *The President, the Congress, and the Constitution.* New York: Free Press, 1984.
Relyea, Harold C. "The Coming of Secret Law." *Government Information Quarterly* 5 (1988): 97.
———. "The Evolution of Government Information Security Classification Policy: A Brief Overview (1773–1973)," in U.S. House of Representatives, Committee on Government Operations, *Executive Classification of Information,* H.Rept. 93-221, 93d Cong., 1st sess., 1973.
———. "National Emergency Powers." *CRS Report for Congress,* July 22, 1999.
———. "National Emergency Powers and Y2K Problems." *CRS Report for Congress,* July 22, 1999.
Rosenberg, Morton. "Assessment of Legal Issues Raised by the President's Directions to the Secretary of Energy with Respect to the Implementation of the National

Nuclear Security Administration Act in His Signing Statement of October 5, 1999." American Law Division, Congressional Research Service, November 1, 1999.

————. "Beyond the Limits of Executive Power—Presidential Control of Agency Rulemaking Under Executive Order 12291." *Michigan Law Review* 20 (1981): 193.

Rubin, Irene S. *The Politics of Public Budgeting: Getting and Spending, Borrowing and Balancing.* 3d ed. Chatham, N.J.: Chatham House, 1997.

Salamon, Lester M. *Beyond Privatization: The Tools of Government Action.* Washington, D.C.: Urban Institute, 1989.

Sandel, Michael J. *Democracy's Discontent.* Cambridge: Harvard University Press, 1996.

Schick, Allen. *The Federal Budget: Politics, Policy, Process.* Washington, D.C.: Brookings Institution, 1995.

Schlesinger, Arthur M. Jr. *The Coming of the New Deal.* Boston: Houghton Mifflin, 1958.

————. *The Imperial Presidency.* Boston: Houghton Mifflin, 1973.

Schulman, Bruce J. *Lyndon B. Johnson and American Liberalism.* Boston: Bedford Books, 1995.

Schweizer, Peter. *Victory.* New York: Atlantic Monthly Press, 1994.

Seidman, Harold. *Politics, Position, and Power.* 3d ed. New York: Oxford, 1980.

Sheffer, David J. "U.S. Law and the Iran-Contra Affair." *American Journal of International Law* 81 (1987): 696.

Simpson, Christopher. *National Security Directives of the Reagan and Bush Administrations.* Boulder, Colo.: Westview Press, 1995.

Smith, Bromley K. *Organizational History of the National Security Council During the Kennedy and Johnson Administrations.* Washington, D.C.: National Security Council, 1988.

Souers, Sidney W. "Policy Formulation and National Security." *American Political Science Review* 43 (1949): 536.

Stanley, David T. *Changing Administrations.* Washington, D.C.: Brookings Institution, 1965.

Storing, Herbert, ed. *The Anti-Federalist.* Chicago: University of Chicago Press, 1985.

Story, Joseph. *Commentaries on the Constitution of the United States, with a Preliminary Review of the Constitutional History of the Colonies and States Before the Adoption of the Constitution.* Boston: Charles C. Little and James Brown, 1851.

Sundquist, James L. *The Decline and Resurgence of Congress.* Washington, D.C.: Brookings Institution, 1981.

Taft, William Howard. *Our Chief Magistrate and His Powers.* New York: Columbia University Press, 1938.

United Church of Christ, Commission for Racial Justice. *Toxic Wastes and Race in the United States: A National Report on the Racial and Socioeconomic Characteristics of Communities with Hazardous Waste Sites.* New York: United Church of Christ, 1987.

U.S. Commission on Civil Rights. *The Battle for Environmental Justice in Louisiana: Government, Industry, and the People.* Washington, D.C.: U.S. Commission on Civil Rights, 1993.

U.S. Department of Justice, Office of Legal Counsel. *The Attorney General's Duty to Defend and Enforce Constitutionally Objectionable Legislation*, 4A Op. O.L.C. 55 (1980).

U.S. Department of State, Office of the Historian. *History of the National Security Council, 1947–1997*. <http://www.fas.org/irp/offdocs/NSChistory.htm> August 18, 2001.

U.S. General Accounting Office. *Hazardous and Nonhazardous Waste: Demographics of People Living Near Waste Facilities*. Washington, D.C.: GAO, 1995.

————. *Siting of Hazardous Waste Landfills and Their Correlation with Racial and Economic Status of Surrounding Communities*. Washington, D.C.: GAO, 1983.

U.S. House of Representatives. Committee on Economic and Educational Opportunities. "Nullifying an Executive Order That Prohibits Federal Contracts with Companies That Hire Permanent Replacements for Striking Employees." 104th Congress, 1st sess., 1995.

————. Committee on Governmental Operations. *Executive Orders and Proclamations: A Study of the Use of Presidential Power*. 85th Congress, 1st sess., 1957. Committee Print.

————. Committee on Government Operations. *Security Classification Policy and Executive Order 12356*. HRept. 97-731, 97th Cong., 2d sess., 1982.

————. Hearings Before the Committee on Government Operations. *Executive Order on Security Classification Policy and Executive Order 12356*. 97th Cong., 2d sess., 1982.

————. Hearings Before the Legislation and National Security Subcommittee of the Committee on Government Operations. *Environmental Protection Agency Cabinet Elevation—Environmental Equity Issues*. 103d Cong., 1st sess., 1993.

————. Hearing Before a Subcommittee of the Committee on Government Operations. *Presidential Directives and Records Accountability Act*. 100th Cong., 2d sess., 1988. Committee Print.

————. Hearing Before the Subcommittee on Immigration, Refugees, and International Law of the Committee on the Judiciary. *Central American Asylum-Seekers*. 101st Cong., 1st sess., 1989.

————. Hearing Before the Subcommittee on Oversight and Investigations of the Committee on Commerce. *EPA's Title VI Interim Guidance and Alternative State Approaches*. 105th Cong., 2d sess., 1998.

————. Hearing Before the Subcommittee on Oversight and Investigation of House Committee on Energy and Commerce. *Role of OMB in Regulation*. 97th Cong., 1st sess., 1981.

————. House Select Committee to Investigate Covert Arms Transactions with Iran, Senate Select Committee on Secret Military Assistance to Iran and the Nicaraguan Opposition. *Report of the Congressional Committees Investigating the Iran-Contra Affair*. H.Rept. 433, S. Rept. 216, 100th Cong., 1st sess., 1987.

————. Special Committee on the Termination of the National Emergency. *Summary of Emergency Powers Statutes*. 93d Cong., 1st sess., 1973.

————. Staff Study for the Permanent Select Committee on Intelligence. *IC21: The Intelligence Community in the Twenty-first Century*. 104th Cong., 1st sess., 1996.

U.S. Senate. Hearing Before the Committee on Governmental Affairs. *National Security Decision Directive 84—Safeguarding National Security Information.* 98th Cong., 1st sess., 1984.

———. Hearing Before the Subcommittee on Immigration and Refugee Affairs of the Committee on the Judiciary. *Central American Migration to the United States.* 101st Cong., 1st sess., 1989.

———. Hearings Before the Subcommittee on Separation of Powers of the Committee on the Judiciary. *The Philadelphia Plan.* 91st Cong., 1st sess., 1969.

———. Report of the Committee on the Judiciary to Accompany S. 332 as Amended. *Providing for a GAO Study on Conditions of Displaced Salvadorans and Nicaraguans, and for Other Purposes.* 100th Cong., 1st sess., 1987.

———. Report of the Special Committee on National Emergencies and Delegated Emergency Powers. *Executive Orders in Times of War and National Emergency.* 93d Cong., 2d sess., 1974. Committee Print.

———. Report of the Special Committee on National Emergency and Delegated Emergency Powers. *National Emergencies and Delegated Emergency Powers.* 94th Cong., 2d sess., 1976.

———. Special Committee on the Termination of the National Emergency. *Summary of Emergency Powers Statutes.* 93d Cong., 1st sess., 1973.

———. Subcommittee on National Policy Machinery. *Organizational History of the National Security Council During the Truman and Eisenhower Administrations.* (Jackson Report.) 86th Cong., 2d sess., 1960. Committee Print.

Walker, David B. *The Rebirth of Federalism.* 2d ed. New York: Chatham House, 2000.

Walsh, Lawrence E. *Iran-Contra: The Final Report of the Independent Counsel.* New York: Random House, 1993.

Warren, Charles. *The Supreme Court in United States History.* 2 vols. Boston: Little, Brown, 1923.

Weaver, Jace, ed. *Defending Mother Earth.* Maryknoll, N.Y.: Orbis Books, 1996.

Westin, Alan F. *The Anatomy of a Constitutional Law Case: Youngstown Sheet and Tube v. Sawyer.* New York: Macmillan, 1958.

White, Leonard D. *The Federalists.* New York: Macmillan, 1956.

Wilber, David N. "Clandestine Service History: Overthrow of Premier Mossadeq of Iran." *New York Times.* <http://www.nytimes.com/library/world/mideast/iran-cia-intro.pdf> January 15, 2001.

Woodward, Bob. *The Agenda: Inside the Clinton White House.* New York: Simon and Schuster, 1994.

Woolf, Malcolm D. "Clean Air or Hot Air?: Lessons from the Quayle Competitiveness Council's Oversight of EPA." *Journal of Law and Public Policy* 10 (1993): 97.

Works Projects Administration. *Historical Records Survey, Presidential Executive Orders.* Vol. 1. New York: Hastings House Publishers, 1944.

OPINIONS CITED

Adarand Constructors, Inc. v. Peña,
515 U.S. 200 (1995), 275 n.23
AFL-CIO v. Kahn, 472 F.Supp. 88 (D.D.C.
1979), 66–67, 257 n.108–109, 111
*A.L.A. Schechter Poultry Corp. v.
United States,* 295 U.S. 495
(1935), 22–23, 252 n.35
*Amalgamated Meat Cutters and
Butcher Workmen of North
America v. Connally,* 337 F.Supp.
737 (D.D.C. 1971), 252 n.31
*American Foreign Service Association
v. Garfinkel,* 490 U.S. 153 (1989),
273 n.160
*American Foreign Service Association
v. Garfinkel,* 732 F.Supp. 13
(D.D.C. 1990), 273 n.160
*American Hospital Association v.
Bowen,* 834 F.2d 1037 (D.C.Cir
1987), 264 n.105
American Pilots' Association v. Gracey,
631 F.Supp. 828 (D.D.C. 1986),
260 n.29
*AMERON, Inc. v. U.S. Army Corps of
Engineers,* 607 F.Supp. 962 (D.NJ
1985), 225, 278 n.93
*AMERON, Inc. v. U.S. Army Corps of
Engineers,* 610 F.Supp. 750 (D.NJ
1985), 278 n.94
AMERON, Inc. v. United States Senate,
809 F.2d 979 (3rd Cir. 1986),
278 n.95
AMERON, Inc. v. United States, 787 F.2d
875 (3rd Cir. 1986), 277 n.86, n.95
Armstrong v. United States, 80 U.S. (13
Wall.) 154 (1871).

*Bean v. Southwestern Waste Management
Corp.,* 482 F.Supp. 673 (S.D.TX
1979), 106, 263 n.74

Bowsher v. Synar, 478 U.S. 714 (1986),
216–217, 276 n.65–66, 277 n.77
Buckley v. Valeo, 424 U.S. 1 (1976),
277 n.77
*Building and Construction Trades
Department, AFL-CIO v.
Allbaugh,* 2001 U.S. Dist. LEXIS
17509 (2001), 238, 278 n.5

*California Department of Human
Resources Development v. Java,*
402 U.S. 121 (1971), 256 n.65
Chamber of Commerce v. Reich, 74
F.3d 1322 (D.C.Cir. 1996), 24, 50,
77, 252 n.45, 255 n.54, 258 n.128
*Chester Residents Concerned for
Quality of Life v. Seif,* 132 F.3d
925 (3rd Cir. 1997), 109,
263 n.91
Clinton v. New York, 524 U.S. 417
(1998), 204, 223, 275 n.15, 277
n.81
*Coalition for Economic Equity v.
Wilson,* 122 F.3d 692 (9th Cir.
1997), 251 n.4, 253 n.80
Cole v. Young, 351 U.S. 536 (1956),
252 n.43, 258 n.142
*Consumer Energy Council v. Federal
Energy Regulatory Commission,*
673 F.2d 425 (D.C.Cir. 1982),
209, 225, 276 n.37, 277 n.91
Consumers Union v. FTC, 691 F.2d 575
(D.C.Cir. 1982), 209, 276 n.37
*Contractors Association of Eastern
Pennsylvania v. Secretary of
Labor,* 442 F.2d 159 (3rd Cir.
1971), 57, 256 n.79
*Cornelius v. NAACP Legal Defense and
Education Fund,* 473 U.S. 788
(1985), 52, 256 n.60

Crosby v. National Foreign Trade Council, 147 L.Ed.2d 352 (2000), 35–36, 254 n.94

Dalton v. Specter, 511 U.S. 462 (1994), 258 n.130
Dames & Moore v. Reagan, 453 U.S. 654 (1981), 23–24, 35, 250 n.35, 252 n.37, n.41, 265 n.114, 266 n.24

Environmental Defense Fund v. Thomas, 627 F. Supp. 566 (D.D.C. 1986), 257 n.92, 93, 260 n.29, n.32
Ex Parte Endo, 323 U.S. 283 (1944), 250 n.44
Ex Parte Milligan, 71 U.S. (4 Wall.) 2 (1866), 250 n.44, 252 n.42

Fleming v. Mohawk Wrecking & Lumber, 331 U.S. 111 (1947), 43, 252 n.40, 255 n.30
Fullilove v. Klutznick, 448 U.S. 448 (1980), 275 n.21

The Grapeshot, 76 U.S. (9 Wall.) 129 (1869), 251 n.23

Haig v. Agee, 453 U.S. 280 (1981), 34–35, 252 n.30, 253 n.61, 254 n.88
Heckler v. Chaney, 470 U.S. 821 (1985), 276 n.61
Hirabayashi v. United States, 320 U.S. 81 (1943), 250 n.41, 252 n.39, 265 n.10
Hodel v. Virginia Surface Mining and Reclamation Ass'n, 452 U.S. 264 (1981), 250 n.40
Hynes v. Grimes Packing Co., 337 U.S. 86 (1949), 252 n.30

Immigration and Nationalization Service v. Chadha, 462 U.S. 919 (1983), 209–210, 223–224, 255 n.35, 276 n.36, 277 n.77
Independent Gasoline Markets Council v. Duncan, 492 F.Supp. 614 (D.D.C. 1980), 250 n.45, 252 n.31
Industrial Union AFL-CIO v. American Petroleum Institute, 448 U.S. 607 (1980), 252 n.36
Isbrandtsen-Moller v. United States, 300 U.S. 139 (1937), 252 n.40

Joint Anti-Facist Refugee Committee v. McGrath, 341 U.S. 123 (1951), 79, 258 n.140

Kendall v. United States ex rel. Stokes, 37 U.S. (12 Pet.) 524 (1838), 224, 252 n.43, 277 n.87
Korematsu v. United States, 319 U.S. 432 (1943), 250 n.41

Laird v. Tatum, 408 U.S. 1 (1972), 253 n.52, 266 n.33
The Lake Monroe, 250 U.S. 246 (1919), 266 n.34
Lear Siegler v. Lehman, 842 F.2d 1102 (9th Cir. 1988), 278 n.96
Little v. Barreme, 6 U.S. (2 Cranch) 170 (1804), 27, 77, 252 n.44, 253 n.58, 258 n.131, 266 n.18

Mammoth Oil Co. v. United States (Teapot Dome), 275 U.S. 13 (1927), 257 n.85, n.86
Marbury v. Madison, 5 U.S. (1 Cr.) 137 (1803), 225
Maryland Casualty Co. v. United States, 251 U.S. 342 (1919)
McLouth Steel Products Corporation v. Thomas, 838 F.2d 1317 (D.C.Cir. 1988), 264 n.105
Menotti v. Dillon, 167 U.S. 703 (1897), 251 n.6, 253 n.59

Midwest Motor Express, Inc. v. International Brotherhood of Teamsters, Chauffeurs, Warehousemen and Helpers of America, Local 120, 512 N.W.2d 881 (MN 1994), 49, 255 n.49

Minnesota v. Mille Lacs Band of Chippewa Indians, 143 L.Ed.2d 270 (1999), 25, 252 n.46

Murphy v. Ford, 390 F.Supp. 1372 (W.D.MI 1975), 134–135, 267 n.45

Myers v. United States, 272 U.S. 52 (1926), 224, 277 n.85

National Federation of Federal Employees v. U.S., 695 F.Supp. 1196 (D.D.C. 1988), 273 n.160

Natural Resources Defense Council v. Ruckelshaus, 1984 U.S. Dist. LEXIS 23589 (D.D.C. 1984), 257 n.92

Norman v. Baltimore & Ohio Railroad, 294 U.S. 240 (1935), 254 n.12

Panama Refining Co. v. Ryan, 293 U.S. 388 (1935), 18–19, 22, 251 n.19, 252 n.34

Pan American Petroleum and Transport Co. v. United States, 273 U.S. 456 (1927), 257 n.85

Perkins v. Lukens Steel Co., 310 U.S. 113, 127 (1940), 257 n.110

Peters v. Hobby, 349 U.S. 331 (1955), 258 n.141

Printz v. United States, 521 U.S. 898 (1997), 216, 276 n.64

The Prize Cases, 67 U.S. (2 Black) 635 (1862), 250 n.43, 266 n.30

Process Gas Consumers v. Consumer Energy Council, 463 U.S. 1216 (1983), 276 n.38, 278 n.92

Proclamations Case, 12 Co. Rep. 74 (1611), 5, 249 n.13

Public Citizen v. Department of Justice, 491 U.S. 440 (1989), 75–76, 258 n.126

Raines v. Byrd, 521 U.S. 811 (1997), 258 n.115, 277 n.78

Richmond v. J. A. Croson Co., 488 U.S. 469 (1989), 275 n.22

Rutan Republican Party of Illinois, 497 U.S. 62 (1990), 33, 254 n.82

Sale v. Haitian Centers Council, 509 U.S. 155 (1993), 115, 120, 265 n.117, 265 n.13, 266 n.25

Schick v. Reed, 419 U.S. 256 (1974), 133, 266 n.41

Southern Offshore Fishing Association v. Daley, 995 F.Supp. 1411 (M.D.FL 1998), 208–209, 275 n.31

Swayne v. Hoyt, 300 U.S. 297 (1937), 252 n.40

United States v. Allied Oil Corp., 341 U.S. 1 (1951), 255 n.31

United States v. Barnett, 376 U.S. 681 (1964), 131, 266 n.32

United States v. Curtiss-Wright Export Corp., 299 U.S. 304 (1936), 35, 124–125, 250 n.42, 254 n.90, 266 n.22–23

United States v. Lee, 106 U.S. 196 (1882), 278 n.94

United States v. Lopez, 514 U.S. 549 (1995), 264 n.110

United States v. Martin, 557 F.Supp. 681 (N.E.Dist. Iowa 1982), 265 n.8

United States v. Midwest Oil Co., 236 U.S. 459 (1915), 36–37, 59, 254 n.96

United States v. Morrison, 146 L.Ed.2d 658 (2000), 264 n.110

United States v. Nixon, 418 U.S. 683 (1974), 224–225, 277 n.89–90

United States v. Oregon and California Railroad, 176 U.S. 28 (1900), 251 n.6, 253 n.253

United States v. Pewee Coal Co., 341 U.S. 114 (1951), 258 n.133

United States v. Reynolds, 250 U.S. 104 (1919), 251 n.10, 254 n.1

United States v. Sperry Corp., 493 U.S. 52 (1989), 35, 254 n.92

United States v. Story, 891 F.2d 988 (2d Cir. 1989), 210–211, 276 n.45

United States v. Symonds, 120 U.S. 46 (1887), 252 n.43

United States v. United Mineworkers, 330 U.S. 258 (1947), 42, 255 n.24

United States v. Wayte, 119–120, 710 F.2d 1385 (9th Cir. 1983), 265 n.8–9

United States of America v. Wayte, 119–120, 549 F.Supp. 1376 (C.D.Cal 1982), 265 n.7

United States ex rel. Skinner & Eddy Corporation v. McCarl, 275 U.S. 1 (1927), 258 n.132

United States Grain Corporation v. Phillips, 261 U.S. 106 (1923), 255 n.25

U.S. Shipping Board Merchant Fleet Corporation v. Harwood, 281 U.S. 519 (1930), 258 n.132

Whitman v. American Trucking Association, 149 L.Ed.2d 1 (2001), 252 n.36

In re Wilson, 140 U.S. 575 (1891), 252 n.38

Wolsey v. Chapman, 101 U.S. 755 (1879), 118, 265 n.2

Woods v. Cloyd W. Miller Co., 333 U.S. 138 (1948), 43, 254 n.18, 255 n.30

Xin-Chan Zhang v. Slattery, 55 F.3d 732 (2d Cir. 1995), 77, 258 n.129

Yakus v. United States, 321 U.S. 414 (1944), 22, 252 n.33

Youngstown Sheet & Tube v. Sawyer, 343 U.S. 579 (1952), 250 n.34, 252 n.29, 264 n.109, 265 n.115, 266 n.37, 277 n.88

INDEX

Abortion, 81, 82–93
Accountability, 76, 162, 196, 234
Administrative law, 70, 75, 233. *See also* Rulemaking
Administrative presidency, 1, 60
Administrative Procedure Act (APA), 17, 58, 229
  judicial review in, 48, 59
  policy statements under, 110
Advice and consent power. *See* Constitution
Affirmative action, 33, 104
  Bush signing statement on, 206
  Lyndon Johnson and, 8, 55–58, 66
  Philadelphia Plan on, 57
Agency for International Development (AID), 81, 175, 192
Allende, Salvador (Chile), 182
Arbenz Guzman, Jacobo (Guatemala), 178–179
Attorney general, 17, 43, 53, 57, 79, 109, 201, 210, 216–217, 200, 222, 225–227
Authority, 75, 234, 242
  constitutional, 4, 21, 24, 34, 76, 185, 204
  delegation of, 22–23
  statutory, 4, 22, 76
  subdelegation of, 28–30, 36

Barber, James David, 9
Black, Hugo, 10
Brownlow Commission, 29
Bryd, Robert, 199–200, 229, 236, 243
Burger, Warren, 34–35
Bush, George, 31–32, 60, 61, 63, 82, 86–90, 90, 93, 100, 102, 120, 150, 152, 156, 166, 195, 201, 203, 207–208, 212, 215, 219, 221, 232, 234
  abortion "Gag Rule" and. *See* Abortion
  Andean Initiative of, 171
  attack on administrative rulemaking by. *See* Rulemaking
  Council on Competitiveness (Quayle Commission) and. *See* Rulemaking. *See also* Regulation
  covert operations and. *See* Covert operations
  Haitian refugees and. *See* Haitian refugee crisis
  Iran-Contra pardons by, 135, 140–141
  Iraq and. *See* War
  "Operation Desert Storm" and. *See* War
  organization of NSC by, 151, 153
  rejection of affirmative action. *See* Signing statements, presidential
  rejection of congressional civil rights standard by. *See* Signing statements, presidential
  Somalia and. *See* War
  Whistleblower Protection Act controversy and. *See* Signing statements, presidential
Bush, George W., 13, 83, 204, 208, 238
  creation of the Office of Homeland Security by, 32
  Faith-Based Initiative of. *See* Faith-Based Initiative
  "Mexico City" Policy reinstatement by, 83
  military arrest, detention, and trial order of, 9
  organization of NSC by, 1
  Regulatory Review Plan of, 83

Bush, George W. (*continued*)
  rulemaking moratorium of. *See*
    Rulemaking
  September 11 attack and, 9, 12, 32

Cabinet, 1, 2, 15, 74, 77, 144, 233
Carter, James Earl, 10, 11, 24, 26, 31,
    34, 61–62, 71, 75, 77, 82, 90, 121,
    142, 144, 150, 153, 156, 166, 183,
    201, 209, 232–233
  anti-inflation orders and
    proclamations of, 66–67, 132
  draft registration proclamation of, 119
  investigation of Three Mile Island
    nuclear plant incident, 54
  Iran Hostage crisis and. *See* Iran
    Hostage crisis
  organization of NSC by, 151
  Petroleum Import Adjustment Program
    of, 8, 13, 22, 121, 133, 137
  regulatory review order. *See*
    Rulemaking
  security classification order of. *See*
    Security classification
Central Intelligence Agency (CIA), 34,
    53, 146, 164–165, 173, 175, 180,
    186, 192
  director of, 153, 157, 181
  inspector general of, 205
Chile
  Salvadore Allende and, 182
  U.S.-sponsored coup in, 182
Civil rights, 26, 90, 103–104, 106–112,
    127
  affirmative action in. *See* Affirmative
    action
  desegregation of the military and. *See*
    Military
  environmental justice and. *See*
    Environmental justice
  equal employment opportunity and,
    55–57
  Franklin Roosevelt order on, 51
  Voting Rights Act and, 56

Civil Rights Act of 1964, 55–57
  Title VI of, 107–108
  Title VII of, 57, 207
Civil Rights Act of 1991, 206–207, 216
Civil War. *See* War
Clinton, William Jefferson, 3, 13, 14,
    15, 17, 31, 32, 35–36, 49–51, 54,
    55, 60, 61, 63, 71, 75, 81–84, 86,
    90, 92, 93, 96, 97–99, 100, 106–
    112, 114, 118, 120, 135, 144,
    145, 150, 156, 166, 171, 185,
    188, 196, 199–201, 206, 208–
    209, 212–213, 215, 217, 219–
    221, 224, 227, 232, 234–235,
    238, 241, 243
  abortion "Gag Rule" and. *See*
    Abortion
  environmental justice directives of.
    See Environmental justice
  ethics order and, 48, 233
  family and children policies
    memoranda of, 103–104
  federal lands proclamations and
    orders of. *See* Public lands
  federalism order of. *See*
    Intergovernmental relations
  fetal tissue experimentation and. *See*
    Memorandum, presidential
  "gays in the military"
    (nondiscrimination on the basis of
    sexual orientation), 82, 92
  gun control and, 101–102
  Gun-Free Schools memorandum, 84,
    102
  Haitian refugee proclamations of. *See*
    Haitian refugee crisis
  HIV/AIDS and military personnel
    controversy of. *See* Signing
    statements, presidential
  human subjects experimentation
    memorandum of, 100
  Internet technology and, 98, 103,
    188–190, 196. *See also*
    Technology

Kosovo policy and, 44, 99
Los Alamos National Laboratories
  nuclear security crisis and. *See*
  Signing statements, presidential
"Mexico City Policy" and. *See*
  Memorandum, presidential
Organization of NSC by, 151
pardons and, 135, 139, 142
Patients' Bill of Rights and, 101
policy of. *See* Military
rejection of congressionally created
  National Nuclear Security
  Administration. *See* Signing
  statements, presidential
RU-486 (abortion pill) and. *See*
  Memorandum, presidential
signing statement on energy security.
  See National Nuclear Security
  Administration
Somalia and. *See* War
striker replacement order of. *See*
  Labor disputes
White Water scandal and, 135
Y2K orders of, 43–44
Cold war, 143, 154, 157, 163, 164–166,
  173–174
NSC 68 and, 147–149, 155, 162
Project Solarium and, 149
Comptroller general, 57, 216–217
Congress, 3, 9, 10, 11, 12, 17, 19, 21,
  22
acquiescence theory and, 10, 24, 35,
  67, 68, 69
appropriations and, 23–24, 67, 86
end-runs around, 55–58, 71, 96, 100–
  102
oversight by, 86
power to declare war of, 7
presidential conflict with, 71, 76,
  100–102, 214–215, 220
war powers resolutions of. *See* War
  powers resolutions
Congressional Budget and
  Impoundment Control Act, 13

Constitution, 7, 22, 32, 76, 176, 202–
  203, 207, 209, 235, 238
advice and consent requirement in, 7,
  30
appointments power in, 30, 207–208,
  222
Civil War amendments to, 127
commander in chief power in, 7, 78,
  208
"duty to take care" clause, 207
executive powers in, 6, 9, 24, 120,
  202, 222, 224
executive privilege under, 72, 222
First Amendment in, 185–186
interstate commerce clause in, 36
judicial powers in, 205
pardon power in, 7, 133. *See also*
  Pardons
presidential foreign affairs power, 12,
  224
veto power in, 7
war power in, 12. *See also* Executive
  orders
"Constitutional Dialogue," 4, 9–10, 12,
  236
Contracts, government, 8, 11, 49, 57,
  61, 184, 188, 241
AMERON controversy and. *See*
  Signing statements, presidential
debarment from, 50, 66–67
Federal Property and Administrative
  Services Act in, 50, 66–67
Office of Federal Procurement Policy
  (OFPP) and, 66
policy as leverage for change, 65–68
Counterstaffing. *See* Administrative
  presidency
Covert operations, 167, 175–182, 235
303 committee and, 176
5412 committee and, 176
Guatemala coup d'etat. *See*
  Guatemala
Iran-Contra. *See* Iran-Contra
Iran coup d'etat. *See* Iran

Covert operations (*continued*)
  new president on the job trap, 191–
    192, 235
  VEIL security classification created
    for, 176
Crisis management. *See* Emergency
Cuba, 164–165, 167, 183
  Bay of Pigs, 149, 179–182, 184
  Fidel Castro, 53, 165, 175
  Missile crisis and, 184

Determinations, presidential, 86, 90,
    92, 105, 116, 121, 122, 135
Directives, presidential, 17, 19, 75, 82,
    83, 91, 99, 105, 144. *See also*
    Executive orders, Memoranda,
    presidential, and national security
    directives
Due process, 75, 78

Eisenhower, Dwight David, 8, 25, 79,
    90, 145, 148, 155, 176–179, 182–
    183, 184, 209
  covert operations and. *See* Covert
    operations
  Guatemala coup and. *See* Guatemala
  Iran coup and. *See* Iran
  "New Look" policy of, 148–149
  organization of the NSC and, 148–
    149, 162
Emergency, 4, 12–13, 15, 34, 39–45,
    61, 69, 71, 79, 96, 121, 127–133,
    232, 234–235, 238
  economic, 13, 40–42, 127, 234
  foreign policy issues as, 44, 99, 234
  memoranda used in the management
    of, 99–100
  military, 12, 23, 33
  natural disasters as, 99–100, 127,
    135
  NSDs as tools for management in,
    184
  transition into or out of, 42–44, 69, 96
Environmental justice, 74, 106–112,
    235

Environmental Protection Agency
    (EPA), 61, 205
Executive agreements, 10, 34, 122
Executive Office of the President, 31,
    60–61
  Office of Information and Regulatory
    Affairs (OIRA), 31, 60, 93–95
  Office of Management and Budget
    (OMB), 17, 58, 60, 79, 82, 93–94,
    101, 114, 226
  Office of Personnel Management
    (OPM), 52, 186
  White House counsel, 79, 141
Executive orders, ix–x, 2, 4, 8, 10, 11, 13–
    14, 15–80, 82, 83, 86, 90, 91, 105,
    106, 112, 116, 118, 122, 123, 131,
    138, 142, 176, 231, 233, 238, 243
  as private bills. *See* Private bills
  codification of, 19–20
  compared to proclamations, 16, 27
  congressional ratification of, 12, 23–24
  congressional rejection of, 23
  continued funding as support for
    validity of, 23–24
  decree inertia principle and, 63, 77
  defined, 16
  disposition tables for, 20, 114
  form of, 17
  government contracts and. *See*
    Contracts, government
  governors and, 16, 33, 80
  in time of war. *See* Emergency. *See
    also* War
  investigative commissions and, 52–
    55, 74
  Japanese internment and. *See*
    Japanese exclusion and internment
    orders
  legal force of, 21
  mayors and, 16, 33, 80
  publication of, 18–19
  security classification and. *See*
    Security classification
  severability of, 25
  symbolic uses of, 48–49, 58, 69, 71, 107

Faith-Based Initiative, 15, 51
Federal Bureau of Investigation (FBI), 52, 157, 186
Federal Register, 81, 85, 105, 110, 118
act establishing, 18–19, 114, 118, 145
materials exempt from publication in, 19
office of, 17
Federalism, 58. *See also* Intergovernmental relations
Federalist Papers, 6, 133
Federation of American Scientists, 14
Fisher, Louis, 9–10, 30, 203–204, 209, 236
Ford, Gerald, 90, 156, 160, 209
Navy expansion directive of, 169
organization of NSC by, 151–153
pardon of Richard Nixon by. *See* Pardons
Vietnam draft proclamations of, 138–139

General Accounting Office (GAO), 106, 195
General Agreement on Tariffs and Trade (GATT), 221
Gingrich, Newt, 215, 221
Gore, Al, 17, 48, 75, 82, 84, 213 *See also* National Performance Review
Governance, 233–234, 237
Governors. *See* Executive orders. *See also* Proclamations
Grant, Ulysses, 17
Great Depression, 40–41, 71, 132. *See also* New Deal
Guatemala, 140, 157
Jacobo Arbenz Guzman and, 178–179
U.S. sponsored coup (Operation PB Success) in, 8, 178–179, 192

Haig, Alexander, 151–152
Haitian refugee crisis, 34, 120, 125, 137
Hamilton, Alexander, 6, 123, 133

Harding, Warren, 59
Hoover, Herbert, 17, 43
Humphrey, Hubert, 56. *See also* Civil rights

Implementation, Policy, 28, 49, 74, 95, 144, 154, 201, 207–208, 212–213, 229–230, 233. *See also* Signing statements, presidential
Indians, 98–99
memorandum on consultation with tribal groups, 90
tribal rights of, 25
Washington's proclamation on respect for rights of, 130, 136
Interest groups, 11
Intergovernmental relations, 4, 10–12
conflict over Clinton orders on federalism and, 72–74
disaster recovery and, 99–100
regulation and. *See* Regulation
state economic activity and, 35–36
tension in, 70, 72–74, 76, 235
International Emergency Economic Powers Act, 36, 44, 79
Iran Hostage crisis, 10, 24, 34, 44, 70, 77, 79, 152
Iran. *See also* Iran-Contra and Iran Hostage crisis
Mohammad Mosadeq of, 177–178
Shah of, 143, 178
U.S.-sponsored coup (Operation Ajax) in, 143, 177–178, 184, 192
Iran-Contra, 143, 150, 163, 166, 167–168, 181, 191, 194–195, 235, 241
Tower Commission on, 54, 176–177, 193–194
Iraq, 164. *See also* War
Bush NSD 54 launching Desert Storm in, 170
Hussein, Saddam in, 170
Israel, 166

Jackson, Andrew, 203
nullification crisis and, 130–131, 136

Jackson, Robert, 10, 23, 24, 211
Japanese exclusion and internment
   orders, 8, 12, 78
Jefferson, Thomas, 123–124
Johnson, Lyndon, 8, 13, 17, 54, 71, 78,
   90, 144, 149, 154, 156, 172–174,
   176, 182, 185, 190, 193, 209
   affirmative action and. See
     Affirmative action
   covert operations and. See Covert
     operations
   creation of Warren Commission by,
     52–53
   Gulf of Tonkin incident and, 173, 192
   psychological warfare and. See
     National security directives
   TFX (FB–111) directive of, 169
   Vietnam and. See War
Judicial review, 48, 59, 70, 75, 76, 107,
   113, 121, 215–220
   case or controversy requirement and,
     205
   exhaustion of administrative
     remedies and, 110–111
   private right of action for, 110–111,
     113
   standing to seek, 58, 70, 76–77, 113,
     120, 138
Justice, U.S. Department of, 52, 119,
   138, 201, 216, 218–219
   Office of Legal Counsel in, 201, 204,
     206–207, 211–213, 215, 220, 222,
     230

Kennedy, John F., 8, 17, 25, 45–48, 59, 76,
   90, 118, 131, 144, 149, 154, 157, 163,
   182–184, 190, 193, 195, 209
   Bay of Pigs and. See Cuba
   Berlin crisis and, 170, 180, 184
   creation of Peace Corps by, 31
   Cuban Missile crisis and. See Cuba
   directive creating counter-guerilla
     forces (Green Berets), 169
   Warren Commission on the
     assassination of, 52–53

Labor disputes, 8, 9–10, 41–42, 45–48
   Taft-Hartley Act and, 9
   Truman steel seizure order and, 9,
     24, 42, 237
   Striker replacement order and, 24,
     49–51, 55, 66, 71, 238
Legislative history, 75
Legislative veto. See Veto
Lincoln, Abraham, 12, 20, 27, 39, 131,
   136, 234
   Emancipation Proclamation of, 8,
     125–127
Line Item Veto. See Signing statements,
   presidential
Locke, John, 7–8
Los Alamos National Laboratories. See
   National Nuclear Security
   Administration

Madison, James, x, 6, 7, 124
Mayors. See Executive orders. See also
   Proclamations
Media, news, 13, 16, 48, 98–99, 103,
   104, 105, 186, 241
Meese, Edwin, 150, 152, 184–185, 241
   AMERON controversy and, 225–227
   presidential signing statements and,
     201–203, 210, 216, 220, 222, 225–
     227
Memoranda, presidential, ix, 2, 14, 32,
   80, 81–116, 121, 125, 135, 137,
   142, 190, 196, 217–218, 231–233,
   238, 243
   abortion "Gag Rule" and. See
     Abortion
   as modifications for executive orders,
     112–114
   as substitutions for executive orders,
     114–115
   codification and, 105
   confusion with executive orders and,
     83–84
   defined, 83
   executive orders compared with, 91
   fetal tissue experimentation and, 81

"Mexico City Policy" and, 81–82, 83
of disapproval, 86–90
presidential determinations as. *See*
Determinations, presidential
public relations uses of, 97–99
quasi-memoranda and, 115–116
symbolic uses of, 81, 90, 96, 99,
102–104, 116
Military, 27, 29, 32, 33, 144, 155, 183,
196
desegregation of, 8, 70, 80, 237
doctrine and deployment of, 168–172
force posture, 156, 168
foreign sales of equipment for, 86,
156, 166–168
lands and reservations for, 33
memorandum on gays in the, 82, 92
peacekeeping forces, 171–172
rules of engagement for. *See* Warfare

National Emergencies Act, 13, 39, 44–
45, 72, 135
National Industrial Recovery Act
(NIRA),
"Hot Oil" case and, 18–19
"Sick Chicken" case and, 22–23
National Nuclear Security
Administration (NNSA), 199–201,
221, 227–229, 236
National Performance Review (NPR),
17, 75, 84–85, 98, 213
National Security Act of 1947, 25, 146,
176
National security classification. *See*
Security classification
National Security Council (NSC), 144,
145–146, 151, 186, 190.
and national security adviser, 148
creation of, 145–146
development by Eisenhower
administration of, 148–149
policy papers. *See* National security
directives
Reagan problems with organization
of, 152–153

National security directives (NSDs), ix,
2, 14, 19, 34, 91, 142, 143–197,
204, 231, 233, 235–238, 243
arms sales and. *See* Military
as basis for NSC organization, 151–153
as distinct from presidential
memoranda, 86
as foundations for negotiations, 160–
162
counterintelligence and, 187, 195–196
country policy and, 157–160, 183
covert operations and. *See* Covert
operations
defined, 144
economic policy and, 162–166. *See*
also Warfare
fact sheets on, 185
Jackson Committee and, 145
National Security Council policy
papers as, 144
nuclear policy and, 172
origins of, 146
polygraph testing of public officials
(NSD 84) and, 186–187, 196, 233
psychological warfare (public
diplomacy) and. *See* Warfare
regional policy and, 157–160, 183
rules of engagement and. *See*
Warfare
varied names for, 144
Neutrality Proclamation. *See*
Washington, George
New Deal, 23, 30, 72
Nicaragua, 164, 181. *See also* Iran-Contra
"Contra" rebels in, 157, 167
Nixon, Richard M., 13, 26, 31, 39, 71,
90, 144, 150, 152, 156, 182, 224
opening to China by, 156
Vietnam protestors and, 26,
131–132
wage/price freeze and, 8, 22, 28, 66–
67, 121, 132–133, 137
Watergate scandal and. *See* Watergate
North American Free Trade Agreement
(NAFTA), 49, 221

Office of Legal Counsel. *See* Justice,
U.S. Department of
Office of Management and Budget
(OMB). *See* Executive Office of
the President
Office of Information and Regulatory
Affairs (OIRA). *See* Executive
Office of the President
Office of Personnel Management
(OPM). *See* Executive Office of
the President

Panama, 161, 193. (War) 171
Paperwork Reduction Act (PRA), 31–
32, 93–94
Pardons, 7, 133–135
of Richard Nixon, 133–134, 139
of Vietnam draft evaders, 133
Peoples Republic of China (PRC), 86,
156, 157–160
Philadelphia Plan. *See* Affirmative action
"Plebiscitary Presidency," 234
Policy communities, 11
Policy mix, 91–92, 120, 137, 138, 175,
181
Policy statements, 110. *See also*
Rulemaking
Policy tools, ix–x, 1, 8, 10, 13, 14, 45,
83, 86, 91–92, 104, 105, 116, 121,
137, 138, 142, 144, 163, 213, 215,
220–221, 231–243
Powell, Colin, 145, 150, 153, 194, 219
Preemption, 36
Prerogative, 4–9, 35
framers' reaction against, 6–8
royal, 5–7, 30, 138
Presidential powers. *See* Constitution
Private bills, 32–33, 78
Proclamations, ix, 2, 4, 8, 14, 19, 34,
90, 91, 117–142, 231, 238, 243
and presidential pardons. *See*
Pardons
as bases for criminal prosecution,
119–121
codification of, 19–20

defined, 117–118
executive orders compared to, 16, 27,
119
publication of, 18, 118
ratification of, 12
Public lands, 27
Clinton controversy over, 36–37
historical use of presidential orders
and proclamations on, 36–37

Randolph, A. Philip, 51
Reagan, Ronald, 10, 13, 14, 17, 24, 30,
31, 52, 54, 58, 60, 61–63, 69, 71,
76, 77, 81–83, 90, 93, 100, 101,
103, 114, 119, 142, 150, 153, 154,
156, 157, 160, 164, 165, 166, 167,
172, 173, 176–177, 181, 183, 185,
188, 194–195, 201, 207–210, 216,
220, 232, 234, 237, 241
AMERON controversy and. *See*
Signing statements, presidential
B-1 bomber and, 168
covert operations and. *See* Covert
operations
deregulation efforts of, 71
Drug-Free Workplace order and, 68,
232
economic warfare and. *See* Warfare
Falklands/Malvinas war and, 164
Grenada invasion and. *See* War
Intermediate-Range Nuclear Forces
(INF) talks and, 161–162
investigation of space shuttle
Challenger disaster and, 54
Iran Hostage crisis and. *See* Iran
Hostage crisis
Lebanon conflict and, 170, 171
"Low-Intensity Warfare" and. *See*
Warfare
Mexico City Policy and. *See*
Memoranda, presidential
MX missile controversy and, 169, 185
polygraph testing of public officials
and. *See* National security
directives

problems related to organization of
NSC operations, 151–153
psychological warfare and. *See*
National security directives
regulatory review orders of, 8
security classification order of. *See*
Security classification
"Star Wars" and. *See* Strategic Defense
Initiative
Strategic Arms Reduction Treaty
(START) and, 160
Strategic Defense Initiative (SDI) of,
162, 169, 173–174
strategic forces modernization policy
of, 155, 168, 184. *See also* Military

Regulation, 27–28, 82–83, 93–96, 101.
See also Rulemaking
intergovernmental model of, 11–12.
See also Intergovernmental
relations
Rehnquist, William, 10, 24
Reinventing government, 82, 98, 213,
232. *See also* National
Performance Review
Roosevelt, Franklin, Delano, 22, 25,
40–41, 51, 53, 60, 61, 72, 77, 117,
136, 145, 211, 219
Chaco conflict proclamation of, 124–
125
civil rights orders of. *See* Civil rights
Japanese internment and. *See*
Japanese exclusion and internment
orders
Lend-Lease and. *See* Signing
statements, presidential
National Industrial Recovery Act
(NIRA) and. *See* National
Industrial Recovery Act
Rulemaking, 13, 15, 17, 31–32, 58, 59,
62, 71, 74, 75, 82, 91, 92, 111,
229, 232–233
Council on Competitiveness (Quayle
Commission) and, 31–32, 94–96,
114

George Bush attack on, 93–96
George W. Bush moratorium on, 83,
232
policy statements as means to avoid,
110
Reagan moratorium on, 93, 96, 232
review of proposed rules, 8, 11, 94, 111
Vice President's Task Force on
Regulatory Relief and, 31
Russia (Soviet Union, USSR), 92, 143,
154, 155, 164–166, 168, 173–174,
183. *See also* Cold war

Scowcroft, Brent, 150, 169, 185
Security classification, 25–27, 76, 176,
192
Carter order on, 26, 233
Clinton order on, 26–27
Reagan order on, 8, 154
Roosevelt order on, 25,
Separation of powers, 30, 68, 209, 222,
224–225
checks and balances in, 30
Severability, 25
Signing statements, presidential, ix, 14,
142, 199–230, 231, 238, 243
as directions for implementation of
statutes, 201–202, 206, 207–208,
210, 212–213, 229
as legislative history, 202–203, 207,
210–211, 216, 242
as line item veto, 203–206, 222
boundary setting for statutes and,
206–210
Bush rejection of affirmative action
in, 206
Clinton rejection of National Nuclear
Security Administration. *See*
National Nuclear Security
Administration
conflicts over appointments and, 205,
207–208
defined, 201
HIV/AIDS and military personnel
controversy and, 217–219

Signing statements, presidential
(*continued*)
legal interpretation and, 201–203, 208–209, 210, 215–220
Reagan administration development of, 200–204
Reagan AMERON controversy and, 225–227
Reagan rejection of congressional constraints on administration nondisclosure rules, 204–205
refusal to enforce statutory provisions and, 206–207
Roosevelt Lend-Lease policy and, 211
severability and, 206
Whistleblower Protection Act controversy and, 212, 230
Social Security,
FDR order creating committee on, 53
George W. Bush order creating commission on reform of, 54–55
Souter, David, 36
Soviet Union. *See* Russia
State, U.S. Department of, 20, 34, 86, 147, 150, 154, 190
passport revocation and, 27
Supreme Court, U.S., 10, 11, 12, 13, 17, 18, 22, 23–25, 27, 33, 34, 42, 44, 52, 53, 70, 77
Sutherland, George, 124–125

Teapot Dome scandal, 8, 59
Technology, 188, 194
Tools. *See* Policy tools
Trade, 27, 35–36, 120–121, 125, 131, 149, 163. *See also* North American Free Trade Agreement and General Agreement on Tariffs and Trade
export-import policy and, 156
sanctions and, 86, 163–164
Trading with the Enemy Act, 22, 79, 132

Transition, 1, 61–65, 68–69, 79, 81–83, 96, 183–184
Treaties, 19, 25, 34, 121, 160, 169, 219, 221–222
Truman, Harry, 13, 14, 25, 39, 41–43, 79, 80, 115, 117, 125, 136, 146–148, 155, 174, 175–176, 178, 182–83, 224, 233, 237
civil rights and. *See* Civil rights
covert operations and. *See* Covert operations
desegregation of the military by. *See* Military
John L. Lewis conflict with, 42
loyalty-security program of, 8, 51–52, 79
NSC 68 and. *See* Cold war
steel seizure order of. *See* Labor disputes
Tyler, John, 25

Unfunded mandates, 73, 74
Union of Soviet Socialist Republics (USSR). *See* Russia

Veto, 204, 211–212, 217, 222. *See also* Signing statements, presidential
legislative, 44–45, 209, 236, 242
presidential, 86
Vietnam. *See* War

War, 23, 42, 132. *See also* Emergency
demobilization from, 66
Falklands/Malvinas. *See* Reagan, Ronald
Grenada, 170–171, 173
Iraq ("Desert Storm"), 99, 170, 195, 236
Korean, 10, 146, 147
Panama, 171
Revolutionary, 122–123
Somalia, 171, 208
U.S. Civil, 8, 12, 27, 39, 131
Vietnam, 66, 143, 172–175, 181–182, 185, 192

WWI, 8, 25, 40, 43, 77, 132, 136
WWII, 8, 12, 25, 28–29, 41, 43, 77,
   117, 132, 145
Warfare,
   cyberwarfare, 189
   economic, 164–166, 175
   environmental, 160
   low-intensity, 169, 172, 192
   psychological (public diplomacy),
      172–175
   rules of engagement for, 171–172
War powers resolutions, 12, 13, 23, 40,
   72

Warren, Earl, 52–53
Washington, George, ix, 14, 15, 27,
   118, 133, 234
   Neutrality Proclamation of, 8, 34,
      117, 120, 122–124
   Whiskey Rebellion proclamations of,
      127–130, 131, 133
Washington rules, 3, 4, 239–242
Watergate, 26, 66, 202, 224. *See also*
   Pardons
White, Walter, 51
Wilson, James, 6
Wilson, Woodrow, 8, 13, 40, 72, 132